Marketing and Feminism

This volume offers the best of current scholarship on feminist perspectives in marketing. Through many stimulating and sometimes controversial discussions, it highlights and challenges assumptions about women and gender in marketing theory and practice from both historical and current contexts.

Marketing and Feminism: Current Issues and Research challenges the received view of the relationship between marketing and feminism, demonstrating that they have much to offer one another.

Key issues and debates include:

- the dark side of female consumption
- women and marketing in socialist economies
- women and advertising
- ecofeminism and marketing
- gender, marketing and cultural diversity.

With an international range of contributors, this collection offers new insights, new challenges and a positive vision for the future relationship between marketing and feminism.

Miriam Catterall is Senior Lecturer in Management at the Queen's University of Belfast, **Pauline Maclaran** is Reader in Marketing at De Montfort University, Leicester and **Lorna Stevens** is Lecturer in Marketing at the University of Ulster.

Routledge interpretive marketing research series

Edited by Stephen Brown
University of Ulster, Northern Ireland
and Barbara B. Stern
Rutgers, the State University of New Jersey, USA

Recent years have witnessed an 'interpretive turn' in marketing and consumer research. Methodologists from the humanities are taking their place alongside those drawn from the traditional social sciences. Qualitative and literary modes of marketing discourse are growing in popularity. Art and aesthetics are increasingly firing the marketing imagination.

This series of scholarly monographs and edited volumes brings together the most innovative work in the burgeoning interpretive marketing research tradition. It ranges across the methodological spectrum from grounded theory to personal introspection, covers all aspects of the postmodern marketing 'mix', from advertising to product development, and embraces marketing's principal sub-disciplines.

Representing Consumers
Voices, views and visions
Edited by Barbara B. Stern

Romancing the Market
Edited by Stephen Brown, Anne Marie Doherty and Bill Clarke

Consumer Value
A framework for analysis and research
Edited by Morris B. Holbrook

Marketing and Feminism
Current issues and research
Edited by Miriam Catterall, Pauline Maclaran and Lorna Stevens

Marketing and Feminism

Current issues and research

Edited by **Miriam Catterall, Pauline Maclaran and Lorna Stevens**

London and New York

First published 2000
by Routledge
11 New Fetter Lane, London EC4P 4EE

Simultaneously published in the USA and Canada
by Routledge
29 West 35th Street, New York, NY 10001

Routledge is an imprint of the Taylor & Francis Group

Typeset in 10/12pt Baskerville by Graphicraft Limited, Hong Kong
Printed and bound in Great Britain by Biddles Ltd, Guildford and
King's Lynn

British Library Cataloguing in Publication Data
A catalogue record for this book is available from the British Library

Library of Congress Cataloguing in Publication Data
Marketing and feminism: current issues and research / edited by
Miriam Catterall, Pauline Maclaran, and Lorna Stevens.
p. cm. — (Routledge interpretive marketing research series)
Includes bibliographical references.
1. Marketing. 2. Feminism. 3. Women consumers.
I. Catterall, Miriam, 1950– II. Maclaran, Pauline. III. Stevens,
Lorna. IV. Series.
HF5415 .M2969 2000
658.8'34'082—dc21 00–020069

ISBN 0–415–21972–8 (hbk)
ISBN 0–415–21973–6 (pbk)

Contents

Illustrations

Figures

Table

Contributors

Janeen Arnold Costa is Associate Professor of Marketing at the University of Utah. She received her Ph.D. in cultural anthropology from Stanford University in 1983 and undertook post-doctoral training in marketing in 1987. Costa founded and chaired the first three conferences on Gender, Marketing and Consumer Behaviour. She has published widely on the social and cultural dimensions of consumer behaviour and marketing.

Shona Bettany is currently undertaking research towards a Ph.D. in the Department of Marketing at Lancaster University. She read marketing with women's studies at Lancaster. Prior to this, and a career break, she worked in Social Services. She has published on feminist perspectives on research and the consumer's voice in relationship marketing.

Stephen Brown (Professor of Retailing at the University of Ulster) witnessed his first bra-burning ceremony at the tender age of 8. His mother, admittedly, wasn't too pleased at the sight of her underwear drawer going up in flames. Pyromania, then, is one of Stephen's many talents, as are kleptomania (other people's ideas a speciality) and monomania ('Is there a paper in it?'). These days, however, he prefers to *flambé* the metaphorical Wonderbras of marketing thought (cross his heart) and, countless accusations of chauvinism notwithstanding, claims that his feminist credentials are impeccable (albeit forgery is yet another of Stephen's non-scholarly fortes).

Miriam Catterall is Senior Lecturer in Management at the Queen's University of Belfast. She has considerable business experience in the market research industry and in management consultancy. Her research interests lie in market research and feminist issues in marketing. She designs computer-based teaching and learning materials and publishes in such outlets as *ALT-J* and the *British Journal of Educational Research* on the ways these can enhance the learning experience.

Susan Dobscha is Associate Professor of Marketing at Bentley College, Massachusetts. Her research interests include the potential negative effects of marketing on consumers' quality of life and consumer-mediated economies such as the Filene's Basement Bridal Event.

Sue Eccles worked for British Gas, Laker Airways and the City and Guilds Institute over a thirteen-year period before commencing an academic career which took her to Oxford and Bradford Universities before her current appointment at Lancaster University where she now lectures in marketing in the Management School. Sue's current research into shopping addiction has attracted widespread media attention and she has contributed to a number of TV documentaries and local and national radio programmes.

Eileen Fischer is Associate Professor of Marketing in the Schulich School of Business at York University in Toronto. She conducts research in the fields of consumer behavior and entrepreneurship that focuses on the discursive practices that create socially constructed understandings, and on the implications of embeddedness in particular socially constructed realities such as gender roles. An outgrowth of this research has been her interest in qualitative methodologies. Her empirical and conceptual work has been published widely in international journals.

Lorraine A. Friend lectures in the Department of Marketing and International Management at the University of Waikato, New Zealand. Her current research and teaching is focused in the areas of services marketing and qualitative research methodology. Lorraine's specific interest in consumption and social issues has recently led to the completion of her Ph.D., where she used memory-work to examine women's 'lived' experiences of clothing retail encounters.

Helene Hill is Senior Lecturer in the Department of Retailing and Marketing at Manchester Metropolitan University. Prior to this she worked as a researcher at the University of Central England. Her research interests are many, and they reflect her preference for merging varied concepts and viewpoints, as opposed to having a unitary perspective. She is particularly interested in exploring the relationship between subcultures, consumers and marketing management.

Margaret K. Hogg lectures in consumer behaviour at Manchester School of Management, UMIST. She read politics and modern history at Edinburgh University, completed an MA in business analysis at Lancaster University and a Ph.D. at Manchester Business School. She has published on relationship marketing, gender issues in advertising and symbolic consumption.

Mihaela Kelemen is Lecturer in Quality Management in the Department of Management and a member of the Centre for Social Theory and Technology at Keele University. She has published numerous articles and chapters on the following topics: critical approaches to quality and re-engineering, identity, morality, gender, community, and Eastern European management. She is currently co-editing a book on Critical Eastern European Management.

George Long is Senior Lecturer and Head of the Department of Marketing at Lancaster University. He read business studies and marketing at Enfield College of Technology, now part of Middlesex University, and completed an MA in educational research at Lancaster University. As well as teaching and consulting he has published articles, conference papers and book chapters in the areas of relationship marketing, services and service quality and issues in marketing education.

Pauline Maclaran is Reader in Marketing at De Montfort University, Leicester. Prior to becoming an academic she worked in industry for many years, initially in marketing positions and then as a founder partner in her own business, a design and marketing consultancy. Her main research interests are feminist perspectives and gender issues in marketing; and the utopian dimensions of contemporary consumption, particularly in relation to the festival marketplace.

Stephanie O'Donohoe is Senior Lecturer in Marketing at Edinburgh University. Her research has explored consumer experiences of advertising, with particular emphasis on issues of advertising literacy and consumers as readers of advertising texts. Her research has appeared in a range of marketing and advertising journals and she has presented her work at numerous international conferences.

Julie L. Ozanne is Associate Professor of Marketing at Virginia Polytechnic Institute and State University. Her past work in consumer research focuses on the philosophical assumptions and goals that underlie research methods and theories. Currently, she seeks to understand how business practices harm consumers.

Lisa Peñaloza is Assistant Professor of Marketing at the University of Colorado, Boulder. She completed her doctorate at the University of California, Irvine. Her research investigates how consumers from one culture adapt to marketplaces associated with another culture and how, in turn, marketers adapt to consumers of another culture. Cultural differences under examination relate to ethnicity/race, nationality, gender/sexuality and, most recently, industry and region in the case of Western culture at a stock show and rodeo. Professor Peñaloza is currently investigating the consumer behaviors of Mexican Americans/Chicanos/as in the US, funded by the Marketing Science Institute.

Linda Scott is Associate Professor of Advertising at the University of Illinois, Urbana-Champaign. Her book, *Fresh Lipstick: Redressing Fashion and Feminism*, is forthcoming. The book is based on an article of the same name that appeared in the Winter/Spring 1993 issue of the *Media Studies Journal*.

Barbara B. Stern is Professor II and Chair of the Marketing Department at Rutgers, the State University of New Jersey, Faculty of Management, Newark. She is on the editorial boards of the *Journal of Consumer Research*, *Journal of Advertising*, *Journal of Marketing* and other publications. Her research has introduced principles of literary criticism into the study of marketing, consumer behaviour and advertising. Additionally, she has focused on gender issues from the perspective of feminist literary criticism, using feminist deconstruction to analyse values encoded in advertising text.

Lorna Stevens is Lecturer in Marketing at the School of International Business at the University of Ulster, Magee College. Prior to embarking on her academic career she worked for ten years as an editor in the book publishing industry in Dublin, Belfast and London. Her research interests lie in the area of feminist perspectives and gender issues in marketing and consumer behaviour, including postmodern perspectives on consumption and popular culture.

Shona M. Thompson teaches sociology of sport and leisure at the University of Auckland, New Zealand. She has recently published a book called *Mother's Taxi* (1999), which is a feminist analysis of how women's unpaid domestic labour services the institution of sport. Shona was a member of a memory-work collective investigating consumer satisfaction and dissatisfaction in women's clothing retail experiences.

Natasha Tolstikova graduated from the Journalism Department of Moscow State University in 1983. Prior to becoming an academic she worked as a copy writer in a private advertising agency in Moscow. In 1993 received an M.Sc. in advertising from the University of Illinois at Urbana-Champaign, where she is currently working on her Ph.D. dissertation. The topic for her study is the Russian women's magazine *Rabotnitsa* and its messages about consumption throughout the first fifty years of existence.

Helen Woodruffe-Burton worked in the areas of banking and computing for eleven years prior to taking up her first teaching appointment in 1989. She currently lectures in marketing at Lancaster University Management School and her research interests are services marketing and consumer behaviour. Helen's current research into shopping behaviour has been widely covered by the press and she has contributed to a number of TV documentaries and local and national radio programmes.

Len Tiu Wright is Professor of Marketing at De Montfort University, Leicester. She is the co-author of *The Marketing Research Process*, which is now in its fifth edition. She has been employed in a variety of industries and has researched widely in Japan, Southeast Asia, Europe and North America. Her papers have appeared in academic journals and international conferences for over a decade. Some of these have been given best paper conference awards. Len Tiu has guest-edited a number of academic journals in the UK and abroad. She is editor of *Qualitative Market Research – An International Journal.*

Preface

Within the past ten years a number of articles advocating feminist perspectives within marketing have been published in leading marketing journals. These articles are usually critical of the ways that marketing theory and research can trivialise and essentialise women and sex/gender issues. In this way momentum has gathered in the whole area of gender and the way gender-based knowledge is constructed and sustained in marketing. Four conferences have been organised on the subject of gender and consumer behaviour and the conference proceedings of the Association for Consumer Research regularly include papers on gender issues in marketing. More recently, we ourselves have edited two special issues of journals, *Marketing Intelligence and Planning* and the *Journal of Marketing Practice: Applied Marketing Science*, devoted to the subject of marketing and feminism.

Researchers from other disciplines writing from feminist perspectives have also contributed to our understanding of how gender is implicated in marketing phenomena. Since the 1970s a considerable feminist literature has accumulated which simultaneously confronts and confirms our marketing assumptions about women as consumers. There are feminist analyses of women and food, diet, body image, eating out, fashion, romance fiction, glossy magazines, savings and debt, home decorating, design, shopping, sport and leisure, and domestic technologies. As these issues come increasingly to the fore, more marketing academics – men as well as women – have expressed dissatisfaction with the ways in which marketing has evolved within the prevailing cultural and social climates and how it has responded to contemporary issues.

There is an upsurge of interest in feminism and in particular 'the new feminism' with its emphasis on pragmatism rather than purity, on diversity rather than political correctness. There is also a growing awareness of the significance of gender in marketing and consumer behaviour. In the light of these important trends in contemporary culture, this book highlights these issues by bringing them to the attention of marketing academics and students in Europe, the USA and Australasia. It sets out to capture, within a single volume, the diversity and variety within both feminism and marketing, and the tensions between them.

The book offers the best of current scholarship on the relationship between marketing and feminism internationally. All of the chapters that follow have been written by leading scholars in marketing and consumer research. Our overall theme is the evolving relationship between marketing and feminism, a relationship that is more subtle and complex than is usually portrayed. Many of our readers may be new to the body of literature that currently exists on marketing and feminism. They may even have certain preconceived and possibly negative ideas about feminism. This book challenges preconceptions and stereotypes and opens up new ways of thinking about the relationship between marketing and feminism.

Through the various contributions contained within, we aim to provide the context and grounding for current and future feminist marketing scholarship. For example, analyses will include how women have been conceptualised and reconceptualised by marketing theorists and practitioners during the lifetime of modern marketing; and the presences and absences of women as contributors to marketing theory and thought.

The principal market for the book is final-year marketing undergraduates, students on post-experience and postgraduate marketing programmes and doctoral students in marketing and consumer research. On these programmes it is likely to be recommended as a supplementary text on modules in marketing theory, research methods, consumer behaviour, ethics, macromarketing/marketing and public policy. The themes addressed in the book will also be of interest to students and researchers in media and cultural studies, women's studies, CAM and consumer studies programmes, given that it reflects and develops current debates in these related disciplines. So, whilst the main focus of the book is directed at the marketing community, it will appeal to anyone who considers women important as an audience or subject of study.

Acknowledgements

We would like to thank the following people for their advice and support throughout the development of this project: Stephen Brown for his continual encouragement and who, along with his co-editor Barbara Stern, supported its inclusion within the Routledge Interpretive Research series; the three reviewers for their constructive and insightful comments; Michelle Gallagher for her infinite patience with us; and Paula Burns at the University of Ulster for all her help with the manuscripts.

The authors and publishers would like to thank the following for permission to reproduce copyright material:

Unilever for figure 2.3; *Mademoiselle* for figure 2.4; Media Education Foundation for figure 2.5; Nine West for figure 2.7; *Rabotnitsa* for figures 10.1–10.5.

Miriam Catterall
Pauline Maclaran
Lorna Stevens

1 Marketing and feminism: an evolving relationship

Miriam Catterall, Pauline Maclaran and Lorna Stevens

INTRODUCTION

On the face of it marketing and feminism is a potentially explosive combination. After all, marketing promotes a system that has traditionally been castigated by feminists for exploiting women. However, all of the chapters in this book demonstrate that marketing and feminism have much to offer one another, specifically by showing us the very positive contribution feminism can make to marketing theory and practice. Feminism is a word that carries many emotive associations, not all of them positive. There can be few words that have been so controversial, so derided and so frequently maligned. Indeed, in common parlance it is often referred to as the 'f' word.

We cannot deny that the relationship between marketing and feminism is a complex one and it is that complexity that we seek to address and explore in this book. Does feminism have any relevance to marketing? Does feminism have any relevance at all in the twenty-first century? Surely gender is no longer an issue in these postmodernist times that consider identity as multiple, fractured and almost infinitely malleable? Perhaps it would be more sensible to recognise that the battles for women's social and economic equality, characteristic of the 1970s and 1980s, have been won? Our main argument in this book is that feminism is as relevant and important at the dawn of the twenty-first century as it was at the dawn of the last century. We believe that talk of battles won and the irrelevance of gender is premature (Wilson 1999), and that so long as this remains the case feminist analyses of marketing theory, research and practice are as important now as they ever were.

One of the avowed aims of feminist academics is to bring the study of women and topics of interest and importance to women into the academic foreground. Since the consumer is usually assumed to be female we should not be surprised that feminist academics study consumers and consumption (Campbell 1995). Nor is this a recent phenomenon. Feminists have engaged in analyses of modern marketing almost from its inception. Betty Friedan's *The Feminine Mystique*, first published in 1963, maintained that marketers and advertisers were complicit in confining women to the home as housewives. This influential book set the tone for many of the feminist analyses of marketing and advertising that followed, from women academics based in such disciplines as sociology, cultural and media studies. Specifically, marketing and advertising have been conceptualised as forms of cultural doping that trivialise women or exploit their vulnerabilities. As might be expected, few of these ideas penetrated the mainstream marketing literature.

It would be wrong to assume, however, that feminist perspectives on marketing are solely or mainly about women consumers. Feminist research is often described as being on, by and for women, and this focus is important at a time when women are increasingly filling marketing classrooms and marketing jobs. The feminisation of marketing continues apace, and more women are moving into positions that were once male bastions. Feminist theories provide frameworks to help us understand how women have been integrated into the marketing profession, and whether and how the profession changes as a consequence.

We should not be embarrassed or defensive about this partisan focus on women and women's issues, or about placing these explicitly on the wider marketing agenda. Too often in the past marketing researchers produced overgeneralised, essentialised and trivialised accounts of women as consumers. In a similar vein, there is a paucity of studies on women in the marketing professions. Indeed, it is often assumed that the marketing manager is male whereas the consumer is female.

Feminist academics may focus on women, but this does not mean that men are excluded, or that feminist perspectives are irrelevant for men. Indeed many men consider themselves feminists (Digby 1998) and many others are empathetic to the aims of feminism. Clearly it is difficult, if not impossible, to study women without also studying men and gender relationships. Furthermore, issues relating to the feminising of the marketing profession and the consequent implications, in terms both of practice and of professional status, are of equal import to the men who work in marketing.

Whilst feminists have examined and commented on marketing phenomena for many decades, it is only within the past decade that feminist analyses from *within* the marketing academy have emerged and developed. Our main aim is to bring together in a single volume the latest thinking and research on feminist perspectives in marketing from marketing academics. It also offers an opportunity to reflect on how the relationship between marketing and feminism has developed and how it might develop in the future.

We have talked about feminist perspectives and the relationship between marketing and feminism and at this point it might be appropriate to discuss in more detail what we mean by feminism and feminist perspectives. We recognise that many of our readers may be unfamiliar with feminist theories and why and how they provide such a compelling framework for the study of gender and women's issues in marketing. For this reason we begin our chapter by reviewing some of the key features of feminist thought. We continue with an examination of the relationship between marketing and feminism in terms of the past, the present and the future. Finally we offer an overview of each of the chapters, with our thoughts on how these contribute to the developing relationship between marketing and feminism.

WHAT EXACTLY IS FEMINISM?

Bracketing feminism is difficult, as there is no single philosophy that can be labelled feminism. Indeed some scholars argue that 'feminisms' may be a more appropriate term since there are many feminist positions (Whelehan 1995). These include liberal feminism, radical feminism, socialist feminism, postmodern feminism, post-feminism, *l'écriture féminine*, and so on. For example, liberal feminists have consistently argued for equality of opportunity for women, particularly in relation to the world of work. Other feminists argue that equality of opportunity is not enough to redress gender asymmetry, and that wider structural and cultural changes are needed that will impact on both genders. This argument is persuasive. The past two decades may have marked a transformation in the lives of many women, but not without some cost. Many women undertake what is termed the 'double shift': paid work outside the home in addition to 'normal' domestic duties in the home. Thus, in the absence of a transformation of wider social systems and values, true equality of opportunity remains a distant goal. The differences between these feminisms can seem substantial and irresolvable. This perception seriously underestimates both the areas of commonality amongst feminists and the capacity within feminism to encourage and embrace diversity.

Common aims

Whatever the differences, feminists agree that women have suffered social injustice because of their sex and thus seek to redress this gender imbalance. Feminism involves a combination of social criticism (of the sources and impact of gender asymmetry) and social action (to highlight and improve the position of women). Thus, politics is inherent in feminism:

> Feminism is a politics. It is a politics directed at changing existing power relations between women and men in society. These power relations structure all areas of life, the family, education and welfare, the worlds of work and politics, culture and leisure. They determine who does what for whom, what we are and what we might become.
>
> (Weedon 1997: 1)

Given its roots in socio-political critique and action, feminism has an uneasy relationship with theory and philosophy; indeed some radical feminists are anti-theory. The more feminists have engaged in social criticism, the more they have identified the inadequacies of mainstream philosophy and epistemology and developed new thought in these areas. Feminist research tends to go beyond the description, explanation or understanding of phenomena (Ozanne and Stern 1993). Just as feminism as a socio-political movement incorporates the twin aims of social criticism and social change, so too does feminist theory and research. As social critics, feminist researchers have exposed knowledge as gendered. As advocates of social change, they seek to redress the gender imbalance in knowledge by offering alternative theories and methods of creating knowledge. This involves a complete rethink of the very basis of disciplinary knowledge and, in particular, its 'male' perspective and gender-blindness.

The assertion that knowledge is gendered and gender-blind needs an explanation. Some readers may recall the early days of the women's movement in the 1960s and 1970s when there were arguments that women were basically no different from men: 'anything you can do I can do better', or at least as well. Differences between males and females were often played down for fear that these would be used as arguments to stifle women's progress. It is easy to appreciate why such arguments arose, since higher value is given to that which is considered male and lower value to that which is considered female. The privileging of male over female is to be found across time and across cultures. Whilst there are many reasons offered as to why this should be the case, one that has considerable support is the way in which philosophers have dichotomised male and female.

Over the centuries philosophers have found dichotomous categories (Jay 1981) or dualisms (Plumwood 1993) useful in analysing and explaining the human condition. Plato used the categories reason/emotion and universal/particular; for Hegel and Rousseau public/private, male/female and reason/nature proved useful; Marx employed production/reproduction, mental/manual, freedom/necessity; and Descartes emphasised mind/body, human/nature and subject/object, to name but a few (Lloyd 1984; Plumwood 1993). The feminist argument is that these dichotomies operate in a way that privileges one of each pair so that, for example, reason, mind and male are deemed superior to emotion, body and female. Indeed they are conceptualised in such a way that the latter of each pair is defined only in relation to the former, by what the former is not, as befits its inferior status. Thus, reason is defined and emotion becomes seen as that which reason is not. The terms are also linked so that 'superior' terms form a kind of coherent group: mind, reason, public and male, in contrast to such 'inferior' terms as body, emotion, private and female. In this way female has come to be defined by what male is not (an incomplete man) and has become associated with other linked inferior terms: emotion, body, object, and so on. Indeed these dichotomies, created by culture and society, have often taken on a 'natural' or biological basis or justification. For example, women are often portrayed as being more emotional than men, as if emotionality was a sex-specific disposition. It remains the case that it is more socially acceptable for women than for men to express emotion, and thus it is a gender difference created in culture rather than a sex difference rooted in 'nature'. This distinction between sex (the biology of a person) and gender (created in culture) is vital to the feminist project for it means that whilst gender differences may be pervasive in culture they are not immutable.

For many feminists the privileging of 'male' values is reflected in knowledge and knowledge production. Academic knowledge is no more perspectiveless than the culture in which it is produced. It has traditionally reflected a dominant 'male' worldview and it is this gendering of knowledge that academic feminists have exposed. Feminist thought and philosophy is particularly influential in the academic world, and disciplines across the academy have been subjected to feminist analyses, highlighting the gendered nature of discipline knowledge previously assumed to be perspectiveless and neutral.

Celebrating diversity

During the 1980s the diversity of feminist positions came to the fore. Women of colour, notably bell hooks, pointed out that talk of shared oppression and universal sisterhood reflected the experiences and perspectives of white, middle-class women. Gender is not a sole defining category or experience, since no woman is only a woman. Race, class and sexuality can intersect with gender in ways that problematise talk of oppression on the basis of gender alone. Indeed, the experiences of black women or working-class women may have little in common with those of white and middle-class women (see Peñaloza, Chapter 3).

Similarly, it was argued that the notion of a universal feminism, largely an Anglo-American feminism, failed to take into account the experiences and perspectives of women in different countries and cultures. In these respects feminism, which had done so much to expose and redress the gender-blindness of academic knowledge and discourse, was forced to recognise its own 'blindness' (Crowley 1999), as new feminist positions and perspectives emerged to challenge such 'traditional' positions as liberal, radical or socialist feminism. This presented a very real challenge to feminism as a unified project. Was it possible to incorporate all these differences into feminist theory or would the vision of what constituted feminist theory and the feminist project need a more radical rethink?

The situation was exacerbated by the growing popularity of postmodernist perspectives. These offered a radical critique of gender and the idea of a shared oppression based on gender, arguments that had always been central to the feminist project. Postmodernists argue that gender is one of those universalising and unhelpful binaries that typify modern Western thought. Many feminists agree with this position but are reluctant to dispense with this binary or to embrace postmodernism, and with good reason. Susan Bordo captured the difficulties for many feminists in accepting a postmodernist analysis of feminism and gender. Bordo (1990: 152) stated that 'like it or not, in our present culture, our activities are coded as "male" or "female". . . . One cannot be gender neutral in this culture'. Feminism is not simply about theory or radical intellectual critique; it is a political practice with the aim of improving the position of women, and it remains the case that women across the globe, whatever their class, race or sexuality, are in a less favourable position than their male counterparts.

Secondly, the search for commonalities amongst women in the face of difference and diversity was proving difficult to abandon. Indeed, it has been argued that feminism might focus on the commonalities of resistance (how women across the globe identify and define their problems and seek to address these) rather than assume a shared oppression amongst women:

> . . . the need to continue moving on from nineteenth century visions of global sisterhood to an understanding of the range of local and global feminisms.

> Although the reality remains that women around the globe are worse off then their male counterparts, future possibilities for building global links are more likely to be found through looking for commonalities of resistance rather than assuming a sameness of oppression.
>
> (Flew *et al.* 1999)

As this brief discussion illustrates there is now a plethora of feminist positions, yet the possibility of unity in diversity remains. In this respect feminism stands at the intersection between modernism and postmodernism with a foot in each camp (Crowley 1999). Additionally, in contrast to the univocality which is all too often symptomatic of many academic discourses, feminists celebrate multivocality. Diversity is regarded as a strength rather than a weakness. Furthermore, this goes some way to ensuring that feminist thought and feminist practice does not remain static but is in constant change, in perpetual transformation. The nascent interdisciplinarity and capacity for perpetual transformation in feminism provide a framework that can help us understand phenomena and, simultaneously, embrace the changes taking place.

THE RELATIONSHIP BETWEEN MARKETING AND FEMINISM

This capacity for embracing change and perpetual transformation is useful when examining the evolving relationship between marketing and feminism. In marketing in the past gender rather than feminism was an issue. In spite of its salience, gender was not well understood or conceptualised in marketing theory, research or practice. Theoretical categories such as sex, gender, sexuality and sex-role were often conflated. Gender was (and still is) one of the most widely used segmentation variables, and most market research studies, even today, employ it as a quota control, or as a face-sheet variable in survey research. Academic and practitioner research studies in marketing that studied sex/gender tended to report that differences either did (or did not) exist between males and females, and left this as the finding, without any real attempt to investigate how, in what way and, importantly, why differences were found. Artz and Venkatesh (1991: 619) observed that studies of gender issues in marketing and advertising generated 'superficial and self-evident inferences', were devoid of theory and were preoccupied with the single issue of sex-stereotyping. Costa (1994) argued that we should stop accepting these findings as important since the field of gender and consumer research had advanced well beyond such simplistic and superficial findings.

The many analyses of gender representations in advertising during the 1970s and 1980s did not refer to the growing body of theory on gender, nor did they draw from the literature on gender and marketing phenomena developed by feminist scholars working in other disciplines. Even Rena Bartos' (1982) groundbreaking work that highlighted marketers' misconceptions about female consumers did not draw explicitly from this literature. The failure to acknowledge the feminist literature on these issues was perhaps due to the fact that the mass entry of women into the business and management professions and into university business and management programmes is a comparatively recent phenomenon (Stern 1996).

The late 1980s and early 1990s saw the introduction of many radical new perspectives on marketing, including feminism. The first publications concentrated on presenting feminist thought to a marketing audience and exploring the possibilities for feminist perspectives in marketing and consumer research (Ozanne and Stern 1993). These papers drew attention to the ways that marketing theory and research trivialised and essentialised women and sex/gender issues. They also argued that theory and knowledge in marketing and consumer research were gendered in unrecognised ways.

Bristor and Fischer (1993) presented a challenge to the way gender-based knowledge is constructed and sustained in marketing, and they recommended that marketing and consumer researchers review their theories and methods. Peñaloza (1994) recommended the use of participatory and dialogic methods to achieve a greater understanding of the consumer. Fischer and Bristor (1994) deconstructed the rhetoric of marketing relationships. They argued that the discourse associated with the marketer/consumer relationship revealed parallels to the male/female relationship, with notions of seduction and patriarchy woven into that relationship.

The situation changed rapidly as an increasing number of marketing researchers applied feminist perspectives to marketing phenomena, particularly within the field of consumer research. Four conferences were organised on the subject of gender, consumer behaviour and, latterly, marketing (Costa 1991, 1993, 1996; Fischer and Wardlow 1998) and the conference proceedings of the Association for Consumer Research now regularly include papers on gender issues in marketing (Dobscha 1993; Larsen 1993). Of course not all studies of gender in marketing refer to feminist work on gender and certainly feminists do not own the gender debate. Whilst undoubtedly contributing to our knowledge and understanding of the relationship between marketing and gender, few of these papers have been written from a feminist perspective.

Feminist marketing academics begin to provide an internal critique in the 1990s, and they do not differ in their basic assumptions and approaches from feminist scholars in other disciplines. The portrayal of marketing as a negative force in the lives of women still holds considerable sway in feminist-inspired analyses of marketing and consumption. This is the case whether they come from within the discipline (marketing and consumer research academics) or without (feminist scholars in areas as diverse as sociology, geography, cultural and media studies). All too often the focus on the negative aspects of the relationship between marketing and women can divert researchers' attention from its positive potential. In other words, we need to identify the possible strengths in the relationship as well as the weaknesses.

Marketing practices have, in many ways, predicated an improvement in the social and political position of women (see Scott, Chapter 2). In stark contrast to other disciplines in the academy, marketers have always studied women's lives; the consumer was and still is assumed to be female. To illustrate, market researchers examined the everyday aspects of women's lives such as doing the family laundry or preparing meals long before housework became an acceptable topic of study in sociology (Oakley 1974). Even today marketers take for granted the importance of studying women's lives – a situation not always experienced by feminists in other academic disciplines (see Peñaloza, Chapter 3). Of course we should not assume that these studies are always positive for women, nor are we suggesting that feminist marketing academics become apologists for marketing. Rather, we argue that the relationship between marketing and women is not quite as simplistic and unidimensional as it is often represented.

More recently feminist scholars working in other disciplines have also argued that women can benefit from marketing and advertising. For example, Nava (1992) and others (Chaney 1983; Lancaster 1995) argue that the development of department stores was beneficial to women, as consumers and as store employees. As consumers, women suddenly had an area of expertise (shopping) that was legitimised in the public sector (Nava 1992). This also led to a heightened awareness of women's entitlement outside the sphere of consumption, and Nava (1992) believes that this made a significant contribution to the conditions for modern feminism.

It is important, therefore, that we examine the subtleties that underpin marketing's relationship with feminism, a relationship whereby marketing can simultaneously be represented in both an exploitative and a liberating light.

Women in marketing

One important aspect of this relationship that has been overlooked is the increasing numbers of women who study and work in marketing. Feminist academics within and outside of marketing have tended to focus on the relationship between marketing and women as consumers. Few studies focus on the women who work in the profession (Maclaran, Stevens and Catterall 1998). There are a small number of studies of women in sales roles in the marketing literature (Dawson 1992), in advertising (Alvesson 1998) and in public relations (Krider 1997).

Similarly, few women are profiled or mentioned in the various histories of marketing thought. It is tempting to assume that women did not figure in this history because they were not present in sufficient numbers (women had only a very small presence in the marketing academy or its mainstream literature until relatively recently) or because their contributions were minimal or irrelevant. Cooke (1999) showed how in recent years women have been written in to the histories of organisation development where previously their 'contributions' were unacknowledged, illustrating that history is socially constructed. In this instance history is reworked and re-presented either to reflect the societal changes in power relations between men and women or to sustain the legitimacy of the activity amongst those on whose behalf they are written (the women as well as the men who study and practise management). There is some evidence that marketing history will follow suit. Women were present as marketing practitioners in marketing past and their influence on marketing theory and practices is only now beginning to be examined. Waller-Zukerman and Carsky (1990) examined the contribution of home economists (predominantly women) to our understanding of consumer behaviour. McDonald and King (1996) pointed out that there were a number of women amongst the founders of the Market Research Society in Britain during the 1940s. Women also made important contributions in the advertising industry (see O'Donohoe, Chapter 5). However, following Cooke (1999), the paucity of historical and current studies of women in marketing is somewhat surprising, given the growing number of women who now study marketing and enter marketing employment.

This feminising of marketing raises a number of issues, including the impact women may or may not have on how marketing is conceptualised. How has it affected the way academics and practitioners talk about and do marketing work? Has it had an impact on professional values and ethics, and on professional status?

Insider perspectives on marketing and feminism

The subtleties in the relationship between marketing and feminism and the feminising of marketing work raise an issue that feminist marketing academics have so far neglected to discuss. Feminists within the marketing academy need to consider whether and in what ways our internal feminist critique of marketing differs from the external critiques provided by feminist scholars in other disciplines. In what ways does our knowledge and experience of marketing as insiders offer opportunities and insights not always available to scholars outside the discipline, and how is this reflected in our feminist critiques of marketing?

One of the hallmarks of feminist scholarship is that it is transdisciplinary. It follows that feminist scholars harbour doubts about a retreat into individual disciplines, which talk of an 'insider perspective' implies. In this respect Whelehan draws attention to one of the contradictions inherent in feminist discourse:

> . . . on the one hand it needs to emphasise its separateness from the disciplines, as they are traditionally defined, because of its nascent interdisciplinarity; and yet on the other hand there exists a strong desire to be credited for attempts to transform and expand those disciplines from within by highlighting the gaps and silences on the subject of women.
>
> (Whelehan 1995: 146)

It remains the case that women's issues are not explicitly on wider marketing agendas, either in academic research or in professional practice. The success of feminism has been largely due to its focus on women and women's issues that were previously ignored or not taken seriously. A feminist presence in marketing is important to raise awareness of these issues. Of course, we need to recognise that many women academics, students and practitioners neither identify with nor support the need for feminist analyses of marketing as a discipline or as a professional practice. If feminist scholarship is to have a future in marketing we simply cannot ignore this issue. After all, our work makes claims to either speak for or reflect the interests and concerns of women who work in marketing and who, as consumers, are the subject of marketing practices. If our work is to begin to realise its emancipatory aims (social change as well as social criticism) it needs to be read, studied and critically analysed and evaluated by our academic and practitioner colleagues, and our students. This will not happen unless we engage with marketing theory, practice and practitioners from a position of understanding based on our 'insider' knowledge.

CURRENT RESEARCH ON THE RELATIONSHIP

The contributors to this volume discuss in detail many of the issues we have raised on the developing relationship between marketing and feminism whilst simultaneously reflecting the heterogeneity that is feminism. Linda Scott and Lisa Peñaloza discuss the developing relationship between marketing and feminism from historical and current perspectives. In Chapter 2 Linda Scott argues that we have too readily accepted the prevailing feminist view that the relationship between marketing and feminism is a negative one, focusing on its weaknesses rather than its strengths. She points out that this perspective has its roots in the history of the feminist movement (particularly in the USA) whereby early feminists, many of whom belonged to a 'leisured class', were disdainful of 'trade' and commercial activity. This position stands in marked contrast to their actions, since leading feminists and the feminist movement itself undoubtedly benefited from commercial and marketing activities. Lisa Peñaloza (Chapter 3) offers us at once a personal and also a political study of feminism, gender and race in the context of the marketing academy, arguing, like Scott, that we need to recognise that the relationship between marketing and feminism is a continually evolving one. She emphasises the need for us to think about how feminism and feminist perspectives in marketing are introduced and represented in the marketing classroom and in marketing scholarship. However, she offers a note of caution about focusing too heavily on what unites us as feminist marketers by pointing out the dangers of overgeneralising women's experiences of and in marketing, experiences that vary considerably between generations, races, classes and sexualities.

Chapters 4 and 5 address issues relating to advertising. Feminist-inspired analyses of advertising tackle a wide range of complex and subtle issues. Barbara Stern has brought feminist literary criticism to the forefront in her analyses of advertising text in the past decade. In Chapter 4 she provides a thorough grounding on the origins and nature of reader-response theory and its relevance for feminist deconstructions of text. Importantly she provides recommendations on how advertisers and their advertising agencies might be more proactive in response to the significant body of theoretical and research work in this area. In Chapter 5 Stephanie O'Donohoe continues on this theme, exploring the complex relationship between texts and readers in relation to the gendered consumption of advertisements. She suggests that women may adopt a 'bi-textual' approach to advertising text and that, in due course, as more and more women become involved in the advertising industry, gynocentric advertising texts will emerge which speak *to* us rather than *at* us as women.

Feminist academics have had considerable impact across the academy on the ways we think about and do research, and particularly in respect of subject/object relationships, research ethics and reflexivity. Lorraine Friend and Shona Thompson (Chapter 6) review this contribution and illustrate how feminist-inspired research can begin to meet its twin aims of social criticism and social change. Using a technique known as memory-work they explore how women can become more empowered in their daily lives, through drawing on their collective strength. Margaret Hogg, Shona Bettany and George Long (Chapter 7) examine these issues in relation to marketing research, illustrating their arguments and reflections with one of the most influential pieces of marketing research to be published in recent years, namely, Susan Fournier's work on consumer–brand relationships.

Both these chapters on feminist methodology raise important issues on the problematics as well as the benefits of implementing dialogic research. An aim of feminist research is the transformation of the researcher/researched relationship. Reinharz (1979) suggested that too frequently academic researchers apply a rape model whereby they hit, take and run on the respondent and offer little or nothing in return for their co-operation. In contrast, feminists attempt to incorporate the respondent into the research process, in a dialogic, inclusive manner. Susan Fournier, who was approached to provide some feedback on the evolving work of Margaret Hogg, Shona Bettany and George Long (Chapter 7), found herself in a 'respondent' role in this dialogic process. She points out that as researchers we can benefit considerably from such role reversal. The dialogic process is an evolving one; we may be in regular contact with respondents over many months and, indeed, the relationship between researcher and respondent is also likely to evolve. Thus, participating in the research process can intrude on our respondents' lives in ways that they can never fully anticipate. Whilst respondents are involved in the analysis and interpretation process, they can be surprised, even shocked, at the way we researchers employ the data they provide. She points out that there is an epistemological issue here that goes beyond what the respondents' feel about how data are used. By its very nature, interpretive research involves employing concepts and frameworks as lenses through which we view and make sense of data. Respondents may find themselves placed in a reactive position, responding within the researcher's framework with its own particular boundaries. Striking an equal balance between the researcher and the researched is clearly never easy. Specifically, the representation of the respondent still risks being a partial one that privileges the researcher. Ultimately it is the researcher who is responsible for the final written account of the research and who has to justify the research to peers and a wider audience.

Stephen Brown further explores the theme and the dilemma of representation in Chapter 8. His focus is not what we write but how we write as academics. It is a widely accepted view that all women learn to read and write according to a male norm (Fetterley 1986). This may be particularly true of academic text, with its rigid adherence to conventional means of expression. Stephen, in a characteristically carnivalesque and indeed controversial chapter, challenges us to embrace the virtues of *l'écriture féminine* against this Western patriarchal tradition of rational and linear writing. Writing in a discursive and circular way he suggests an alternative 'feminine' way to approach academic writing. His historical 'bouillabaisse' weaves together a discussion of the long-forgotten American feminist Victoria Woodhow with other, better-known (male) figures, including Karl Marx, Thorstein Veblen and P. T. Barnum.

Chapters 9 and 10 address issues relating to global feminism and global marketing, and Len Tiu Wright and Mihaela Keleman examine the advertising industry in these contexts. They discuss the advertising strategies of Western companies in Malaysia and Romania, arguing that they need to encompass a clearer understanding of the ways in which individuals make sense of the world in particular social and cultural contexts. Focusing specifically on women consumers, they suggest that there needs to be a greater emphasis on how values are constituted by the religious, political, demographic, economic and ideological environments of these indigenous cultures.

In the 1980s and early 1990s a number of feminist studies of Western women's magazines argued that these magazines were part of a social, cultural and economic mechanism designed to control and tyrannise women (McRobbie 1991; Winship 1987; McCracken 1993). Increasingly, however, women's magazines are celebrated for their liberatory potential, their ability to offer multiple choices, multiple identities, and multiple pleasures for women (Moore 1986). In her historical analysis of a Soviet magazine, *Rabotnitsa*, Natasha Tolstikova examines the connection between political systems and the status of women. Drawing on parallels with the contribution of American magazines to women's oppression, she illuminates the factors that reinforce political ideologies.

Chapters 11 and 12 examine aspects of consumer research. Helen Woodruffe-Burton and Sue Eccles have developed the consumer research literature on compulsive and compensatory consumption as it relates to women. They offer fascinating insights into why women go shopping, discuss the many facets of 'retail therapy' for women consumers, and explore the nature of shopping addiction. They conclude that women's reasons for this shopping behaviour may be as diverse as the lived experiences of individual women themselves.

The concept of servicescape has considerable currency, having been brought to our attention by Bitner (1992) and developed more recently by Sherry (1997). Helene Hill, in Chapter 12, examines the concept of women-focused spaces in her work on cafés/bars in Amsterdam. In so doing she raises a number of interesting gender issues about the relationship between women and the servicescape, and the relationship between heterosexual and lesbian servicescapes, discussing both the commonalities and the differences between them. She concludes by suggesting that gender identity and sexual identity play a large part in determining what we expect from the servicescape.

The next two chapters examine aspects of marketing theory that have emerged as strong and fruitful areas of research over the past decade, namely, relationship marketing and green marketing. These areas have rarely been subject to critical feminist analyses. The recent rise and rise of relationship marketing can be seen as part of the feminising of management discourse (Fondas 1997). Just a decade earlier Ries and Trout (1986) talked about marketing as warfare. Eileen Fischer, in Chapter 13, offers a note of caution about the new relationship paradigm. Marketers have ignored or have deliberately deselected 'unpromising' target markets, notably poor consumers who tend also to be women. Drawing an analogy with John Fowles' novel *The Collector*, Eileen argues that mass-customisation can be a powerful means of capturing and disenfranchising individual consumers. Given that women continue to be a disadvantaged market this is particularly pertinent from a feminist perspective. Eileen suggests that those who escape marketers' one-to-one attentions may in fact be the fortunate ones, as 'promising' targets can become trapped in relationships with suppliers.

Ecofeminists argue that the interests of women and nature should be aligned and that the patriarchal systems that dominate and devalue both must be challenged. Taking an ecofeminist perspective, Susan Dobscha and Julie Ozanne explore the mind/body disconnection and how this is reinforced in the marketplace, to the extent that women's relationship to their bodies is often framed in terms of consumer decision-making problems. Needless to say, the solutions offered to these problems exact a price that harms both women and the environment. Based on interviews with women consumers who have opted out of consumerism in order to be more in tune with nature and their own bodies, their work highlights the subversive power of women to transform themselves and their relationship with nature and the marketplace.

Some time in the future a marketing historian may choose to look back at the origins and evolution of gender research in marketing. One name will be writ large in that analysis – Janeen Arnold Costa. Her contribution to this field is considerable, not just in terms of her own research on gender, culture and consumption but also in terms of her sheer determination to encourage and inspire others to develop this field. Janeen organised the first three conferences on gender and consumer research and has edited a book in the area. It is fitting, then, that Janeen should have the last word in this particular volume. In Chapter 15 she presents the results of an extensive study on the interaction of culture, gender and consumption. Through this she offers a framework designed to assess overall cross-cultural differences and similarities in gender and consumption in traditional and developing societies around the globe.

CONCLUSIONS

It seems to us that the core theme running through these chapters is how we, as marketing academics, are in a unique position to renegotiate the relationship between marketing and feminism. We believe the book will offer new insights, new challenges, and a positive vision of the future of this relationship. We hope this will provide inspiration, not only to those who are simultaneously marketers and feminists but also to those in the broader academic and indeed practitioner communities.

REFERENCES

Alvesson, M. (1998) 'Gender relations and identity at work: a case study of masculinities and feminities in an advertising agency', *Human Relations* 51, 8: 969–1005.

Artz, N. and Venkatesh, A. (1991) 'Gender representation in advertising', in R. H. Holman and M. R. Solomon (eds) *Advances in Consumer Research* 18, Provo, UT: Association for Consumer Research, 618–23.

Bartos, R. (1982) *The Moving Target: What Every Marketer Should Know about Women*, New York: Free Press.

Bitner, M. J. (1992) 'Servicescapes: the impact of physical surroundings on customers and employees', *Journal of Marketing* 56: 57–71.

Bordo, S. (1990) 'Feminism, postmodernism and gender-scepticism', in L. J. Nicholson (ed.) *Feminism/Postmodernism*, London: Routledge, 133–56.

Bristor, J. M. and Fischer, E. (1993) 'Feminist thought: implications for consumer research', *Journal of Consumer Research* 19, March: 518–36.

Campbell, C. (1995) 'The sociology of consumption', in D. Miller (ed.) *Acknowledging Consumption: A Review of New Studies*, London: Routledge, 96–126.

Chaney, D. (1983) 'The department as cultural form', *Theory, Culture and Society* 1, 3: 22–31.

Cooke, B. (1999) 'Writing the Left out of management theory: the historiography of the management of change', *Organization* 6, 1: 81–105.

Costa, J. A. (ed.) (1991) *Proceedings of the First Conference on Gender and Consumer Behavior*, Salt Lake City: University of Utah Printing Press.

—— (1993) *Proceedings of the Second Conference on Gender and Consumer Behavior*, Salt Lake City: University of Utah Printing Press.

—— (1994) 'Gender issues: gender as a cultural construct', in C. T. Allen and D. R. John (eds) *Advances in Consumer Research* 21, Provo, UT: Association for Consumer Research, 372–3.

—— (1996) *Proceedings of the Third Conference on Gender, Marketing and Consumer Behavior*, Salt Lake City: University of Utah Printing Press.

Crowley, H. (1999) 'Women's studies: between a rock and a hard place or just another cell in the beehive?', *Feminist Review* 61, Spring: 131–50.

Dawson, L. M. (1992) 'Will feminization change the ethics in the sales profession?', *Journal of Professional Selling and Sales Management* 12, 1: 21–33.

Digby, T. (1998) *Men Doing Feminism*, New York: Routledge.

Dobscha, S. (1993) 'Women and the environment: applying ecofeminism to environmentally related consumption', in L. McAlister and M. L. Rothschild (eds) *Advances in Consumer Research* 20, Provo, UT: Association for Consumer Research, 36–9.

Fetterley, J. (1978) *The Resisting Reader: A Feminist Approach to American Fiction*, Bloomington: Indiana University Press.

—— (1986) 'Introduction', in P. P. Schweickart and E. A. Flynn, *Gender and Reading: Essays on Readers, Texts and Contexts*, Baltimore, MD: The Johns Hopkins University Press.

Fischer, E. and Bristor, J. (1994) 'A feminist poststructuralist analysis of the rhetoric of marketing relationships', *International Journal of Research in Marketing* 11, 4: 317–31.

Fischer, E. and Wardlow, D. L. (eds) (1998) *Proceedings of the Fourth Conference on Gender, Marketing and Consumer Behavior*, San Francisco: Association for Consumer Research.

Flew, F., Bagilhole, B., Carabine, J., Fenton, N., Kiyzinger, C., Lister, R. and Wilkinson, S. (1999) 'Introduction: local feminisms, global cultures', *Women's Studies International Forum* 22, 4: 393–403.

Fondas, N. (1997) 'Feminization unveiled: management qualities in contemporary writings', *Academy of Management Review* 22, 1: 257–82.

Friedan, B. (1982) *The Feminine Mystique*, Harmondsworth: Pelican.

Jay, N. (1981) 'Gender and dichotomy', *Feminist Studies* 7, 1: 39–56.

Krider, D. S. (1997) 'The experiences of women in a public relations firm: a phenomenological explanation', *Journal of Business Communication* 34, 4: 437–54.

Lancaster, B. (1995) *The Department Store: A Social History*, London: Leicester University Press.

Larsen, V. (1993) 'A sociolinguistic approach to gender and personal selling', in L. McAlister and M. L. Rothschild (eds) *Advances in Consumer Research* 20, Provo, UT: Association for Consumer Research, 48–51.

Lloyd, G. (1984) *The Man of Reason: 'Male' and 'Female' in Western Philosophy*, London: Methuen.

McCracken, E. (1993) *Decoding Women's Magazines from* Mademoiselle *to* Ms., Basingstoke: Macmillan.

McDonald, C. and King, S. (1996) *Sampling the Universe: The Growth, Development and Influence of Market Research in Britain since 1945*, London: NTC Publications.

Maclaran, P., Stevens, L. and Catterall, M. (1998) 'The glasshouse effect: women in marketing management', *Journal of Marketing Practice: Applied Marketing Science* 4, 5: 134–47.

McRobbie, A. (1991) *Feminism and Youth Culture*, London: Macmillan.

Moore, S. (1986) 'Permitted pleasures', *Women's Review* 10: 9–10.

Nava, M. (1992) *Changing Cultures: Feminism, Youth and Consumerism*, London: Sage.

Oakley, A. (1974) *The Sociology of Housework*, London: Robertson.

Ozanne, J. L. and Stern, B. B. (1993) 'The feminine imagination and social change: four feminist approaches to social problems', in L. McAlister and M. L. Rothschild (eds) *Advances in Consumer Research* 20, Provo, UT: Association for Consumer Research, 35.

Peñaloza, L. (1994) 'Crossing boundaries/crossing lines: a look at the nature of gender boundaries and their impact on marketing research', *International Journal of Research in Marketing* 11, 4: 359–79.

Plumwood, V. (1993) *Feminism and the Mastery of Nature*, London: Routledge.

Reinharz, S. (1979) *On Becoming a Social Scientist*, San Francisco: Jossey-Bass.

Ries, A. and Trout, J. (1986) *Marketing Warfare*, New York: Penguin.

Sherry, J.F., Jnr (ed.) (1997) *Servicescapes: The Concept of Place in Contemporary Markets*, Chicago: NTC Business Books.

Stern, B. B. (1996) 'Curriculum change: feminist theory in the classroom', in J. A. Costa (ed.) *Proceedings of the Third Conference on Gender, Marketing and Consumer Behavior*, Salt Lake City: University of Utah Printing Press, 228–137.

Waller-Zuckerman, M. E. and Carsky, M. L. (1990) 'Contribution of women to U.S. marketing thought: the consumers' perspective, 1990–1940', *Journal of the Academy of Marketing Science* 18, 4: 313–18.

Weedon, C. (1997) *Feminist Practice and Poststructuralist Theory*, Oxford: Blackwell.

Whelehan, I. (1995) *Modern Feminist Thought: From the Second Wave to Post-feminism*, Edinburgh: Edinburgh University Press.

Wilson, F. (1999) 'Genderquake? Did you feel the earth move?', *Organization* 6, 3: 529–41.

Winship, J. (1987) *Inside Women's Magazines*, London: Pandora.

2 Market feminism: the case for a paradigm shift

Linda Scott

INTRODUCTION

The most salient aspect of this moment in human history is the globalisation of the market economy. Because human economic interaction inevitably involves an exchange of technology, culture and politics, as well as goods, the moment might be propitious for the globalisation of feminism, too. The feminist movements that have typified political life in the post-industrial Western nations during the twentieth century have left women with unprecedented power to influence world events. The potential for females in relatively advantaged positions to assist those who remain under truly crippling forms of patriarchy is more palpable than it has ever been. Certainly the need is great: the new world information systems horrify us with stories of honour killings, genital mutilations and other brutalities visited upon women in the developing nations. In the wake of the break-up of the former Soviet Union, women from the former Eastern bloc countries are dislocated, disempowered and, too often, forced into prostitution.

In contrast, the achievements of feminism in Western Europe and North America – in government and academia, but particularly in the private sector – have been impressive. Over the past twenty-five years, the number of women holding responsible positions in business, especially in market-related areas, has mushroomed. Finding a woman at the helm of a major corporation is still newsworthy, but happens more frequently. Though women still get neither the pay nor the prestige that men do, the progress made in a single generation has been dramatic. Women in the private sector of the global economy are now positioned to effect change in important ways.

The tragedy is that, for many, feminist thought remains chained to an anti-market prejudice. Numerous writers have asserted the fundamental incompatibility between market economics and feminism. Yet, as surveys of global feminism clearly demonstrate, the movement has had a wider, more lasting impact in those very societies where capitalism and consumer culture are most fully developed (Chafetz and Dworkin 1986). In truth, between the abysmal conditions for women in the developing nations and emerging accounts of women under the Soviets, it is less clear than ever that capitalism and the market offer the worst socio-economic conditions for the advancement of feminism. This obvious contradiction between theory and data should cause questions to be raised, but so far it has not. In the present political environment, therefore, using momentum provided by the market to spread the acceptance of feminist values remains unthinkable.

Indeed, the prejudice against the marketplace in contemporary feminist thought, rather than empowering feminists in the private sector, thrusts upon them a dilemma. How is one to act as a feminist while working for an ad agency? Or while managing a line of toys? Today's feminism is so unbendingly negative in its approach to market activity that steps taken to present positive imagery in ads or make progressive toys for girls are sweepingly dismissed: women who try to act on their feminism through marketing activities are often seen as merely co-opting feminism for private profit. While such an attitude may give abstract comfort to academics, it does legions of working women a disservice – and shuts off an avenue for the advancement of feminism already shown to be broadly effective. We are thus ill-equipped to rise to the opportunity before us.

The purpose of this chapter is to help create an intellectual environment where the unthinkable may be considered and the unspeakable may be articulated: Can the market be used to advance feminism? And, if so, how? I will approach the issue with a two-pronged argument. First, I will raise questions about whether feminism itself is (or has ever been) 'outside the market' by unmasking the ways that leading feminists have advanced their cause as well as their own financial interests through the shrewd use of marketing. By doing this, I hope to inspire a little healthy scepticism in my readers and to give them some ammunition for future essays and policy discussions. My second tactic will be to show how women in the private sector historically have expressed their feminism through market activities. By this, I hope to open others up to attitudes and strategies more in keeping with the trajectory of global politics (and the empirical record of global feminism). After identifying the contradictions inherent in the anti-market stance I will suggest how a paradigm shift in feminist outlook – toward what we could call 'market feminism' – might be realised.

What is offered in this chapter can only be a sketch, given the limits of space. It's a suggestive outline, however, and one that I hope will be provocative enough to spur on others to investigate further. One of the most noticeable shortcomings is that I will only be retracing American feminist history here, rather than British or French or, certainly, global feminism. My excuses are both personal and strategic. I write about American feminism because that is my area of expertise. Nevertheless, I think the United States is a good place to begin for two reasons: (1) the movement in America is often noted as the most visible, radical and widespread among historical efforts to advance the cause of women and (2) American culture is often pinpointed as 'ground zero' of capitalism, marketing and consumer culture. To begin in the place that is home to both the most virulent capitalism *and* the most virulent feminism seems somehow appropriate.

CONTRADICTIONS IN ANTI-MARKET FEMINISM

The women who first organised on behalf of American women's rights were atypical. Though the women of nineteenth-century America were culturally diverse and predominantly working folk, the early feminists were uniformly of British descent, Puritan-Quaker religion and leisure-class status (Hersh 1978). Their attitude to commerce was coloured, predictably, by both the ideology of their tradition and the challenges of their historical situation.

The tradition of the 'founding feminists' held that only commonfolk participated in commerce, while aristocrats like themselves remained above it. Working people produced what they could from their own labours, but most had to trade with others in order to survive. Aristocrats, in contrast, were usually large landowners whose tenants and capital were supposed to supply them with all they needed. In reality, of course, the ruling class participated in the market through the rents they collected from tenants, the interest they made on capital, and the trades they made for luxuries even they could not produce themselves. Though the gentry's claim to a position 'outside the market' was an ideological fiction, their assertion of commercial neutrality was used to support their further claim to superior morality, which in turn justified their domination of both government and cultural life (Wood 1992).

The American Revolution destroyed the infrastructure of this social hierarchy by removing its anchor point, the British monarchy. Thus, the ancestral aristocracy abruptly and unexpectedly lost their hegemony over American life at the end of the eighteenth century. Until well into the 1800s, however, the former ruling class struggled to regain control while the commonfolk – made bold by democratic rhetoric and independent by the burgeoning modern economy – challenged the aristocrats' 'inborn' right to rule. By the mid-nineteenth century, when the first feminist meetings were being held, the country was being further challenged by a staggering influx of immigrants, who came to seek their freedom and fortune in the new market democracy. Over the next seventy years, immigrants continued to arrive in undiminished numbers from all parts of Europe. The new arrivals represented a further challenge to the old order because they were predominantly Catholic or Jewish and thus unimpressed by the moral authority of the Protestant hierarchy that had ruled for the previous 200 years. Thus, as the market system picked up more steam, the old colonial elite became increasingly vituperative in their charges against the 'immorality' of commerce.

The founding feminists were personally, demographically and politically aligned with the conservative Protestants who resisted the new order. They were, therefore, also heavily involved in Whiggish efforts to regain control through 'reform' movements focused on the recreation, consumption, reading material, child-rearing practices and market behaviour of working-class people and immigrants. The anti-commercial origin of American feminism, therefore, predates the current fashionability of Marxism by at least 100 years, and is rooted in sectarian, ruling-class interests, not redistributive radicalism.

Just as their fathers and grandfathers had consistently overlooked their own commercial activities when they asserted their moral superiority, so did the early Puritan feminists. The 'female reform societies' not only raised money through bazaars; they took shrewd advantage of a new economic form, the corporation (Ginzberg 1990). By incorporating, these women could shed the liabilities of the individual, including the many legal disadvantages of female gender, allowing them to collect and manage large sums of money in a way that would have been impossible for an individual female. Today, of course, American feminist organisations are also corporations – who now further benefit from later legislation allowing 'non-profit' corporations to avoid taxes. Consequently, the corporate form so hated by feminist theorists has actually been a key facilitating factor in the organisation and perpetuation of the movement.

The earliest media vehicles of the industrial age were religious newspapers, many of which were dedicated to covering the reform movements that the feminists and their men were initiating. The first feminist publication, *The Lily*, began as a temperance newspaper. Published by Amelia Bloomer, *The Lily* included contributions from leading feminists, especially Elizabeth Cady Stanton. The paper had a tiny circulation, limited to the Puritan reform community, until Ms Bloomer printed a picture of a new 'dress reform' – a pair of full trousers worn under a short skirt. This outfit, which quickly became known as 'bloomers', became a fashion fad that spread throughout the United States and even to Europe (Hersh 1978; Gattey 1967; Griffith 1984).

Feminist histories seldom acknowledge the popularity of the bloomer, but the resulting success of *The Lily* and its publisher leave no doubt as to the positive financial outcome of this sartorial innovation. The publisher promoted the bloomers by printing patterns for making them, daguerreotypes of herself and Stanton wearing them, and articles suggesting design and accessories. The circulation of *The Lily* skyrocketed as the fad spread: during the first year, subscriptions grew from 500 to 4,000 and the paper went from a monthly to a twice-monthly schedule. When Bloomer sold *The Lily* three years later, it had a national circulation of 6,000, which would have brought an attractive annuity of $6,000. During the same period, Bloomer was invited to give speeches at a number of prestigious venues. Appearing at the Metropolitan Hall in New York, for instance, she drew a standing-room-only crowd of 3,000, which produced a tidy sum in ticket sales. Soon, Bloomer could command fees for her speeches that were equal to the most respected male lecturers of the day. The *New York Journal* wrote:

> If ever a lady waked up one morning and found herself famous, that woman was Mrs. Bloomer; she has immortalised her name, and the Bloomer Costume will become as celebrated as Mary Queen of Scots' Cap, the Elizabeth Ruff, or the Pompadour Robe.
>
> (Gattey 1967: 82)

We could, therefore, say that Amelia Bloomer's good fortune derived not only from her feminism but from clear-cut promotional activities, including the fetishising of a pair of trousers and the commoditisation of her own speaking skills. There seems little here that is 'outside the market'.

Lecturing was a recognised 'get rich quick' activity in the nineteenth century. So, although feminist leaders of that period certainly took social risks by speaking for women's rights, they also reaped financial benefits. Lucy Stone, a prominent abolitionist and feminist, worked the popular lecture circuit in both the US and Canada. Though an impassioned activist, she delighted audiences everywhere, drawing huge crowds. In the mid-1850s, she attracted the largest audiences ever assembled in both St Louis and Toronto. Some said she even outdrew Jenny Lind, the Swedish opera singer famously promoted by P. T. Barnum. All this success translated into dollars, of course. Over the first three years of her career as a speaker, Stone managed to save $7,000 – an enormous sum at that time. Indeed, the press used her financial success as a point of criticism: she was accused of taking money from rural innocents and even charged with selling discounted 'season tickets'. By the time of her Southern tour in 1854, Stone was netting between $500 and $1,000 a week. She retired from lecturing when she gave birth, but was forced to return because of her husband's poor money management. Though all her savings had been wiped out, she quickly recovered that money and then some. Stone was quite wealthy when she died – yet she had no means of support other than what she earned as a speaker and as publisher of her own feminist vehicle, the *Woman's Journal* (Gattey 1967; Kerr 1992).

Elizabeth Cady Stanton did not take advantage of the money-earning opportunities offered by the movement until her children were grown up. She was engaged by the New York Lyceum Bureau in 1869 and she earned $2,000 in her first seven months. She continued to lecture for twelve years – eight months out of every year – earning $3,000 to $4,000 per annum. In the crucial women's convention year of 1871, in fact, Stanton did not want to forego income by interrupting her lecture tour, so she sent a $100 donation instead (Lutz 1940).

By the turn of the century, Elizabeth Cady Stanton and her close associate, Susan B. Anthony, were not only well known in the traditional public service sense but were also celebrities in the modern mass-market sense: Stanton even appeared in a national advertising campaign for Fairy Soap (Figure 2.1). Struggling for a reason to justify this transgression, feminist historian Mary Ryan writes: 'The common-sense advertisements of the Fair [sic] Soap Company even resorted to feminism, picturing Elizabeth Cady Stanton extolling the virtue of their pure, simple cleansing product, unadulterated by perfume' (1983: 155). It seems, however, that appealing to feminist sentiments was not a desperate measure at all. Fairy Soap was the leading brand at that time; the campaign seems to have been a straightforward celebrity appeal, and Stanton was only one among many marketable figures who were signed to hype the soap.

Feminism's high-class origins had, furthermore, given it clear social cachet by 1900 – and the market authority that goes with status. The ideal of the movement, known then as 'The New Woman', appeared often in the popular press, usually wearing bloomers, smoking or riding a bicycle. The New Woman's

Figure 2.1 Advertisement for Fairy Soap featuring Elizabeth Cady Stanton
Source: *Ladies' Home Journal*, September 1899, p. 31

upper-class credentials, university education and 'progressive' ideas made her quite chic. Though today's critics like to claim that the New Woman was antithetical to capitalism, she did, in fact, appear in ads – then and later (Figures 2.2 and 2.3). Such contradictory evidence usually prompts the charge that industry 'co-opted'

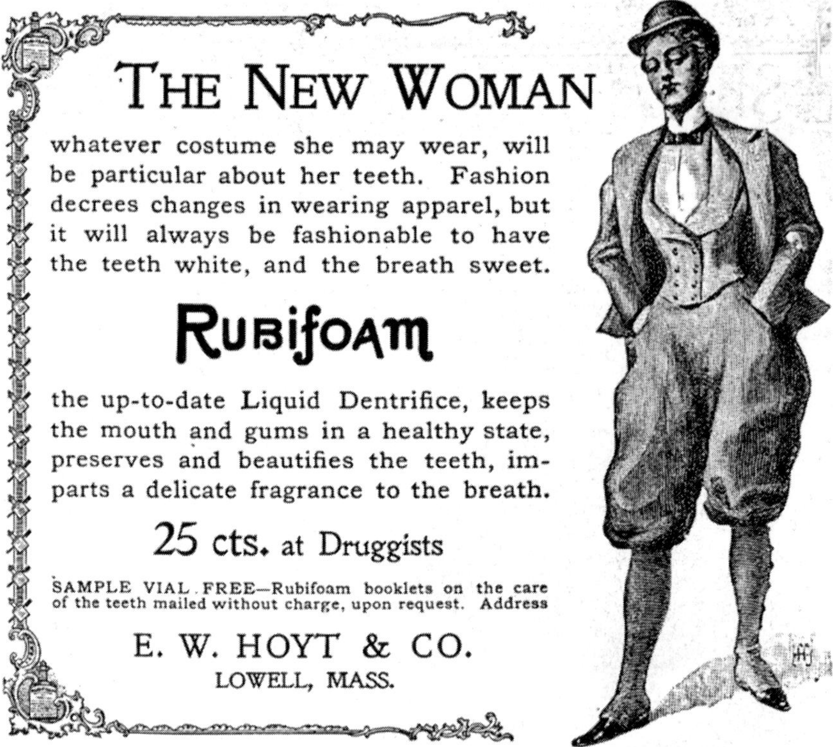

Figure 2.2 Advertisement for Rubifoam
Source: *Ladies' Home Journal*, April 1894, p. 35

feminism for private profit. Let's bear in mind the humbling information that feminism's founders did the same.

Feminist leaders continued to benefit from the marketability of the movement during the Second Wave. Press coverage focused on fresh college graduates entering the movement in late 1969 and early 1970. Having been involved in leftist politics on campus, the 'New Feminists' brought an affinity with Marxism and insisted that women's liberation be subject to the destruction of the whole socio-economic system (Cohen 1988). Yet the leaders of the New Feminism were, even then, benefiting financially from the interest that the media took in their movement.

In 1970 alone, the new wing of the feminist movement produced three books: Kate Millett's *Sexual Politics*, Shulamith Firestone's *Dialectic of Sex* and Robin Morgan's *Sisterhood is Powerful*. These books were published not by radical underground presses but by Doubleday, William Morrow and Random House, respectively. Since none of these books had been started before 1969 and all of them were available for purchase in 1970, it seems smart editors at major houses recognised the commercial potential of the new movement immediately and jumped to sign contracts with its leaders. After that, though most media interest reflected the

Figure 2.3 Advertisement for Pond's cream
Source: *Mademoiselle*, November 1969, p. 107

newsworthiness of feminism, some of it was undoubtedly engineered by publicity agents representing radical feminists who had signed contracts with big publishers.

The first of these books, Kate Millett's *Sexual Politics*, debuted in 1970 and quickly found a place on the best-seller list, making its author, in her own words, 'shamefully, pointlessly rich' (Cohen 1988: 251). The book was positively reviewed,

Figure 2.4 Advertisement for panty hose
Source: *Mademoiselle*, August 1971, p. 172

particularly by *Time* magazine, who put Millett's picture on the cover of their 31 August 1970 issue. During the next six months, Millett appeared on the *Dick Cavett Show* and *David Susskind*, as well as the *Today Show*. In February 1971, *Mademoiselle* ran a feature called 'A Day in the Life of Kate Millett'. '*Sexual Politics* is one of those books that change irrevocably and forever one's way of seeing things', exuded the fashion magazine, 'It casts a light so brilliant and penetrating that it illuminates not just a single corner but a whole landscape. Everything is different' (p. 138).

That year, *Mademoiselle* chose four books that were 'must-reads for the times'. *Sexual Politics* was one of them. But it was Robin Morgan's *Sisterhood is Powerful* that, arriving in time for the Christmas rush, won the place on *Mademoiselle*'s 'plan to give/hope to get' list. Ironically, when this collection of radical feminist chapters with the woman sign on the cover appeared, the same symbol had already been 'co-opted' for a panty hose package (Figure 2.4). Both were popular commodities. Not to be outdone, other leading publishers brought out still more feminist books. Basic Books published Vivian Gornick's *Woman in Sexist Society* in 1971, which was followed in the same year by Karen Decrowe's *The Young Woman's Guide to Liberation* and Lucy Komisar's *The New Feminism*. It appears that feminist books, no matter how radical, were good business.

Germaine Greer's 1971 American tour was a full-blown marketing event in the tradition of P. T. Barnum. The fanfare opened with a cover of *Life* magazine touting the 'Saucy feminist even men like'. One of Greer's first appearances was a debate moderated by Norman Mailer and attended by the most well connected of New York's avant-garde. Tickets on the main floor went for twice what popular Broadway shows were charging and, even so, were in short supply. The whole evening was captured by a British film crew for a documentary to be called 'Germaine Greer versus the United States'. The American media, as well as her documentary crew, proceeded to follow Greer around the US as she stumped for feminism and dallied rather publicly with an assortment of attractive men (Cohen 1988). Needless to say, Greer's book, *The Female Eunuch*, became a best seller.

Speech-making for feminism was still lucrative during the Second Wave. Like the founding feminists, speakers such as Gloria Steinem, Germaine Greer and Betty Friedan were highly sought after, particularly on college campuses. The 'take' for these events must have been enormous, because the speakers themselves often reaped higher incomes from speaking than from their regular work. For instance, Steinem already made an above-average income writing for magazines like *Esquire*, *New York* and *Vogue*. On the feminist lecture circuit, she earned double that amount (Cohen 1988). (To her credit, Steinem returned her speaking fees in donations to the movement. Others similarly remunerated were not so generous.)

The most long-lasting commercial endeavour of the Second Wave is now touted by academics as the most commerce-free. Clay Felker, Gloria Steinem's former editor at *Esquire* and *New York*, came up with the idea for 'a slick, commercial magazine' devoted to the feminist movement (Cohen 1988: 324). Felker chose Gloria for the editorship largely because he thought her fame as a feminist and a member of the 'Beautiful People' would bring publicity. After a prototype inserted in *New York* sold out in eight days and 35,000 women mailed in requests for subscriptions, Warner Communications put up $1 million dollars to publish *Ms.* magazine on a monthly basis. Betty Friedan promptly accused Gloria Steinem of 'ripping off the movement for private profit' (ibid.: 336). Yet Friedan had once quit her publisher because he wasn't prepared to market *The Feminine Mystique* aggressively enough: 'I remember him pleading with me . . . and I remember looking him right in the eye and saying, "George, you made me feel Jewish for trying to sell that book. Go fuck yourself" ' (ibid.: 96). Today, of course, Friedan's classic has been reprinted many times and in multiple languages, providing no doubt plenty of 'private profit'.

A few New Feminists ended up with successful careers in the media. More went back to the universities where they began to write feminist theory, criticism and history. Over the next two decades, university professors researching their topics with a feminist perspective produced a remarkable body of work, contributing vastly to our knowledge of women in several fields, including history, literature, anthropology, sociology and psychology. With the power of print behind them and the captives of the classroom beneath them, however, academics could focus the feminist agenda with a perspective uniquely their own and even begin to assert the right to define feminism. Because this cadre of academic feminists was still loyal to Marx, a prominent characteristic of post-Second Wave feminist writing is its persistent attack upon the market economy, particularly the corporations behind it.

During the same timeframe, the female employees of those same corporations have gone from representing only 3 per cent of corporate management jobs to 40 per cent (Towery 1998). Many marketing specialities, like public relations, have become female-dominated (58.6 per cent of public relations professionals are women) (Cline and Toth 1993). In advertising, the area of the economy which draws the most feminist fire, more than half of all managers (57 per cent) are now women (Hernandez 1997). The effects of this 'feminisation' in the marketplace are visible in Nike campaigns and Barbie themes, but feminist academics have either ignored or discounted the efforts of working women to bring a feminist perspective to bear on the objects and messages that the market actually produces. Instead, anti-market feminist literature has generalised on a 'theoretical level' until nothing produced by capitalist consumer culture can be considered feminist. Various other rhetorical strategies have also negated the efforts of women in corporations. For instance, feminist authors belittle the clothes and taste of female corporate leaders, calling them 'homeovestites' if they aren't masculine (see Lord 1994 on Jill Barad). Or, they equate market activity with maleness, implying that women in corporations are 'really men' (Ehrenreich 1990). Or, they dismiss the very real power of some women in the private sector – arguing that corporations are still, after all, dominated by men (as if universities *were not* dominated by men) (Duffy 1994).

To my mind, the most problematic aspect of the whole situation is that feminist writers consistently condemn others for 'commoditising' or 'co-opting' feminism in order to make a profit, as if they themselves are not doing the same thing. Yet feminist books continue to be published by major publishers, and the authors are commoditised in lecture tours and talk shows. For example, in spite of her charges that the publishing industry stokes the fires of anti-feminism Susan Faludi's *Backlash* was a runaway success. Her frequent appearances on television and in magazines were not, I'm sure, entirely attributable to her good credentials as a feminist, but had some little to do with the efforts of her publisher, Doubleday. Similarly, *The Beauty Myth*, also a best seller, quickly propelled its pretty author, Naomi Wolf, to celebrity status, from which she could display herself in classic Hollywood glamour style in the pages of *Esquire*. Wolf, five years later, has already published her third book, which suggests that her publishers, both Doubleday *and* Random House, are making some money.

Jean Kilbourne's (1979) advertising critique, *Killing Us Softly*, was casually reissued in almost identical form as 1987's *Still Killing Us Softly*. Now *Killing Us Softly 3* is upon us like a movie sequel. These videotapes can be purchased for $299 or rented from Cambridge Documentary Films for $46 a day plus shipping and credit charges. If you rent the tapes, they arrive plastered with stickers warning that they are both copy-protected and copyrighted. It would seem that a profit motive is at work: if all Kilbourne wanted was to further 'the cause', there would be no need to guard property rights so jealously. Indeed, one might think that it would be in the interests of the movement if these tapes were copied and circulated as freely and widely as possible. But in spite of the profit motive that is clear from the moment you open the box, a major point of Kilbourne's argument is that corporations who do include a feminist message in their ads are 'co-opting' the movement for private gain.

bell hooks also offers a videotape on the commoditisation of women and blacks in commercial culture. Her own direct mail piece, however, rather effectively commoditises feminism, critical studies and even hooks herself (Figure 2.5). The distribution company is a 'non-profit organisation', to be sure, but that term merely describes a particular tax status with special post office privileges – and in no way means that hooks is not profiting from the sale of this tape.

The price tags on Kilbourne and hooks' videos would seem to put them out of reach for most women. That's because the real market for these expensive tapes is not individual consumers, but university libraries – hardly an 'alternative' market. The fantastic popularity of women's studies programmes virtually guarantees an audience for these tapes, as well as a market for feminist books and lecture tickets. Since women's studies was first established in the mid-1970s, more than 670 undergraduate and 111 graduate programmes have been established at 250 colleges nation-wide (Worthington 1997). Feminists have been 'big box office' on college campuses for thirty years now, producing robust income for the speakers and, sometimes, the university groups who engage them.

The idea that any of this activity is taking place 'outside the market' is a naive delusion. Yet most of these feminists are making money off women – by complaining about *other people* making money off women. Then they expect us not to notice the paradox.

Figure 2.5 bell hooks' direct mail piece
Source: Media Education Foundation, www.mediaed.org

MARKET FEMINISM

In contrast to the prevailing view, I would argue that industrialisation and the market system are what made the success of American feminism possible. There are several reasons why this is true. One of them, as we have seen, is that the market-driven media (including newspapers, books, television, lecture circuits and magazines) has provided an efficient conduit for feminist ideas since the first days of the movement. Of at least equal importance, however, was the creation of a large class of educated, motivated women with the leisure time to devote to politics. As nearly every history of the modern economy shows, one of the most important effects of industrialisation was the creation of a large middle class. In America, the women of this class chose to stay home in order to emulate the prevailing ideas of gentility. Not satisfied with merely staying home, and freed by the labour-saving devices of consumer culture to devote themselves to other activities, middle-class housewives were the foot-soldiers of the First Wave. These women picketed, canvassed, circulated petitions, organised groups, initiated referenda, and, in short, provided the woman-power for suffrage as well as other women's issues. Histories of American feminism are unequivocal about the importance of these volunteers. Thus, to a significant degree, American feminism rests upon the political possibilities created by the material abundance of industrialisation.

American feminism also rests upon the opportunities for work the modern economy created for another large group. Though the traditional wisdom insists that the modern economy required women stay in the 'domestic sphere' (Cott 1977), the actual statistics point in a different direction. Since the first factory in America opened in 1814, women have been employed by industry in significant numbers – and not only as factory operatives, but as designers, marketers, writers, advertising agents, illustrators, print-makers and craftspersons. The percentage of women in the American labour force has grown steadily over the last hundred years (Figure 2.6). Certainly there is no question that some areas of the economy were closed to women. And, women, like men, were often employed in unsafe and underpaid jobs. Nevertheless, it is also unquestionably true that the modern economy has offered women a level of economic autonomy undreamed of in pre-industrial American culture.

The modern economy has also produced many new cultural forms. Here, too, women have benefited. Even the women's magazines so reviled in feminist writing have been havens for women's employment and staunch supporters of women's advancement. Though the feminist literature has repeatedly asserted that the women's magazines are merely the prostitutes of corporate capitalism, the most recent histories are now debunking that myth. In books like Jennifer Scanlon's history of the *Ladies' Home Journal* (1995), we find that the predominantly female writers, editors and advertising agents behind the early women's magazines were sympathetic to the movement (and were sometimes activists). They carried the feminist spirit into their hiring practices and market strategies, and into the pages they produced. Scanlon shows, for instance, that both the biggest women's

Figure 2.6 Women's labour trends in the US, 1890–1990
Source: US Census

magazine in the early century, the *Ladies' Home Journal*, and the biggest advertising agency, J. Walter Thompson, were led by women with developed feminist consciousness. These women, Louisa Knapp Curtis and Helen Lansdowne Resor, surrounded themselves with other feminists as colleagues and contributors, thus advancing the cause of feminism in the private sector. Their readers, including their advertisers, seem to have responded positively. As I have demonstrated in my forthcoming book, *Fresh Lipstick*, the women's magazines that supported feminism during the suffrage years experienced an increase in subscriptions as well as advertising revenues, while those which opposed women's rights declined and even closed. Furthermore, by putting their activism to work in the mainstream press, women in the media have spread the word about feminism to a far larger audience than was possible through sectarian or scholarly publications.

After discovering the support provided by women like Curtis and Resor, it is unsettling to find that the First Wave was marked by the same schism between 'scholastics' and secular women that concerns us here. The academics of the early twentieth century were not inclined to acknowledge or document the support they received from women in the private sector – and their counterparts later in the century have been disinclined to redress the balance in their histories.

Take, for instance, Miriam Leslie. Once a dancer in New Orleans who called herself 'Minnie Montez', she led what some would delicately call 'a colourful life'. But in 1865, Miriam became editor of a magazine in Frank Leslie's enormous publishing empire. She and Leslie became lovers, and their affair was a national scandal. After marrying her boss, Mrs Leslie was one of the industrial *nouveau riche* the aristocratic feminists so thoroughly despised. Frank Leslie, however, eventually ran into financial difficulties and died in bankruptcy. Upon his death, Miriam took over the business and assumed all his debts. Under her close direction, the publishing company was brought back to its former power. When Miriam died in 1914, she left her entire estate to the women's suffrage movement and named its leader, Carrie Chapman Catt, as trustee. This generous behest was a major factor in putting the movement 'over the top', paying for educational and promotional materials that went out around the country in support of suffrage. The money also figured quite prominently in the consolidation of Ms Catt's power in the movement (Fowler 1986). Yet most histories of the suffrage movement never mention Mrs Leslie or her generous gift.

Jane Cunningham Croly was the most famous newspaperwoman in nineteenth-century America. She was the first woman to work daily for a newspaper and she was the first to teach journalism at the college level. She was the originator of the women's page and the syndicated column. Though this is all well-known in media history, Croly's equally important contribution to the women's movement is known only to those who read the footnotes of feminist histories.

Croly founded the first non-sectarian organisation devoted exclusively to advancing the interests of women. Called 'Sorosis', this club's members were very different from the Puritan feminists (Croly 1898). Most worked for pay: doctors, journalists, designers, editors, illustrators and poets. They were not necessarily Anglo-Saxon Protestant or born in America. They were more pragmatic than ideological in orientation – what critics today call 'atheoretical'. Within a year of its founding, Sorosis had grown to 83 members, almost entirely professionals. Soon, however, the membership expanded to include middle-class women who wanted to invest their energies outside the home. Like brushfire, the women's club idea spread to other towns. In 1880, Jane Croly took the first step toward forming the General Federation of Women's Clubs by calling a national conference. Non-partisan and non-denominational, the GFWC started with 52 member organisations. Within a dozen years, the Federation had 180 clubs and 20,000 members. By the turn of the century, it had 150,000 members. There were one million women in the GFWC by 1910 and two million by 1915. Thus, it was Jane Croly who started the biggest organisational movement for women in American history (O'Neill 1969). Ultimately, it was through the GFWC that the suffrage movement got most of its money, workers, publicity and influence.

In a very concrete sense, the feminist organisations of today, like the National Organisation for Women, are the descendants of Sorosis. Historians should have been studying the history of Sorosis with the same respect and intensity with which they have pored over the early reform groups. But they have not. One reason for this, I believe, is that the lives of these women do not fit the ideology of feminism as it has developed. These women were neither Puritans, academics nor ideologues. Perhaps most incriminating, they were intimately involved in the burgeoning commercial and consumer culture.

One of the most successful feminist organisations that emerged within the framework of the GFWC was the National Consumers' League. The League was founded on the concept that the biggest political weapon middle-class women had was their spending power. Using boycotts, lobbying and other governmental pressure, including the drafting of protective legislation, the NCL became, in feminist historian Eleanor Flexner's words, the 'militant and highly articulate conscience of the buying public' (1975: 213–14). Florence Kelly, leader of the NCL during its heyday, was a Marxist. Though she retained her belief in the long-range goals of socialism, she directed her activities in the NCL to putting an end to abuses as she found them. Her choice draws criticism today. As feminist historian William O'Neill remarks:

> She needed immediate results, and they were to be gotten only through bourgeois reformist organisations like the NCL. . . . This response, so typical of American radicals, might well be called the pragmatic fallacy, because by concentrating on reform at the expense of revolution one ended up with neither. Nonetheless, Mrs. Kelley's decision did her credit. It requires a certain hardness of character to put abstract propositions, like The Revolution, ahead of human wants, and to work for a distant event when present evils are so compelling.
>
> (O'Neill 1969: 136–7)

Here we have another paradox produced by the Marxist loyalties of recent feminist writers. In spite of the long and admirable record of American feminism in putting pressure upon both business and government, today's feminists belittle 'liberal' reform efforts as a matter of principle. In their view, it is preferable to do nothing toward alleviating human suffering, in order that 'The Revolution' may come about sooner. In this way of thinking, virtually none of the major feminist initiatives – suffrage, the Equal Rights Amendment, the pro-choice movement, the anti-pornography movement, the push for equal education rights, the work toward divorce reform, the assertion of property rights, and so on – can be held to be anything but weak liberal backsliding. Furthermore, according to this viewpoint, the huge numbers of professional women who were in the American work-force by 1970 may as well have stayed at the office, conducting business as usual, instead of coming out as they did for the re-emergent feminist movement.

Just as middle-class housewives formed the backbone of the First Wave, the strength of the Second Wave came from growth in the number of educated working women joining the movement (Chafetz and Dworkin 1986). The National Organisation for Women, for instance, was founded by business and professional women. NOW's victories in extending anti-discrimination protection to women in the workplace, in establishing the right to equal pay for equal work and in knocking down gender classifications for employment notices were all achieved while NOW was still under the guidance of successful working women, rather than campus radicals. In those early days, public relations for NOW was professionally managed by nationally known PR people such as Muriel Fox. Media support was ensured by such members as Shana Alexander, Marlene Sanders and Helen Gurley Brown (Cohen 1988). (Contrary to the prevailing myth, the women's magazines generally supported the Second Wave, just as they did the First, particularly in their dramatic rally around the Equal Rights Amendment.) As the critique of the marketplace first emerged from the campus radicals, NOW members in marketing, such as Rena Bartos, used the power of their professional positions to perform studies and make changes that would reflect the feminist agenda in messages, magazines and products (Figure 2.7).

The businesswomen of that early Second Wave generation proceeded in their careers – some of them reaching the summits of American corporations. Linda Wachner, for instance, was one of the earliest advertisers to support *Ms.* magazine. She is now head of Warnaco, the multinational that owns both Victoria's Secret and Calvin Klein underwear. Other women now run some of the largest ad agencies on the face of the globe, like Charlotte Beers at Ogilvy & Mather. Jill Barad, who had a progressive impact on the design of Barbie as a marketing manager, is now head of Mattel.

Barbie. Victoria's Secret. Ogilvy & Mather. Having women in the forefront of enterprises like these was a pipe dream when the Second Wave first burst on the scene. In those early days, the idea that women in such positions might make a difference in the design of toys, the comfort of clothes or the depiction of women was heady stuff. Yet now the day has arrived and no one seems to care what, if anything, these women do for feminism. Indeed, academic feminists appear to be intent upon discounting any progress that women in these positions are able to make – and will demean them personally for trying.

All the while, more American women are training for careers in business, especially marketing. Today, women represent 34 per cent of MBA enrolment. Women have long dominated college programmes in public relations (where they now outnumber men ten to one) and advertising (68 per cent of advertising majors in America are female) (Cline and Toth 1993; Lazier and Kendrick 1993). If these women should also show an interest in women's studies while on campus, however, they must listen to diatribes against the market – and precious little, if anything, to guide them as feminists in their future careers. If they're smart, they learn early to compartmentalise their feminism *from* their work, instead of learning to look for ways to implement feminism *at* work. And it's a shame – because, as we have seen, the history of feminism is replete with examples of how the market was used to advance the cause: through the media, through products, through book publishing and lecturing, through employment practices or through advertisements. Much could be gained by having something productive to say to these young women before they go out into the global economy.

AND, IF SO, HOW?

Let's return now to the original questions: Can the market be used to advance feminism? And, if so, how? It seems to me that a paradigm shift towards 'market feminism' could have an impact on theory, activism, research and education.

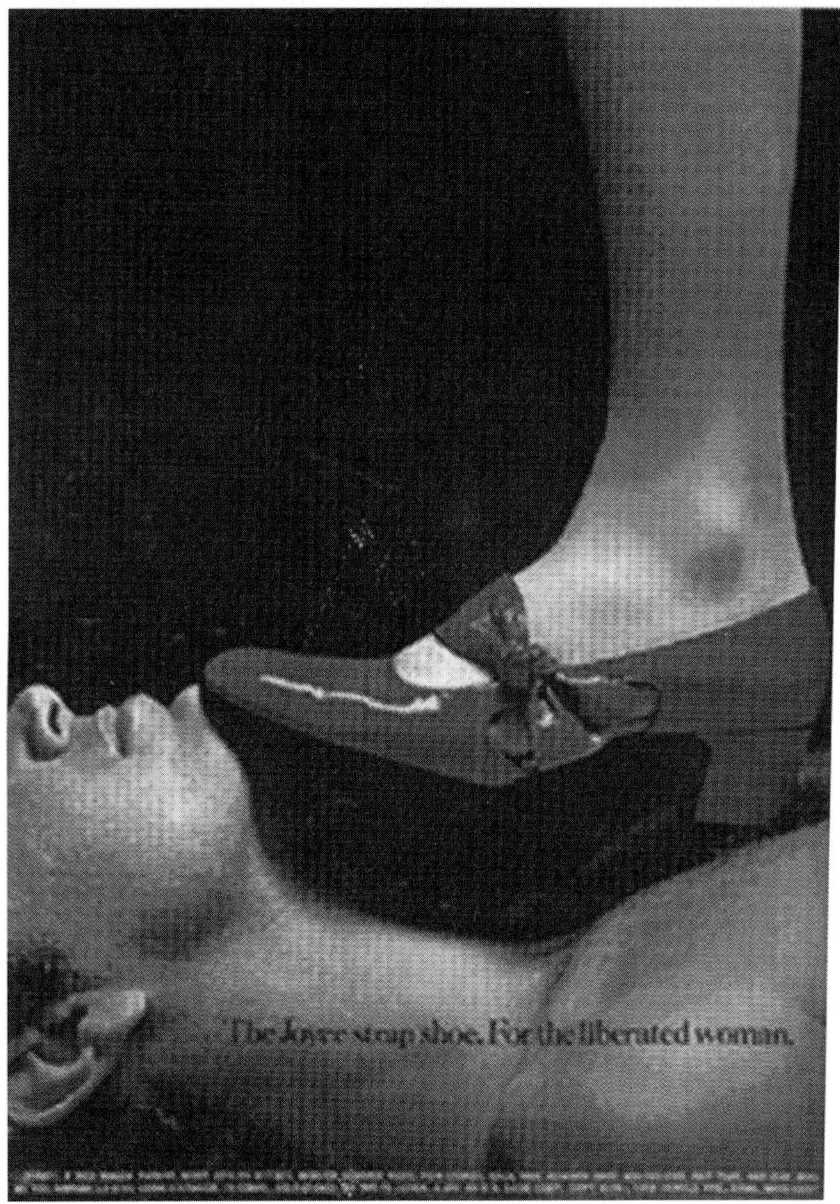

Figure 2.7 Shoe advertisement
Source: *Glamour*, February 1971, p. 68

The overriding consideration, perhaps, is theory, since that is where the problem is centred.

The first step towards retheorising feminism's relations with the marketplace is to acknowledge a single awful fact: women have been oppressed in every form of government or economy that is known to us. From a purely feminist (and not necessarily Marxist) perspective, there is simply no reason for the overwhelming emphasis on criticising capitalism. As Gayle Rubin wrote in her classic 1975 chapter:

> Women are oppressed in societies that can by no stretch of the imagination be described as capitalist. . . . Capitalism has taken over, and required, notions of male and female which predate it by centuries. No analysis of the reproduction of labour power under capitalism can explain foot-binding, chastity belts, or any of the incredible array of Byzantine, fetishized indignities, let alone the more ordinary ones, which have been inflicted upon women in various times and places.
>
> (Rubin 1975: 163)

Capitalism is not the cause; it is merely the current circumstance. So, the second step, perhaps, is recognising yet another awful fact: it is sometimes necessary to act under imperfect conditions. By letting go of the expectation that right action can occur only in the context of total system destruction ('The Revolution'), the 'bourgeois reform efforts' which have historically been feminism's stock in trade can be reinstated and redignified. If this small generosity could be extended to activism within the confines of a corporation, then a window could open somewhere for feminism in the workplace. Such a shift would necessarily require that feminist theorists allow the possibility of progress within a market- and profit-oriented framework. The fact that a change occurred within a business organisation or an advertising campaign could not, *ipso facto*, discredit the activism that led to it.

Academic authors might find for the first time that they could write about positive changes in the marketplace without the need to find some means – any means – to condemn them. Thus, corporate feminists might be recognised for their efforts on behalf of the movement. Having others who recognise and support their efforts 'on the inside', as it were, could only produce more positive motivation for women in the private sector. The cause of activism would be well served.

Feminist criticism would not need to lose its teeth by such a switch, however. Instead, a smarter, more worldly-wise approach to economics would vastly improve both the critical edge and the practical contribution of the literature. Though economists like Julie Nelson and Marianne Ferber (1993) have made important initial efforts to marry feminist politics and economic theory, most critics still approach economics with language theory – with disastrous results. As part of an overall effort to bring real economic theory into feminist thought, promiscuous use of terms like 'co-opt' and 'commodities' might be curbed in favour of more acute analysis. Under the current intellectual fashion, words like 'commoditise' have come to be used so carelessly that they no longer mean anything at all.

The whole area of advertising criticism could benefit from more 'market feminist' knowledge and techniques. As Margaret Duffy pointed out in her exhaustive review of feminist advertising studies, one of the biggest ongoing problems is the embarrassing lack of knowledge about how marketing and advertising are actually done (1994). Lazier and Kendrick (1993) further suggest there is a real need to improve our investigation of consumer response to commercial messages; but under today's theoretical perspective it's the critic's view that counts, not the reader's. After thirty years of polemics, more research into the actual response of feminism's constituency – that is, ordinary non-academic women – is probably in order.

Changes in terminology, method and theory could result in a more inclusive perspective. Consider, for instance, that charging a woman with 'co-opting' feminist language or imagery because she used it in the course of private-sector work necessarily implies that feminist academics, who *also* use feminist language and imagery in the course of their work, are 'outside the market', and so cannot 'co-opt' feminism. This, as we have seen, is pure ideology. But the criticism further implies that feminism is not open to all women, only to those of a certain class. Such distinctions inevitably lead toward selective discussions of who is 'inside' and who is 'outside', a path that should be forbidden to a social movement that hopes to encompass the world.

It would be my hope that another outgrowth of the shift to 'market feminism' would be the retrieval of women like Jane Croly and Helen Resor from obscurity. Let's find out more about the women who expressed feminism in the marketplace. Who were they? How did they envision their activities as political statements? What did they contribute to the organised movement? Learning more about these women may point up further directions for both research and activism. For instance, learning the history of the National Consumers' League (and the many other consumer advocacy initiatives of the First Wave) made me wonder why and how feminism lost that approach. Bringing a focused consumer advocacy perspective back into feminism – instead of just bemoaning 'consumers' and 'consumer culture' in general terms – would surely improve conditions as these objects and habits spread around the world.

Last, but perhaps most important, I would hope to see a pedagogical perspective develop that could ground and guide the next generation of marketing managers. As it is, when you look through the literature for ways to teach feminism in a market context, you come up empty-handed. There is nothing there but condemnation. When confronting a classroom of female faces already committed to business training and marketing careers, just standing there dogmatically condemning the market economy seems inadequate, out of touch, intellectually lazy and even cowardly. Those are the times when the cost of this lost opportunity seems entirely too high.

Seizing this moment, therefore, could have historic results matching the dimensions of the global economy itself. Continuing to adhere, ostrich-like, to a viewpoint that lacks empirical validity, ignores the realities of the past and is so grossly out of touch with the present can only impede the movement's progress into the future. Adopting a fresh perspective could instead help push feminism into a paradigm for the new millennium.

REFERENCES

'A day in the life of Kate Millett', *Mademoiselle*, February 1971, 138ff.

Chafetz, J. S. and Dworkin, A. (1986) *Female Revolt: Women's Movements in World and Historical Perspective*, Totowa, NJ: Rowman & Allanheld.

Cline, C. G. and Toth, E. L. (1993) 'Re-visioning women in public relations', in P. Creedon (ed.) *Women in Mass Communication*, New York: Sage, 183–98.

Cohen, M. (1988) *The Sisterhood*, New York : Simon & Schuster.

Cott, N. (1977) *The Bonds of Womanhood*, New Haven, CT: Yale University Press.

Croly, Mrs J. C. (1898) *The History of the Woman's Club Movement in America*, New York: Henry G. Allen & Co.

Duffy, M. (1994) 'Body of evidence: studying women and advertising', in *Gender and Utopia in Advertising*, Lisle, IL: Procopian Press.

Ehrenreich, B. (1990) 'Sorry, sisters, this is not the revolution', *Time*, Fall: 15.

Flexner, E. (1975) *Century of Struggle: The Woman's Rights Movement in the United States*, Cambridge, MA: Harvard University Press.

Fowler, R. B. (1986) *Carrie Chapman Catt: Feminist Politician*, Boston: Northeastern University Press.

Gattey, C. (1967) *The Bloomer Girls*, London: Femina Books.

Ginzberg, L. D. (1990) *Women and the Work of Benevolence*, New Haven, CT: Yale University Press.

Griffith, E. (1984) *In Her Own Right: The Life of Elizabeth Caoly Stanton*, New York: Oxford University Press.

Hernandez, D. G. (1997) 'Advertising's "dirty little secret"', *American Advertising*, Fall/Winter: 8–13.

Hersh, B. (1978) *The Slavery of Sex*, Urbana: University of Illinois Press.

Kerr, A. M. (1992) *Lucy Stone*, New Brunswick, NJ: Rutgers.

Kilbourne, J. (1979) *Killing Us Softly: Advertising's Image of Women*, Cambridge, MA: Cambridge Documentary Films.

Lazier, L. and Kendrick, A. G. (1993) 'Women in advertisements: sizing up the images, roles, and functions', in P. Creedon (ed.) *Women in Mass Communication*, New York: Sage.

Lord, M. G. (1994) *Forever Barbie*, New York: Avon Books.

Lutz, A. (1940) *Created Equal*, New York: John Day & Co.

Nelson, J. and Ferber, M. (1993) *Beyond Economic Man: Feminist Theory and Economics*, Chicago: University of Chicago Press.

O'Neill, W. L. (1969) *Everyone Was Brave*, Chicago: Quadrangle Books.

Rubin, G. (1975) 'The traffic in women', in R. Reiter (ed.) *Toward an Anthropology of Women*, New York: Monthly Review Press, 157–210.

Ryan, M. P. (1983) *Womanhood in America: From Colonial Times to the Present*, 3rd edn, New York: F. Watts.

Scanlon, J. (1995) *Inarticulate Longings*, New York: Routlege.

Towery, M. (1998) *Powerchicks: How Women Will Dominate America*, New York: Longstreet.

Wood, G. S. (1992) *The Radicalism of the American Revolution*, New York: Knopf.

Worthington, R. (1997) 'Colleges' battle for sexes becoming gender neutral', *Chicago Tribune*, 4 February: 1.

3 Have we come a long way, baby? Negotiating a more multicultural feminism in the marketing academy in the USA

Lisa Peñaloza

INTRODUCTION

Penning this chapter has given me an opportunity to reflect upon my own ambivalent relationship with feminism. Although I feel alienated by feminists at times, I remain seduced by their attempts to create alternative, woman-centred ideas and spaces, and to alter the many forms of male-domination evident here and in other countries.

The changes over the past five decades have been particularly profound. I recently interviewed three Mexican American women in their eighties,[1] revisiting their stories of first working outside the home during the Second World War. The three women shared a number of firsts common at the time: earning the 'good money' of what had been men's jobs, which they enjoyed because it enabled them to buy things for the house although it took them away from their family; wearing trousers, which enabled physical movement although they preferred dresses at the time to please their husbands; and owning cars, which gave them greater independence. They also spoke of segregation. Historically, economic conditions have fostered opportunities for women, which in turn have set the context for altering the complex social fabric of gender expectations and personal ambitions, with marked ethnic and class differences in women's experience.

Over the past three decades feminists have broadened our concerns in synchrony with those of other progressive movements, yet often at the pace of one step forward, two steps back. Despite conflicting goals and perspectives, feminists' concerted challenges to 'looksism', classism, racism and heterosexism have contributed to an ongoing ethic of engaged, critical consciousness combined with social action through which more and more *women and men* experience fewer limitations put upon them solely based on their gender. Many contemporary feminists are motivated by a strong sense of egalitarianism and meritocracy, such that one's race and class should be as irrelevant as gender in defining one's social opportunity and standing.

Differences in approach as well as goals, such as revaluing women's experience, pursuing social reform versus radical changes, and advocating assimilation versus outright separatism have proven to be as divisive as differences in class and race/ethnicity among feminists. These persistent internal differences, coupled with external perceptions of the successes of the movement and the sentiments of the present generation of young women that feminist concerns are obsolete, map the complex terrain in which feminist marketing academics presently find ourselves.

As for me, I've got my own beefs with feminism. I'm very uncomfortable with the moralising overtones and exclusionary tactics exhibited from time to time. Having stepped away from some social roles and worldviews, I am disappointed to find others imposed upon me in their place. In this chapter I make a few critical observations regarding the place of feminism in the contemporary marketing academy. I begin with an overview of various historical developments of feminism as a jumping-off point for discussing some ways in which feminist ideals and practices can enrich our lives as feminist marketing academics in the activities of research, teaching and service.

WHOSE FEMINISM/WHAT FEMINISM?

If anything has been gleaned over the last century, at the fore should be the nonsingularity of feminism. From the suffragists at the turn of the century, to the gender egalitarians of the 1970s, to contemporary transgender liberationists, feminists have confronted a range of opportunities and challenges stemming from within and outside the movement.

Contemporary feminist marketing academics also face opportunities and challenges from within and without. For us, helping bring about a 'coming of age' of feminism in marketing requires a full interrogation of each of its composite domains – as subject position, social movement, discipline of study and research paradigm play into the others in generating understanding (Peñaloza 1994).

In marketing, Bristor and Fischer (1993), Hirschman (1993) and Stern (1993) have touched on all these areas, although their emphasis was on feminist research, and their focus was primarily on commonalties across women's experience. In contrast, this chapter cuts across these four domains with attention to particular configurations of gender, class and colour. My goal is not to exacerbate our differences, but neither is it to resolve them. I bring forward these important differences among women as a necessary precursor to building mutual understanding.

Feminism as a subject position

Being a feminist is no easy feat at present! It seems that even mention of the word conjures up profound disaffection or apathy. In contrast to the hotbed of social activism through the 1970s and early 1980s, today many young women brazenly express the sentiment that feminism is obsolete. It's hard not to agree with them, especially when much of their sense of the feminist dialogue consists of a select few professional white women (e.g., Roiphe 1993; Patai 1998) recentering their neo-conservative positioning within the movement, not by taking on their predecessors – Second-Wave feminists, such as Millett (1970), Daly (1973) or Steinem (1983) – but by wrestling down straw (wo)man caricatures of their ideas.

Identity itself has so been problematised by post-structuralist mandates that it is as refreshing as it is tortuous to see a person writing from a self-identified feminist subject position. Woman-ness is not as simple as it used to be. Generalising about women's experience is only possible after thinking through intersections of gender, class and colour. At issue then, is how we situate our own sense of feminism within our gender, class and colour, and in consideration of other configurations.

Further complicating the picture is the increasing prevalence of persons whose feminist identities are situated across groupings. Importantly, feminism, like the Black, Latino/a and gay movements, has been built upon a paradigm of singular identity, with much work over the last two decades aimed at incorporating the complexities of members' multiple subject positions (James and Busia 1993; Schulman 1994; Peñaloza 1994, 1996; Trujillo 1998). While there are persons who identify themselves more on one dimension than others, increasingly people are refusing to split their allegiances. An example is a person whose maleness is as important to him as being a feminist and a Latino. Other examples would be a Black lesbian feminist or a white working-class feminist. Further, when followed over time, a person's identification with various dimensions of his/her subject position often changes.

Feminism as a social movement

Historically, feminists have organised around a number of political issues including enfranchisement, equal pay for equal work, sexual expression, reproductive rights and domestic violence. Over time, issues come and go, and feminists have made gains and experienced some disappointments.

In the 1970s by comparison, the simple, straightforward reversals of male-for-female-bias abounded. Woman-centeredness was where it was at! The main objective was to revalue women; that is, to work from the inside out, putting women's positions, experiences and perspectives forward, articulating obstacles to women's development and self-actualisation, and working to overcome them.

Lesbian-baiting proved an anathema for feminists (Brown 1976). Those already struggling with mainstream social disapproval succumbed to the logical fallacy that being *for women* automatically meant one was *against men*. Lesbians epitomised the ultimate terror to the nuclear family in not being economically or emotionally dependent on men. Yet, rather than take the offensive, emphasising the social benefits of lifestyle choices, both hetero- and homosexual, made from desire as opposed to role-conformity or economic necessity, feminists remained in a defensive posture, constantly responding to charges of destroying the sacrosanct family.

By the early 1980s feminism dovetailed with modernism in ways that would prove as fascinating to social theorists as they would be challenging to those concerned with advancing the feminist agenda. By then we feminists had, as the advertising slogan for Virginia Slims cigarettes put it, 'Come a long way, baby!' even though some would later admit, if somewhat grudgingly, that the grass wasn't so green on the other side.

At that time feminists advocated a way of being necessarily counter to the traditional roles of serving others, cooking, cleaning house and having children. Notably, the movement was largely middle-class in nature, although some feminists were attuned to working-class women's relatively longer history of juggling work outside the home with household chores (Brown 1976). Even so, feminists were not so much out to decry those women having made traditional choices as to direct attention to the role of social norms in rendering actions less than fully conscious. Their approach emphasised broadening the options of women over tackling larger issues of economic constraints. Externally, conservative critics continued to rail against feminists for the impact women working had on home life, conveniently ignoring the role of the increasingly demanding economy.

Internally, feminists' efforts for gender equality in the workplace and in intimate relations were condemned as 'out-manning men', ultimately belittling biological and social gender qualities that many had accepted as the source of women's identity, some unquestioningly and others fully consciously. By the end of the 1980s the notion that women could have it all had fallen from grace, splintered as much by conflicting choices between career and family commitments as by clashes between those living out choices to have both a career and family versus those opting for one or the other.

Feminism as a discipline of study

Women's studies programmes emerged in major universities in the USA and abroad in the 1970s on the heels of student activism for civil rights and against the Vietnam War at the end of the previous decade. Following closely behind were Chicano studies and African American studies programmes. Underlying each of these programmes of study was a sense that members of the respective social group were worthy of study in their own right and had been either neglected or maligned in traditional academic departments (MALCS 1993; James and Busia 1993).

In the case of women's studies, issues such as women's health and psychological development, and the impact of such social constraints as gender roles and cultural rituals were given priority in a network of courses, newsletters, magazines, journals and books. Courses that had been offered in various departments across campus, such as women's literature and history, found a new home in women's studies, supplemented with courses more specifically tailored to the history of the women's movement and feminist theory. Journals such as *Signs*, *Sage:*

A Scholarly Journal on Black Women and *Sinister Wisdom*, and books such as Millett's *Sexual Politics* (1970), Daly's *Beyond God the Father* (1973) and Gilligan's *In a Different Voice* (1982) are examples of the feminist canon that flowered at the time, partly due to the institutional support of the university and to the resulting social legitimisation. However, it is sobering to note that then, as well as now, women's studies programmes come under attack on the grounds of limited career potential and academic rigour, mostly as the result of their overtly political agenda.

Feminism as research strategy and method

Feminist research emerged in the 1980s from developments in women's studies curricula. Extending from the perspective that women were worthy of study in our own right and from the work of predominantly women academics, there was growing recognition that inherent in our research perspectives and approaches were gender differences in content as well as method. Differences among feminists within this domain may be traced to the disparate approaches of making research adhere to scientific rigour versus challenging the scientific approach outright. Examples of the former include such strategies as including women as subjects to assure generalisability, or at least qualifying male studies and perspectives with attention to their unspecified male bias. Examples of the latter deride scientific practice as inherently masculinist and instead argue for the propriety of subjective phenomena, dialogic methods and alternative ways of writing. Exemplary texts include Belenky *et al.*'s *Women's Ways of Knowing* (1986), Harding's *The Science Question in Feminism* (1986) and Gergen's *Feminist Thought and the Structure of Knowledge* (1988).

CUT TO THE PRESENT

In feminism, Blacks, Latinas and lesbians have been at the vanguard of thinking and working through multiple dimensions of feminist subjectivity, largely as the result of negotiating the competing pulls of their respective communities with those of feminism (Anzaldúa and Moraga 1983; James and Busia 1993). Women of colour have had to be attuned to white culture to succeed. The reverse is not true; and when this has occurred it has been a function of genuine interest or opportunism, at times by both parties.

Black scholars Cade-Bambara (1970) and Smith (1983), and more recently McKay (1993) and James and Busia (1993), have written of conflicting loyalties to the Black and women's movements. While Black men subordinate them as women, white women denigrate and/or ignore them. As McKay writes:

> The wounds inflicted by generations of privileged women on less privileged women, and the continued insensitivity of many white women today are embedded in race, and retard progress toward unity. Anxious to avoid further rifts between them, many white women still deny differences based on

> past experiences between themselves and others, and focus on the commonalties of gender.
>
> (McKay 1993: 273)

Continuing, she quotes Johnetta Cole (1986), 'To address our commonalties without dealing with our differences is to misunderstand and distort *that which separates as well as that which unites us as women*' [emphases added].

A particularly troubling area has been white women's lack of understanding regarding women of colour's allegiance to men of colour and their respective ethnic/racial communities. White women simply do not have to contend with the marginalisation of white men; they are after all at the centre of racial power. McKay concludes, 'Black women cannot choose between their commitment to feminism and the struggle with their men for racial justice' (1993: 276).

Latinas have faced somewhat similar oppositions. On one hand are the pulls of machismo and community-centeredness within the Chicano community demanding commitment and work while denying voice and agency. On the other hand, the women's movement promises sisterhood, yet painfully excludes Chicanas and omits issues specific to our culture (MALCS 1993; Trujillo 1998). Latinas have criticised white women for their overreliance on gender, exclusion of ethnicity/race and class and individualistic ethos, forwarding instead a collective, family-based struggle for community empowerment (Pesquera and Segura 1993).

Sadly, these tensions continue today. Poised at the nexus of these contradictions, contemporary feminists must turn a critical eye to the legacy of the past while developing a unique posture regarding our differences. From the outside, what may appear to be an uneasy relativism should be viewed with the historical recognition that trying to work through these differences has proved unnervingly futile. Instead, by grasping the particular socio-historical conditions within which they are embedded, we can maintain our differences in conjunction.

I suspect this is what cultural theorists mean when they argue that identity politics are obsolete. Although identification affords the opportunity to define oneself and attribute meanings and value to one's subject position and activities, doing so often brings about reactionary moves from others. These complexities confound us, yet we must ask: How can feminists privilege the category woman without specifying which women and thus excluding others? How can we privilege woman without reifying biological qualities which have been and continue to be the basis of oppression? How can we privilege woman without threatening the heterosexual world? Alternatively, for those intent upon separating from the latter because they believe doing so at least partially denies it power: How to avoid recreating its oppressive hierarchies? In short, do we deal with the limitations of our physical bodies and social communities, even as we revel in their sheer sensuality and joyous pleasures in mindfully realising our interests?

With hindsight can we say that all feminist policies are good things? Superwomen, indeed! Catching up with men in our incidence of heart disease, strokes and other illnesses has accompanied the gains we've made in wages. Even so, these gains are marked by persistent racial and class differences. Currently, while white women make 70 cents to the white man's dollar, Black and Latina sisters make 97 and 91 cents to every dollar a white woman makes (Robles 1999).[2]

And what of our identities as women? Our personal relationships? Our careers? These issues are no easier. I suspect we've all experienced strained or broken ties to family, friends and colleagues on these counts, disappointments, feeling compelled to provide explanations for being different and thinking differently, having to correct sexist jokes, to raise consciousness regarding the ways many advertisements degrade women, and initiate discussions when confronted with the daily injustices of racism and classism. Still, even if we could, I doubt many would trade the joys and pains our life choices have brought, for with each we have learned.

There is another reason. Each of our communities plays a role in our personal and academic development, often in surprising ways. Recognising the workings of power in relation to various subjective positionings, material conditions, marketing practices, beauty standards, sexualities, job demands and even the demands of leisure have been important steps in a growing consciousness of feminism. Throwing off the limitations of mainstream dogma and social norms has proved important for our growth and development. Remembering how far we've come is important, not so much to reify the past as to provide some tangible basis for understanding where we want to go in the future and how we might get there. In the next section I playfully reword Freud's question, 'What do women want?', and discuss ways in which feminist practices can enrich our lives.

What then does the feminist marketing academic want?[3]

Articulating the place for feminism in marketing is a complex task. Convincing anyone of their bias is daunting in itself, much less within a discipline like marketing that so prides itself on its objectivity and rigour. Challenges from outside are as pressing as those originating from within our ranks, as previously discussed. Even opposition to patriarchy, the one thing Second-Wave feminists could count on, has been called into question in the kinder, gentler, make-no-waves, get-in-and-get-mine, neo-conservative strands of feminism emerging in the late 1990s. While the women's, Black, Chicano/a and gay/lesbian movements have been built upon a foundation of shared identity and experiences of discrimination, a rejection of society's rationale for their circumstances and a recognition of the need for group solutions (Pesquera and Segura 1993), feminist marketing academics have much work to do on all counts.

Do feminists have an identifiable presence in the marketing academy?

This book on marketing and feminism presumes a unique position for feminists in marketing. Yet, feminism cuts across domains of subjective positions, politics, topics of study and the means by which we do research.

At the risk of being difficult, seeking to articulate a sense of feminism in the marketing academy is perhaps somewhat self-defeating, as the more we seek to articulate what is feminism, the more we may bring on internal and external conflicts. What can be said, after all, beyond placing gender equality at the fore? Dare we go so far as to privilege feminist work over non-feminist work in journals or in academic departments? How can/should we respond to the fairly widespread and persistent occurrence of gender inequities in work and pay?

Here things get particularly rocky as a function of feminism's difficulty with competition and power. In an ironic twist, competition and power are inherent to market exchanges, just as they are inherent to our jobs as marketing academics. Yet I do not see that feminism, as currently construed, adequately prepares us for these challenges, as all too often it denigrates competition without articulating a replacement.

A colleague recently related her litmus test of women's collegiality: competitive sports. Team sports, she argued, help women compete by offering lessons of being able to do so while working together and relating collegially. In the absence of being able to work out our differences in sports, it is my intention that by articulating the place of feminism in the marketing academy we can better recuperate its complex potential.

THE MULTICULTURAL GENDERED MARKETING ACADEMY

While some feminist marketers are academics, many more are practitioners. My focus in this work is on marketing academics, although the two institutional settings share many opportunities and challenges. Women are increasingly prevalent in advertising and marketing research agencies, marketing departments of large firms and entrepreneurial ventures, although the 'glasshouse phenomenon' remains tightly in place for most (Maclaran, Stevens and Catterall 1997).[4]

In the marketing academy, women have made gains, even though we continue to be primarily located in non-tenured and non-administrative staff positions. As a doctoral student I attended two of the early sessions on gender issues in the profession, one entitled 'Research, teaching and professional issues for women in consumer behaviour: do women have a different experience?' at the 1989 Association for Consumer Research conference, and the other a breakfast at the 1991 Winter American Marketing Association conference. The sessions comprised a star-studded panel of our finest: Beth Hirschman, Valerie Zeithaml, Mary Gilly, Alice Tybout and Barbara Stern addressed a standing-room-only audience.

Yet, unlike previously expressed perceptions of 'tangible feelings of goodwill and solidarity' (Stern 1991), I walked away from these sessions with less positive sentiments. Most of the participants had been denied tenure or were in the midst of difficult reviews, and lawsuits were not uncommon. While the obvious conclusion was that the academic deck is stacked against women, it remains a curiosity that women, like ethnic and racial minorities, somehow seem to salvage a sense that things will be different for us as individuals. Often unconscious and unspoken is the assumption that with enough hard work, individually we'll somehow transcend any limitations or mistaken attributions put upon us as a function of our gender, social class or race/ethnicity.

Most importantly, these assumptions preclude the development of coping strategies. Such conventional solutions as networking and building coalitions remain important strategies in inculcating feminist ideals and practices in our academic disciplines, departments, institutions and professional associations. Both explicit and implicit communication forums are valuable in passing on the torch of feminism in the marketing academy. The conference sessions mentioned above were two of the few formal venues where I'd heard women faculty members speak of their difficulties. Doing so takes courage, and comes from a place of strength, not weakness. This many women of colour know, for it is the shamed silence that works further to constrain us.[5]

Generations of marketing feminists

Three generations of feminists are delineated among our ranks. It should be noted that these generations do not correspond directly to the First, Second and Third waves of feminists; nor do they correspond to respective generations of women in marketing, due to a lag in incorporating feminist ideals and practices within our field. It is important here to recognise generational differences in how we bring feminism to bear in our work.

The first generation consists of the first women to work as university professors in marketing and their allies within the institution. Many are full professors now and can tell amazing stories of 'breaking in' their institutions. Their advances came with a heavy price, however; many have experienced contested tenure rulings and lawsuits. Their allies, many of whom are senior professors, with the rest being peers, staff and administrators, took a visionary stance and refused to let the male-dominated status quo prevail. At the time these women were rising through the ranks in their universities, feminism meant access and was commonly considered something just for women.

I'd count myself among the second generation. This group is composed of senior assistant and associate professors and is more evenly split between women and men. We share a sense that feminist ideals and practices make the institution more hospitable for us all, and that the rate of such changes, while encouraging, is not inevitable. Confident that time is on our side, we second generationers are put off by the stalwart ways of 'good old boy' senior colleagues, and are concerned at what we see as members of the third generation taking gender, race and class egalitarianism for granted.

The third generation is formulating itself even as this is written. This group is composed of graduate students and junior faculty. They have been raised on the dicta of multiculturalism and political correctness, and are suspicious of any form of identity politics based on gender, race or class that does not cast itself in relation to other groups. Gender is taken as the full spectrum of possible subject positions, to include the range of identities, sexualities, roles and domestic living arrangements, rather than its narrow framing in terms of the dualistic biological categories of sex.

Recognising these generational differences is necessary in building important bridges and coalitions. Further, this recognition should help defuse the troublesome sentiment that, because feminists do not all share a particular perspective or priority, we are either alone or worse, feminism in marketing does not exist.

Utopian dreams of sisterhood

For me good relations and mutual support among women colleagues is one of the goals of feminism in marketing. Now, perhaps this appears overly idealistic when it comes to the notion of sisterhood. Yet, I do not believe this to be the case. The personal is political, right?! Unfortunately, solidarity among women tends to be selectively manifest. More often than not I have experienced tremendous support from other women in the field. But when I have met with disappointment, a strong factor has been misunderstanding of our respective experience.

There is much irony here, and it is less than poetic. Much of the work of accommodating gender differences in organisations posits implicit yet quite specific positions, even as the state-of-the-art research on gender advances a multidimensional range of expression. There is much work to be done to remedy this disjunction, and doing so is important in our research and interpersonal relations.

There are clearly important distinctions in the choices and the lack thereof we experience, in our advantages and disadvantages. These distinctions are packed into the multiple experiences of class, race and gender, and evident in such life issues as having children; caring for an ailing parent; remaining single; being a person of colour in a predominantly white university; living as gay, lesbian or transgendered; and being the first in one's family or hometown with a Ph.D. Further complicating the situation are the ways these life issues are experienced confluently. While I am uncomfortable ranking people's circumstances, appreciating the range of gender expression is important in gaining understanding of how our own subject positions are played out in all aspects of our work.

The relationality of gender

One of the emerging tenets of feminism is that gender is not just about women. Recognition of the inherent relationality of masculine and feminine gendered subject positions, roles and identities is an important part of advancing feminist ideals and practices within the marketing academy. They do not make sense separately; after all, the masculine and feminine evolved in tandem, with particular expressions evolving distinctly within particular socio-economic systems.

In recognising the inherent relationality of gender, some women's studies faculties are considering renaming and reorienting their departments. This is also the result of the increased legitimacy of queer studies within women's studies departments, as gay, lesbian and transgendered subject positions, roles and identities present a challenge to ideals and conventions of feminism.

Nevertheless, probably due to the way women's studies emerged separately in the university and the more generalised lack of attention to powerful groups,[6] there is much resistance to the way masculinist ideology and roles constrain men as well as women. To this day, men's studies lag in development to women's studies. It is unlikely that we will gain meaningful understanding of feminist concerns, in the marketing academy as well as outside it, in the absence of concerted investigations of the relationality of gender.

Classism

As feminist marketing academics, we occupy upper-middle-class subject positions, while most women are not so privileged. Yet, we represent marked differences in class background. While some of us represent the first generation to go to college, much less graduate school, others are second- or even third-generation academics. It is important to keep in mind these differences in our thinking and writing about feminism.

Recognising class differences is critical, as from each respective subject position come transitions and points of growth, both in terms of individual and community development and intellectual thought. A telling example of this appears in a dialogue between Black feminist bell hooks and rap musician Ice Cube (hooks 1994). hooks distinguishes between marketing Blackness, the appropriation of which she condemns, and self-determination, which she lauds. She illustrates her point with a story of being chided for buying a BMW because her writing is so overtly political. 'We all deserve the best', she concludes. Ice Cube agrees:

> Just because we black and we write the way we do doesn't mean we don't want the finer things in life . . . if we work, and earn the money, then we should be able to buy these things without the neighbourhood saying, 'why you going around in this?' I don't think the way we spend money as individuals is even relevant.
>
> (hooks 1994: 126–7)

But are our personal lives irrelevant to our work? Surprisingly, hooks does not invoke the feminist litany that the personal is political. A dangerous rift emerges within feminism when the workings of class are eclipsed by the workings of race. Positionality matters. Upper-middle-class women's concerns with not having greater access to resources, while important, often fall flat when cast in contrast to the class differences among whites, and between whites and people of colour.

Race matters

Analogous to increasing recognition that gender is not about just women is recognition that race and ethnicity are not about just people of colour. Just as the study of gender relations is steadily making gains in women's studies programmes, so studies of race relations are making headway in ethnic studies, Chicano studies and African American studies programmes. Much of this work has entailed an interrogation of white privilege as an invisible but nevertheless crucial aspect of social power.

The guilt of whites has been identified as a key factor sabotaging recognition of the workings of racial power. Rios (1999) cleverly deflects this guilt, noting how it diverts attention from the racial issues which whites prefer to cast themselves outside of, even as they occupy racially privileged positions. All too often, racial issues in feminism become dominated by this guilt, which Rios terms the 'easy way out for white women'. Instead, she calls for meaningful dialogue between white feminists and feminists of colour.

Equally important are the colour schemes within and between racial/ethnic groups. Blacks have a history of the paper bag and ruler tests (Graham 1999). For Latinos/as the güera/o (light skinned) is valued over the prieta/o (dark skinned).[7]

In addition to these colour hierarchies are differences in socio-economic status and educational attainment for the two groups. Regarding representation in the marketing academy, Blacks have made important educational advances over Latinos/as, numbering approximately fifty Ph.D.s, for every seven Latinos/as with Ph.D.s in marketing, according to figures kept by KPMG Peat Marwick Foundation's Ph.D. project, a doctoral consortium geared to bolstering the numbers of minorities in the profession. Why these numbers differ so markedly is a key question, particularly given that the groups maintain similar numbers within the US population.[8]

The gap likely reflects the unique historical circumstances of both groups – slavery versus colonisation and immigration, as well as differences of language, colour and way of life. Another important distinction became evident to me recently, while watching an interview with Lawrence Otis Graham, author of *Our Kind of People* (1999). The book provides a fascinating account of elite Black social clubs, universities, sororities and fraternities, summer camps and even pre-school programmes.

Latinos/as also have an upper class – the late Robert Goizueta, former CEO of Coke; Frederico Peña, former US Secretary of Transportation; and Henry Cisneros, current President of Univision, immediately come to mind. Yet, we have no universities in the US, although there are longstanding academic traditions in Spain and Central and South America dating back to the sixteenth century, and there is a tradition dating to the mid-nineteenth century of elites from these countries sending their children to preparatory schools and colleges in the US and Europe.

Ultimately, both Latino/a and Black populations remain skewed, with the majority in the working classes and in poverty. It is important to retain a sense of the internal variation in characteristics and experiences of racial groups, necessarily including whites, to avoid the reductionism of race equals persons of colour, and views of these subcultures solely in relation to whites.

My identity as a Chicana is as convoluted as is my feminism. I grew up speaking English in a middle-class neighbourhood in a small town in Central Texas, although Spanish was my parents' first language. Of the 150 students in my high school class, only one other person was Latino. I remember first being asked my ethnicity in completing the application for the doctoral programme at the University of California, Irvine, wondering what I should put down. As an undergraduate and MBA student at Texas A&M University, I'd had no part of any Mexican American student groups, but even in that then predominantly white institution times were changing. In the late 1980s my dissertation topic on Mexican immigrants was initially turned down. A year later, the discovery of the 'Sleeping Giant', as the Hispanic market was then called, made it acceptable. My own ethnic consciousness rose with the group's commercial potential.

Even so, I was stunned by a peer's remark years later at the doctoral consortium that I'd only got my interviews because I was Latina. I was struck speechless, already intimidated by the intense interviewing process. It took years for me to come up with the response I now share with students, 'I suppose my work has nothing to do with it!' Meanwhile, the students tell me, the disparaging remarks continue. So much for the post-affirmative action era. The erosions in affirmative action programmes at the university and in government procurement continue, juxtaposed with persistent gaps between whites, Blacks and Hispanics in wages, employment and educational attainment, and in contrast to the growth of 'minority' populations and markets.

Research

Regarding research, by now we have reached a point in which it is no longer necessary to justify feminist methods. Certainly this is one of the advantages of breaking into the mainstream, and for this such pioneering feminist scholars as Bristor and Fischer (1993), Hirschman (1993) and Stern (1993) deserve much credit.

Amidst this success, we must actively guard against the tendency to become as rigid and exclusionary in our constructions of feminist research as some of the defenders of the paradigm seeking to exclude us have been at times. In a marked sleight of hand, strategic marketing researchers claim objectivity even as they readily take on masculinist subject positions and those of marketers in actively furthering their objectives. At the same time, when scholars take on the perspectives of feminists or market critics, the charge of practising non-science often is levelled.

For feminist marketing researchers it is as much a contribution in specifying the implicit masculine bias in research and holding positivism to its scientific tenets as challenging them with alternative research practices. Both decentring manoeuvres are important in doing research from a feminist subject position. Further, despite many advances, many studies continue to employ the terminology of gender even as they implement the dichotomy of sex, i.e., male versus female decision making and information processing. Relatively scarce are multidimensional, continuous treatments of gender that embrace its performative, ritualised dimensions and socialisation dynamics while not losing sight of either cultural roles or biological imperatives.

Perhaps due to the market imperative favouring research investigating women, we in marketing experience much less admonishment against work on women by women than colleagues in the social sciences. Its corollaries, discrediting of 'brown on brown' research (research on Latinos/as by Latinos/as), and 'Black on Black' research (research on Blacks by Blacks) are equally less prevalent in marketing, probably for the same reasons (Venkatesh 1998).

The market imperatives favouring research investigating women and ethnic/racial minorities should give us some cause for concern, however, regarding our roles in the marketing institutional apparatus (Valdivia 1995). 'How could I sleep at night if I thought marketers created needs?' I was once asked by a female colleague, visibly uncomfortable with her own role. We had been talking about the differences between objective, scientific research and subjective, action-oriented research.

Why does the marketing canon continue to skirt this issue philosophically, echoing the refrain that marketers tap into latent needs, yet at the same time it is clear that creating needs is increasingly expected of marketers as their central social responsibility in a capitalistic society? Attending to our roles *vis à vis* consumers and marketers is an important step in building a greater consciousness of the general workings of power in our personal and professional domains (Murray and Ozanne 1991).

We will and should differ regarding where we come out with respect to furthering marketers' objectives and/or championing consumers' rights, and our levels of comfort with our positions. Nor should they be viewed as mutually exclusive. The important point lies in developing conscious awareness of the political implications of our actions and positions as feminists within the marketing academy.

Teaching

With time, I have learned to let students raise differences of opinion regarding the sensitive topics of gender, social class and cultural diversity, instead of preaching the dictum of informed knowledge and enlightenment. This valuable lesson came serendipitously. I had just returned from a conference on ethnic studies, participating in a plenary session on immigration. Until then I'd never presented my work to an audience consisting predominately of Blacks and Latinos/as. But my appreciation for the audience was cut short when I encountered the obligatory test of my own economic politics.

Traditionally, Black and Latino/a studies departments have been populated with persons from the social sciences and humanities, and the strong Marxist training of many is a telling factor in their critical anti-business positioning. As a result, many ethnic studies scholars view business as something other people do to minority communities, with the siphoning out of capital as the result. There are exceptions, of course, and recent trends suggest that business can play a role in minority community development, largely at the hands of minority-owned entrepreneurial businesses and with increased representation of minorities in schools of business and economics. Even so, the anti-business stance is predominant among minority academics.

Talking about this with my students, I was surprised to learn of their similar experiences with their peers in the humanities and social sciences. They noted that they had been the target of much criticism and condescension for being greedy and willing to exploit others. While a minority of the students admitted they were out to make money, many had other goals of having a positive impact on the world through their participation with large businesses, as well as their own firms, and were offended by these characterisations. At the same time, they acknowledged that the criticisms were not without some basis, as some marketers were responsible for reprehensible business practices. By soliciting and orchestrating the already existing differences of opinions regarding sensitive issues of gender, race, class and business ideology among the students, I've learned to be more effective in advancing class discussion.

Service

Anne Huff's (1991) paper on women as the caretakers of the university is a timely, eye-opening introduction to the gender politics of service in the academy.[9] Huff suggests that part of the reason women do not – and should not – get promotions and raises is that we have not learned to do what matters to the organisation. All too often we are the caretakers, the wives of the organisation, as she terms it, focusing on interpersonal relationships over more substantive work. While some organisational theorists suggest these interpersonal skills will come to be more valued in the current era of rapid technological change and relationship marketing (Handy 1994; Freeman and Varey 1997), so far the evidence does not support them (Maclaran, Stevens and Catterall 1997). Learning when to say yes and when to say no is of the utmost importance if one is to survive in the marketing academy, given the tendency for women to be assigned – and take on – service tasks in higher proportions than men. This is further compounded by the challenges of family and career. Huff's article contains some very useful advice based on her experience and observation, and continues to be relevant today, even as women academics increase in numbers and prominence.

Notably, women of colour and those from working-class backgrounds routinely experience challenges in addition to the gender issues shared by all women. It is difficult, but necessary, for us to say no to many university activities, given the low percentages we see or – more often – do not see among our colleagues and in our classes at the university. Such activities as mentoring minority students and speaking on topics of diversity, while also done by white faculty, fall disproportionately on us. Couple that with added calls for participation on committees that 'need to hear our voices', and those stemming from our ethnic/racial communities, and we are often left overextended, more so because many of us want to participate and are troubled by our low percentages in our disciplines and in our institutions. As an acid test, simply take a look at a few curricula vitae –

compare white men and women with men and women of colour. With few exceptions the results should be an eye-opener to us all.

CONCLUSIONS

This chapter has explored a number of issues impacting the future of feminism in the marketing academy. Its overview of feminist thought and its personal reflections are offered in the interests of stimulating discussion on issues affecting contemporary feminist marketing academics. It is encouraging to note the diffusion of feminist ideals throughout society and in the marketing academy specifically, although this is tempered somewhat by ambivalence and sporadic backlash.

As feminist marketing academics, we will continue to confront challenges from within as well as outside our ranks. While the challenges raised by our internal differences in race/ethnicity, class and sexuality are great, they also afford tremendous opportunities for growth and meaningful connections with others. Such connections are basic to what Audre Lorde termed the 'erotics of work', and they are powerful indeed.

> For once we begin to feel deeply all the aspects of our lives, we begin to demand from ourselves and our life-pursuits that they feel in accordance with the joy which we know ourselves to be capable of.
>
> (Lorde 1984: 57)

It is towards the goal of achieving that joy that this chapter is offered.

NOTES

1 The interviews are part of a study of Mexican American consumers.

2 The figures are mean earnings ratios from the 1998 Current Population Reports of the US Bureau of the Census, controlled for income by comparing those with Master's degrees. As such, they represent conservative comparisons, given persistent differences in education between white men and women, and between white women and women of colour.

3 I thank Kathryn Rios for providing the inspiration for this heading. In a 1999 paper intended to build bridges between white feminists and feminists of colour she uses the phrase, 'What do women of colour want?'

4 Maclaran, Stevens and Catterall (1997) coin the term glasshouse effect in reference to gender-related obstacles to horizontal as well as vertical advancement.

5 This is not to say that women of colour have a monopoly in understanding the politics of silence and shame. Perhaps it is a class-based, rather than racial tendency to speak about what we have learned, invoking personal experience in overcoming adversity.

6 Part of this may well be the result of who tends to do scientific research, as well as who tends to be its focus, as inherent to the workings of power is staying invisible (Faugeron

and Robert 1978). Whatever the case, less is known about powerful groups such as men, whites and the upper classes than less powerful segments of society.

7 My experience is as a güera.

8 Just this year the number of Latino/a youth in the US surpassed the number of Black youth, indicative of a future trend that Latinos/as will soon be the nation's largest minority group.

9 Informal potlucks with other women in the College of Business at the university have been a valuable source of information as well.

REFERENCES

Anzaldúa, G. and Moraga, C. (eds) (1981) *This Bridge Called My Back: Writings by Radical Women of Colour*, Watertown, MA: Persephone Press.

Belenky, M., Clinchy, B., Goldberger, N. and Tarule, J. (1986) *Women's Ways of Knowing*, New York: Basic Books.

Bristor, J. M. and Fischer, E. (1993) 'Feminist thought: implications for consumer research', *Journal of Consumer Research* 19, 4: 518–36.

Brown, R. M. (1976) *A Plain Brown Wrapper*, Oakland, CA: Diana Press.

Cade-Bambara, T. (1970) *The Black Woman: An Anthology*, New York: New American Library.

Cole, J. B. (ed.) (1986) *All-American Women: Lines that Divide, Ties that Bind*, New York: Free Press.

Costa, J. (ed.) (1994) *Gender Issues and Consumer Behaviour*, Thousand Oaks, CA: Sage.

Daly, M. (1973) *Beyond God the Father: Toward a Philosophy of Women's Liberation*, Boston, MA: Beacon Press.

Faugeron, C. and Robert, P. (1978) 'La justice et son public et les representations sociales do systeme penal', Paris: Masson; cited in M. Wittig 'The straight mind', in R. Ferguson, M. Gever, T. T. Minh-ha and C. West (eds) *Out There: Marginalization and Contemporary Cultures*, Cambridge, MA: MIT Press.

Freeman, S. and Varey, R. (1997) 'Women communicators in the workplace: natural born marketers?', *Marketing Intelligence and Planning* 15, 7: 318–24.

Gergen, M. McC. (ed.) (1988) *Feminist Thought and the Structure of Knowledge*, New York: New York University Press.

Gillligan, C. (1982) *In a Different Voice: Psychological Theory and Women's Development*, Cambridge, MA: Harvard University Press.

Graham, L. O. (1999) *Our Kind of People: Inside the Black Upper Class*, New York: HarperCollins.

Handy, C. (1994) *The Empty Raincoat: Making Sense of the Future*, London: Hutchinson.

Harding, S. (1986) *The Science Question in Feminism*, New York: Cornell University Press.

Hirschman, E. (1993) 'Ideology in consumer research, 1980 and 1990: a Marxist and feminist critique', *Journal of Consumer Research* 19, 4: 537–55.

hooks, bell (1994) *Outlaw Culture: Resisting Representations*, London: Routledge.

Huff, A. S. (1991) 'Wives – of the organisation', paper presented at the Women and Work Conference, Arlington, TX, 11 May.

James, S. M. and Busia, A. P. A. (1993) *Theorizing Black Feminisms: The Visionary Pragmatism of Black Women*, London: Routledge.

Lorde, A. (1984) *Sister Outsider: Essays and Speeches*, Freedom, CA: The Crossing Press.

McKay, N. Y. (1993) 'Acknowledging differences: can women find unity through diversity?', in M. J. Stanlie and A. P. A. Busia (eds) *Theorizing Black Feminisms: The Visionary Pragmatism of Black Women*, London: Routledge, 267–82.

Maclaran, P., Stevens, L. and Catterall, M. (1997) 'The "Glasshouse" effect: women in marketing management', *Marketing Intelligence and Planning* 15, 7: 309–17.

MALCS (Mujeres Activas en Letras y Cambio Social) (1993) *Chicana Critical Issues*, Berkeley, CA: Third Woman Press.

Millett, K. (1970) *Sexual Politics*, New York: Doubleday.

Murray, J. B. and Ozanne, J. (1991) 'The critical imagination: emancipatory interests in consumer research', *Journal of Consumer Research* 18, September: 129–44.

Patai, D. (1998) *Heterophobia: Sexual Harassment and the Future of Feminism*, Lanham, MD: Rowman & Littlefield.

Peñaloza, L. (1994) 'Crossing boundaries/drawing lines: a look at the nature of gender boundaries and their impact on marketing research', *International Journal of Research in Marketing* 11, 4: 359–79.

—— (1996) 'We're here, we're Queer and we're going shopping: a critical perspective on the accommodation of gays and lesbians in the US marketplace', *Journal of Homosexuality* 31, 1/2: 9–41.

Pesquera, B. M. and Segura, D. M. (1993) 'There is no going back: Chicanas and feminists', in MALCS, *Chicana Critical Issues*, Berkeley, CA: Third Woman Press, 95–116.

Rios, K. (1999) 'Confrontations and collaborations between women of colour and others', Women's Studies Spring Colloquium, University of Colorado, Boulder, 2 February.

Robles, B. (1999) 'Latinas in higher education: faculty, student and the graduate pipeline', working paper, Austin, TX: LBJ School of Public Affairs.

Roiphe, K. (1993) *The Morning After: Sex, Fear and Feminism on Campus*, Boston, MA: Little, Brown & Company.

Schulman, S. (1994) *My American History: Lesbian and Gay Life during the Reagan/Bush Years*, New York: Routledge.

Smith, B. (1983) *Home Girls: A Black Feminist Anthology*, New York: Kitchen Table.

Steinem, G. (1983) *Outrageous Acts and Everyday Rebellions*, New York: Holt, Rinehart & Winston.

Stern, B. B. (1991) 'Déjà vu: feminism revisited', in J. A. Costa (ed.) *Gender and Consumer Behaviour*, Salt Lake City: University of Utah Printing Service, 341–9.

—— (1993) 'Feminist literary criticism and the deconstruction of ads: a postmodern view of advertising and consumer responses', *Journal of Consumer Research* 19, 4: 556–66.

Trujillo, C. (1998) *Living Chicana Theory*, Berkeley, CA: Third Woman Press.

Valdivia, A. N. (1995) *Feminism, Multiculturalism and the Media: Global Diversities*, Thousand Oaks, CA: Sage.

Venkatesh, A. (1998) 'The market value of diversity: a cultural analysis', in A. K. Gardner (ed.) *Investing in Diversity: Advancing Opportunities for Minorities and the Media*, Washington, DC: The Aspen Institute, 193–216.

Wolf, N. (1993) *Fire With Fire: The New Female Power and How it will Change the Twenty-first Century*, New York: Random House.

4 Advertisements as women's texts: a feminist overview

Barbara B. Stern

INTRODUCTION

Until the 1990s, researchers studied advertisements in accordance with the underlying and largely unquestioned assumptions (Stern 1992, 1993) that language neutrality enables transmission of the 'same' information to all recipients and that meaning can be universally and 'correctly' comprehended by all consumers, notwithstanding the tendency of some consumers to miscomprehend some messages. These assumptions are embedded in the modernist premise of a single right reading in which consumers respond to stable advertising text. Only within the last decade have advertising researchers challenged these assumptions, introducing feminist and multicultural ideas about reading that cast doubt on the existence of stable language and universally comprehensible meanings.

Articles by Mick and Buhl (1992), Stern (1992, 1993, 1994), Stern and Holbrook (1994), Holbrook and Stern (1997), Brown, Stevens and Maclaran (1999), and Kates (1999) draw from such sources as deconstruction, feminist criticism, queer theory, Bakhtinian analysis and psychoanalytic theory to question language neutrality, universal meaning and fixed signification. The new wave of interdisciplinary scholarship in advertising and consumer behaviour was influenced by earlier feminist research that sought to integrate studies of popular culture into social, political and literary theory (Goffman 1976; Allen 1987). In this way, its theoretical roots can be traced via the feminist agenda of integrating literary and cultural criticism first activated in the study of literature (Modleski 1982; Radway 1984; Schweickart and Flynn 1988; Ruthven 1990). These studies are 'cross-disciplinary in practice and feminist in perspective, and they signal a move away from disciplinary boundaries which threaten to keep the most informed textual readings from their fullest cultural contexts' (Allen 1987: 296). However, even though feminist criticism has entered advertising research, it has done so in a scattered way, with theoretical innovations introduced piecemeal. The purpose of this paper is to step back a bit and review feminist ideas applicable to advertising text that may pave the way for the integration of humanities theory (Stern 1989) and social science empiricism.

The chapter will begin by presenting background information about feminist theory to contextualise what we know about women's writing (text production) and women's reading (text interpretation). Note that 'reading' is a term borrowed from literary criticism and used as a generic descriptor for consumer responses to advertising text. Feminist theories of reading and writing will be summarised, and research suggestions from multicultural studies will be proposed. In addition, in conformance with the political aim of most feminist theory, a prescriptive research agenda for advertising will be suggested.

GENDER AND READING: UNSTABLE TEXTS AND VARIABLE READERS

Prior to the revolution in literary criticism in the 1960s and 1970s, 'reading' was for the most part assumed to consist of a correct audience response to a stable text. Within this framework, an advertisement, like any other species of text, was assumed to have an agreed-upon, officially sanctioned meaning, one that consumers were expected to 'get' if they read it correctly, that is, comprehended it. The major problem was 'whether consumers accurately comprehended the advertisements that they see, read, and hear' (Jacoby and Hoyer 1987: 3). However, reader-response criticism in the 1970s (Bleich 1978) and deconstructive criticism in the 1980s challenged the concept of 'correct' readings, positing a more dynamic – and more problematical – relationship between the reader and the text (Schweickart 1988). The combined weight of postmodern schools of criticism exploded the notion that the reader is a passive recipient of a single right reading of the same text. Instead, each reader was assumed to be a dynamic participant in the reading process, seeing 'phenomena through a filter of concerns and awarenesses' that shaped his or her response (Donovan 1975: 76). The deconstructive critics dealt a death-blow to the concept of finite language meaning, claiming instead that every reading is a misreading (Bloom 1976). The confluence of feminism and deconstruction engendered a re-examination of reader–text relationships, with the focus on analysis of the way that a reader's sex functions as a significant determinant of the process of making meaning.

Problematisation of the relationship entered consumer/advertising research in the 1990s, when the concept of gendered text was adapted from literature to advertising (Stern 1992, 1993). Just as products are assigned gender on the basis of product category, spokesperson and/or sex of potential user (see Iyer and Debevec 1986, for review), so too can advertising text be assigned gender as either male-centred or female-centred. Following the research on gendered products, I propose that advertising be studied as sex-specific rather than sex-neutral, based on interactions between the gender of text and that of the reader analogous to interactions hypothesised in literary criticism. That is, in so far as advertising texts are likely to differ based on androcentricity (male-centred) versus gynocentricity (female-centred), male readers are likely to read male advertising text 'as a man', but female readers are likely also to read male advertising text 'as a man' (Culler 1982).

To trace the influence of feminist theory in our own discipline, we must return to the roots of sex-linked analysis. In literary criticism, as in other disciplines, feminists first brought to light the repressiveness of 'women's place' in a culture so automatically patriarchal that male dominance was taken for granted as the norm (Russ 1972). The norm implies that both men and women accept a single point of view as dominant: the male one. It is embodied in the concept of a patriarchal society; the model for all historically documented cultures (Bullough 1974). In patriarchal culture, reality is construed in terms of a male-centred perspective and, in so far as the female perspective is developed or articulated at all, it represents a minor, unofficial and often aberrant point of view (Firestone 1971; Stern 1992, 1993, 1994). Prior to the feminist identification of culture as relentlessly male, a question such as Culler's, 'If the meaning of the work is the experience of a reader, what difference does it make if the reader is a woman?' (1982: 42), would have made no sense.

Feminist critics offered new and radical insights to uncover heretofore unexamined masculinist formulations of reality, often using the simple method of sex-role reversal to expose the presence of two distinct male and female cultures coexisting side by side (Fetterley 1978; Stern 1993, 1996). They reread texts in light of the sexual power system and used theories of sexual difference to offer new interpretations (Allen 1987). This method was applied to advertising in a rereading of the macho Marlboro Man icon (Stern 1996). The postulation of two separate cultures was taken to mean that any text true to the female experience could be expected to differ from one true to the male experience, both in subject-matter and style as well as in perceived meaning. The rationale is that different cultural experiences influence both *what* each sex reads and *how* each one reads. The synthesis of feminist, reader-response and deconstructive criticism suggests that understanding different modes of reading based on the reader's sex is likely to have important consequences for researchers bent on studying differences between consumer segments in response to advertising messages as well as to literary ones.

The issue of what it is that different readers *get out* of the text is a mainstay of feminist criticism, which divides texts and readers according to gender, locating differences in male and female readers' responses to male and female texts. Let us begin with a discussion of gendered texts, and then move to the more complex issue of reader gender and its relation to text.

TEXTUAL GENDER: ANDROCENTRIC VERSUS GYNOCENTRIC

Androcentric text: reading 'as a man'

For feminists, the question of *how* we read can only be answered by first answering the question of *what* we read. The feminist insistence on breaking apart the monolith of 'culture' into 'male' and 'female' stems from historical evidence of separate spheres, the 'cult of true womanhood' (Welter 1966), that enshrined sexual differences based on appropriate societal roles. These spheres, simply put, were domestic life for women and everything else for men, evident in advertising as well as literature. Woman's sphere was home and hearth, and her functions were limited to those concerning household affairs. Early feminist criticism aimed at documenting the pervasive androcentricity in the literary canon (Showalter 1977) that socialised readers into accepting women's place as normal and natural. Influential early studies of images of women in male-authored literature, such as Kate Millett's book (1971), documented stereotypical portrayals in works by such authors as D. H. Lawrence and Norman Mailer and pointed out the sexism of phallic criticism. Feminist critics accepted Fish's (1980) notion that reading strategy is regulated by canons of acceptability in the reading community, but set out to show that these canons were androcentric. They concluded that the reading process socialises male and female readers alike by exposing everyone to male-dominant texts. Kolodny summarises the process: 'In so far as we are taught to read, what we engage are not texts but paradigms. . . . In so far as literature is itself a social institution, so, too, reading is a highly socialised, or learned activity' (1980: 451). In so far as androcentric texts comprise the majority of our cultural icons, both male and female readers learn to read androcentric texts, the majority of our cultural products, *as a man* (Fetterley 1978). Advertising, too, fits into the androcentric tradition, for, as Friedan points out (1963), it reflects the male vision of gender division.

For male readers of androcentric text, the phrase 'reading as a man' does not contain the same ambiguity as does 'reading as a woman' (Culler 1982). The reason is that androcentric text serves as a meeting ground of the personal and the universal: maleness is equated with humanity, and male readers feel affinity with what is presented as the universal paradigmatic human norm. Reading as a man can be considered the default, for a man (almost) always reads as a man, and women have been trained to read androcentric text in this manner. However, although both men and women nearly always read 'as a man', men almost never read 'as a woman'. Thus, 'reading as a man' is the norm, whereas 'reading as a woman' is a minority activity, a manifestation of otherness. In advertising, persuasive appeals before the 1970s depicted women viewed through the lens of male-determined 'norms'. Feminist critics pointed out that the empowerment of androcentricity as the norm teaches women 'to think as men, to identify with a male point of view, and to accept as normal and legitimate a male system of values' (Fetterley 1978: xx). For female readers, the process of reading as a man, far from being normal, provides evidence of the 'immasculation' of the woman reader. Feminist critics view text itself as imbued with the cultural version of what constitutes a woman, pointing out that men have historically controlled the signifying practices that construct woman (Allen 1987). The power of male control of textuality is demonstrated by the symbiotic relationship between the androcentric literary canon controlled by DWEMs (Dead White European Males) and male modes of reading. This critical tradition (Baym 1981) – the 'male club of literary criticism' (Heilbrun and Stimpson 1975: 65) – perpetuates not simply the production of androcentric texts, but also the body of scholarship about reading. Similarly, marketing scholarship reinforced androcentricity, if not by overt manipulation of women to suit male wants and needs (Friedan 1963) than by covert acceptance of women in pre-designated roles. Ironically, the more women read and learn about reading, the more likely they are to see things 'his way'. When the text is male, when the commentary is male and when the generic reader is assumed to be male, the female reader can scarcely avoid accommodation to the male viewpoint.

Gynocentric text: reading 'as a woman'

If androcentric works were the only ones available, feminist criticism could do no more than accentuate the negative, affirming 'women's point of view [only] by revealing, criticising, and examining its impossibility' (MacKinnon 1983: 637). However, early feminist critics set out to discover a body of gynocentric writings largely ignored or undervalued in the patriarchy. By the 1970s, feminist critics began to uncover neglected or 'lost' women writers and began making the case for a 'women's tradition by literature' (Allen 1987: 288). Their goal was the discovery, codification and publication of a canon of woman-centred literature, usually defined as works written by, for and about women. The recovery of a sizeable body of women's literature permitted formulation of new theories of reading based on responses to texts representative of women's culture, and arguments were made for including women writers in the literary pantheon. Once women's texts gained acceptance as a literary canon in its own right, a central feminist question could be framed: What does it mean for a woman, reading as a woman, to read literature written by a woman writing as a woman?

The concept of 'reading as a woman' (Culler 1982) permits entry into women-centred text that, unlike male-centred mainstream works, does not immasculate women. However, an important caveat is that this mode of reading is likely to apply only to *women's readings of women's writings*, for feminist critics assume that this situation alone presents pressure neither to adopt the male viewpoint nor to negate or resist it. In consequence, women are likely to read women's writings differently from the way they read men's writings. In so far as this difference applies only to gynocentric text *and* to women readers, feminist studies (Radway 1984; Radford 1986) often focus on women writing/women reading. Indeed, one can criticise the power of advertising to imitate women's writing as an illegitimate means of persuading women to buy into the patriarchal economy.

However, an interesting question arises in reference to the opposite situation: How do male readers respond to gynocentric text? That is, if women readers adopt androcentric perspectives when they read men's texts, do men readers adopt gynocentric perspectives when they read women's texts? The answer appears to be that they do not: men are 'resisting readers' (Fetterley 1978) of women's texts, for men almost never read 'as a woman' (Culler 1982: xxv). The reasons are embedded in the patriarchal value system that socialises members of a culture from early childhood experiences on up through adult developmental stages.

Male resistance to gynocentric text seems to be inculcated from childhood, for the child's acquisition of literacy is said to help form gender identity, and reading is viewed in our culture as a vehicle for proper sex-role socialisation. Children's books (like toys) have been segregated by sex since the mid-nineteenth century (Segel 1988), and males are as averse to female books ('sissy lit') as they are to female toys. Even in today's relatively enlightened intellectual milieu, taboos against boys who read girls' books and play with girls' toys are more stringent than the reverse – witness the Moral Majority's condemnation of Tinky Winky (a male Teletubby) as gay because he carries a red purse. So, too, with books. Although many books are consciously written for unisex audiences, if a book is perceived as a 'girls'' book (Judy Blume's works, for example), boys are discouraged from reading it. Advertising and marketing practices continue to reflect not only the division between male and female spheres – witness toy store layouts – but also the implication that whereas boys can be boys, girls are only girls when they fit the mould that boys create.

Not surprisingly, adult men tend to denigrate 'women's literature', such as weepies, soap operas or 'gothics', and to avoid the bookstore section labelled 'romances'. Most men dismiss women's magazines as trivial, and readership of *Vogue, Allure* and so forth is overwhelmingly female. However, note that a category of 'men's fiction' (Cawelti 1976), including spy stories, military and police adventures and science fiction, parallels that of women's fiction. Holland and Sherman (1988) have pointed out that gothics appeal primarily to women readers and that men consign romance novels to the alien and inferior category of 'women's fiction'. Holland (1975) explains this in terms of a psychoanalytic theory of reading that posits readers as unconsciously in search of pleasure during the reading process. Pleasure occurs when readers are able to see their fantasies become 'real' in fiction that shows their wishes fulfilled and/or their fears overcome. Many categories of women's fiction such as romances, family sagas and soap operas (Lavin 1995) maximise pleasure for women readers by featuring experiences of family relationships and fantasies about love and marriage. Male aversion to female texts is said to result from the failure to derive pleasure from such themes and fantasies (Holland and Sherman 1988). Men avoid reading not simply gynocentric texts but also works written by men that are considered women's literature (ibid.).

The existence of gynocentric advertising text has been identified in terms of characteristic themes and structures adapted from literature. For example, advertisements have been found that conform to the soap opera (Stern 1991a; Lavin 1995) and romance genres (Stern 1991b). Genre conventions such as narrative structure, nature of characters, kind of language used, and themes and values have been transferred nearly intact from literature, albeit miniaturised to suit advertising constraints. In so far as both romances and soaps are considered women's literature, we propose that a gynocentric advertising category exists parallel to another, but not yet well-explored, category of androcentric advertisements. In this regard, gynocentric text is likely to show formal affinities with genres categorised as 'women's literature,' and female readers are likely to read female (gynocentric) advertising text 'as a woman' and male (androcentric) advertising text 'as a man'. However, male readers are likely to read all advertising text 'as a man'.

CONTROL OF THE TEXT

Efferent versus aesthetic reading styles

The gender of a text is but one factor that affects the reading process. According to reader-dominant critics such as Fish (1980), the other and possibly more important influence is the reader, said to supply much if not all of the meaning. The meaning of the text is conceptualised as a function of the interpretive strategies used by the reader (Taylor and Taylor 1983), which Crawford and Chaffin call 'schemata' (1988: 5). From this perspective, schemata lie within the reader and are imposed on the text. However, if schemata are seen as internal to the reader, the problem of what readers of each gender (and other demographics) get out of text arises.

Rosenblatt (1978) was one of the first to recast the controversy in feminist terms by formulating a dichotomy that differentiated reading styles according to the gender of the reader. She labelled the two opposing modes of reading *aesthetic* (feminine) versus *efferent* (masculine), claiming that they grow out of different approaches to text: cognitive versus affective activity. Aesthetic reading is characteristic of female readers, for it is an affect-based style in which a reader experiences the text fully by living through the described events. This entails an emotional willingness to participate vicariously in the characters' lives and to eschew insistence on a goal-oriented ending. Efferent reading, on the other hand, is characteristic of male readers, for it is a cognitive style in which a reader engages in the process in order to take away something useful from the reading. Here, an ending is required to reassure readers that they have reached a goal worthy of their expenditure of time and effort on the text.

These opposing strategies were said to flow from differences in the way men and women conceive of themselves and their relations with others (Chodorow 1978; Gilligan 1982) based on different values. For example, men value autonomy and define themselves through individuation and separation from others, whereas women value relationships and define themselves in terms of affiliation and contact with others. The concept of different male/female values was extended to models of reading (Crowder 1982; Downing and Leong 1982), for the male preoccupation with control over text (the drive to get it right) calls for a cognitive style directed towards an informational goal, whereas the female desire for intimacy between the reader and the text (the drive to connect with others) calls for an affective style directed towards an experiential goal (Rosenblatt 1978). Male and female readers are said to differ on the basis of the experiential versus utilitarian approach to text – that is, whether they read to enjoy the trip or to get to the destination.

These values are discussed in the consumer research literature (Hirschman 1991) under the rubric 'agentic' (male) versus 'communal' (female), following Bakan's (1967) formulation. Agentic values predominate when interaction with others is viewed as a conflict in which one must fight for individual rights, whereas communal values predominate when interaction with others is viewed as a mediation of conflict in which one aims at maintaining relationships. These sex-based differences in values have been found to affect not only the language of marketing research but also its goals and methods, as evidenced by the metaphors (man-as-machine), themes (war, conflict) and methodologies (quantitative, rational) that dominate the literature (Hirschman 1991). The feminist delineation of different reading styles based on gender rounds out the picture of different agentic/communal research modes by adding the domain of advertising text – *what* is being studied – to that of the research process – *how* it is being studied. As such, differentiating between efferent versus aesthetic reading styles contributes to consumer behaviour research by revealing a new way to think about readers as consumers of advertising text. To sum up, aesthetic style refers to reading for the experience, whereas efferent style refers to reading for information. When gender is factored in, aesthetic reading style is characteristic of female readers, and efferent reading style is characteristic of male readers.

DETACHMENT VERSUS PARTICIPATION: READER ENGAGEMENT WITH TEXT

Male and female reader responses are said to differ based not only on reading style but also on interactions between the text and the reader that determine the mode of reader engagement with text. Bleich (1988) and Flynn (1988) conducted empirical studies of student responses to short narratives in which they found significant gender-related differences in willingness to engage with the stories. Bleich labelled the male response 'detachment' to express the idea that men read (evaluate, retell) a story from an outside perspective. Flynn labelled the female response 'participation' to express the opposing idea – that women read (experience, feel, empathise with) a story from an inside perspective.

Bleich used short stories in his study of the response patterns of men and women, and he found significant differences in 'response statements' based on the reader's gender, rather than the author's. Differences occurred in four areas: authorial intent, information seeking, inferencing, and evaluation (Clark 1977). Men tended to read for authorial intent, were more intent on acquiring information from a story, were less likely to draw inferences and more likely to make evaluative judgements. In contrast, women did not search for authorial intent, were more intent on experiencing a story's personal relationships than on getting its 'point', were more likely to draw inferences, and were less likely to evaluate than to experience a story. These differences relate to areas of interest to consumer researchers, such as inferencing, attitudes to advertisements, experiential consumption, empathy, comprehension and processing strategies (Meyers-Levy and Maheswaren 1991), which will now be discussed more fully.

Authorial voice

The most salient difference in the way men and women read prose fiction appears to be the way in which each sex perceives the authorial 'voice', the imputed teller of a tale (Booth 1961). Men perceive the presence of a strong authorial voice, and read a novel or story for what it tells them about the intent of the teller. They construe a story's meaning and logic in terms of consequences that result from the teller's actions, presumed to be purposeful. The male reader's orientation begins with the author, for he first seeks to ascertain whether or not an author is in accord with his own values. Men appear to be 'distant' from a text, intent on discovering the author's hand behind it and demanding linear structure and coherence. Male readers thus detach from the story by remaining outside its action to see what the author intended and to determine if that meshes with their own view of life.

In contrast, women construe a story as a world unto itself in which authorial intent is less important than the story's existence in its own right. That is, the story takes precedence over the storyteller. The female reader's orientation centres on her personal growth, and her response to fiction is based on a sense of participation in the story's relationships. Women are thus more likely than men to enter into the world of the novel; they 'lose themselves' in books, and experience this fictional world as a given, something 'there' for an experiential purpose. Thus, the female reader's response to fiction is based on a sense of participation in the story and on affective responses to its human relationships. Women, unlike men, enter into a story rather than remain on the outside. If this difference can be applied to advertising, women may be the more vulnerable market. The tendency to value the story over the storyteller and to enter into the story world suggests that women may be less focused on why advertisers are telling them this than on what it is that they are being told.

Information, relationships and inference

Detachment and participation are evidenced not only in terms of attitudes to an author (extrinsic to text) but also in attitudes to the plot and characters (intrinsic to text). These responses are elicited by the simple expedient of asking readers to 'retell the story in your own words'. In so far as men define fiction teleologically by imputing a 'reason why' to the author's presentation of characters and events, when men retell a story, they do so as if its purpose were to deliver a clear chain of information. Their primary concern is the informational one of getting the facts 'straight'. One consequence of men's concern with matters of fact is that they also tend to be more literal in interpretations of text. They are more cautious about retelling with accuracy and tend to retell only what can be documented literally. To this end, men avoid inferencing or 'putting' things into a story. This suggests that men may read advertisements with more suspicion about persuasive intentions because they are accustomed to searching for authorial purposes.

On the other hand, when women retell a story they do so as if it were an experience and draw inferences without strict regard for the text's literality, but with regard for their affective sense of human relationships. Inferencing is more regularly considered part of women's readings, for women make inferences about stories and consider it legitimate to do so. These inferences are seen as integral to the story, not as excrescences added by the reader. Thus, women participate more fully than men in stories by adding their own interpretations to fill in textual gaps and to arrive at meaning. The habit of interpolation may indicate a wider latitude of acceptance among women, who are perhaps more likely than men to ascribe credibility to spokespersons and product appeals.

Evaluation and comprehension

Detachment and a focus on authorial intent accord with the male tendency to judge characters, for they read a story as something 'other' (told by another) that is being presented to them. Male readers tend to define their role as one of approval/disapproval of the author's presentation, and they are likely to evaluate what they read. As a result, men are more distant from their readings, as the abstractions in their retellings indicate. Men seem more frustrated by a failure to understand what they are reading than are women (see Flynn 1988), perhaps because the need for literal comprehension accompanies the distancing impulse. If men tend to hover on the outside of stories, detached from the life within, they are more likely to want to dissect the fiction as an object to be understood rather than, as women do, go with the flow and enter into relationships even when these are not fully comprehended.

In contrast, both Flynn (1988) and Bleich (1988) found women less likely to insist on comprehending a story and also less likely to pass evaluative judgement when they fail to understand it fully. Women respond affectively to human relationships presented in the story and are more inclined to enter into the experience of these relationships than to remain detached and take a judgmental stance. This is signalled by women's readiness to retell a story less in terms of an abstract summary of what it was about than in a concrete discussion of the way it was experienced, and they interpolate judgements as one part of the retelling, not its main purpose. In so far as women participate in a story's human situations more readily, their retellings deal more with interpersonal motives and less with the author's intent or their critique of that intent. Women seem to have a less urgent need to comprehend a story and are less likely to condemn author or story if they fail to understand it fully.

In sum, reader engagement with the text is likely to differ based on the reader's gender as a determinant of participation in or detachment from what is being read. Male detachment from text as opposed to female participation (Flynn 1988) suggests that patterns of response exist along gender lines that may be important in advertising. One such area is attitude to the advertisement (AAd), a construct that can be enriched by adding gender as a variable contributing to attitudes toward the ad, the sponsor and advertising in general. In this regard, women's acceptance of the authorial presence as a given in contrast to men's determination to seek out the author's purpose has implications for advertising credibility. It suggests that women are more disposed to accept text as authoritative because it exists, whereas men are more disposed to question the motives of the author(ity) responsible for the text.

MODELS OF READING: DOMINANCE, SUBMISSION, INTERACTION, RESISTANCE

Feminist reader-response critics view the reading process as one in which the gender inscribed in the text interacts with that of the reader to determine control (or lack thereof) over the text. Some feminists conceptualise reading in de Beauvoir's terms ([1949] 1952) as a confrontation between the 'self' (reader) and the 'other' (text), and aim at a description of the process in conflict/resolution terms (Flynn 1988). Four models of reader response have been proposed: dominance, in which the reader dominates the text; submission, in which the text dominates the reader; interaction, in which both interact in a dialogue; and resistance, in which a reader resists reading a text as it was meant to be read (Schweickart 1988), instead reading it against itself to take a stand against male dominance. This feminist process involves 'taking control of one's reactions and inclinations' and is a re-reading that comprises 'a kind of therapeutic analysis' (Schweickart 1988: 50). These models are based on the way that readers, divided by sex, respond to gendered text.

The first model, dominance, occurs when a reader dominates the text by refusing to enter it and, hence, remains unchanged as a result of the encounter. It is characteristic of the detached reader, who observes a story from a distance. This reader imposes a predetermined structure on the text, with the reader's memory and expectations taking precedence over anything to be found in the words themselves. Dominant readers may be bored by a text because they approach it with hostility and distaste for experiential engagement. They may be unwilling to accept the possibility of learning something new, for they unpack judgements based on previously established norms rather than leaving themselves open to empathetic involvement with new material. There is minimal communication here, for the reader is 'reading' the contents of his/her own mind rather than the story.

The second model, submission, occurs when a reader submits to the text and allows it to become so powerful that the text overwhelms the reader and effaces the personal self. In contrast to dominant readers, submissive ones are overly involved, so enmeshed in the events of the story that they are unable or unwilling to step back and make evaluative judgements. Submissive readers tend to be anxious rather than bored when faced with new material, for they are too overwhelmed by a text to assign a meaning to it. Here, too, there is minimal communication, for the reader is attempting to read the story without the benefit of input from his/her own mind.

The third model, interaction, occurs when a reader interacts with the text and balances empathetic involvement with critical detachment, thereby learning something from the encounter. Here, the reader engages in active participation in the construction of meaning (Flynn 1988). The reader communicates with the text in an iterative process of self-correction, with the reader's perspective shifting in response to textual cues. The flux of readjustments permits the reader to discover a pattern of meaning by the end of the story (Iser 1972). Readers succeed in comprehending the pattern when they resolve the tensions and understand textual cues not as unrelated elements but, rather, as parts of a meaningful whole. In contrast to detachment and reader domination of the text or engagement and reader domination by the text, interaction balances detachment and engagement to attain comprehension. This model enables the reader to integrate the self and the text by invoking personal feelings and values during the course of reading and merging them with the new experience that the story presents. The model is one that advertisers aim for when they commission texts designed to evoke empathy by drawing the reader into the ad.

The fourth model, resistance (Fetterley 1978), describes a situation in which interaction in the conventional sense is not possible for a female reader. Feminist theories of reading depart from mainstream reader-response theory by focusing on the experience of the woman reader in reading male texts. Fetterley terms this experience 'immasculation,' an interpretive process whereby the woman reader is forced to identify, against herself, with the male experience because we have all learned to read as men. She describes a revisionist reading process that offers women readers a more authentic view of their own experience when they become 'resisting readers'. The resisting reader reads a text as it was not meant to be read (Schweickart 1988) and, thus, reads it against itself to take a stand against male dominance. This feminist process involves 'taking control of one's reactions and inclinations' and is a rereading that comprises 'a kind of therapeutic analysis' (Schweickart 1988: 50). What occurs is that although the reader reads male texts (impossible to avoid) and absorbs androcentric reading strategies (also impossible to avoid), as she becomes a resisting reader, she develops awareness of the androcentricity that dominates interpretative strategies and reads both as a man (we are all trained this way) and as a woman (resisting the male subjectivity implicit in the text).

Models of reading and sex of reader

Feminist critics have found these models associated with characteristic responses by male and female readers. To begin, dominance is typical of men's responses to both androcentric and gynocentric texts (Flynn 1988). This corresponds to the detachment Bleich (1988) saw in his male subjects, as well as to Holland's antipathy to gothic romances (Holland and Sherman 1988). Dominant readers refuse to engage with a text and feel little empathy for the characters. They tend to judge characters harshly rather than make an effort to understand them. When readers are dominant, they superimpose their own values on the text, thus interfering with their ability to make sense of it. The concomitant tendency is dismissiveness, in which a story is condemned as meaningless or nonsense by a dominant reader who refuses to expend whatever effort might be necessary to resolve the tensions and comprehend a meaningful pattern.

Whereas male readers have occasionally been found submissive to androcentric text (see Flynn 1988), they virtually never submit to gynocentric text. Men tend to be unwilling to treat women's literature as worth serious concern, and they are likely to react antagonistically rather than empathetically to stories about vulnerable women characters or abusive male protagonists. When they pay attention to women's literature at all, they tend to judge it derogatorily.

On the other hand, submissiveness is the model characteristic of women readers, who readily submit to immasculation by androcentric texts (Fetterley 1978). Furthermore, women try to understand male texts before passing judgement. Even though women are more likely than men to resolve tensions in a story and to comprehend its pattern (Flynn 1988), the danger in submission is that they become so entangled in the text that they doubt their own attributions of meaning. Thus, although comprehension may be attained, women are so accustomed to read submissively that they do not have faith in their own readings of androcentric texts.

In contrast, when women approach gynocentric text, they adopt an interactive reading strategy, balancing detachment and involvement. The interactive reader is one who encounters not simply a text, but 'the heart and mind' of another woman. The hedging characteristic of women's speech (Lakoff 1975) is transformed into the useful interpretive strategy of interlarding critical assessment of a text with receptivity to a plurality of meanings. Feminists suggest that this model of interactive reading affirms the connection among all women and forms an alternative valid paradigm of human existence – the female one – different from the one assumed by earlier theorists.

When these ideas are translated to fit advertising, the same four models are likely to describe consumer engagement with advertising text and the models are likely to vary by gender of reader/gender of text. That is, male readers are likely to dominate androcentric and gynocentric advertising text (refuse to engage), whereas female readers are likely to submit to androcentric advertising text (be overwhelmed by it), but to interact with gynocentric advertising text. However, female readers, especially those with some exposure to feminist thought, are likely to resist androcentric advertising text (read against meaning). The concepts from feminist reader-response criticism that deal with alternative reading styles, gendered text and gendered responses to text underlie a research agenda in which a prescriptive outline of research topics is developed to further the aim of feminists who seek not merely to understand the world, but to change it.

CONCLUSION: FEMINISM AND HUMANISM

The praxis of feminist criticism as a change agent openly avows its political agenda (Schweickart 1988), in which consciousness raising (Holly 1975) is the first step. The discovery of heretofore unrecognised but fundamental beliefs about the nature, character and destiny of women forces men and women alike to confront what was formerly hidden on a conscious level. When feminist critics move into 'the prophetic mode' (Donovan 1975) by way of prescriptive criticism, they often call for a new order of literary reality, in recognition of the fact that neither men nor women have been treated realistically in the standard sexual myths and stereotypes that dominate Western culture.

These stereotypes also dominate advertising, for here feminists view the sexist ideology as particularly ubiquitous, accessible and dangerously influential. Because advertising is a dominant feature of the mass media, its influence on daily life through the creation of role models and the depiction of social interaction probably affects real-life power relationships (Holly 1975) even more pervasively than does literature. Feminist practical criticism suggests changes in advertising necessary to transform it from an oppressive patriarchal institution to one that serves the cause of men's and women's liberation (Register 1975). Non-sexist advertising, an ideal not yet achieved, would do the following:

1. *Present authentic female experience*
   Non-sexist advertising can only express the female experience authentically in all of its varieties by excluding denigrative sex-role stereotypes ('sex kitten,' 'brainless housewife') and instead presenting realistic, multifaceted women characters. Feminist critiques encourage the development of advertising that is true to the fullness of women's experience by depicting what it feels like to be a woman. If advertising were to emphasise such honest self-expression rather than focusing on women reflected through male eyes (the 'gaze'), it might serve as a forum for women's voices.
2. *Show positive female role models*
   Authenticity in advertising would also entail a focus on positive female role models, not only for adults but also for children. The wasteland of advertising to children hammers home both incessant messages to consume and caricatures of women. Only when young children become socialised by seeing women who are 'self-actualising, and whose identities are not dependent on men' (Register 1975: 67) can they be expected to develop a positive sense of feminine identity and high self-esteem.
3. *Reflect co-operation among women*
   The depiction of women's communality is necessary to overcome the animosity of women for each other as a result of isolation, competition for male attention and belief in female inferiority. If women are repeatedly shown as rivals for male attention, their sense of self-worth is eroded and their self-actualising goals are implicitly derogated.

4 *Represent a new humanity*
Emphasis on high esteem as the hallmark of feminine identity would permit advertising to be a force for humanising culture rather than for perpetuating sexism. It has the potential for furthering the feminist agenda that calls for nothing less than the creation of a new social order founded on humanistic values, some of which are traditionally female and not respected in contemporary society. This new order is posited as de-emphasising traditional male values such as competition and aggression in either sex, based on the realisation that macho women may be as bad for society as macho men. The advertising goal is to depict the humanisation of both sexes, so that values such as nurturance, kindness and co-operation can be given a chance to change the world for the better.

REFERENCES

Allen, C. J. (1987) 'Feminist criticism and postmodernism', in J. Natoli (ed.) *Tracing Literary Theory*, Urbana: University of Illinois Press, 278–305.

Bakan, D. (1967) *The Duality of Human Existence*, Chicago: Rand McNally.

Baym, N. (1981) 'Melodramas of beset manhood: how theories of American fiction exclude women authors', *American Quarterly* 33, Summer:123–39.

Bleich, D. (1978) *Subjective Criticism*, Baltimore, MD: Johns Hopkins University Press.

—— (1988) 'Gender interests in reading and language', in E. A. Flynn and P. P. Schweickart (eds) *Gender and Reading: Essays on Readers, Texts, and Contexts*, Baltimore, MD: Johns Hopkins University Press, 234–66.

Bloom, H. (1976) *A Map of Misreading*, New York: Oxford University Press.

Booth, W. (1961) *The Rhetoric of Fiction*, Chicago: University of Chicago Press.

Bordo, S. (1999) *The Male Body*, New York: Farrar, Straus, & Giraux.

Brown, S., Stevens, L. and Maclaran, P. (1999) 'I can't believe it's not Bakhtin! Literary theory, postmodern advertising, and the gender agenda', *Journal of Advertising* 28, 1: 11–25.

Bullough, V. (1974) *The Subordinate Sex: A History of Attitudes Toward Women*, Baltimore, MD: Penguin.

Cawelti, J. G. (1976) *Adventure, Mystery, and Romance: Formula Stories as Art and Popular Culture*, Chicago: University of Chicago Press.

Chodorow, N. (1978) *The Reproduction of Mothering: Psychoanalysis and the Sociology of Gender*, Berkeley: University of California Press.

Clark, H. H. (1977) 'Inferences in comprehension', in D. Laberge and S. J. Samuels (eds) *Basic Processes in Reading: Perception and Comprehension*, Hillsdale, NJ: Lawrence Erlbaum Associates, 243–63.

Crawford, M. and Chaffin, R. (1988) 'The reader's construction of meaning: cognitive research on gender and comprehension', in E. A. Flynn and P. P. Schweickart (eds) *Gender and Reading: Essays on Readers, Texts, and Contexts*, Baltimore, MD: Johns Hopkins University Press, 3–30.

Crowder, R. G. (1982) *The Psychology of Reading: An Introduction*, New York: Oxford University Press.

Culler, J. (1982) *On Deconstruction: Theory and Criticism after Structuralism*, Ithaca, NY: Cornell University Press.

de Beauvoir, S. ([1949] 1952) *The Second Sex*, trans. H. M. Parshley, New York: Alfred A. Knopf, Inc.

Donovan, J. (1975) 'Afterword', in J. Donovan (ed.) *Feminist Literary Criticism: Explorations in Theory*, Lexington: University Press of Kentucky, 74–82.

Downing, J. and Leong, C. K. (1982) *Psychology of Reading*, New York: Macmillan.

Fetterley, J. (1978) *The Resisting Reader: A Feminist Approach to American Fiction*, Bloomington: Indiana University Press.

Firestone, S. (1971) *The Dialectic of Sex: The Case for Feminist Revolution*, revised edn, New York: Bantam Books.

Fish, S. E. (1980) *Is there a Text in this Class? The Authority of Interpretive Communication*, Cambridge, MA: Harvard University Press.

Flynn, E. A. (1988) 'Gender and reading', in E. A. Flynn and P. P. Schweickart (eds) *Gender and Reading: Essays on Readers, Texts, and Contexts*, Baltimore, MD: Johns Hopkins University Press, 267–88.

Friedan, B. (1963) *The Feminine Mystique*, New York: Norton.

Gilligan, C. (1982) *In a Different Voice: Psychological Theory and Women's Development*, Cambridge, MA: Harvard University Press.

Goffman, E. (1976) *Gender Advertisements*, Cambridge, MA: Harvard University Press.

Heilbrun, C. and Stimpson, C. (1975) 'Theories of feminist criticism: a dialogue', in J. Donovan (ed.) *Feminist Literary Criticism: Explorations in Theory*, Lexington: University Press of Kentucky, 61–73.

Hirschman, E. C. (1991) 'A feminist critique of marketing theory: toward agentic-communal balance', in J. A. Costa (ed.) *Gender and Consumer Behavior Conference Proceedings*, Salt Lake City: University of Utah Printing Service, 324–40.

Holbrook, M. B. and Stern, B. B. (1997) 'The Paco Man and what is remembered: new readings of a hybrid language', in K. T. Frith (ed.) *Undressing the Ad: Reading Culture in Advertising*, New York: Peter Lang, 66–84.

Holland, N. (1975) *Five Readers Reading*, New Haven, CT: Yale University Press.

Holland, N. and Sherman, L. F. (1988) 'Gothic possibilities', in E. A. Flynn and P. P. Schweickart (eds) *Gender and Reading: Essays on Readers, Texts, and Contexts*, Baltimore, MD: Johns Hopkins University Press, 215–33.

Holly, M. (1975) 'Consciousness and authenticity: toward a feminist aesthetic', in J. Donovan (ed.) *Feminist Literary Criticism: Explorations in Theory*, Lexington: University Press of Kentucky, 38–47.

Iser, W. (1972) 'The reading process: a phenomenological approach', *New Literary History* 3, Winter: 279–99.

Iyer, E. and Debevec, K. (1986) 'Gender stereotyping of products: are products like people?', in N. K. Malhotra and J. M. Hawes (eds) *Developments in Marketing Science* IX, Atlanta, GA: Academy of Marketing Science, 40–5.

Jacoby, J. and Hoyer, W. D. (1987) *The Comprehension and Miscomprehension of Print Communications*, Hillsdale, NJ: Lawrence Erlbaum Associates.

Kates, S. M. (1999) 'Making the ad perfectly queer: marketing "normality" to the gay men's community?', *Journal of Advertising* 28: 35–7.

Kolodny, A. (1980) 'A map for rereading: or, gender and the interpretation of literary texts', *New Literary History* 11, Spring: 451–67.

Lakoff, R. (1975) *Language and Woman's Place*, New York: Harper & Row.

Lavin, M. (1995) 'Creating consumers in the 1930s: Irna Phillips and the radio soap opera', *Journal of Consumer Research* 22, June: 75–89.

MacKinnon, C. A. (1983) 'Feminism, Marxism, method, and the state: toward feminist jurisprudence', *Signs* 8, Summer: 635–58.

Meyers-Levy, J. and Maheswaran, D. (1991) 'Exploring differences in males' and females' processing strategies', *Journal of Consumer Research* 18, June: 63–70.

Mick, D. G. and Buhl, C. (1992) 'A meaning-based model of advertising experiences', *Journal of Consumer Research* 19, December: 63–70.

Millett, K. (1971) *Sexual Politics*, Garden City, NY: Doubleday.

Modleski, T. (1982) *Loving with a Vengeance: Mass-Produced Fantasies for Women*, Hamden, CT: Archon.

Radford, J. (1986) 'Introduction', in J. Radford (ed.) *The Progress of Romance: The Politics of Popular Fiction*, London: Routledge & Kegan Paul, 1–22.

Radway, J. (1984) *Reading the Romance: Women, Patriarchy, and Popular Literature*, Chapel Hill: University of North Carolina Press.

Register, C. (1975) 'American feminist literary criticism: a bibliographical introduction', in J. Donovan (ed.) *Feminist Literary Criticism: Exploration in Theory*, Lexington: University Press of Kentucky, 1–28.

Rosenblatt, L. (1978) *The Reader, The Text, The Poem: The Transactional Theory of the Literary Work*, Carbondale: Southern Illinois University Press.

Russ, J. (1972) 'What can a heroine do? Or why women can't write', in S. K. Cornillon (ed.) *Images of Women in Fiction: Feminist Perspectives*, Bowling Green, OH: Bowling Green University Popular Press, 3–20.

Ruthven, K. K. (1990) *Feminist Literary Studies: An Introduction*, Cambridge: Cambridge University Press.

Schweickart, P. P. (1988) 'Reading ourselves: toward a feminist theory of reading', in E. A. Flynn and P. P. Schweickart (eds) *Gender and Reading: Essays on Readers, Texts, and Contexts*, Baltimore, MD: Johns Hopkins University Press, 31–62.

Schweickart, P. and Flynn, E. A. (1988) 'Introduction', in E. A. Flynn and P. P. Schweickart (eds) *Gender and Reading: Essays on Readers, Texts, and Contexts*, Baltimore, MD: Johns Hopkins University Press, ix–xxx.

Showalter, E. (1977) *A Literature of Their Own: British Women Novelists from Bronte to Lessing*, Princeton, NJ: Princeton University Press.

Segel, E. (1988) 'As the twig is bent . . . gender and childhood reading', in E. A. Flynn and P. P. Schweickart (eds) *Gender and Reading: Essays on Readers, Texts, and Contexts*, Baltimore, MD: Johns Hopkins University Press, 165–86.

Stern, B. B. (1989) 'Literary criticism and consumer research: overview and illustrative analysis', *Journal of Consumer Research* 16, December: 322–34.

—— (1991a) 'Literary analysis of an advertisement: the commercial as soap opera', in R. H. Holman and M. Solomon (eds) *Advances in Consumer Research* 18, Provo, UT: Association for Consumer Research, 164–71.

—— (1991b) 'Two pornographies: a feminist view of sex in advertising', in R. H. Holman and M. Solomon (eds) *Advances in Consumer Research* 18, Provo, UT: Association for Consumer Research, 384–91.

—— (1992) 'Feminist literary theory and advertising research: a new reading of the text and the consumer', *Journal of Current Issues and Research in Advertising* 14, Spring: 9–22.

—— (1993) 'Feminist literary criticism and the deconstruction of advertisements: a postmodern view of advertising and consumer responses', *Journal of Consumer Research* 19, March: 556–66.

—— (1994) 'Advertising to the other culture: women's use of language and language's use of women', in B. G. Englis and D. F. Baker (eds) *Global and Multinational Advertising*, Hillsdale, NJ: Lawrence Erlbaum Associates, 67–81.

—— (1996) 'Deconstructive strategy and consumer research: concepts and illustrative exemplar', *Journal of Consumer Research* 23, September: 136–47.

Stern, B. B. and Holbrook, M. (1994) 'Gender and genre in the interpretation of advertising text', in J. A. Costa (ed.) *Gender and Consumer Behavior*, Beverly Hills, CA: Sage, 11–47.

Taylor, I. and Taylor, M. M. (1983) *The Psychology of Reading*, New York: Academic Press.

Welter, B. (1966) 'The cult of true womanhood: 1820–1860', *American Quarterly* 18, Summer: 151–74.

5 Women and advertising: reading the relationship

Stephanie O'Donohoe

INTRODUCTION

Barbara Stern's chapter in this volume addresses recent shifts in literary studies away from notions of stable texts evoking singular 'correct' interpretations by passive readers. Reviewing various perspectives on text–reader relationships, Stern considers how women and men respond to androcentric and gynocentric texts and describes different styles and models of reading. This chapter seeks to develop her argument that literary theories and research have implications for the gendered consumption of advertising. It begins by revisiting questions of text–reader relationships and the reading experience, relating these to advertising consumption. The difficulties of classifying ads as androcentric or gynocentric are examined, and this chapter then considers how advertisements position women as readers, and how women respond; some textual strategies which encourage the adoption of particular vantage-points for women as readers of ads are considered, along with research on gendered attitudes and readings with respect to advertising.

As Buikema (1995: 9) points out, 'Black, white, lesbian, heterosexual, older and younger, more and less educated women are not in every respect concerned with the same struggle'. Much feminist writing unintentionally replicates patriarchy's 'unequal relationships of central and peripheral, inclusion and exclusion' (Eagleton 1996: 14) by failing to take into account different perspectives and experiences *between* women (Kemp and Squires 1997; McDermott 1998). This chapter discusses how 'women' are positioned by texts and how we read texts, but the literature it draws upon does not fully represent the diversity of women's identities, alignments and experiences. Thus, it cannot presume to speak for all women, or about all women's encounters with advertising texts. Instead, it is hoped that readers who identify gaps in this text will respond by creating other texts, thereby expanding our understanding of relationships between women and advertising.

TEXTS, READERS AND THE READING EXPERIENCE

A text, according to Barthes (1971: 163) is 'a space where language circulates'; it invites readers to engage in a 'practical collaboration . . . producing text, opening it out, *setting it going*'. The complex relationship between texts, readers and contexts continues to fascinate literary, media and cultural critics (Tompkins 1980; Moores 1994; Jensen and Pauly 1997). Discussing the balance of power between text and reader, Stern (1993: 557) advocates a moderate position, with meaning 'anchored by the text at one endpoint and by the reader at the other'. Others emphasise the struggle for control over meaning. Culler (1983) rejects any 'compromise formulation' involving shared control, while Pearce (1997) sees the relationship as dialogic but power-inscribed and 'always already gendered'.

If text–reader relations are power-inscribed, this raises questions concerning the sources of textual power. Writing about television, Hall (1973) suggests that the structure of communication elements delimits their meanings, and that all societies or cultures try to impose certain views about the social, cultural and political world on their members. Thus, messages are encoded to suggest 'preferred readings', reinforcing the institutional, political or ideological order. Althusser (1971) argued that we internalise ideological messages because they constantly 'hail' or 'interpellate' us, hollowing out an interpretive space for us to occupy and inviting us to recognise ourselves as the imaginary self constructed by the text (Morris 1993). In the 1970s, Althusser's ideas were applied to film by various theorists writing in *Screen*, the British film studies journal. *Screen* theory held that a media text 'interpellates' its audience by containing a single ideological vantage-point from which it makes sense. By adopting that position, audiences are 'sutured' or stitched into the text; drawn towards making particular inferences, they become bound up with or implicated in the text's structures of meaning (Christie 1994; Moores 1994).

Althusser's argument has been a useful starting-point for feminist literary and cultural critics examining how textual features such as narrative point of view, plot structure, camera position and editing encourage women to align themselves with male interests and perspectives (Mulvey 1975; Fetterley 1978; Morris 1993). Texts differ in the extent to which they constrain interpretive freedom, however. Barthes (1975) characterised *readerly* texts as relatively conventional and closed, inviting essentially passive, receptive and disciplined readers to accept their meanings as already made. He compared these to *writerly* texts, which tend to transgress rather than adhere to conventions; they highlight their own artifice, and constantly challenge readers to rewrite or co-create them in the process of making sense of them. In any case, regardless of the extent to which messages encode preferred meanings, they remain polysemic: readers do not always take the preferred meaning (Hall 1973).

Turning to the interpretive strategies available to audiences, De Certeau (1984) uses the term *decipherment* for reading someone else's language according to their rules, and *reading* for occasions where we bring our own oral vernacular culture to bear on the written text (Fiske 1989). Hall proposes three 'ideal-type' positions from which audiences may decode television messages. *Dominant* readings occur when viewers accept the preferred meaning 'full and straight'. *Oppositional* readings translate messages from the dominant code to an alternative, critical frame of reference, while *negotiated* readings combine adaptive and oppositional elements.

There are some overlaps and differences between the categories used by Hall and the models of reading described by Stern in this volume; Hall's *dominant* readings seem similar to Stern's *submissive* model, and there are also parallels between his *oppositional* category and her model of *resisting* reading.

Much media reception research has demonstrated how texts are interpreted quite differently by different audiences and audience members. Certainly, the position of audience members in the social structure may set parameters to their experiences and influence the cultural codes available to them. These factors can never determine their readings, however; as they also depend on how audience members feel about their position. Furthermore, we do not occupy a single vantage point with respect to texts: audiences are composed of various overlapping subgroups, in terms of class, age, gender and ethnic origin, for example (Morley 1980, 1986). A post-structuralist perspective develops the idea of readers' shifting identities, since it views the self as a constantly negotiated, ever-changing repertoire of subject positions (Fuss 1989).

Much media studies research has addressed the practices of 'active' audiences, often engaged in oppositional or negotiated reading (Morley 1980, 1986; Hobson 1982; Lull 1990; Fiske 1993; Livingstone 1998). Some critics have highlighted the dangers of romanticising the 'active audience' and conflating textual resistance with real political power (Seaman 1992). None the less, various studies have demonstrated the varied, often quite subtle and empowering pleasures which women, as individuals or as members of interpretive communities, derive from texts, even those which seem to work against their interest (Radway 1984; Ang 1985; Steiner 1988; Gledhill 1992).

Christie (1994) notes that research in this tradition tends to focus on how *resistance* rather than *interpretation* occurs. Arguing that greater attention to interpretation is crucial, Christie champions Sperber and Wilson's (1986) linguistic theory of relevance. This treats a text's features as just one piece of evidence available to readers; others include knowledge or assumptions regarding the author's intentions. In making an interpretation, readers make inferences from a selection of the available evidence, based on the perceived 'relevance' of the evidence to the task at hand.

Although viewing text–reader relationships as a struggle for control over meaning may be useful, the cognitive emphasis in much of this work offers a deceptively limited view of the reading experience. As Culler observes, the experiences reader-oriented critics describe are not those of:

> . . . feeling shivers along the spine, weeping in sympathy, or being transported with awe, but having one's expectations proved false, struggling with an irresolvable ambiguity, or questioning the assumptions on which one had relied.
>
> (Culler 1983: 39)

A model of reading which ventures 'beyond interpretation' is presented by Pearce (1997). Characterising the reader as a lover rather than a semiotic sleuth, she seeks to reclaim the full emotional range of reader–text relationships. Drawing on *A Lover's Discourse* (Barthes 1978), Pearce describes in detail the *ravissement* of 'falling in love' with particular texts (including novels, a photography exhibition and a film), and the devotion and fulfilment associated with this phase of a relationship. As with a romance, the relationship depends on first identifying a 'textual other' to whom we are attracted. This may be a character in the text, a textual positioning, an author-function or even an empty scene inviting our own fantasy projections. Pearce also describes the sequel to *ravissement*, including states of anxiety, frustration, jealousy and disappointment. She also cautions that the pleasures of textual engagement may conflict with desires to read as a feminist:

> . . . our enchantment by a textual other . . . may blind us to the contexts (gendered, raced, classed, sexualised) in which those relationships operate. It may cause us to forget that every nuance of the power-dynamic in which we are engaged – and which *seems* such an intimate, private and unique thing – will have its end in some material chain of power relations . . .
>
> (Pearce 1997: 255–6)

ADVERTISING TEXTS AND READERS

As the 'literature of consumption' (Scott 1994), advertising can be described as a distinctive discourse or literary genre (Cook 1992; Myers 1994). Many ads do more than extol the virtues of brands; they often take the form of dramas, inviting us as consumers to project ourselves into situations or emotions (Boller and Olson 1991). Increasingly, advertising and consumer researchers are questioning the adequacy of positivistic, psychological (and predominantly cognitive) theories in accounting for the range, depth and richness of consumers' experiences of ads. Many arguments employed against traditional theories resonate with, and borrow concepts from, literary, media and cultural studies (Stern 1993, 1996; Scott 1994; Ritson and Elliott 1995; Brown 1998). Mick and Buhl (1992) argue that consumers negotiate the meaning of ads in light of their particular life themes and life projects. This suggests that when a consumer looks at advertising, he or she may be seeking:

> . . . concepts of what it is to be a man or a woman, concepts of what it is to be middle aged [or] a member of a community and a country . . . he or she is looking for symbolic resources, new ideas and better concrete versions of old ideas with which to advance their project.
>
> (McCracken 1987: 122)

Scott (1994) makes a particularly compelling case for the act of reading ads as a complex and sophisticated exercise in informed inference. She argues that the inscribed reader of advertising is selective, active and sceptical, and capable of drawing on various cues to make inferences. Advertising consumers are necessarily agile readers, changing expectations, interpretive frames and strategies as the textual task suggests. They draw on a wide interpretive repertoire and are capable of highly metaphorical, imaginative thinking. For Scott (1994: 475), 'being the reader' of advertising texts may involve testing imaginative selves, assuming particular social roles, experiencing particular moods or attitudes, or sharing certain problems; crucially, it may also mean 'rejecting the text'. Uses and gratifications theory and the concept of advertising literacy also emphasise the agency and potential subversiveness of advertising consumers (Buttle 1991; O'Donohoe 1994a; Ritson and Elliott 1995; O'Donohoe and Tynan 1998).

Since contemporary advertising debates are bound up with themes of texts, readers and contexts, it should not be surprising that literary, media and cultural studies offer useful lenses for viewing the 'always already gendered' relationship between advertising texts and readers. Before reviewing research in this area, however, this chapter outlines the difficulties of categorising ads as male or female texts.

GYNOCENTRIC AND ANDROCENTRIC ADVERTISING TEXTS

The distinction between *androtexts* (texts written by men) and *gynotexts* (those written by women) was first made by Elaine Showalter (1977). Applying this categorisation to advertising, it seems that American agency J. Walter Thompson was producing gynotexts more than eighty years ago, when Helen Landsdowne Resor organised the agency's female copywriters into a Women's Editorial Department. Run by women, it was responsible for advertising products aimed at women, and by 1918 it accounted for $2,264,759 of the agency's total $3,902,601 copy billings. In her account of the department's history and celebrated campaigns, Scanlon (1995) notes that most of the women hired by Resor were unmarried college graduates who had been active in many feminist and suffragist campaigns. They saw the consumer culture as an extension of their progressive politics, and approached their work with missionary zeal. Ironically, by writing ads, which persuaded other women to consume, Resor's staff obtained a degree of personal and economic autonomy that many of their readers lacked.

Theories of intertextuality challenge the notion of a single author for any text (Worton and Still 1990), and there is increasing recognition that women's texts are 'bi-textual', in dialogue with male and female traditions (Meijer 1995). Contemporary advertising presents practical as well as philosophical authorship problems, however: the identity of those who create ads is not generally known to the public, and many people are involved in the production process. Given the small proportion of women in creative and senior managerial positions within the industry (Baxter 1990; Clifton 1995), it would be difficult to identify many female-authored advertising texts. As Hatfield (1999a) notes, agencies often face accusations that they have overtly macho cultures or encourage laddishness in the creative department. He sees a recent 'execrable' ad for Smirnoff Red as fuelling such concerns:

> I wanted to like this, but it's tosh . . . a man takes a very long time to walk into a tattoo parlour and have '666' removed from his head. We then cut to a nunnery, where a beautiful nun offers 'brother Damien' a cherry from her basket. . . . Devil takes nun's cherry! Grow up! Where are all the women creatives? We desperately need you.
>
> (Hatfield 1999b: 20)

It may be thought that the need for women creatives would be recognised at least in traditionally female product sectors. Even in the case of a product as exclusively female as sanitary protection, a furore was created recently when a client insisted that only all-female creative teams could pitch for a new account. Not only were there accusations of 'discrimination against men', but many agencies faced problems putting together an all-female team (Green 1997). In any case, the collaborative process involved in making an ad means that a female creative team is not enough to produce a gynotext. Dougary (1994: 196) tells the story of a commercial for Vivas body spray produced by Saatchi and Saatchi. According to Rita Clifton, then director of planning at the agency, the team working on the ad was almost totally female: 'It was researched by a woman, the senior account handler was a woman, the planners were women and the creative was a woman'. The idea was to depict a woman lost in her own personal fantasy. However, the commercial's director was male, and the way he shot the ad led to a change in 'the whole tone of the ad, from one of female personal involvement to male observation'.

If the circumstances of advertising production mitigate against exclusively female-authored texts, perhaps we need a broader definition of female texts in advertising. For Pearce (1997: 47), women's writing is 'not writing by women, or about women, but, more especially, writing *for* them'. In this context, Meyers-Levy (1989) and Clifton (1995) suggest how ads can target women more effectively, while Bellizzi and Milner (1991) 'gendered' ads by varying the sex of characters, voiceovers and emphasising different brand benefits. Stern (2000) distinguishes between andro*centric* and gyno*centric* or female-oriented ads that borrow themes and structures from other women's texts, such as romances and soap operas. Stern (1993) analyses an androcentric Marlboro cigarette ad featuring the legendary solitary cowboy, arguing that it reflects male values and a male vantage-point on the world. A 'gynocentric' Dakota cigarette ad features and targets women, but a male vantage-point is still inscribed within it. There is no solitary Dakota woman, but four women and two men. The most prominent woman presents a 'feminised version of frontier values'. She is not depicted as self-sufficient, but leans on the man next to her who has an arm around her neck. This raises the obvious point that an ad *for* women, even if produced in part *by* women, still may not be in our interests. Commenting on ads and features in the *Ladies' Home Journal* between 1916 and 1930, Scanlon argues that:

> Women's inarticulate longings for sensuality, independence, and social worth found a voice in these advertising campaigns, forming, like the magazine's advice and fiction, an undercurrent of revolt in a finely packaged and tremendously successful message of accommodation.
>
> (Scanlon 1995: 227)

In this way, Resor's female copywriters were implicated in the creation of 'a particularly female, and, by most accounts, particularly disempowering twentieth-century consumer culture' (Scanlon 1995: 171). Thus, it seems that if we are to read ads as a feminist, there is no safe haven of 'women's texts' that we can visit to recharge our critical batteries or lower our defences with impunity.

HOW DO ADS POSITION WOMEN AS READERS?

Examining stereotyped gender roles in advertising has been an important part of the feminist agenda. This section considers another way in which gender is inscribed in ads, namely, how women are addressed as readers of advertising texts. An early airing of this issue is found in Berger who suggests that:

> The spectator-buyer is meant to envy herself as she will become if she buys the product . . . the publicity image steals her love of herself as she is, and offers it back to her for the price of the product.
>
> (Berger 1972: 134)

Williamson (1978) offers a more thoroughgoing analysis of how ads position their readers, relating this to questions of gender. Drawing on Marxism, structuralism and psychoanalysis, her classic text offers a detailed analysis of how advertising performs its ideological work. She argues that ads address us as 'active receivers' who relate their content to 'referent systems' beyond the world of advertising. She describes a process of audience *appellation*, an exchange between ourselves as individuals and the imaginary subjects addressed by ads:

> Every ad necessarily assumes a particular spectator: it projects into the space out in front of it an imaginary person composed in terms of the relationship between the elements within the ad. You move into this space as you look at the ad . . .
>
> (Williamson 1978: 50)

Ads constitute their audiences by using themes and images from the world beyond advertising; they assume we will understand allusions to particular lifestyles, concerns and aspirations, be drawn into the world of the brand promoted in the ad, and make connections between ourselves and the product. Although ads are designed to promote goods and services, they deal in social identities and relationships and thus gender is inevitably inscribed in them.

Williamson's analysis covers over 100 ads, many product categories and print media, and a range of issues besides gender relations. Several recent studies focus on how women are positioned as readers of particular ads or kinds of advertising. It has been suggested, for example, that despite their rhetoric of freedom, sanitary protection ads rely on a woman reader steeped in the 'invisible taboo' surrounding menstruation who has internalised a sense of shame and anxiety concerning her monthly cycle (Treneman 1988).

Advertisers' attempts to 'turn the discourse of feminism into hard currency' have been explored by Goldman, Heath and Smith (1991: 336) who argue that the feminism which ads present to women has been 'cooked to distil out a residue'; all that remains is a style or attitude which can be communicated through the consumption of objects. One example of advertisers' attempts to appropriate feminism is the trend towards presenting the female body, and female sexuality, as not simply the object of the male gaze, but as a site of women's own pleasure and empowerment; this rhetoric, for example, surrounds the Wonderbra advertising campaign (Hailstone 1995). Goldman, Heath and Smith (1991: 349) argue that many advertisers have adopted this more reflexive approach to positioning female audiences since it allows them to 'disarm viewer resistance to a male gaze carrying meanings of submissiveness or subordination'. They analysed ads from a 1987 issue of *Mademoiselle* magazine, which they see as targeting women who want to be both objects of desire and subjects in control of their social situation. Many of the ads used signifiers of feminism to modify the appearance and meaning of the male gaze. None the less, more than half the ads offered some visual representation of a male gaze or presumed it as the motivation for consuming the brand (see also Goldman 1992). According to 'commodity feminism' then, the rules of the game for women seem to have changed. However, we are still encouraged to play the card of our appearance, enhancing the one dealt by nature through the constant purchase and use of commodities. More recently, Winship (1999) examines three campaigns addressing women that were commercially successful and culturally significant, at least in terms of the media debate that they provoked. All three campaigns – 'Dress to kill' for Wallis fashions, 'Ask before you borrow it' for Nissan Micra cars and 'Hello boys' for Wonderbra – foreground tensions between different ways of being a woman: 'independent and dependent, strong and weak, active and passive, desiring and desirable, optimistic and pessimistic' (1999: 11). For example, the 'dress to kill' ads feature men placing themselves or others at risk because they are distracted at vital moments by admiring a well-dressed woman oblivious to their gaze. As Winship observes:

> . . . our look, as well as the look of the camera, is the privileged one having access to a knowledge she does not have and which is also the key to the humour of the ad. We laugh at men's predicament. We relish the exercise of power our organising gaze grants us.
>
> (Winship 1999: 15)

She also suggests, however, that:

> . . . the female spectator's pleasure in looking at the Wallis ads is that the woman (in the ad and the spectator herself) dramatically holds attention and power. But there is also reassurance in the male gaze which holds her. His look which confirms feminine identity is still necessary.
>
> (Winship 1999: 18)

Other detailed readings of advertising texts include Wicomb's (1994) analysis of a 1989 ad for family planning in a popular black South African magazine. She notes that race as well as gender is inscribed in the text, since white magazines did not carry ads for family planning. The ad takes the form of a young black woman teacher advocating birth control; she is shown surrounded by pupils, with the male children's body language indicating that they may be dominating the scene. The smiling teacher looks out of the ad and the text purports to offer her views on having children. The ad's headline – *I love children far too much to have one before I'm ready* – is written as if on a blackboard, enhancing its authority. The rest of the text tells us that the teacher looks after and loves all her pupils, and hopes to give her own children the material advantages of being 'planned'. It also makes clear that her husband approves of this. In her analysis, Wicomb shows how the ad's visual and verbal elements reconcile its various contradictions, including love of children and the undesirability of becoming pregnant, tradition and change, family and career, material and emotional needs and freedom and deference. Overall, she argues that:

> the gendered reader constructed by the text . . . is crucially aware of another reading over her shoulder . . . a male to whom the text is not directly addressed but whose role as surrogate reader is crucial to the female's production of meaning.
>
> (Wicomb 1994: 101)

Thornborrow (1994) examines two Filofax ads, one explicitly aimed at women, the other implicitly at men. Her detailed analysis of the ads' stylistic features shows their positioning of readers based on gender stereotypes. Thus, drawing on the conventions of informal chat, the 'female' ad engages the reader with tag questions (often associated with women's speech) and thirteen references to 'you' and 'your'. The world that these textual features draw the reader towards is one of unmitigated domesticity. The woman addressed by the text is concerned only with activities limited to the home and family; the ad's words and phrases are from domains of home furnishing, home entertaining and domestic chores. Furthermore, the implied reader is not the initiator of actions; sentence constructions position Filofax as the agent, helping the reader to serve her family better. The second version of the ad never touches the world of mundane domesticity. It takes the form of excerpts from a personal diary. Thornborrow argues that the inscribed reader is one who identifies with that lifestyle, and that this is undoubtedly male. The narrator is engaged in various high-status actions; the text draws on the language of business, finance and information technology, and there are references to cricket, concerts, dates in restaurants with women, long-distance travel and casual shopping at irregular hours. The text contains puns, alliteration, rhymes and other literary devices, and the reader is positioned as consuming the text for pleasure rather than advice; Filofax's role in facilitating this lifestyle is indicated in a much more subtle way than in the female ad.

Using the tools of literary criticism on ads allows us to identify the ways in which ads position women readers ideologically. The story does not end there, however, as indicated by O'Barr's (1994: 7) criticism of Williamson: 'She tells, but never asks, her readers what the advertisements mean.' In the next section, we turn to women as actual readers rather than inscribed subject positions of advertising texts.

GENDERED READINGS OF ADVERTISING TEXTS

Without subscribing to the view that gender *determines* the way in which a text will be read, this section considers research findings concerning male and female readings of ads. Turning first to attitudes towards advertising in general, Shavitt, Lowery and Haefiner (1998) found little evidence of gender differences in American consumers' overall attitudes to advertising, with women marginally more positive than men (45 per cent of women and 43 per cent of men claimed to like advertising to some extent). However, 57 per cent of women and 45 per cent of men reported that they were 'often' or 'sometimes' offended by ads, and women were also more supportive of government regulation of advertising. In Britain, the Advertising Association (1996) found that among British consumers, 81 per cent of men and 76 per cent of women approved of advertising 'a lot' or 'a little'. Men seemed more enthusiastic, with 34 per cent approving 'a lot' compared to 24 per cent of women. A few years earlier, the Advertising Standards Authority (1990) examined British attitudes to advertising and its portrayal of women. Men seemed less concerned than women about the social influence of advertising: 46 per cent of male respondents agreed that 'advertising cannot have any real effect on the way people view the world' compared with only 25 per cent of women. Female respondents were more critical of female portrayals in ads and of the use of female nudity and sex appeal as attention-getting devices. However, when shown a number of particular ads, including some which had been banned by the ASA for their sexist imagery or language, men and women responded in quite similar ways.

Turning to studies of particular ads, Brown, Stevens and Maclaran (1997) present three readings – one male, two female, all from academics – of a Moet & Chandon ad featuring an illustration of a woman in the style of Alphonse Mucha. Their readings differ from others discussed in this section, since they draw directly on literary, marketing and postmodern theory, and are undoubtedly intended to amuse, provoke and inform an academic audience. None the less, they emphasise the dangers of attributing different reading strategies simply to differences in gender. Stephen's Bakhtinian and positively bacchanalian reading sees the woman in the ad as sensual and inviting. Pauline offers a parody of 'reading as a man', identifying but ridiculing aspects of the text which pander to a lecherous male gaze. Lorna reads the ad as a woman, and finds in the illustration an empowered woman, a subject rather than an object, whose attitude to the implied male spectator is disdainful and remote rather than inviting.

Moving on to more prosaic readings, Mick and Politi (1989) found some gender differences in response to a print ad showing a young woman seated at an easel on a beach, with a young man sitting on the ground and tugging her hem. Male students tended to interpret the scene as erotic, but women saw it as romantic; they also emphasised the female character's artistic talent and control over the situation. Other studies have found similarities between male and female response to ads featuring overt sexuality (Elliott *et al.* 1995), sex role stereotypes (Kolbe and Langefeld 1991; Cosgrove 1991), and male and female endorsers (Carsky and Zuckerman 1991). One interesting application of Stern's (2000) taxonomy of gendered texts and readers is provided by Bellizzi and Milner (1991), who compared male and female responses to differently 'gendered' ads. The 'female-explicit' ad (female spokesperson, copy points and brand name) was considerably more successful with women than the 'male-explicit' or neutral versions. Male respondents were only somewhat less positively disposed to the female ad than to the male version, leading the authors to suggest that such ads could attract women without unduly antagonising men.

Commenting on the tendency for research on gender differences to find weak effects, Carsky and Zuckerman (1991) suggest that this may be due to increasingly blurred gender boundaries, particularly among younger consumers, or to research methods which were not sensitive enough to the nuances of difference. They also suggest that as details from various studies accumulate, new patterns of difference might emerge. Stern (2000) suggests some patterns to look out for; she hypothesises that women will be more likely to identify with an ad's characters and situations, respond emotionally to vicarious stimuli, make inferences and suspend judgement till the end of an ad. We may expect men, on the other hand, to search more for authorial intent, to activate the 'schemer schema' (Wright 1986) more, and to respond with greater cynicism and counter-arguments than women. Research examining these issues is considered below.

Elaboration and inferencing

Krugman (1966–7) was one of the first researchers to note that women elaborated more on ads than men. More recently, Meyers-Levy and Sternthal (1991) conducted experiments on simulated ads for a new television programme. They found that women had a lower threshold for elaborative processing of message cues, and made greater use of those cues in making judgements. A related study (Meyers-Levy and Maheswaran 1991) found that women's processing often involved substantial elaboration of message content, and in some cases greater sensitivity to detail in message claims. Male processing was more likely to be driven by overall message themes or schema. Mick and Politi (1989) found women were more attuned to the body language in the print ad they were shown. Both male and female students made inferences about the ad, however, constructing 'mini stories' around the scene.

In contrast to studies examining specific gender differences in relation to particular ads, O'Donohoe's (1994b) findings are based on a broader study of young adults' everyday experiences of advertising. This study combined individual interviews and small group discussions, using age, gender and occupational status quotas. Rather than focusing on pre-selected ads, informants were asked to describe any ads they remembered for any reason, and subsequent discussion revolved around those accounts. In the group discussions, women tended to embellish their descriptions of ads more than the men, and to describe how their interpretations changed as they watched an ad. This young woman exemplifies Scott's (1994) agile reader:

> 'It's an empty bed and Sean Connery says "So-and-so, aged such-and-such, car crash". But there's nobody in bed . . . you think these people have died for some reason. And then it shows you another bed and it says "dismissed due to a blood transfusion". You're thinking that everyone's died but they've all been released. Cos it's quite a sad one.'
>
> (female worker 21–4 years)

However, male groups also offered many detailed descriptions and interpretations of ads, and in the individual interviews, male informants were no less prone to elaboration than the women. In fact, some of the longest accounts of particular ads came from male informants, and these were rich in detail and inferences. This excerpt is from a particularly long and detailed description of a beer ad:

> 'It starts off, they go to – it looks as if it's a wine bar, but the old-fashioned type bar as well. The barman's behind the bar with the old apron on. It basically immediately puts forward quality. Quality bars are basically better than the disco bars you get now . . .'
>
> (male worker 18–20 years)

It may be that differences in the groups between male and female informants had less to do with elaboration propensities or thresholds and more to do with how they communicated among themselves, especially given the more expressive cultural codes of femininity (Morley 1986).

Empathy and participation

As Pearce (1997) points out, men as well as women have access to more 'intimate' modes of reading. Certainly, many of O'Donohoe's (1994b) male informants expressed empathy with the characters or situations in ads. An ad for Tennent's lager depicting a homesick Scot giving up his career in London to return home certainly 'struck a chord' with many male informants: detailed accounts of the ad were provided, words were put into the character's mouth, and there were often references to friends who had been in that situation. Despite this, women tended to demonstrate greater involvement with ads, and with advertising characters or situations in particular. They were more likely than men to engage with ads emotionally, and they offered the richest and most nuanced readings of advertising characters. For example, in the case of Rutger Hauer, the actor who for several years personified a pint of Guinness:

> 'He's very different. He's very good-looking I think and he's got striking sort of grey hair. His eyes are really sort of piercing. Very fine, quite a sculptured face I see. Also he's old which is even better. Slightly haggard. Been places, you know. . . . He's really, really cool. He just knows where it's at. He's calm . . . you couldn't imagine him getting stressed out and making a fool of himself.'
>
> (unemployed female 21–4 years)

Female informants' engagement with ads also tended to be characterised by a greater sense of playfulness and creativity. They described how they had cut up ads to create collages or posters for their walls, and they talked more than the men did about singing along with ads, particularly when they were watching television with friends. Most examples of 'dreadful' ads being celebrated as a cult akin to the B-movies treasured by film buffs (O'Donohoe 1994a) came from women.

Authorial intent

Elliott *et al.* (1995) noted that men and women drew on different 'interpretive repertoires' in group discussions about sexuality in ads. For women, humour appeared to be the means through which issues of men and sex could be discussed, while men – in the group discussion context at least – tended to resort to intellectualism, focusing on the motivations of advertisers and the creative techniques used. This provides some support for Stern's (2000) belief that a male concern with the authorial voice would be expressed through an interest in 'schemer schema'. Further support is provided by O'Donohoe's study (1994b). Male informants did not lack a sense of humour or playfulness in their dealings with ads, but at the same time they seemed to approach advertising from a more informative and analytical perspective. While advertising was not considered particularly informative, it was the men who tended to emphasise its educational potential, such as cereal ads highlighting the benefits of fibre in peoples' diets. Although informants generally expected themselves to understand ads, the men expressed more concern about not being able to 'get' particular ads. Male informants also adopted the roles of 'surrogate strategists' and 'casual cognoscenti' (O'Donohoe and Tynan 1998) more often; they were more likely to discuss advertising objectives, brand positions, market contexts, campaign scheduling and timing, for example, and they offered more background stories about the making of ads and comments about likely advertising costs.

Counter-arguments

O'Donohoe's (1994b) male informants were more prone to counter-arguing, particularly in the group discussions. A typical comment in this category came from a student who was not impressed by 'isotonic' drinks:

> 'The whole advert strikes me as being a load of crap anyway: "This drink is in balance with all your body fluids." It's just, well, a fizzy drink. It's got lots of sugar in it, that's it.'
>
> (male student 18–20 years)

This pattern conforms to Stern's (2000) expectations of more analytical and cynical responses from men. However, women were certainly at ease making counter-arguments, particularly in the individual interviews. For example, in the case of cosmetics, a young female worker commented that 'It might make you look younger, but it's not going to make you look beautiful, is it?' Rather than head-on confrontation, however, female informants appeared to favour more subtle ways of challenging advertising claims and messages: often using humour, they identified the conventions or propositions at work in an ad, thereby showing their ability to see through the ad. For example, a group of students commented on a coffee ad:

> – 'Become sophisticated by buying Gold Blend!'
> – 'And you'll instantly have gold earrings to take off when you answer the phone or whatever. That's kind of dodgy.'
>
> (female students 21–4 years)

This deconstructive approach was also used to make 'resisting readings' of advertising, by identifying and critiquing stereotyped portrayals, particularly though not exclusively relating to women. For example:

> 'They're taking it from one extreme to another. The good-looking girl is just the epitome of everything we want to be. Whereas the normal-looking person, who could be any one of us sort of thing, is made out to be really sick, part of a really tacky advert and "God, who wants to look like her?" sort of thing.'
>
> (female students 18–21 years)

Reading as/like a woman

In general, female informants expressed more concern about stereotyped portrayals in advertising than their male counterparts. They were very critical of the way ads portrayed women as constantly washing, cooking and cleaning up for their husbands and children. Portrayals of women as glamorous and attractive to men came in for even more criticism. There were indications that they did not always read ads 'on behalf on feminism' (Pearce 1997), however; they still tended to treat the women in ads as role models, comparing themselves with advertising's idealised images, even as they recognised that these were unattainable. Various comments indicated that advertising's male gaze was more than an abstract academic concept for them. Thus, ads showing women taking off their clothes were 'obviously directed at men'. There were also some indications that they turned this gaze on themselves:

> 'I know this sounds really bad and people will think I've not much confidence or something like that. But you see these totally perfect people on the adverts . . . and really it makes you think "oh no, what must I be like?" I mean, you're sitting with your boyfriend, and he's saying "Oh look at her, what a body".'
>
> (female students 18–20 years)

Some men expressed concern about the portrayal of women in ads, and discussed this in detail. Indeed, one male group began with someone commenting that he found sexism in ads annoying. Several men suggested that women may feel insulted or resentful of their portrayals, and that idealised portrayals may make real women feel inadequate and encourage diets or eating disorders. Their comments on such matters may be interpreted as examples of 'reading like a woman'. Indeed, since the researcher was a woman, there is always the possibility that such readings were performances staged for her benefit. However, less progressive attitudes towards women were also expressed at times, particularly in the groups, as indicated by passing references to women as 'wifies' or 'birds'.

CONCLUSION

> We read, it seems to me, in the hope/expectation that we will be *spoken* to; and it is the weight of that expectation, and the knowledge that it frequently will *not* be met, that has made it such a fraught, as well as potentially pleasurable, activity.
>
> (Pearce 1997: 254)

Reading ads as a woman seems to involve a similar triumph of hope over experience. This chapter has explored some aspects of the dialogic, power-inscribed and gendered relationships between women and advertising. Within the world of advertising there seems to be no semiotic sanctuary for women in the form of 'women's texts'. Several scholars have offered readings of advertising texts 'on behalf of feminism', identifying various patriarchal pitfalls inscribed in ads. The last part of this chapter has addressed real rather than inscribed readers of ads. Some support was found for the gender differences hypothesised by Stern in this volume, but a more subtle, playful style of engagement and resistance with respect to ads was also observed among women. However, readers' interpretations and articulations will always be context-dependent; we have seen here, for example, different patterns emerging in individual and group research settings. Further research, especially within the ethnographic tradition, is needed to explore patterns of readership *among* and *between* women. Given the diversity of our experiences, identities and alignments, research on repertoires of reading styles within particular interpretive communities may help us understand what it means to be literate, agile and active readers of advertising texts.

While *reading* ads 'as a feminist' is an important way of redressing the textual balance of power, it seems that we also need more women *writing* ads, and doing so as women and as feminists. Clifton (1995) suggests that the gender composition of the advertising industry in Britain is gradually changing. In the meantime, she suggests that advertisers must address women as *people* rather than a crude demographic segment, and to ensure that women's voices are heard in the early stages of advertising development and research. It will be interesting to see how, or whether, this participative paradigm takes root, and if it does, whether it means that ads will speak to us rather than at us.

REFERENCES

Advertising Association (1996) *Public Attitudes to Advertising 1996*, London: Advertising Association.

Advertising Standards Authority (1990) *Herself Reappraised*, London: Advertising Standards Authority.

Althusser, L. (1971) *Lenin and Philosophy, and Other Essays*, London: Verso.

Ang, I. (1985) *Watching Dallas: Soap Opera and the Melodramatic Imagination*, London: Methuen.

Barthes, R. (1971/1977) 'From work to text', in *Image, Music, Text*, London: Fontana Press, 155–65.

—— (1975) *The Pleasure of the Text*, New York: Hill & Wang.

—— (1978) *A Lover's Discourse: Fragments*, Harmondsworth: Penguin.

Baxter, M. (1990) *Women in Advertising*, London: Institute of Practitioners in Advertising.

Bellizzi, J. and Milner, L. (1991) 'Gender positioning of a traditionally male-dominant product', *Journal of Advertising Research* 31, 3: 72–9.

Berger, J. (1972) *Ways of Seeing*, London: Penguin.

Boller, G. and Olson, J. (1991) 'Experiencing ad meanings: crucial aspects of narrative/drama processing', in R. H. Holman and M. Solomon (eds) *Advances in Consumer Research* 18, Provo, UT: Association for Consumer Research, 172–5.

Brown, S. (1998) *Postmodern Marketing Two: Telling Tales*, London: International Thompson Business Press.

Brown, S., Stevens, L. and Maclaran, P. (1997) 'If I said you had a beautiful body: literary theory, Mikhail Bakhtin and the gender agenda', in R. Ashford *et al.* (eds) *Marketing Without Borders: Proceedings, First Annual Academy of Marketing Conference*, Manchester: Manchester Metropolitan University, 113–28.

Buikema, R. (1995) 'Windows in a round house: feminist theory', in R. Buikema and A. Smelik (eds) *Women's Studies and Culture: A Feminist Introduction*, London: Zed Books, 3–13.

Buttle, F. (1991) 'What do people do with advertising?', *International Journal of Advertising* 10, 2: 95–110.

Carsky, M. and Zuckerman, M. (1991) 'In search of gender differences in marketing communication: an historical/contemporary analysis', in J. Costa (ed.) *Gender and Consumer Behavior*, Salt Lake City: University of Utah Printing Service, 43–52.

Christie, C. (1994) 'Theories of textual determination and audience agency: an empirical contribution to the debate', in S. Mills (ed.) *Gendering the Reader*, New York: Harvester Wheatsheaf, 47–66.

Clifton, R. (1995) 'Do we need another article about women?', *Admap* 30, 354: 23–5.

Cook, G. (1992) *The Discourse of Advertising*, London: Routledge.

Cosgrove, J. (1991) 'Stereotype images from advertising: a reaction to female role portrayals', in J. Costa (ed.) *Gender and Consumer Behavior*, Salt Lake City: University of Utah Printing Service, 53–64.

Culler, J. (1983) *On Deconstruction: Theory and Criticism after Structuralism*, London: Routledge & Kegan Paul.

De Certeau, M. (1984) *The Practice of Everyday Life*, Berkeley, CA: University of California Press.

Dougary, G. (1994) *The Executive Tart and Other Myths: Media Women Talk Back*, London: Virago Press.

Eagleton, M. (1996) 'Who's who and where's where: constructing feminist literary studies', *Feminist Review* 53, Summer: 1–23.

Elliott, R., Jones, A., Benfield, A. and Barlow, M. (1995) 'Overt sexuality in advertising: a discourse analysis of gender responses', *Journal of Consumer Policy* 18: 187–217.

Fetterley, J. (1978) *The Resisting Reader: A Feminist Approach to American Fiction*, Bloomington: Indiana University Press.

Fiske, J. (1989) *Reading Popular Culture*, Boston: Unwin Hyman.

—— (1993) *Power Plays, Power Works*, London: Verso.

Fuss, D. (1989) *Essentially Speaking: Feminism, Nature and Difference*, London: Routledge.

Gledhill, C. (1992) 'Pleasurable negotiations', in F. Bonner, L. Goodman, R. Allen, L. Janes and C. King (eds) *Imagining Women: Cultural Representations and Gender*, Cambridge: Polity Press, 193–209.

Goldman, R. (1992) *Reading Ads Socially*, London: Routledge.

Goldman, R., Heath, D. and Smith, S. (1991) 'Commodity feminism', *Critical Studies in Mass Communication* 8: 333–51.

Green, H. (1997) 'Sanpro – or the difference between boys and girls', *Campaign* 8, August: 9.

Hailstone, S. (1995) 'The Wonderbra: how thinking big ensured the survival of the fittest', in C. Baker (ed.) *Advertising Works* 8, Henley-on-Thames: NTC Publications, 263–78.

Hall, S. (1973) 'Encoding and decoding in the television discourse', stencilled occasional paper, *Media Series SP 7*, University of Birmingham: Centre for Contemporary Cultural Studies.

Hatfield, S. (1999a) 'It's not clever and it's not funny either', *Campaign* 5, November: 33.

—— (1999b) 'Turkey of the week', *Campaign* 5, November: 20.

Hobson, D. (1982) *'Crossroads': The Drama of a Soap Opera*, London: Methuen.

Jensen, J. and Pauly, J. (1997) 'Imagining the audience: losses and gains in cultural studies', in M. Ferguson and P. Golding (eds) *Cultural Studies in Question*, London: Sage, 155–69.

Kemp, S. and Squires, J. (eds) (1997) *Feminisms*, New York: Oxford University Press.

Kolbe, R. and Langefeld, C. (1991) 'Female roles in television advertising: viewers' use of gender role cues in appraising stereotypic and non-stereotypic role portrayals', in

J. Costa (ed.) *Gender and Consumer Behavior*, Salt Lake City: University of Utah Printing Service, 65–76.

Krugman, H. (1966–7) 'The measurement of advertising involvement', *Public Opinion Quarterly* 30, Winter: 583–96.

Livingstone, S. (1998) *Making Sense of Television: The Psychology of Audience Interpretation*, London: Routledge.

Lull, J. (1990) *Inside Family Viewing: Ethnographic Research on Television's Audiences*, London: Routledge.

McCracken, G. (1987) 'Advertising: meaning or information?', in M. Wallendorf and P. Anderson (eds) *Advances in Consumer Research* 14, Provo, UT: Association for Consumer Research.

McDermott, P. (1998) 'The meaning and uses of feminism in introductory women's studies textbooks', *Feminist Studies* 24, 2: 403–27.

Meijer, M. (1995) 'A manual for self-defence: feminist literary theory', in R. Buikema and A. Smelik (eds) *Women's Studies and Culture: A Feminist Introduction*, London: Zed Books, 26–39.

Meyers-Levy, J. (1989) 'Gender differences in information processing: a selectivity interpretation', in P. Cafferata and A. M. Tybout (eds) *Cognitive and Affective Responses to Advertising*, Lexington, MA: Lexington Books, 219–60.

Meyers-Levy, J. and Maheswaran, D. (1991) 'Exploring differences in males' and females' processing strategies', *Journal of Consumer Research* 18, June: 63–70.

Meyers-Levy, J. and Sternthal, B. (1991) 'Gender differences in the use of message cues and judgements', *Journal of Marketing Research* 28, February: 84–96.

Mick, D. and Buhl, C. (1992) 'A meaning-based model of advertising experiences', *Journal of Consumer Research* 19, December: 317–38.

Mick, D. and Politi, L. (1989) 'Consumers' interpretations of advertising imagery: a visit to the hell of connotation', in E. Hirschman (ed.) *Interpretive Consumer Research*, Provo, UT: Association for Consumer Research, 85–96.

Moores, S. (1994) 'Texts, readers and contexts of reading: developments in the study of media audiences', in D. Graddol and O. Boyd-Barrett (eds) *Media Texts: Authors and Readers*, Clevedon: Multilingual Matters, 256–72.

Morley, D. (1980) *The Nationwide Audience: Structure and Decoding*, London: British Film Institute.

—— (1986) *Family Television: Cultural Power and Domestic Leisure*, London: Comedia.

Morris, P. (1993) *Literature and Feminism: An Introduction*, Oxford: Blackwell.

Mulvey, L. (1975) 'Visual pleasure and narrative cinema', *Screen* 16, 3: 6–18.

Myers, G. (1994) *Words in Ads*, London: Edward Arnold.

O'Barr, W. (1994) *Culture and the Ad*, Boulder, CO: Westview Press.

O'Donohoe, S. (1994a) 'Advertising uses and gratifications', *European Journal of Marketing* 28, 8/9: 52–75.

—— (1994b) 'Postmodern poachers: young adult experiences of advertising', unpublished Ph.D. thesis, University of Edinburgh.

O'Donohoe, S. and Tynan, C. (1998) 'Beyond sophistication: dimensions of advertising literacy', *International Journal of Advertising* 17, 4: 467–82.

Pearce, L. (1997) *Feminism and the Politics of Reading*, London: Arnold.

Radway, J. (1984) *Reading the Romance: Women, Patriarchy and Popular Literature*, Chapel Hill: University of North Carolina Press.

Ritson, M. and Elliott, R. (1995) 'A model of advertising literacy: the praxiology and co-creation of advertising meaning', in M. Bergadaa (ed.) *Proceedings of the 24th Conference of the European Marketing Academy*, Paris: ESSEC, 1035–54.

Scanlon, J. (1995) *Inarticulate Longings: The* Ladies' Home Journal, *Gender, and the Promises of Consumer Culture*, New York and London: Routledge.

Scott, L. M. (1994) 'The bridge from text to mind: adapting reader-response theory to consumer research', *Journal of Consumer Research* 21, December: 461–80.

Seaman, W. (1992) 'Active audience theory: pointless populism', *Media Culture and Society* 14: 301–11.

Shavitt, S., Lowrey, P. and Haefiner, J. (1998) 'Public attitudes toward advertising: more favorable than you might think', *Journal of Advertising Research* 38, 4: 7–22.

Showalter, E. (1977) *A Literature of Their Own: British Women Novelists from Bronte to Lessing*, Princeton, NJ: Princeton University Press.

Sperber, D. and Wilson, D. (1986) *Relevance: Communication and Cognition*, Cambridge, MA: Harvard University Press.

Steiner, L. (1988) 'Oppositional decoding as an act of resistance', *Critical Studies in Mass Communication* 5, 1: 1–15.

Stern, B. B. (1993) 'Feminist literary criticism and the deconstruction of advertisements: a postmodern view of advertising and consumer responses', *Journal of Consumer Research* 19, March: 556–66.

—— (1996) 'Deconstructive strategy and consumer research: concepts and illustrative exemplar', *Journal of Consumer Research* 23, September: 136–47.

—— (2000) 'Advertisements as women's texts: a feminist overview', in M. Catterall, P. Maclaran and L. Stevens (eds) *Marketing and Feminism: Current Issues and Research*, London: Routledge.

Thornborrow, J. (1994) 'The woman, the man and the Filofax: gender positions in advertising', in S. Mills (ed.) *Gendering the Reader*, New York: Harvester Wheatsheaf, 128–52.

Tompkins, J. (ed.) (1980) *Reader-Response Criticism: From Formalism to Post-structuralism*, Baltimore, MD: Johns Hopkins University Press.

Treneman, A. (1988) 'Cashing in on the curse: advertising and the menstrual taboo', in L. Gamman and M. Marshment (eds) *The Female Gaze: Women as Viewers of Popular Culture*, London: Women's Press.

Wicomb, Z. (1994) 'Motherhood and the surrogate reader: race, gender and interpretation', in S. Mills (ed.) *Gendering the Reader*, New York: Harvester Wheatsheaf, 99–127.

Williamson, J. (1978) *Decoding Advertisements*, London: Marion Boyars.

Winship, J. (1999) 'Women outdoors: advertising, controversy and disputing feminism in the 1990s', paper presented at the First International Conference on Consumption and Representation, University of Plymouth, September.

Worton, M. and Still, J. (eds) (1990), *Intertextuality: Theories and Practice*, Manchester: Manchester University Press.

Wright, P. (1986) 'Schemer schema: consumers' intuitive theories about marketers' influence tactics', in R. Lutz (ed.) *Advances in Consumer Research* 13, Provo, UT: Association for Consumer Research, 1–3.

6 Using memory-work to give a feminist voice to marketing research

Lorraine A. Friend and Shona M. Thompson

INTRODUCTION

Part way through a research project investigating women consumers' satisfaction and dissatisfaction in clothing retail encounters, Helena explained to others in the group how her participation in the project had helped her to be more confident and assertive in a recent experience of shopping with her mother. Helena was involved in the research as a member of a group utilising a qualitative research method known as memory-work (Haug and Others 1987). This method requires those involved to write specifically focused texts about recalled experiences which are read, discussed and analysed in a collective research group. In one of her memory texts, evoked by the theme 'a pressure buy', Helena wrote:

> Once again the shop assistants are engaged in their mysterious tasks, of reorganising the clothes or something, and show no interest in Helena and her Mom who are not, once again, dressed well for the occasion. However, Helena, after attending the empowering memory-workshops on shopping, decides not to be another victim of dominance by distant and secluding shop assistants. She determinedly interrupts one of these customer servants and asks her to help Mom.

In the ensuing group discussion, Helena elaborated:

> 'She knew . . . that her mom would never ask anything from a busy shop assistant. . . . She fought for herself too. . . . Three times she asked, "Why can't I buy the skirt by itself?" [without the knit top which she did not want]. . . . And she didn't feel ashamed [as she had in an earlier experience] that she wasn't dressed for the shopping occasion.'

Helena demonstrates how her involvement in this research process, as a member of a memory-work research group, positively changed her approach to clothing retail encounters. The details of memory-work method will be discussed later in the chapter, and will illustrate how research methods based on principles that are designed to be emancipatory can give voice to marginal groups, challenge and reform traditional research practices, generate new knowledges and help change inequitable social relations by empowering those involved. Such outcomes are in line with those principles recognised as being feminist principles.

BRINGING FEMINISM TO MARKETING RESEARCH

Previous research on consumer satisfaction and dissatisfaction has mostly examined this phenomenon by using a predictive, objective, aggregatable model, emphasising the performance of the product/service and the internal psychological processes of the satisfaction/dissatisfaction response. Neglected in this model is how the consumer's background experience and identity, as well as the sociocultural context, contributes to our understanding of the satisfaction/dissatisfaction phenomenon (Vezina and Nicosia 1990; Deighton 1992; Granbois 1993; Burns 1994). Also absent have been analyses of women's experiences from a feminist perspective, and an understanding of how consumer behaviour and its research are influenced by gender.

For several years now there has been a call for research in marketing and consumer behaviour to embrace feminism and adopt feminist principles (e.g. Bristor and Fischer 1991, 1993; Hirschman 1991, 1993; Stern 1996; Woodruffe 1996; Catterall, Maclaran and Stevens 1997). These calls have recognised the immense relevance of gender as a point of analysis, and the need to acknowledge the specificity of women's experiences, even in their diversity.

As noted by Bristor and Fischer (1993), there are a number of diverse feminist viewpoints in the marketing and consumer behaviour literature, reflecting various assumptions and motives. While feminist researchers do not argue for a definitive set of research methods, they are united in their efforts to examine women's lives and concerns, to minimise harmful research, to promote change that improves women's status and to empower women in positions of subjugation and oppression (Ramazanoglu 1992; Reinhartz 1992; Cancian 1992; DeVault 1996; Oakley 1998). Grossman *et al.* (1997) noted three main purposes of feminist research. The first is to generate new knowledge about aspects of women lives that are invisible, not addressed and/or are deemed unimportant; the second is to give 'voice' to women who are marginalised by their social, cultural, generation and/or class positions; and the third is to identify and critique androcentric biases in theory, concepts and methods. An additional motive, particularly professed by feminists from a radical perspective, is to be emancipatory and to facilitate change.

While past research in marketing and consumer behaviour has focused on and been subjected to feminist critiques, illustrating how marketing has contributed to the adverse effects and neglect of women and their roles, feminist analysis is not just a critique. It also provides a 'framework for generating knowledge, uncovering assumptions, and understanding epistemological, empirical, and theoretical claims' (Schroeder 1997: 357).

FEMINIST RESEARCH

While feminist research is usually associated with qualitative enquiry, a variety of perspectives has been used to produce feminist knowledge (Reinhartz 1992; DeVault 1996; Grossman *et al.* 1997). Key features include: a focus on women's lives and experiences; the significance of gender in understanding inequalities; the recognition of power relations as being the basis of our patriarchal society; the understanding and use of language in relation to power; a critique of the research process, including a rejection of hierarchical relationships in the research process and the promotion of participatory methods; and the goal of empowerment or action for societal change (Roberts 1981; Stanley and Wise 1983; Cook and Fonow 1986; Nielsen 1990; Worell and Etaugh 1994; Worell and Johnson 1997).

Early feminist work aimed to redress imbalances of power as formulated in research and theory by focusing exclusively on women (Gelsthorpe 1992). More recently, however, feminists have argued that gender differences frame expectations and response patterns, structuring personal experiences and beliefs (Worell and Etaugh 1994). As such, a focus on gender and how it mediates other sources of inequity (e.g. class, race, age) is considered essential to a thorough social analysis (Cancian 1992; Gelsthorpe 1992).

Gender has also been identified as an important construct in consumer and marketing research. In the past decade a number of researchers (e.g. Hirschman 1991, 1993; Bristor and Fischer 1993; Fischer and Bristor 1994; Peñaloza 1994) have shown how theory and knowledge in marketing and consumer research are gendered, sometimes in unrecognised ways (Catterall, Maclaran and Stevens 1997). Others have illustrated how consumer and marketing activities are influenced by and 'construct' gender identities (e.g. Stern 1993; Sparke 1996; Friend 1997; Woodruffe 1997).

Because of the past dominance of men in social science it is argued that women's voices have been suppressed, resulting in 'masculine' knowledge (Oakley 1998). Early social science has marginalised or excluded women's experiences and lives by focusing on the 'public world' of paid labour rather than the private world of home and domestic labour (Elshtain 1981; Stacey 1981). The areas of social life that are of common concern to women, such as caring, emotions, the body, sexuality and discrimination have mostly been ignored (Oakley 1998). Consequently, many feminist research projects examine 'the personal, everyday experiences of women (and men) . . . to validate feelings and activities that have been ignored or devalued in traditional research, and to understand the broader context of people's actions' (Cancian 1992: 627).

In their commitment to making women's experiences and concerns a more visible and legitimate focus of enquiry, many feminist scholars have argued for alternative approaches to traditional scientific methods (e.g. Cook and Fonow 1986; Nebraska Sociological Feminist Collective 1988; DeVault 1990, 1996; Smith 1990; Fonow and Cook 1991; Cancian 1992; Worell and Etaugh 1994; Oakley 1998). Data collection and analysis methods have also been rigorously scrutinised. They have been criticised for ignoring gender (Eichler 1980; Stanley and Wise 1983;

Bristor and Fischer 1993), for being reductive (Eisner 1997) and for '"context stripping" through laboratory approaches that reduce complexity and individuality' (Worell and Etaugh 1994: 447). Also for the ways by which some methods disregard the significance of language, dismissing the power differentials that may be inherent in its use (Worell and Etaugh 1994). In their listed goals for future consumer research, Bristor and Fischer (1993: 533) suggest incorporating, 'Data collection methods that recognise emergent subjective experiences of women and minority groups as epistemologically valid, and instruments that are sensitive to the effects of gendered, or otherwise biased, language'.

INTRODUCTION TO MEMORY-WORK

Memory-work is a method which was specifically developed by a collective of feminist researchers (Haug and Others 1987) in response to considered inadequacies of traditional scientific method, and as a critique of the ways by which women's lives had been theorised and women's experiences were being understood. It involves participants in small collective groups, who analyse written texts about their memories of specific experiences. The process of writing the memories, followed by each participant's and the group's reflections on them, is important for uncovering meaning and its construction. Through details in the text we are able to document the taken-for-granted and the conflicts that occur between dominant cultural and oppositional meanings. The resultant analysis can be related to existing theory and/or may lead to new theory development (Haug and Others 1987; Crawford *et al.* 1992). Written memories provide texts about women's everyday lives which often appear to be unimportant and uninteresting, adding value and allowing women to take themselves seriously (Haug and Others 1987; Kippax 1990; Crawford *et al.* 1992). Moreover, women become no longer the 'subject' of others' writing which is often objectionable (Koutroulis 1993) and can 'arrive at perceptions of self . . . without appearing inadequate' in relation to cultural views (Haug and Others 1987: 43).

Memory-work rejects the view that the subject and the object designate independent entities (Kippax 1990: 93). It also bridges the gap between 'theory' and 'experience' (Haug and Others 1987), providing a base from which to theorise about experience (Stephenson, Kippax and Crawford 1996). As Crawford *et al.* (1990) explained, memory-work is not just a technique for data collection, but rather a method, which analyses and theorises through its interpretation and reinterpretation of the data. It uses a phenomenological hermeneutic process that bridges the subject–object dichotomy by engaging the researcher(s) in the interpretation of both self and others.

The lines of objectivity that separate the researcher from the subjects in memory-work are explicitly removed. Group members actively share and interpret their memories, identifying themes and meanings which underlie the events and actions that are described in their written text (Friend and Rummel 1995). As such, the collective of participants are viewed as 'co-researchers' or 'co-workers' where they are their own subjects and have equal status in the research process (Haug and Others 1987; Crawford *et al.* 1992; McCormack 1998). Aligned with feminist principles, memory-work 'takes the subject and what the subject has to say seriously' (Kippax 1990: 93). Thus, participants are viewed as being authorities regarding their own lives (McCormack 1998) and 'experts in everyday life' (Haug and Others 1987: 54).

Knowledge produced from experience, however, is also contextual, where 'relative truths' or 'multiple truths' exist rather than one single value-free objective law. Relative truth is framed from an individual's experience and perspective in a given time and place, and as such leads to multiple perspectives or truths regarding an actual event, episode or action. Moreover, the meanings attributed to an episode determine the resultant attitudes, emotions and behaviours. Contextual relationships of knowledge allow generalisation to particular groups of women rather than being applicable to all women (Stanley and Wise 1983; Personal Narratives Group 1989; McCormack 1998). In reflecting on their memories, individuals tell stories to understand and give meaning to their and others' actions, emotions and beliefs within the social discourse (Madison 1990). Stories are told to explain what happened within their experience, to unravel many of the interrelated events and components of the process (Lallijee and Abelson 1983; Trabasso, Secco and Van Den Broek 1984; Read 1987). Gabriel (1991) and Allaire and Firsirotu (1984) noted that the understanding of a story, and thus its truth and value, develops not through the accuracy of the account of its past events but through its reconstructed symbolic meanings.

'DOING' MEMORY-WORK

Writing text

Memory texts are written according to a set of rules to ensure that a detailed description is provided rather than a general abstracted or justified account (Crawford *et al.* 1992). These rules are to write: 1) about a particular episode related to a selected 'trigger' topic; 2) in the third person; 3) in as much detail as possible, including circumstantial and trivial detail; and 4) without interpretation, explanation, biography or autobiography.

The process of memory-work begins with selecting, in consultation with the research group, a 'trigger' topic which is related to the research focus and objectives. Clichéd or obvious triggers are avoided as they are rooted in popular prejudices and may provide apparent or overrehearsed answers which may not be useful for analysis (Haug and Others 1987). Participants in Friend and Eummel's (1997b) study of consumer satisfaction/dissatisfaction of clothing retail encounters wrote memory texts using five different trigger topics: 1) a quick exit; 2) a nasty experience; 3) a pressure buy; 4) exhilaration; and 5) an impulse buy or an unusual experience. In that triggers are selected collectively, they become generalisable and significant to the general topic being examined (Haug and

Others 1987). Moreover, this allows the participants to be more in control of the research process, determining what is relevant to examine.

By writing a memory, rather than presenting it verbally, the self is de-emphasised. When talking about oneself it is difficult not to get involved in self-presentation, or to automatically justify and interpret our stories. Writing gives the participant 'permission not to bother to make things "normal" or proper' (Crawford *et al.* 1992: 47). Writing memory texts in the third person encourages participants to provide a 'bird's eye view' as an observer, and to describe rather than warrant (Crawford *et al.* 1992). It also protects the author from painful past events by distancing her from them, but at the same time allowing her to write fully about her past experiences (Haug and Others 1987). Participants are specifically asked to write without interpretation or autobiography as this often brings unproductive cohesion to the text. It may lead to smoothing over the rough edges and covering up absences and inconsistencies which later limit analysis and understanding of the episode (Crawford *et al.* 1992).

Analysing texts

After writing the memory texts for each trigger, the participants collectively analyse their memory texts. At the beginning of the session each participant reads in turn and 'reflects' on her memory text. The group ask questions, express ideas and opinions and compare the gathered information against the other memory texts, obtaining the necessary details to uncover the social meanings and the processes by which these meanings are arrived (Crawford *et al.* 1992).

One of the first steps in the analytical process is for the participants to question the memory texts for forgotten and repressed information. This provides the collective with additional details required for analysis, and provides the 'initial corrective focusing discussion on the credibility of the situation as well as its typicality' (Haug and Others 1987: 56). Haug and Others (1987) warn against the use of certain analytical techniques such as queries that convey criticism, 'amateur' psychoanalysis and sympathy to access the 'forgotten' and the 'repressed' from each memory text. These techniques place the author of the memory text in a defensive and/or subordinate role, thus discouraging her to remember and produce the details that are so vital to a successful collective analysis. It is also necessary during the collective interpretive process for the group to 'adopt temporarily the same standpoint as the writer' (Haug and Others 1987: 57). This is done partly by the use of pseudonyms in the group analysis, to help ensure the discussion occurs at the collective rather than the personal level.

As the group session progresses, the level of discussion gradually becomes more analytical. The collective identifies and analyses clichés, generalisations, contradictions, cultural imperatives, metaphors, and gaps or absences in the memory texts. For example, clichés and abstract generalisations must be challenged because they assume consensus and conformity to rigid views of what are considered appropriate feeling and desires. An examination of the meanings derived from the language employed (or absence of it) is important. It is through our everyday language that the ideological character of objects is formed (Haug and Others 1987). Attention to the language employed allows participants to explore contradictions or conflicts that occur within their lives, and to identify the non-recognised, the denied and the repressed. This helps to make visible the unconscious structures that underlie a 'fanaticised harmony' in women's lives (Haug and Others 1987: 69).

Silence is also a method of coping with the incompatible or the unacceptable. Analysis of absences in the text as well as what is written can be important to its interpretation. These absences are noted when participants expand upon and discuss each others' stories, discovering different vantage-points to their own. By examining stories from the vantage-point of others, participants alter their ideas about their own and others' actions.

As the collective is presented with each individual participant's memory text, and with there being no given criteria as to what is essential to its interpretation, the collective finds itself tracing new and exciting linkages which are 'immediately recognised by the group as credible, since they . . . form part of all [the participants'] meanings' (Haug and Others 1987: 54). The group also begins to identify similarities, differences and/or patterns across the memory texts as they search for explanations of their experiences. Thus, they endeavour to gain an understanding of how the whole (i.e., society or social experience) gives meanings to its parts (i.e., individual experiences) (Crawford *et al.* 1992). They do so through the process of intersubjectivity, by noting shared understandings rather than individual circumstances of the actors (Stephenson, Kippax and Crawford 1996). However, as each memory is discussed, its owner validates or invalidates the interpretation. In so doing, 'Memory-work transcends the oppositions between the individualistic bias in psychological theory and structural theory that does not recognise agency' (Crawford *et al.* 1992: 53–4).

In the final stage, the researchers then relate the interpretations, to pre-understandings of different theoretical positions (Crawford *et al.* 1992). Kippax (1990: 97) views this process as an evaluation of the collective's theorising. These new theoretical understandings are then tested against other stories in the group and/or other collectives and adjusted accordingly (Haug and Others 1987). This recursive process can lead to the construction of the researchers' own theoretical stance. Priority is given to neither subjective experience nor theory; rather, these are set in a reciprocal and mutually critical relationship. The process aims at both modifying and building theory (Crawford *et al.* 1990).

HELENA'S MEMORIES

During research on consumer satisfaction and dissatisfaction in women's clothing retail encounters, Helena wrote the following two connected stories in response to the trigger 'a quick exit'. The first describes a clothing store experience and the second involves a health club. Helena wrote the second, about the health club, to contrast and explain her avoidance of the clothing store, as depicted in the first story. The examination of Helena's memory text below, therefore, is twofold. First, it illustrates how not having any expertise or experiences in purchasing 'nice' clothes and shopping in 'nice' clothing stores lead to her feelings of not 'belonging', and thus her avoidance and dissatisfaction with this clothing store experience. Second, it describes how Helena experienced dissatisfaction in her health club experience when her sense of belonging was not reconfirmed in the encounter.

Helena's memory text[1]

She was standing in front of a large window of a clothing store mall. The clothes on the mannequins looked exactly what she had been looking for: natural white silk-cotton long sleeved blouse and blue ankle length skirt with a slit in the back. The blouse was loose and flowed nicely on the contours of the overly skinny mannequin. The skirt hugged the mannequin's long sleek legs. The clothes fit her newly awoken sense of style. She stretched her neck without moving from the front of the window to peek inside the boutique. No music inside the store, no neon lights, but soft yellow lights. No customers were in there, only the saleswoman at the counter filling out some forms, her spectacles hanging in a chain from her neck. She had very blond, short hair, permed and perfectly in place and her face was covered with perfect, but clearly noticeable make-up. The colors of the make-up weren't too offensive, like her lipstick was pink, but not bright pink. She was frowning over her papers. She was about 40 and clearly projected classy, expensive taste. The saleswoman scared her. She walked quietly away avoiding the open door so she wouldn't be seen inside of the shop. She was wearing a blue T-shirt tucked into her loose jeans that stayed up with her hipbones. Her once white aerobics shoes were worn out into every day street colours. She certainly didn't want to bother the lady.

She always hesitated to go into clothing stores, although she liked nice and usually expensive, good quality clothes, but she never had any apprehension about going into a health club. She was one of them with the right gear. This time she had on her black cotton bike shorts, just long enough to cover the whole length of the quadriceps; a white T-shirt and a blue sweat shirt on top of it as it was cold inside. It was fall. She carried her pink water bottle in her hand, paid at the counter, marched into the aerobics class. She left her water bottle on the side and took a place toward the mid front of the rectangular large aerobics room. The well acclaimed athletes smiled at her from all of the four walls. Were they supposed to inspire someone? The room was full of people, mostly women – young – but also men. It was packed. She felt like a fish in an overcrowded aquarium where the fish were trying to stay in one spot by paddling their little fins nervously back and forth. The instructor was a sinewy, fit, lean small short man, probably Polynesian descent. His mannerism was quick, so was his way of talking. One of her students stood in front of her. This student seemed very muscular. This wasn't the usual surroundings for an encounter with a student, she avoided looking at her. The instructor started to blast his music; the usual rappy, hip-hoppy aerobics stuff. She could barely see him moving, although he pranced back and forth on an elevated instructor floor; there were so many people. She couldn't move her arms without hitting somebody. The others didn't seem to worry about hitting her (she hated when people aren't considerate like that), they didn't even notice. Their eyes were glued to the instructor, who changed his quick moves in quick bursts and gave his instructions after these bursts; quick words aided with constant, rapid hand gestures. Everyone was doing the moves wrong, moving into wrong directions and facing the wrong directions but she noticed their eyes were shining; they were looking at 'God' up there and they were all following his lead with determined, ambitious smiles on their faces – two beats behind or some were two measures behind him. The mass of bodies moved around her in an ever closing circle that was going to squeeze her in its centre, but no one looked at her. She looked down at the pink and rose carpeted floor. She felt she was suffocating, she hated these moves, she thought the instructor was no god, he actually sucked. She tried to understand why people loved this, but got too irritated and angry and aggravated and pushed her way through the uplifted, enthusiastic faces to pick up her water bottle next to the erector spinae machine – this machine was closest to the door of all the white training machines – and ran out after five minutes. She had never done that before, left the class like this without giving it a chance. She did not look at anybody on her way out. She felt bad, like culturally insensitive.

Discussion of Helena's memory text

Helena uses the second part of her memory text, the 'quick exit' from the health club, to explain her general avoidance of clothing stores which is represented in her first memory text. Helena's avoidance of clothing stores in this case can be viewed as a pre-formulated type of an exit.[2] Leading into the discussion, Helena explained:

> 'This is a bit different. . . . Why are both memories here? Well that was because Helena had lots of general memories about clothing stores and they all related to this kind of thing, that she didn't even go in. She couldn't remember even getting herself, even wanting to face a situation where somehow she had to leave. She'd always felt very unempowered according to those things. . . . She won't even go in it [a clothing store]. She won't let them intimidate her like that!'

Because of the way she contrasts these memories, the 'quick exit' from the health club will be discussed first.

Along with the disconfirmation of Helena's expectations of her health club experiences, Helena's memory text reflected two main injustice concepts, inequity and social comparison, which 'grounded' her 'fleeing'. Specifically, it was Helena paying for the service, receiving the unexpected appropriate performance attributes, and at the same time comparing and judging herself to the other clientele who appeared to be satisfied. This led to Helena's perceived inequity in the encounter. In addition, Helena compared herself to the other clientele and the instructor, which resulted in her feelings of being uncomfortable and not belonging to this health club's 'culture'. It was this combination of Helena not belonging, and the disconfirmation of her expectations, that led to her aggravation, and resulted in her quick exit. Helena reflected:

> 'This [health club memory] . . . is sort of a story where you "buy services" and she clearly remember this time that she got so angry and just marched out, and she never did that.'

Helena went along to the session feeling comfortable, enthusiastic and confident, she 'belonged'. She reflected, 'Helena had her uniform on. She was one of them.' Furthermore, Helena had committed herself to the encounter by paying for the session. As Helena consumed her paid-for experience at the club, the physical environment, the clientele's performance and the instructor made her uncomfortable. Her training in physical education, dance and aerobics intensified her expectations and reinforced her judgement of the appropriate quality performance attributes which should be offered. 'Because she was the expert, she had the power to judge' [Helena]. Two others in the research group, Annabel and Wendy, noted respectively, 'it was that the service and the facilities were not what they should have been', and 'not what Helena expected'. Thus, there was negative disconfirmation of Helena's expectations.

On a personal basis Helena compared her social self to the other clientele and the instructor. This contributed to her feelings of the inequitable exchange, and not belonging to this specific encounter. While Helena considered herself 'one of them,' her description in her memory text of what she was wearing, how she reacted, her lack of enjoyment, the other clients' body images, their reactions and enjoyment, and the instructor's image illustrated how Helena differed from them. While the others appeared confident about their images and abilities, she did not appear so, even though she was an 'expert', and a teacher. Helena's muscular framed body was covered and protected, while theirs were not. Her clothing blended into the background, again protecting her image. The others, however, were young, full of self-confidence and ability.

Helena felt that 'everyone else was really enjoying it', even though, according to her, they were doing things wrong. She also felt as if she was being abused, squeezed out, suffocated and ignored by this 'culture' in which she supposedly belonged and to which she was committed.

Nor was Helena able to fit into the group or enjoy the experience by adhering to her personal values: '*she couldn't move her arms without hitting somebody*'. She was actually striking and pushing others away, and not performing to her perceived standard. Comparing herself to others, '*she tried to understand why people loved this*'. For Helena, having not received the expected experience for which she had paid, having been squeezed and suffocated into feeling she did not belong, and having been threatened as to whom she was, she became too '*irritated and angry and aggravated . . . and ran out after five minutes*'. Helena rationalised that she had due cause to 'flee'. After all, she was the expert. She 'clearly knew that it was terrible!' [Helena]. As '*she pushed her way through the uplifted, enthusiastic faces*', she reconfirmed her actions and fairness by noting her expertise by being able to name the '*erector spinae machine*'.

Although Helena externally blamed the health club for her 'bad' experience and thus exits the session with pride, she flees from this exchange feeling guilty. In response to her own description of herself she reflected:

> 'She felt totally bad, although she knew that it wasn't good. She felt guilty. "Oh gosh, I wasn't nice", and you know, maybe this is because this is just

> different than what she was used to. You know, maybe it is her fault. Maybe she should try to adapt! So totally putting the blame on herself.'

Helena's avoidance of the clothing store is conceptualised from the two interlinked injustice concepts, inequity and social comparison, which were the main source of her quick exit from her health club experience. First, by not 'bothering' the saleswoman Helena did not commit herself, and as such avoided an inequitable exchange where she felt obligated to participate. Unlike the health club, Helena felt insecure about entering into the clothing store. Rather than marching in, full of confidence, Helena stood '*in front of a large window of a clothing store mall. . . . She stretched her neck without moving from the front of the window to peek inside the boutique*'. Second, by comparing her image to the store's image, Helena felt inadequate, insecure and uncomfortable with the encounter. Helena's image of herself was incongruent with her perception of the store's display and saleswoman's image. Helena wrote, '*[The saleswoman] . . . was about 40 and clearly projected classy, expensive taste. [Helena] . . . was wearing a blue T-shirt tucked into her loose jeans that stayed up with her hipbones. Her once white aerobics shoes were worn out into every day street colours.*'

Helena acknowledged that she frequently avoids clothes shopping because she has neither the knowledge nor the skills that enable her to know what to look for and thus to ask the appropriate questions. In this experience, she lacked the expertise and the confidence in (a) knowing what she wanted to purchase for her newly aquired sense of style, (b) her knowledge of how to judge the appropriateness of the clothing, and (c) her skills to interact with the saleswomen. Due to these feelings of 'inadequacy', Helena did not feel in control of her shopping encounter. She felt that the saleswoman would recognise that she did not have the fashion expertise and shopping experience to belong in this fashion boutique. As such, Helena feared being manipulated, pressured, and/or belittled by the saleswoman. Helena reflected in the group discussion:

> 'Well, Helena could tell you a story about the last time she actually went clothing shopping. She avoided the whole business. . . . She didn't really want to go. And like with these clothes [described in the memory text], Helena could have very well afforded them. So it was not because of the price that she didn't go in. . . . Helena went shopping in San Francisco, actually, and the only things that she came out with were leotards . . . because they are easy for her to buy. She knows exactly what she wants. These are good quality, these are bad quality, these look nice and these are useful. But thinking of some other clothes, and having to go and ask the salespeople something . . . , Helena would rather buy it large, because she knows it fits! So she doesn't have to try it on. (Laughing) She knows they're big and that they are going to bag, but she . . . [doesn't care]. "Oh, these are good."'
>
> (Helena)

> 'So Helena would not go into this store because she didn't know what she wanted to buy?'
>
> (Annabel)

> 'That's part of it.'
>
> (Helena)

> 'And Helena didn't want to have to approach them?'
>
> (Annabel)

> 'Bother the lady. . . . Right, because if Helena knew . . . what she wanted, she wouldn't need to bother her, sort of.'
>
> (Helena)

Helena was not wearing what she considered to be appropriate clothes, nor did she know how to interact comfortably with the saleswoman. Rather, Helena felt inadequate and ashamed by her dress that symbolised her lack of fashion knowledge and shopping experience. By comparison, the salesperson's appearance and paperwork symbolised her expertise. The group reflected on appearance, specifically what the consumer and the salespeople were wearing in regard to a consumer's sense of belonging in the encounter. Priscilla commented:

> 'What I find interesting in the three of yours [Helena's, Annabel's and Wendy's 'quick exit' memory texts], is the way they described what they were wearing. To me they all felt inadequate in the clothes that they were shopping in . . . and I found that very interesting. That they have all commented that: Helena was wearing a blue T-shirt tucked into her loose jeans that stayed up with her hipbones; Annabel was in her overalls – her stonewashed baggy overalls; and Wendy was in her . . .'
>
> (Priscilla)

> 'Wendy didn't give details, but she would have been in jeans.'
>
> (Wendy)

> 'But Wendy gave that feeling of being scruffy. So when they set off shopping, they must have felt okay about themselves. But those stores intimidated the way they felt about what they were wearing. But they were in comfortable clothes when they set out, you know.'
>
> (Priscilla)

> 'Yeah. Sometimes you think that if they wore really nice stylish clothes already when they went shopping, that somehow the salespeople would take them more seriously and give them more, you know, service or something. Which is kind of strange because why would you go buy new ones if you

> already had something nice on? But that I guess is the way Helena thinks about it.'
>
> (Helena)

> 'There is some sort of disparity between the sort of "regular out there on the street" women going shopping and the clothes they are comfortable in, and the image that is being presented by the retailing stores. Yeah, I imagine that it is to try and lure them in to buy their wonderful clothes. But there is such a difference.'
>
> (Wendy)

> 'But they actually scare you off. Most of the time Helena feels ashamed of herself. Mostly because she knows she can't go home and change into other clothes, and totally appear like the lady the next day, and go into the same store because she doesn't have any of those clothes. But I think it was also like when Helena went to the health club, she had her uniform on. She was one of them.'
>
> (Helena)

> 'Helena was more comfortable there?'
>
> (Priscilla)

> 'Yeah. But she didn't have her uniform on when she went shopping.'
>
> (Helena)

Helena's feelings of inadequacy were also grounded in her lack of skill and confidence in knowing what she wanted in a '*boutique . . . [which] clearly projected classy, expensive taste*', and in what she felt was her inability to judge if a garment is appropriate. That is, she didn't have the fashion expertise to know what to ask for and what to purchase. Helena reflected:

> 'The hardest thing for Helena is that she doesn't really know what she wants (laughing). She has this idea that maybe she should get some other clothes. But like in that sense she doesn't know how to shop like Priscilla,[3] with a mission. Then Helena would feel better.'
>
> (Helena)

> 'Mm, like when Helena buys leotards and things like that?'
>
> (Priscilla)

> 'Yeah, or if Helena knew something . . . that would sort of help. Because that would give her more power, sort of. . . . If she knew exactly what she wanted – the "look" and what material and what length, and all that stuff. It was something like . . . not having the expertise, having no knowledge; so she wouldn't be totally at the saleswoman's mercy. Sort of. . . . So

> she doesn't have to end up having to try on something that she doesn't like, and she doesn't have to say, "I don't really need this".'
>
> (Helena)

If Helena avoids becoming committed to the clothing store encounter by not bothering the saleswoman, she need not feel guilty for not being nice, as she felt in her health club experience. In this case, Helena does not need to break the reciprocity exchange rule of equity. Furthermore, in her avoidance of the encounter, she does not place herself in a situation where she is at the mercy of the saleswoman who has the power to hurt her by judging her inappropriately according to who she is culturally and personally, as she herself judged others in her health club experience.

In summary, it was Helena's expertise and experience that allowed her confidently to enter and exit from the health club experience. Due to her past skills and knowledge she felt as if she belonged, and thus was comfortable entering and partaking in the aerobic experience. It was also Helena's professional expertise and experience that allowed her to attribute blame to the health club, and thus exit from an incompetent encounter. In contrast, in Helena's clothing store experience she lacked the knowledge and skills in fashion and clothes shopping to feel as if she belonged, and as such avoided entering into the encounter. She had neither the knowledge nor the skills to select and judge appropriate garments, and to leave the store without feeling that she might be pressured, manipulated, and/or intimidated by the salesperson. Overall, she did not want to feel guilty about not doing the 'womanly' thing of 'being nice', and judging people inappropriately. Nor did she want to feel guilty for her appearance, actions and emotions – who she is.

CONCLUSION

By the time Helena came to write a later memory text, for the trigger 'a pressure buy', her involvement in the collective memory-work process had helped her develop an understanding of the meanings within her social context, and an enhanced awareness of her own agency. She wrote, as quoted at the beginning of the chapter, how she was able to be more assertive and take greater control in a subsequent retail encounter. She had, as she said, attended 'the empowering memory-workshops on shopping'. As Kippax (1990: 94) noted, memory-work 'gives insights into the way we appropriate the social world and in doing so transform ourselves in it'.

The above memory-work analysis illustrates how this research process works for a feminist agenda by giving voice to women as the co-researchers, by understanding the significance of language and by investigating issues of power, including those related to hierarchies in the generation of knowledge. It also shows how the collective process, which could be viewed as a structured form of 'consciousness raising', works to encourage and support reflectivity which can lead to individual empowerment, enhanced personal agency and social change. At the same time, memory-work allows us to engage in critical self-reflection that provides a greater understanding of marketing phenomena such as consumer satisfaction and its gendered construction. It allows us to redefine and understand women's experiences of consumer satisfaction in a way that other methods could not.

Following the work of Haug and Others (1987), memory-work has been successfully applied to research in a number of disciplines, including psychology (Kippax *et al.* 1988; Crawford *et al.* 1992), education (Ingleton 1994), leisure studies (McCormack 1998) and nursing (Koutroulis 1993) as well as in consumer behaviour (Friend and Rummel 1995, 1997a, 1997b, 1997c, 1999; Friend 1997). All these studies have been done by women with the deliberate aim of creating theory grounded in the actual experience and language of women by addressing women's lives and experiences in their own terms, which, as noted by Du Bois (1983: 108), 'is the central agenda for feminist social science and scholarship'. In so far as feminist research investigates and explores variations among women, such as how ethnic and racial identities, socio-economic status, sexual orientation, disability, age, parenthood and employment status differ from the majority group (Worell and Etaugh 1994), it is important to develop a research process that recognises marginal status (Kirby and McKenna 1989).

Stern's (1996: 144) review of consumer research reminds us that 'One much-needed direction is inclusion of the silenced voices', suggesting that consumption will only be fully represented if 'the panoply of otherness' is recognised. This follows Bristor and Fischer's (1993: 533) plea for 'theoretical and methodological approaches capable of capturing rich and complex consumption phenomenon, as well as engage in ongoing and critical self-reflection'. We suggest that memory-work is one such approach.

NOTES

1 The authors acknowledge and thank their co-workers for their contribution in the writing and/or analysis of the memory-work data used in this paper. Helena's memory text is distinguished from the memory-work group discussion by the use of italics.
2 Huefner and Hunt (1992: 228) also refer to avoidance as a 'persisting' exit.
3 Helena refers to Priscilla's 'Quick Exit' memory text and discussion where Priscilla is viewed as an 'expert'. She knows what she wants, where to go, what to ask for. Through her fashion and retail experience, Priscilla knows how to shop confidently for clothing.

REFERENCES

Allaire, Y. and Firsirotu, M. E. (1984) 'Theories of organisational culture', *Organisational Studies* 5, 3: 193–226.

Bristor, J. and Fischer, E. (1991) 'Objectivity and gender in consumer research: a feminist deconstruction critique', in J. A. Costa (ed.) *Gender and Consumer Behavior Conference Proceedings*, Salt Lake City: University of Utah Printing Service, 115–23.

—— (1993) 'Feminist thought: implications for consumer research', *Journal of Consumer Research* 19, 4: 518–36.

Burns, M. J. (1994) 'Exploring self (dis)satisfaction as an outcome of product use experiences', *Journal of Consumer Satisfaction, Dissatisfaction and Complaining Behavior* 7: 252–6.

Cancian, F. M. (1992) 'Feminist science: methodologies that challenge inequality', *Gender and Society* 6, 4: 623–42.

Catterall, M., Maclaran, P. and Stevens, L. (1997) 'Marketing and feminism: a bibliography and suggestions for further research', *Marketing Intelligence and Planning* 15, 7: 369–76.

Cook, J. A. and Fonow, M. M. (1986) 'Knowledge and women's interests: issues of epistemology and methodology in feminist sociological research', *Sociological Inquiry* 56, 1: 2–29.

Crawford, J., Kippax, S., Onyx, J., Gault, U. and Benton, P. (1990) 'Women theorising their experiences of anger: a study using memory-work', *Australian Psychologist* 25, 3: 333–50.

—— (1992) *Emotion and Gender: Constructing Meaning from Memory*, London: Sage.

Deighton, J. (1992) 'The consumption of performance', *Journal of Consumer Research* 19, 3: 362–72.

DeVault, M. L. (1990) 'Talking and listening from women's standpoint: feminist strategies for interviewing and analysis', *Social Problems* 37, 1: 96–116.

—— (1996) 'Talking back to sociology: distinctive contributions of feminist methodology', *Annual Review of Sociology* 22: 29–50.

Du Bois, B. (1983) 'Passionate scholarship: notes on value, knowing and method in feminist social science', in G. Bowles and R. Duelli Klein (eds) *Theories of Women's Studies*, London: Routledge & Kegan Paul, 105–16.

Eichler, M. (1980) *The Double Standard*, New York: St Martin's Press.

Eisner, E. W. (1997) 'The new frontier in qualitative research methodology', *Qualitative Inquiry* 3, 3: 259–73.

Elshtain, J. B. (1981) *Public Man, Private Woman*, Oxford: Martin Robertson.

Fischer, E. and Bristor, J. (1994) 'A feminist poststructuralist analysis of the rhetoric of marketing relationships', *International Journal of Research in Marketing* 1, 3: 317–31.

Fonow, M. M. and Cook, J. A. (eds) (1991) *Beyond Methodology: Feminist Scholarship as Lived Research*, Bloomington: Indiana University Press.

Friend, L. A. (1997) 'Realities of women's clothing shopping experiences: implications for understanding consumer satisfaction and dissatisfaction', unpublished doctoral dissertation, University of Otago, NZ.

Friend, L. A. and Rummel, A. (1995) 'Memory-work: an alternative approach to investigating consumer satisfaction and dissatisfaction of clothing retail encounters', *Journal of Consumer Satisfaction, Dissatisfaction and Complaining Behavior* 8: 214–22.

—— (1997a) 'Social comparison as a construct in the dynamic and complex satisfaction/dissatisfaction of retail encounters', paper presented at the 1997 Consumer Satisfaction/Dissatisfaction and Complaining Behavior Conference, Snowbird, Utah, July.

—— (1997b) 'Memory-work: understanding consumer satisfaction and dissatisfaction of clothing retail service encounters', paper presented at the Three American Marketing Association Special Conferences, Dublin, Eire, June.

—— (1997c) 'Threatened self identities: an underlying determinant of dissatisfactory service encounters', paper presented at the 4th Recent Advances in Retailing and Services Science Conference, Scottsdale, Arizona, June/July.

—— (1999) '"Exhilarating" women's clothing retail encounters: stories to better understand consumer satisfaction', paper presented at the 1999 Consumer Satisfaction/Dissatisfaction and Complaining Behavior Conference, Las Vegas/Zion National Park, June.

Gabriel, Y. (1991) 'Turning facts into stories and stories into facts: a hermeneutic exploration of organisational folklore', *Human Relations* 44, 8: 857–75.

Gelsthorpe, L. (1992) 'Response to Martyn Hammersley's paper "On feminist methodology"', *Sociology* 26, 2: 213–18.

Granbois, D. H. (1993) 'Integration, model development and behavioral advice: three directions for satisfaction research', *Journal of Consumer Satisfaction, Dissatisfaction and Complaining Behavior* 6: 34–9.

Grossman, F. K., Gilbert, L. A., Genero, N. P., Hawes, S. E., Hyde, J. S., Marecek, J. and Johnson, L. (1997) 'Feminist research: practice and problems', in J. Worell and N. G. Johnson (eds) *Shaping the Future of Feminist Psychology: Education, Research and Practice*, Washington, DC: American Psychological Association, 73–91.

Haug, F. (1992) *Beyond Female Masochism: Memory-work and Politics*, London: Verso.

Haug, F. and Others (1987) *Female Sexualization: A Collective Work of Memory*, London: Verso.

Hirschman, E. C. (1991) 'A feminist critique of marketing theory: towards agentic-communal balance', in J. A. Costa (ed.) *Gender and Consumer Behavior Conference Proceedings*, Salt Lake City: University of Utah Printing Service, 324–40.

—— (1993) 'Ideology in consumer research, 1980 and 1990: a Marxist and feminist critique', *Journal of Consumer Research* 19, 4: 537–55.

Huefner, J. and Hunt, K. H. (1992) 'Brand and store avoidance: the behavioral expression of dissatisfaction', *Journal of Consumer Satisfaction, Dissatisfaction and Complaining Behavior* 5: 228–32.

Ingleton, C. (1994) 'The use of memory-work to explore the role of emotions in learning', *Research and Development in Higher Education* 16: 265–71.

Kippax, S. (1990) 'Memory-work, a method', in J. Daly and E. Willis (eds) *The Social Sciences and Health Research*, Ballart, Victoria: Public Health Association of Australia Inc., 93–7.

Kippax, S., Crawford, J., Benton, P., Gault, U. and Noesjirwan, J. (1988) 'Constructing emotions: weaving meaning from memories', *British Journal of Social Psychology* 27, 1: 19–33.

Kirby, S. and McKenna, K. (1989) *Experience, Research, Social Change*, Toronto: Garamond Press.

Koutroulis, G. (1993) 'Memory-work: a critique', in B. Turner, L. Eckermann, D. Colquhoun and P. Crotty (eds) *Annual Review of Health Social Science. Methodological Issues in Health Research*, Deakin, Victoria: Deakin University Press, 76–96.

Lallijee, M. and Abelson, R. P. (1983) 'The organisation of explanations', in M. Hewstone (ed.) *Attribution Theory: Social and Functional Extensions*, Oxford: Blackwell, 65–80.

McCormack, C. (1998) 'Memories bridge the gap between theory and practice in women's leisure research', *Annals of Leisure Research* 1: 37–50.

Madison, G. B. (1990) *The Hermeneutics of Postmodernity: Figures and Themes*, Bloomington: Indiana University Press.

Nebraska Sociological Feminist Collective (1988) *A Feminist Ethic for Social Science Research*, Lewiston, NY: Edwin Mellen.

Nielsen, J. (1990) *Feminist Research Methods: Exemplary Readings in Social Sciences*, Boulder, CO: Westview Press.

Oakley, A. (1998) 'Gender, methodology and people's ways of knowing: some problems with feminism and the paradigm debate in social sciences', *Sociology* 32, 4: 707–31.

Peñaloza, L. (1994) 'Crossing boundaries/drawing lines: a look at the nature of gender boundaries and their impact on marketing research', *International Journal of Research in Marketing* 9, 1: 359–79.

Personal Narratives Group (1989) 'Truths', in Personal Narratives Group (ed.) *Interpreting Women's Lives. Feminist Theory and Personal Narratives*, Bloomington: Indiana University Press, 261–4.

Ramazanoglu, C. (1992) 'On feminist methodology: male reason versus female empowerment', *Sociology* 26, 2: 207–12.

Read, S. J. (1987) 'Constructing casual scenarios: a knowledge structure approach to causal reasoning', *Journal of Personality and Psychology* 52, 1: 288–302.

Reinhartz, S. (1992) *Feminist Methods in Social Science*, Oxford: Oxford University Press.

Roberts, H. (ed.) (1981) *Doing Feminist Research*, London: Routledge & Kegan Paul.

Schroeder, J. E. (1997) 'Review of *As Long as it's Pink: The Sexual Politics of Taste*', *Public Policy and Marketing* 16, 2: 356–60.

Smith, D. E. (1990) *The Conceptual Practices of Power: Feminist Sociology of Knowledge*, Boston, MA: Northeastern University Press.

Sparke, P. (1996) *As Long as it's Pink: The Sexual Politics of Taste*, San Francisco, CA: Pandora/HarperCollins.

Stacey, M. (1981) 'The division of labour revisited or overcoming the two adams', in P. Abrams, R. Deem, J. Finch and P. Rock (eds) *Practice and Progress: British Sociology 1950–80*, London: George Allen & Unwin, 173–204.

Stanley, L. and Wise, S. (1983) *Breaking Out: Feminist Consciousness and Feminist Research*, London: Routledge & Kegan Paul.

Stephenson, N., Kippax, S. and Crawford, J. (1996) 'You, I and she: memory-work and the construction of self', in S. Wilkson (ed.) *Feminist Social Psychologies. International Perspectives*, Bristol, PA: Open University Press, 182–200.

Stern, B. B. (1993) 'Feminist literary criticism and deconstruction of ads: a postmodern view of advertising and consumer responses', *Journal of Consumer Research* 19, 4: 556–66.

—— (1996) 'Deconstruction strategy and consumer research: concepts and illustrative exemplar', *Journal of Consumer Research* 23, 2: 136–47.

Trabasso, T., Secco, T. and Van Den Broek, P. (1984) 'Causal cohesion and story coherence', in H. Mandl, N. Stein and T. Trabasso (eds) *Learning and Comprehension of Text*, London: Lawerence Erlbaum Associates, 83–111.

Vezina, R. and Nicosia, F. (1990) 'Investigations of the social determinants of consumer satisfaction and dissatisfaction', *Journal of Consumer Satisfaction, Dissatisfaction and Complaining Behavior* 3: 36–41.

Woodruffe, H. R. (1996) 'Methodological issues in consumer research: towards a feminist perspective', *Marketing Intelligence and Planning* 14, 2: 13–18.

—— (1997) 'Compensatory consumption: why women go shopping when they're fed up and other stories', *Marketing Intelligence and Planning* 15, 7: 325–34.

Worell, J. and Etaugh, C. (1994) 'Transforming theory and research with women: themes and variations', *Psychology of Women Quarterly* 18, 4: 443–50.

Worell, J. and Johnson, N. G. (eds) (1997) *Shaping The Future of Feminist Psychology. Education, Research and Practice*, Washington, DC: American Psychological Association.

7 Shifting the discourse: feminist perspectives on consumer behaviour research

Margaret K. Hogg, Shona Bettany and George Long[1]

FEMINIST MARKETING – CAPITAL F CAPITAL M

In her seminal paper in anthropology Marilyn Strathern distinguished between feminist anthropology, which she defined as an anthropological subdiscipline whose goal was 'trying to shift discourse, not improve a paradigm';[2] and what she called anthropological feminism, 'whose aim is to build a feminist community, one whose premises and goals differ from, and are opposed to anthropology' (Strathern cited in Rabinow 1986: 254; see also Strathern 1985, 1987).

We start with this anthropological reference because it allows us to pose an important question for all researchers in marketing and consumer behaviour. Are we concerned with 'feminist marketing' – that is, developing a marketing subdiscipline which contributes to the discipline's advancement from within the boundaries of its own ideology? Or, are we interested in 'marketing feminism', that is, with building a feminist community whose premises and goals are opposed to the fundamentals of marketing ideology? In the interests of declaring our own 'positionality' (Skeggs 1995: 23) as members of a collaborative research group[3] we do not adopt a separatist or exclusionary approach here. Rather, we espouse 'Feminist Marketing' because we want to contribute to research in consumer behaviour from an inclusive position within the marketing community by 'shifting the discourse' in a spirit of transformation rather than opposition.

FEMINIST THEORY IN MARKETING

The transformatory potential of feminist research for marketing has already been recognised (Brown 1998: 59; Bettany 1999; Long *et al.* 1999) although 'feminist analyses' of marketing 'are unlikely to make for comfortable reading' (Catterall, Maclaran and Stevens 1997: 374; 1999). Most feminist-inspired work in marketing has been directly concerned with gender (Costa 1993), patriarchy (Bristor and

Fischer 1993) and representations of women (Hirschman 1993; Brown 1998). Our approach can be distinguished from these earlier applications, as will be shown.

Our central contention is that the contribution of feminist theory to sociology, anthropology and psychology – which coincidentally are all key disciplines in marketing – can be used to transform research practices and enrich epistemological debate in marketing and the study of consumer behaviour. This, we believe, can be achieved by altering 'the nature of the audience, the range of readership and the kinds of interactions between author and reader, and [thereby] *altering the . . . conversation* in a way that allows others to speak' (Strathern 1984, cited in Rabinow 1986: 255 [emphasis added]). In other words, we concentrate on the voices in *the conversation* of research practice in order to identify and then shift the discourses in our field.

SHIFTING THE DISCOURSE: CHANGING THE CONVERSATION

One of the main contributions of feminism to other social science disciplines has been to recognise the neglected 'other' in research, most notably the disenfranchised in terms of gender, ethnicity, sexual orientation and class. Of particular interest to feminist theorists was the question of locating the voice of the disenfranchised in the 'tales from the field' (Van Maanen 1988). With a few exceptions (e.g. Stern 1998), however, such issues have been largely neglected in consumer research. We believe that through the process of 'finding the voices of the epistemology makers' we will 'uncover the processes of theory and knowledge production' (Code 1991: 155) and thus identify those voices hitherto excluded in marketing and consumer research. However, if we are going to embark on a transformation of the way the *consumers'* voices are represented, it is vital to examine the techniques, issues and rules for collecting the data on which our interpretations are based, as well as having frameworks for interpreting that data. Therefore we discuss the development of an interrogative framework (Figure 7.1) from feminist perspectives on research practices (derived from Fonow and Cook 1991) as a means of achieving our goals.

In Figure 7.1 we present the components that form the parameters of contemporary feminist practice (Fonow and Cook 1991). These are used as the foundation for our examination of epistemological and methodological issues in marketing and consumer behaviour research. Pursuing the anthropological motif, we follow Geertz, 'to muse on texts, narrative, description and interpretation' (cited in Rabinow 1986: 242) and take marketing and consumer researchers, through the medium of their academic texts, as our 'natives and informants' (Geertz in Rabinow 1986: 242). Therefore, we adopt the role of anthropologists, undertaking a critical, but productive feminist quasi-ethnography[4] using the feminists' descriptive categories, as shown in Figure 7.1, to examine the textual productions and communications of our fellow researchers in the field of consumer behaviour.

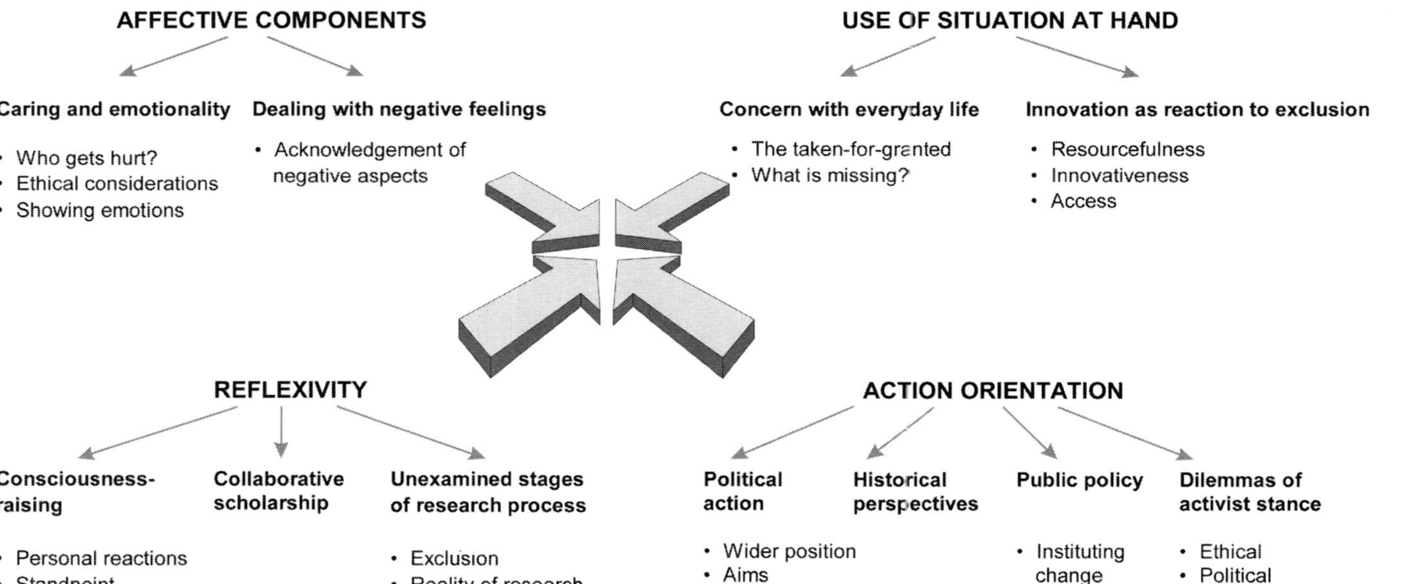

Figure 7.1 Components of feminist research
Source: adapted from Fonow and Cook 1991

FEMINIST RESEARCH PRACTICES

Feminist research practices are typified by a number of components (Fonow and Cook 1991). However, 'there is no one particular model of what feminist research should be like' (Maynard 1994a: 1). As such, the framework below should not be taken as a *fait accompli*, but only as our interpretation of the feminist literature.[5]

Reflexivity

Reflexivity requires researchers to be explicit about the process of the research *in its entirety*, and what influenced or informed the ends reached. It involves, first, reflection at the epistemological level of the research project; for example, what is studied and why, recognizing that 'all knowledge is produced from social and cultural relations' (Skeggs 1995: 2) and that researchers need to not only reflect on these relations but also 'examine critically . . . the *nature* of the research project' (Fonow and Cook 1991: 2 [emphasis added]). In addition, reflexivity should be overt in all stages of the research process from research design and data collection through to writing up and dissemination (Kelly, Regan and Burton 1994; Skeggs 1995: 2). Feminist research also emphasises interactivity and collaboration which should involve participants reflecting on their experience and evaluation of the different stages of the research process (Kelly, Regan and Burton 1994: 36). This should include joint interpretation (if possible) and consultation regarding dissemination of results, particularly where issues of a sensitive nature are under investigation. Moreover, reflexivity is concerned with avoiding 'hygienic research [which involves] censoring out . . . the mess, confusion and complexity of doing research' (Kelly, Regan and Burton 1994: 46) so that the reader is presented with a 'clean, crisp, neatly presented finished product' (Skeggs 1995: 2).

Action orientation

This involves a commitment to praxis, while recognising the dilemmas this brings to the dialectic between the researcher and the researched. Feminist research argues for an 'activist stance' because 'the aim of feminist research is liberation' (Fonow and Cook 1991) concerned with 'facilitating social change and empowering the participants' (Maynard 1994b: 17). Some researchers have called for action in the form of 'construct[ing] research which involves questioning dominant/oppressive discourses' (Kelly, Regan and Burton 1994: 39–40), thus encompassing the political process of challenging and transforming academia both within the specific discipline and as a part of the academy as a whole.

Use of the situation at hand

This reflects an opportunistic, innovative and creative use of research settings and projects demonstrating a concern for the 'taken-for-granteds' in research. For example, feminist researchers have had to be innovative in seizing research opportunities when faced with violence or exclusionary tactics (Fonow and Cook 1991:

11). This theme also highlights the benefits that can be gained from acceptance of non- or semi-formal research settings used overtly in the final research product. For example, researchers complain that the 'best' information is often gained when the interview is over or while the researchers are 'off duty'. Feminist researchers attempt to include these episodes overtly but with a close regard for ethics.

Attention to the affective components of the research act

This advocates the inclusion of the emotional responses to research into academic discourse as a way of achieving greater richness (Fonow and Cook 1991: 11). Feminist researchers have sought to restore the role of emotion in knowledge creation: as a source of reflection, as a method of consciousness-raising and as an object of study. Affective components used include emotion and feelings – negative and positive – involving 'caring and emotionality' (Fonow and Cook 1991: 9). These are linked to ethical concerns and reflection on: who gets hurt by the research, where the balance of benefit lies and how to avoid the researchers' potential abuse of their power (Skeggs 1998). It is important in feminist research practices that negative feelings are dealt with *explicitly* (e.g. Thompson in Reinharz 1992: 34).

INTERROGATIVE FRAMEWORK

From this review of the four major components of feminist research practice (Figure 7.1) we developed questions with which to interrogate the texts in our research field. These questions include: How does the literature reflect wider discourses (i.e., in whose interests does the research appear to have been carried out) and do the texts subsequently reinforce those discourses (Skeggs 1998)? Is there any acknowledgement of how the research has been funded? What issues and interests appear to have informed and influenced the researchers' ends, and are these made explicit (Fonow and Cook 1991)? Where does the power of interpretation lie – with the researchers and/or the respondents (Holland and Ramazanoglu 1994)? Do the authors acknowledge their own values? Is the relationship between the subjects and researchers explicitly discussed in terms of power imbalances? And are the implications of the balance of power on the research discussed?

A WORKED EXAMPLE

Fournier, S. (1998) 'Consumers and their brands: developing relationship theory in consumer research'

Susan Fournier's *Journal of Consumer Research* paper (1998) was chosen for the initial application of the interrogative framework developed from our review of the feminist literature (Bettany 1999; Long *et al.* 1999).[6] We chose Susan Fournier's article because it was one of the very, very few in the canon of work on relationship marketing that included the voice of the consumer. We also thought it was one of the best papers in its field. Fournier's article is also important because it has already been through a very rigorous double-blind review process for one of the major journals in the field; as such, it is a product of the epistemological 'machinery' in the field of marketing. This article therefore helps us to identify 'the voices of the epistemology makers' involved in 'processes of theory and knowledge production' (Code 1991: 155). In addition, Susan Fournier's paper received the accolade of a 'special commendation' in the Robert Ferber awards for the publication of the best *JCR* paper based on dissertation research; which means it carries additional authority because it has been re-reviewed independently by a different group of expert reviewers from the *JCR*.

Although our worked example (both in Long *et al.* 1999 and here) is based around Susan Fournier's article (1998), we recognise that our comments are equally applicable to many other articles which report qualitative data in consumer behaviour research. We would like to emphasise this point, in case it should seem that we have sought to make this particular paper a 'scapegoat'. This is quite the opposite of what we are trying to do here. We would like to reiterate that we chose Susan Fournier's paper for its research excellence. We also acknowledge that some issues, which we discuss below, can only be raised because of the inclusion of respondents/informants in Susan Fournier's article, and without her reports of the consumers' voices in her *tales from the field* (and her generous informal responses to our initial paper) our worked example would have been considerably less substantial. Thus, we do not seek to offer a critique *ad hominem* but would rather use this opportunity to open up a debate about some important issues that surround feminist research practices and the representation of the consumer's voice in our field.

Abstract of Susan Fournier's article

> Although the relationship metaphor dominates contemporary marketing thought and practice, surprisingly little empirical work has been conducted on relational phenomena in the consumer products domain, particularly at the level of the brand. In this article, the author: (1) argues for the validity of the relationship proposition in the consumer-brand context, including a debate as to the legitimacy of the brand as an active relationship partner and empirical support for the phenomenological significance of consumer-brand bonds; (2) provides a framework for characterizing and better understanding the types of relationships consumers form with brands; and (3) inducts from the data the concept of brand relationship quality, a diagnostic tool for conceptualizing and evaluating relationship strength. Three in-depth case studies inform this agenda, their interpretation guided by an integrative review of the literature on person-to-person relationships. Insights offered through application of inducted concepts to two relevant research domains – brand

> loyalty and brand personality – are advanced in closing. The exercise is intended to urge fellow researchers to refine, test, and augment the working hypotheses suggested herein and to progress toward these goals with confidence in the validity of the relationship premise at the level of consumers' lived experiences with their brands.
>
> (Fournier 1998: 343)

Analysis and interpretation

In this section we will work through the themes and issues outlined in the interrogative framework (Figure 7.1).

Questions of reflexivity (1): Epistemological issues – who counts and who knows?

For Fournier's study 'informants generated 112 brand stories for analysis' (1998: 361). The author describes how her analysis started with an 'impressionistic reading of the transcripts' (1998: 347) which was conducted by the researcher herself. Fournier states that 'member checks gauged the credibility of the author's interpretive claims against the views of those sharing their stories' (1998: 348). This seems at first sight to be in line with Baker's (1998) and Skeggs' (1998) comments about the agency of the respondent. However, our interpretation of this process would seem to be unfounded as the paper continues by explaining that: 'Three colleagues reviewed interview transcripts and interpretive summaries in a peer debriefing process [causing] reanalysis of the data towards the goals of mutual comfort, objectivity and recognisability' (1998: 348).

So in answer to our opening questions of 'who counts?' and 'who knows?', it would seem to be the researcher and her peers who 'count' and who 'know' because they are the ones who are used for evaluating the representation of the consumers here, and not the respondents themselves.

However, it is important to consider the counter argument that a postmodern perspective has possibly been adopted here. First, in postmodernism lived experiences are deconstructed within a field of competing discourses and vested interests. Unfortunately, if this is so, these interests – represented in the peer debriefing – remain unexamined and unexaminable. What seems to emerge from the article is that the experts' view prevailed and it is from their 'standpoint' that we have to read and understand how consumers view their relationships with brands. Second, the premises of feminist postmodernism also address the issue of indeterminacy and how 'differences have been repressed in texts'. In this study the author argues from a respondent pool of three. So how were Jean, Vicki and Karen selected? The answer is 'purposively . . . to maximise chances of uncovering insight' (1998: 347), and the subsequent interpretation suggests that the three women can be classified into 'brand relationship styles or patterns as either traditional (Jean), postmodern (Vicki) or transitional (Karen)' (1998: 360).

Questions of reflexivity (2): To what extent does the author reflect on the nature of the project?

At various points the research is framed as addressing 'the limited work that currently exists' (1998: 343) in a way that is 'managerially useful' and 'for the advancement of marketing theory' (1998: 365). The debt is clearly acknowledged to the 'three women who shared their stories' (1998: 343, footnote). However there is no indication that the three women have been involved in an activity that is 'consciousness-raising' or that they have benefited in any way from the research other than by receiving 'specially tailored gifts valued at $100 in exchange for . . . a total of 12–15 hours of home interview' (1998: 347). If marketing is about exchange then we might ask about the balance of power in this particular set of transactions and what effects, if any, such payments might have had on the respondents.

Questions of reflexivity (3): To what extent can the paper be described as being a piece of 'hygienic research'?

Have the 12–15 hours of interviews 'degenerated' into the 'crisp finished product'? (Skeggs 1995). This paper contains several passages that appear to be transcriptions of parts of interviews. However, these quotes have been tidied up since they do not resemble 'real talk' with its associated pauses, stutters and fillers. Stern (1998) has also criticised authors on this count and notes that 'non-verbal accompaniments (smiles, sighs, vocal tone) may or may not be included'. Standing (1998) recounts the dilemma she faced when deciding whether or not to represent the respondents' words as they were spoken.

Other aspects of the paper show extensive editing – for example, the analysis of Vicki. Here, the author consistently refers to Vicki's professed loyalty to Crest toothpaste. Vicki's allegiance is stressed in several quotes and comments, yet the very last quote provided by Vicki is, 'Oh did I tell you I am into this new toothpaste? Mentadent . . .' (1998: 359). This sudden 'reversal' is explained by the comment that 'Vicki is loyal to the process of loyalty itself' (1998: 359). Vicki's own reaction to this comment isn't recorded.

The author explains how 'coding schemes were modified as analysis progressed and new concepts were uncovered' (1998: 347). How this changed the work or the findings isn't indicated other than in the comment 'the ties the author has drawn between the informants and their brand-scapes are tidy ones' (1998: 361).

Action orientation

There is no overt activist stance taken in this paper.

Use of the situation at hand

In terms of the third theme, *using the situation at hand*, there is little evidence of opportunistic use of the research setting.

Attention to affective components (1): a commitment to ethical research?

The issue of research ethics is important, as the researcher is 'free to leave the field at any time and is generally the final author' (Stacey 1988: 21–7). To what extent is the author implicated in a process of the researcher as 'voyeur' (Skeggs 1998) or 'research tourism'? One measure of distance between the researched and the researcher can be found in the degree to which the researcher adopts a judgmental stance. Are the three respondents in this paper allowed to speak for themselves? The answer to this question would seem to be 'no'. Here are some edited descriptions of the three respondents. These extracts are chosen from the paper particularly to illustrate evaluative comments. We acknowledge that these quotes are selective, but nevertheless we feel that they reflect on the issue under discussion.

Karen is described as having 'transitional brand relationship styles' (1998: 360); and she is seen as being 'narrowly focussed on the present' (1998: 354) and 'not knowing what she wants to become' (1998: 352). Karen's 'brand relationship portfolios' are later described as 'largely superficial' (1998: 360) resulting from her being part of a group of women that can be typified by 'abandonment of tradition and community [which] may also cultivate an empty sense of self . . . and "a pathological absence of intimacy, emblematic of a contemporary failure to relate" (Alper 1996)' (1998: 360).

Jean is described as having 'traditional brand relationship styles' (1998: 360) and she is seen as an 'expert consumer' (1998: 352) who 'remains true to the cleaning products that support her performance' (1998: 351); and her use of the 'best brands provide evidence that Jean has made it' (1998: 351). Jean's words are interpreted thus: '"Falling in love" with brands that can provide perceived self efficacy and self esteem (Aron, Paris and Aron (1995)) allows Jean to move towards the resolution of her feelings of marginality and the expression of autonomy in her life world' (1998: 359).

Vicki is described as having 'postmodern brand relationship styles' (1998: 360) and she is seen as 'a master of advertising slogans. She is especially adept at constructing and announcing identities through brand symbols' (1998: 357) although 'she swears loyalty to the brands she holds most central, even when caught occasionally "fooling around"' (1998: 358). It seems from the author's perspective that 'Although Vicki's life story forces appreciation of her personal commitment to the fundamental notions of loyalty and faithfulness, Vicki denies herself exclusivity and longevity in her brand loyalty expressions' (1998: 360).

In her interpretation the author appears to approve of two of her respondents whilst disapproving of the other. Karen seems to be seen as an *other* who is tainted by her lack of 'loyalty and faithfulness'.

The use and interpretation of the respondents' words and the way that their 'voice' is represented suggests the type of power imbalances and 'voyeurism' that feminist research warns against.

Attention to affective components (2): the agency of the respondent and the power relations of the research relationship

With reference to the fourth theme, agency and power relations, some insights into this issue are suggested by the description of the research in terms of a rhetoric of control and of collaboration. The researcher, for example, 'instructed informants to tell the story . . .' (1998: 347). Although later 'the remaining course of the interview was set by the informants' (1998: 347).

The paper is not entirely clear about the extent to which respondents participated in their representations. What is clear is that three colleagues were used jointly to validate the representation of the interviewees' words.

It is interesting that the three women were used as exemplars before an attempt was made to generate models and theory. The research analysis and interpretation are not presented as concurrent with the research data collection and interviews. The implied time sequence is one of data collection followed by analysis. The story of the researched is followed by the story of the researcher. The dialogue between the researcher and the respondents is difficult to elicit from what is presented here. It is also difficult to estimate the extent to which the relationships described have been co-created. The only direct reference to collaborative construction of theory comes in the preliminary acknowledgement, which is made to fellow academics: 'Special thanks to the author's thesis committee, to David Mick, to the JCR reviewers and the editors who helped shape the manuscript' (1998: 343 footnote).

Concluding commentary

Looking at this analysis what conclusions can be drawn? This article (Fournier 1998) represents one of the few attempts to include consumers' voices in a study of relationship marketing. For that, her work is important. Nevertheless, perhaps because of the *JCR* reviewers and editors who shaped the paper (Fournier 1998: 343 footnote), the methodology adopted, whilst phenomenological in intent, is still firmly controlled by the researchers, whose ends predominate. The control of the representation of the 'voices' lies clearly with the author and the reviewers; the makers of epistemology in the field of consumer research can be clearly identified within the mainstream of the academy. In contrast, although the voices of the consumers are not entirely excluded – their representation is shaped by authorial control; and their impact on the discourses in the field is necessarily restricted.

DISCUSSION[7]

Developing a dialogue – giving 'others' a voice

As feminist ethnographers we are aware that ethnography is '. . . a writing practice in which *the other* is inscribed within and explained by, the power of the ethnographer' (Grossberg 1989: 23 [emphasis added]). Therefore, as a reflection of our own power as ethnographers and 'epistemology makers' (Code 1991: 155), we reiterate our commitment to include the voices of those with whom we engage in the spirit of true co-construction of meaning. This follows Arnould's (1998: 89) contention that 'ethnographies . . . issue from a dialogue, argument and confrontation between strategies of representation and the local voices of informants'. We also recognise the importance for feminist-inspired research to pursue reciprocity, accountability and equality – and this section is about that endeavour.

To this end in this section we pursue reflexivity by introducing a variation on a dialogic strategy (Bettany 2000). This is predicated upon the notion of 'selves in relation' (Ruddick 1989: 211), which aims to understand individuals as situated within a social (or professional) context, rather than as individuals 'context-free'. Within feminist scholarship examples of this method are manifold (e.g. Hallam and Marshment 1995; Hamer 1999) and reflect the dynamic nature of epistemological, philosophical and methodological debates in that field. Here we try to initiate the beginnings of a dialogue. We discuss some general issues which have been raised in response to the various drafts of our chapter via the processes of informal and formal peer review. In this attempt at a 'research conversation' we try and map out the research journey in a way which allows 'all voices and perspectives' to be 'listened to, maintained and respected' (Mauthner and Doucet 1998: 140).

The balance of power: interpretation and use of qualitative data

One issue which emerged in the reviews revolved around how data is dealt with in qualitative studies – most notably the power relations involved in the interpretation of data. We posed the questions above: 'who counts?' and 'who knows?' We argued that it is clearly the researcher and institutional peers who 'count' and 'know' because they are the ones who are used for evaluation and interpretation (indeed, 'validation') of the representations of the respondents. It seemed that the 'expert's view' prevailed.

In response to this, one reviewer responded that the issues which we had raised – about doing research which is informed by feminist thinking – are found across the field of marketing and consumer research and are not specific to one paper, and that this needed to be made explicit and clear. Another reviewer commented that academic journals themselves encourage authors to use triangulation and external peer reading in pursuit of increasing the academic standing of the analysis and interpretation of the data. A third point was that data predominates and peer reviews are used in order to support the interpretation of the material (and not to direct it). From this viewpoint researchers are essentially interpreters of the data, but all the interpretations have to be grounded in the data (and the role of peer review is to check that this has happened).

We accept fully that this is the case and academic norms dictate practice. However, we would note that in recent feminist practice it has become imperative to encourage the agency of the respondents with regard to the interpretation process.[8] Beverly Skeggs (1995: 7–8) argues for returning with tapes of interviews to her respondents, not only to clarify meanings but also to help expose the inherent research power balance. This close contextuality is thought preferable to triangulation with individuals who have never been part of the research conversation. Feminist researchers aver that the process of reaching conclusions is 'political, contested and unstable' (Maynard 1994a: 7) and have heavily criticised research that assumes that the values of the researcher do not affect interpretation and data co-construction within the research context. To address this issue feminist researchers strive for 'strong objectivity' (Harding 1987, 1991), that is, the overt inclusion of the researchers' own positionality and values within the disseminated findings, as well as that of all participants. It would seem that we need to call for 'consciousness-raising' amongst editorial boards (and academic reviewers) of the eminent journals in our field if these issues are to be addressed in our part of the academy.

The balance of power: what to include and what to excise

Another issue which emerged from the reviews revolved around the choices researchers have to make when presenting their data in an article. We had argued, using Fournier's paper as a worked example, that only a proportion of the data can be presented in the context of an academic publication. We felt that this leads to what feminist researchers have described as 'hygienic research' which excludes the messiness of the research process and the data from the finished product (Stanley and Wise 1993: 266; Kelly, Regan and Burton 1994: 46; Skeggs 1995: 2).

In response to this, our reviewers noted that it is the conventions of the academic journals in our field that determine how knowledge is created via the choices which are made on the presentation of data – thus to direct this critique at one paper alone was unfair. Current academic practices in our field largely require careful editing of transcripts to remove the 'messiness' (e.g. hesitations, interjections) – and it remains a careful analytic judgement which necessarily rests with the authors (and reviewers) of a paper.

We accept that 'language as it is spoken is impossible to produce on the written page' (Standing 1998: 190), imbued as it is with 'laughter, slang, pauses and idioms'. However, when presented in a 'neutralised' fashion much of its rich contextuality and thus its meaning is lost. This dichotomy is further exacerbated by the power/knowledge inequalities that surface when decisions are made over how radically respondents' words are homogenised (cf. Skeggs 1997). Feminist researchers are generally reluctant to reify the register of academia by putting words into their respondents' mouths and have started to criticise the 'tendency . . . to simplify the complex processes of representing the voices of research respondents' (Mauthner and Doucet 1998: 124). This centres on the 'fantasy that it is possible to have unmediated direct knowledge' (James and Prout 1990 cited in Marks 1996: 115). For example, a particular event or experience may lead to 'ambivalent, contradictory and changing' accounts (Marks 1996: 115). This highlights the difficulties we face as researchers when we seek to 'penetrate the manifest content in order to reveal its hidden kernel' (ibid.) by placing words on a page. As a way out of this dilemma some researchers have called for a challenge to the academic 'meta language . . . writing in ways that are accessible to those outside the university setting' (Standing 1998: 200).

FUTURE DIRECTIONS – THE WAY FORWARD: A CAUTIONARY TRAIL

The editors of this volume warned against the use of marketing feminism as a sterile critique of current practice, and asked for feminist marketers to find a 'way out' or a 'way forward' (Catterall, Maclaran and Stevens 1999). In doing so, they posed three key questions about the future of feminism within our discipline:

1 How might feminist theory and thought enrich and inform marketing theory and research in the coming decades?
2 How might a feminist inspired marketing be the same as or different from what we have currently?
3 How might we reach, or achieve, a feminist informed marketing theory and practice?

In answer to these questions we have proposed (and given a worked example of) an interrogative framework. We have also attempted to include – if only indirectly and in a rudimentary way – the voice of our 'native' and 'informant', Susan Fournier.

The crux of all our reviewers' comments was the importance of achieving reciprocity, accountability and equality in order to fulfil the ideals of feminist scholarship we had outlined in our own paper. Through dialogue among the authors and reviewers we hope we have provided a rich weave which hints at (even if it cannot detail) the flow of point and counterpoint in our own 'research conversation'. This has demonstrated an auditing of the research processes in consumer behaviour from a feminist perspective in a proactive and transformatory manner and illustrates our own search for reflexivity. This remains essentially work in progress. That is our initial 'way out': examining research practices in consumer behaviour through textual interrogation. These interrogations do not constitute a sterile, apolitical academic exercise, but provide a research protocol to illustrate how 'a feminist inspired marketing' could be 'different from what we have currently', and provide guidelines for 'a feminist informed marketing . . . practice' (Catterall, Maclaran and Stevens 2000). In doing so, we seek to enrich marketing research in the coming decades.

As our chapter has shown, what we have 'borrowed' from feminist research is a set of debates that are longstanding, lively and dynamic. These debates are crucial to the health of feminist research practices and scholarship. In introducing our framework as a possible means of shifting the discourse, we remain acutely aware of the dangers such a reduction of these debates to a single framework can pose. Although we stand by its usefulness, the framework is not intended to be dry or deterministic. Rather, we have identified that each component represents a current debate within contemporary feminist thought. As such, our 'way forward' is the intention to open up some of these debates for discussion within the marketing arena to interested parties. As has been illustrated here, within our worked example, methodological and epistemological debates are far more useful when extrapolated beyond a simple question format into a 'live' discussion. Therefore, to enrich the dialogue amongst those within our 'discourse community', we suggest 'returning to the framework' to provide a 'way out' from and a 'way in' to some of these debates.

POSTSCRIPT

We would close by reiterating our opening concern with *altering the nature of the conversation* in Feminist Marketing (Capital F, Capital M) by exploring 'who talks' and 'who listens'. With regard for this concern we have developed an interrogative framework based around four major components of feminist research practice (Figure 7.1) which we offer to our fellow researchers and scholars as a tool (or research protocol) for auditing research practices in marketing, particularly in order to identify 'who talks'. In this chapter we have also tried to offer an example and discussion of feminist research in practice. We believe this is probably the first example within the marketing arena, and represents an attempt to change how the audience in our discourse community 'listens' to research findings. In effect, we are changing the research conversation, *shifting the discourses* to allow others both to *speak* and *listen.* Doing so has not been easy. In trying to tread a dialogic path we have encountered unanticipated issues. This has been a dynamic journey in which our directions have changed to accommodate the concerns of all the parties involved: authors, respondents and editors. Throughout our journey we have tried to adopt a reflexive stance to ensure a fair representation of all of the parties to the project. The process of checking and modification has at times been a frustrating one. Ultimately, whilst in marketing there is no clearly established path to follow a full dialogic strategy, we hope that our own efforts have been sufficiently groundbreaking to encourage other researchers to make further attempts to introduce this and other feminist-inspired research practices into our own field of study. And by doing so, put the consumer's voice centre stage in the study of marketing.

NOTES

1 *Acknowledgement:* Although there are three authors cited here, this chapter would not have been possible without the generosity of Professor Susan Fournier of Harvard

Business School, both in her original article (1998) and in her subsequent willingness to engage in an informal dialogue with the authors as part of a process of informal peer review of earlier drafts of this chapter. We present some of the issues and concerns raised by Professor Fournier at greater length in the Discussion section of this chapter (alongside some issues raised by anonymous reviewers of earlier versions of this paper). This represents an attempt to 'give voice' to the researched in this chapter, without breaching the ethics of confidentiality involved in personal correspondence. However, please note that the responsibility for all the views, analyses and interpretations presented in this chapter lies entirely with the authors, as they retained the 'final editorial cut' and thus inevitably shaped the 'research conversation' as it is presented here by their authorial decisions.

2 We follow Strathern (1985: 8) in avoiding any direct challenge to or discussion of paradigms here, and rather refer to 'discourse communities' (Ellerby and Waxman 1997: 204).

3 Contemporary feminist research is concerned not only with *how the knowledge is produced* but *how the research is produced* (Ellerby and Waxman 1997) [emphases added].

4 'Quasi' because unlike most ethnographers we are unable to leave the field at any time.

5 We acknowledge the contribution of Penelope Eccles (1999) to the development of our thinking in this section and the refinement of Figure 7.1.

6 As a recognition that our work is embedded in the discourse community within which it was produced and to reiterate the value of multiple interpretations, interested readers may wish to access our original CMS conference paper (http://www.waikato.ac.nz/ejrot/cmsconference). In addition, by reading the original Susan Fournier (1998) paper there is the opportunity to make your own interpretations. In the spirit of academic engagement we would welcome and appreciate comments/views/opinions.

7 In developing this section of the chapter we would like to thank three anonymous reviewers who offered us comments on a previous version, including their encouragement to us to pursue 'reciprocity, accountability and equality' in developing the work. We would stress, however, that the entire and sole responsibility for all the views expressed here rests with us.

8 Following these feminist research practices we can at least be aware of the dangers of 'stealing the words out of women's mouths' (Reay 1996).

REFERENCES

Arnould, E. J. (1998) 'Daring consumer oriented ethnography', in B. B. Stern (ed.) *Representing Consumers*, London: Routledge, 85–126.

Baker, P. (1998) 'Hearing and writing women's voices', *Resources for Feminist Research/Documentation sur la recherche feministe* 26, 1 and 2: 31–49.

Bettany, S. M. M. (1999) 'Subversive readings of the consumer as other: construction of an interdisciplinary in(terror)gative framework to challenge contemporary relationship marketing discourse', unpublished dissertation, University of Lancaster.

—— (2000) 'Feminist theory and methodology in consumer research', working paper, University of Lancaster.

Bristor, J. and Fischer, E. (1993) 'Feminist thought: implications for consumer research', *Journal of Consumer Research* 19, March: 518–36.

Brown, S. (1998) *Postmodern Marketing Two: Telling Tales*, London: International Thompson Business Press.

Catterall, M., Maclaran, P. and Stevens, L. (1997) 'Marketing and feminism: a bibliography and suggestions for future research', *Marketing Intelligence and Planning* 15, 7: 369–76.

—— (1999) 'Marketing and feminism: past, present and future', First International Critical Management Studies Conference, UMIST, 14–16 July (http://www.mngt_waikato.ac.nz/Research/erjot/cmsconference/papers_mrktg.htm).

—— (2000) Personal correspondence.

Code, L. (1991) *Rhetorical Spaces: Essays on Gendered Locations*, London: Routledge.

Costa, J. A. (ed.) (1993) *Proceedings of the Second Conference on Gender, Marketing and Consumer Behavior*, Salt Lake City: University of Utah Printing Press.

Eccles, P. (1999) 'A feminist insight on relationship marketing texts: reading in subversive ways', unpublished dissertation, University of Lancaster.

Ellerby, J. and Waxman, B. (1997) 'Collaboration+feminism=new voices, new truths', *New Discourses Women's Studies* 26: 203–22.

Fonow, M. M. and Cook, J. A. (eds) (1991) *Beyond Methodology: Feminist Scholarship as Lived Research*, London: Taylor & Francis.

Fournier, S. (1998) 'Consumers and their brands: developing relationship theory in consumer research', *Journal of Consumer Research* 24, March: 343–73.

Grossberg, L. (1989) 'On the road with three ethnographers', *Journal of Communication Enquiry* 13, 2: 23–6.

Hallam, J. and Marshment, M. (1995) 'Questioning the ordinary woman: oranges are not the only fruit, text and viewer', in B. Skeggs (ed.) *Feminist Cultural Theory*, Manchester: Manchester University Press, 154–69.

Hamer, M. (1999) 'Listen to her voice: an interview with Carol Gilligan', *Women: A Cultural Review* 10, 2: 173–84.

Harding, S. (1987) (ed.) *Feminism and Methodology*, Bloomington: Indiana University Press.

—— (1991) *Whose Science? Whose Knowledge?*, Buckingham: Open University Press.

Hirschman, E. C. (1993) 'Ideology in consumer research, 1980 and 1990: a Marxist and feminist critique', *Journal of Consumer Research* 19, 4: 537–55.

Holland, J. and Ramazanoglu, C. (1994: 133) quoted in Reay, D. (1996) 'Insider perspectives or stealing the words out of women's mouths', *Feminist Review* 53, Summer: 67.

—— (1994) 'Power and interpretation in researching young women's sexuality', in J. Maynard and A. Purvis (eds) *Researching Women's Lives from a Feminist Perspective*, London: Taylor & Francis, 125–49.

James, A. and Prout, A. (1990) 'Re-presenting childhood: time and transition in the study of childhood', in A. James and A. Prout (eds) *Constructing and Re-constructing Childhood: Contemporary Issues in the Sociological Study of Childhood*, London: Falmer Press, 216–37.

Kelly, L., Regan, L. and Burton, S. (1994) 'Researching women's lives or studying women's oppression? Reflections on what constitutes feminist research', in M. Maynard and J. Purvis (eds) *Women's Lives from a Feminist Perspective*, London: Taylor & Francis, 27–49.

Long, G., Hogg, M., Bettany, S. and Eccles, P. (1999) 'Transforming relationship marketing via subversive readings', CMS Conference, UMIST, 14–16 July (http://www.waikato.ac.nz/ejrot/cmsconference).

Marks, D. (1996) 'Constructing a narrative, moral discourse and young people's experience of exclusion', in E. Burman, G. Aitken, P. Alldred, R. Allwood, T. Billington, B. Goldberg, A. J. Gordo Lopez, C. Heenan, D. Marks and S. Warner (eds) *Psychology, Discourse, Practice: From Regulation to Resistance*, London: Taylor & Francis, 114–30.

Mauthner, N. and Doucet, A. (1998) 'Analysing maternal and domestic voices', in J. Ribbens and R. Edwards (eds) *Feminist Dilemmas in Qualitative Research*, London: Sage, 119–47.

Maynard, M. (1994a) 'Introduction', in M. Maynard and J. Purvis (eds) *Researching Women's Lives from a Feminist Perspective*, London: Taylor & Francis, 1–10.

—— (1994b) 'Methods, practice and epistemology: the debate about feminism and research', in M. Maynard and J. Purvis (eds) *Researching Women's Lives from a Feminist Perspective*, London: Taylor & Francis, 11–26.

Rabinow, P. (1986) 'Representations are social facts: modernity and post-modernity in anthropology', in J. Clifford and G. E. Marcus (eds) *Writing Culture: The Poetics and Politics of Ethnography*, Berkeley: University of California Press, 234–61.

Reay, D. (1996) 'Insider perspectives or stealing the words out of women's mouths: interpretation in the research process', *Feminist Review* 53, Summer: 57–73.

Reinharz, S. (1992) *Feminist Methods in Social Research*, New York: Oxford University Press.

Ruddick, S. (1989) *Maternal Thinking: Towards a Politics of Peace*, Boston, MA: Beacon.

Skeggs, B. (1995) *Feminist Cultural Theory*, Manchester: Manchester University Press.

—— (1997) *Formations of Class and Gender*, London: Sage.

—— (1998) 'Introduction to feminist research', unpublished paper, University of Lancaster.

Stacey, J. (1988) 'Can there be a feminist ethnography?', *Women's Studies International Forum* 11, 1: 21–7.

Standing, K. (1998) 'Writing the voices of the less powerful: research on lone mothers', in J. Ribbens and R. Edwards (eds) *Feminist Dilemmas in Qualitative Research*, London: Sage, 186–203.

Stanley, L. and Wise, S. (1993) *Breaking Out Again*, London: Routledge.

Stern, B. B. (ed.) (1998) *Representing Consumers: Voices, Views and Visions*, London: Routledge.

Strathern, M. (1985) 'Dislodging a world view: challenge and counter-challenge in the relationship between feminism and anthropology', *Australian Feminist Studies*, December: 1–25.

—— (1987) 'An awkward situation: the case of feminism and anthropology', *Signs: Journal of Women in Culture and Society* 12, 2: 276–92.

Van Maanen, J. (1988) *Tales of the Field: On Writing Ethnography*, Chicago: University of Chicago Press.

8 The laugh of the marketing Medusa: men are from Marx, women are from Veblen

Stephen Brown

Behind every great man, so they say, is a great . . . carbuncle. In Karl Marx's case, at least. As his most recent biographer makes clear (Wheen 1999), the carbuncle on the backside of capitalism suffered from painful pustules on his own protuberant posterior. So bad was this plague of suppurating boils that the revolutionary's revolutionary often found himself unable to sit down, which was a bit of a bummer in the British Library Reading Room, as you can well imagine. On doctor's orders, indeed, he once repaired to his boudoir for three weeks' rest, recuperation and (temporary) renunciation of revolutionary thoughts. Marx, in short, wasn't so much a red under the bed as a red on top of the bed, writhing in agony for good measure. God is a capitalist, after all.

The rash on Marx's rump may seem like a trivial matter, but history hinges on such ostensible inconsequentialities (see Diski 1999; Durschmied 1999; Ferguson 1998). Martin Luther, we are reliably informed, owed his Roman Catholic-hating cantankerousness to occasional outbreaks of chronic flatulence. Charles Darwin suffered from a severe case of Delhi Belly and, presumably, spent long hours in the smallest room pondering the origin of faeces. When it comes to Hitler's famous missing testicle, furthermore, what can one say except that he went to extraordinary geo-political lengths in order to find it. True, it seems excessive to blame the Russian Revolution, the Stalinist purges and Mao Tse-tung's Long March on the state of Karl's ass. Nevertheless, it is chastening to think that for want of a tube of Savlon, the Romanovs could still be holding court in the Winter Palace, *The Battleship Potemkin* would never have been made (where, indeed, would Hollywood be without all those sub-Eisensteinian steps sequences?) and McDonald's might well have opened a branch in Red Square at least fifteen years before they did. That's history for you.

While few would deny that carbuncles can change the course of history, many might wonder about the continuing relevance of Karl's carbuncles, monumental though they were. Ten years ago, the dramatic fall of the Berlin Wall and the concomitant collapse of 'actually existing' communist regimes signalled the end of Marxism as a significant intellectual force, or so it seemed (Aronson 1995;

Berman 1999; Sakwa 1999). Granted, some left-leaning academicians tried to overlook the cerebral débâcle as a little local difficulty. The actually existing communist regimes were aberrations, after all, and Marxism could hardly be held responsible for their ignominious failure. Other academic apparatchiks effectively gave up the Marxian ghost and appeared content to bellow to each other over the pages of once radical journals, like disorientated dinosaurs in the immediate aftermath of the meteorite-precipitated Cretaceous extinction. And yet others, perhaps the majority, placed their faith in proletariat-free micro-politics – feminist, gay and post-colonial in particular. In fact, it is fair to say that feminism, more than any other post-communist constituency, has kept the red flag flying, albeit at half mast (see Beasley 1999; Ebert 1996; Tong 1989; Watkins, Rueda and Rodriguez 1992).

Without doubt, however, the most unexpected outcome of the Marxian implosion is its recent recuperation by the very forces of capitalism that it once opposed (Diski 1999; Harvey 1999; Wheen 1999). Dialectical materialism, admittedly, might lead us to expect some kind of synthesis between the thesis of crisis-stricken capitalism and the antithesis of heroically struggling communism (Bloomingdale's decision to sell shrink-wrapped bits of the Berlin Wall was surely a straw in the wind). But few expected it to be unfettered, unexpurgated, unreconstructed consumerism.[1] Fewer still would have suspected that the *New Yorker* – hardly a hotbed of communist insurgency – would describe Marx as the 'next big thinker' (Cassidy 1997). And fewer still that the captains of capitalism would eventually be doffing their caps to Karl Marx, of all people (see Harvey 1999). Some diehards doubtless consider the appropriation, commodification and recirculation of Marxism as the ultimate indignity, the final insult, the vanishing point of hero to zerodom. However, Highgate cemetery's finest would surely beg to differ. Carbuncles, as the great man almost said, may make history, but not under conditions of their own oozing.

Although Marx rarely troubled the marketing journals when his pronouncements were in their pomp – except when refracted through a feminist lens (e.g. Hirschman 1993; Stern 1993) – perhaps the time is right to re-examine his marketing qualifications. Not a lot of people know this, but in the fateful winter of 1852, four years after publishing *The Communist Manifesto*, the hirsute one set his sights on becoming a marketing man. Down on his uppers, with nary a pot to piss in, the penurious prophet seriously considered going into the cosmetics business, by acquiring the rights to a new and improved nail varnish! True, this gives a whole new meaning to his descriptions of capitalism red in tooth and claw and, as for Opium of the masses, it is evident that future diversification into fragrances was a definite possibility. Sadly, the champion of the proletariat never became the Coco Chanel of the mid-nineteenth century, communism's Calvin Klein, or even the Avon Lady of the Academy (which could do with a makeover, let's be honest). A back-hander from Friedrich I-bet-he-wears-Harmony-hairspray Engels was never far away and, apart from his subsequent attempt to become a railway clerk – the application was rejected on account of old boily bottom's illegible handwriting – Marx successfully avoided the life of 'trade' that stolid, middle-class, Victorian gentlemen such as himself so heartily despised.

The irony, of course, is that Marx would have made – and in many ways was – an excellent marketing man. From the attention-grabbing misdemeanours of his rambunctious youth to the shameless promotional stunts that surrounded the publication of *Capital* (he penned anonymous newspaper reviews of his masterpiece and 'persuaded' Engels to do likewise), there is more than a touch of P. T. Barnum about Karl Marx.[2] Like Barnum, he had a brilliant way with words and proved to be a self-advertising sloganiser par excellence. He shamelessly exploited the cupidity of the media, the curiosity of the public and the stupidity of his competitors to promote a brand of anti-capitalism that still enjoys a substantial market share more than 150 years after its launch. Marx, moreover, was a superb raconteur, blessed with boundless self-belief and, as many contemporaries observed, endowed with seemingly inexhaustible reserves of energy, just like his American alter ego. Both men, indeed, lived peripatetic lifestyles that vacillated between profligate affluence and abject penury; both were brow-beating bullies, incorrigible hypocrites and inveterate practical jokers, not to mention extremely dangerous opponents; and, both had their posthumous reputations sullied by rumours of illegitimate offspring. At the same time, both men had a wonderful way with children. By all accounts, Marx was a devoted father who concocted intricate bedtime stories for his daughters, whereas the magnificent showman successfully marketed himself as 'The Children's Friend' some sixty years before Walt Disney (Brown 2000).

Marx and Barnum, of course, were exact contemporaries, and these parallels may be more attributable to early Victorian mores, middle-class career paths and expectations concerning personal advancement than anything else. Nevertheless, it is wonderful to think that one of the titans of Western capitalism and one of its most trenchant critics should be working for the same newspaper, at the same time and in much the same capacity (both men served as foreign correspondents for Horace Greeley's *New York Tribune*). Even more remarkable, perhaps, is Karl Marx's connection to Victoria Woodhull, the P. T. Barnum of the women's movement. Now almost forgotten, thanks to her expurgation from the pantheon of such American feminist pioneers as Susan B. Anthony, Elizabeth Cady Stanton and Paulina Wright Davis, Woodhull was the joker in the suffragette pack, who ran for the US presidency in 1872, brought the campaign for women's rights into ruinous disrepute and, as if that weren't enough to be getting along with, was appointed President of the International Workingmen's Association by Karl my-carbuncles-are-killing-me Marx himself. She was also a marketing maestro, *sans sauci*.

As everyone knows, the roots of modern marketing can be traced back to the dawn of time, when the first stone axes were traded across enormous geographical distances and proto-urban civilisations developed at convenient places of proto-commercial exchange (Brown 1995). It is widely accepted, however, that the US patent medicine industry, with its branding, barking and boosterism, did much to engender the cures-all-known-ills, one-size-fits-all, buy-one-get-one-free marketing mindset and, moreover, helped stigmatise practising marketers as snake oil sellers, Fuller Brush pushers and Tupperware party animals. Whatever else she may have been, Victoria Woodhull was a snake oil seller in excelsis. From the age of 10 she was forced to work for her father's travelling medicine show, where she specialised in mind reading, mesmerism and making up batches of 'Miss Tennessee's Magic Life Elixir', an alcohol- and laudanum-laden pick-me-up that sold for the then premium price of $2 per bottle. Soothsaying, however, was Victoria's speciality and, after absconding from the family firm, fleeing her feckless first husband and failing to make ends meet as a 'showgirl' in San Francisco, she established herself as a leading light of the spiritualist movement that flourished in the immediate aftermath of the American Civil War (Gill 1998; Washington 1993; Winter 1998).

Indeed, such was Woodhull's ability to commune with the dear departed that she attracted the attention of Cornelius Vanderbilt, reputedly the richest man in America, who appointed her as his spiritual, financial and, ultimately, erogenous adviser. Many cynics, admittedly, maintained that the appointment had more to do with Victoria's exceptionally good looks and infinitely flexible morals than her credentials as a clairvoyant. But given the appalling oppression that American women endured in the mid-nineteenth century – no vote, no property rights, no legal standing, etc. – spiritualism was one of the few means by which women's voices could be heard and attended to. Vanderbilt, certainly, proved more than willing to attend to Victoria's otherworldly voices (and her rather more worldly vices). Invigorated, apparently, by her coital largesse, the ageing Croesus readily ministered to her pecuniary needs, managed her bulging investment portfolio and encouraged high-roller stockbrokers to patronise Woodhull's 'salon', where injudicious pillow talk was turned to insider dealing advantage.

Thus relieved of the tiresome task of earning an honest crust, and notwithstanding a string of impecunious husbands, Victoria Woodhull applied her not inconsiderable talents to promoting the women's movement. National celebrity, deep pockets, stage training, personal magnetism and a history of parental-cum-spousal abuse (she was starved by her father to inculcate the glazed expression expected of seers and she was repeatedly beaten by one of her husbands, the memorably monikered Colonel Blood) made Woodhull the perfect spokesperson for the faltering woman's movement, which had split over the issues of 'free love' and African-American emancipation.[3] Empowered, what is more, by her reputation as an especially gifted spiritualist, she managed to transcend the feminist faction fighting that then prevailed and almost single-handedly revitalised the National Woman Suffrage Association. Elizabeth Cady Stanton, no less, predicted that 'In the annals of emancipation the name Victoria Woodhull will have its own high place as a deliverer'. Susan B. Anthony described her as a 'bright, glorious, young and strong spirit'. And, Paulina Wright Davis presciently observed that 'you were raised up of God to do wonderful work and I believe you will unmask the hypocrisy of a class that none others dare touch' (see Goldsmith 1998: 3).

Woodhull's good works may well have been motivated by pecuniary gain and personal aggrandisement but her emancipatory achievements cannot be denied. She was the first woman to address the Judiciary Committee of the Joint Houses of Congress; she ran for the presidency, against Ulysses S. Grant and Horace Greeley, with the renowned African-American activist Frederick Douglass as a running mate; she established a newspaper, *Woodhull and Caflin's Weekly*, and used it to advance the cause of feminism in general and free love in particular; and, she founded a highly successful financial services brokerage, which specialised in investments for women and exploited her high public profile to brilliant promotional effect. As noted previously, moreover, she persuaded Karl Marx to place the fate of the International Workingmen's Association in her eminently capable hands. This appointment, it must be stressed, was not tokenism or some kind of recompense for Woodhull's decision to publish the first American edition of *The Communist Manifesto*. On the contrary, she actively campaigned against prominent department store owners, such as R. H. Macy and A. T. Stewart, who paid their employees less than a living wage; she aligned the NWSA with the American Labour Reform League, much to the former's chagrin; and she repeatedly took to the streets in support of the doomed Paris Communards, amongst many others.

There is no doubt that Woodhull was a great show(o)man, in the mould of P. T. Barnum, albeit the exhibitionist extraordinaire strongly disapproved of her exhibitionism (too close for comfort, presumably). She was larger than life at a time when larger than life was run-of-the-mill. She was a first-wave feminist icon, a *fin de siècle* firebrand, a forceful personality who problematised the pedestalisation of pretty women. Most importantly perhaps, she was a marketer through and through – a veritable Marketing Medusa – who robbed the robber barons, tricked the tricksters of Wall Street, met Victorian hypocrisy with hypocrisy *de luxe* and, in keeping with her feminised marketing credo, developed a range of intra-uterine contraceptive devices for the prostitute population of New York City. Her conspicuously extravagant lifestyle, what is more, suggests that she was an early convert to the cause of retail therapy. As Goldsmith observes about her 1870 'conquest' of American high society:

> The next weeks were filled with shopping sprees for Oriental rugs, oil paintings and Venetian glass chandeliers. The downstairs rooms were hung throughout with purple velvet. And everywhere there were mirrors, even on the ceiling of the mahogany-panelled library. In the main salon, incense burners hung from the gilded ceiling . . . [and] . . . featured a wondrous dome painted in the most exquisite colours, depicting the loves of Venus in delicate lines. Victoria's bedroom was lined in green velvet with a matching green velvet and gold fringed bedspread and gilt chairs, while [her sister's] bedroom was draped in deep purple velvet and lilac-patterned silk imported from France. The *Star* called their house a 'Modern Palace Beautiful'.
>
> (Goldsmith 1998: 209)

Yet, despite her astonishing achievements, this P. T. Barnum in petticoats is remembered, if at all, as a woman who suffered for suffrage but tarnished the Gilded Age and set the cause of feminism back several decades. In sum, the 'prostitute who ran for president'. Ironically, Woodhull's precipitous fall from grace commenced when she accepted the Marxian mantle and her robber baron backers became fearful of feminist-led working-class insurrection. Not long after, she was exposed by a muckraking newspaper as a former streetwalker who had used her ample physical endowments to make a fortune. Ever the battler, Victoria responded in kind by publishing details of the extra-marital affairs of America's pre-eminent pastor (and notorious philanderer), Henry Ward Beecher. A libel trial ensued; the forces of patriarchy prevailed in what was the Monica Lewinsky/O. J. Simpson/Heidi Fleischmann imbroglio of its time; and the disgraced Mrs Woodhull was consigned to non-personhood thereafter. Her subsequent attempt to stand for the presidency in 1892 was boycotted by the women's movement and she ended her days – believe it or not – as a semi-respectable member of the English aristocracy, whose antecedents were never mentioned in polite company (see Goldsmith 1998).

For all her faults, Victoria Woodhull was a feminist activist; she may have been a money-grubbing marketer at heart but she also campaigned ceaselessly for women's rights. She was a lion of the Lyceum circuit, established by James Redpath in 1868, and proselytised for the cause in packed auditoriums all over the country, where she propounded a progressivist model of female emancipation. In this regard, of course, she owed a considerable intellectual debt to her European mentor, Karl Marx. As every teenage rebel surely recalls, Marx posited a five-stage model of historical development in his famous 1859 preface for *A Contribution to the Critique of Political Economy* (Cohen 1979; Gottleib 1992; Singer 1980). Four of these stages, Asiatic, Ancient, Feudal and Modern Bourgeois, had previously come to pass, and the other, Socialism, was inevitable, since the modes, forces and relations of production were inherently unstable, the owners' extraction of workers' surplus labour ensured antagonistic class relations, and (all together now) guaranteed the eventual overthrow of the bourgeoisie by the proletariat. Or so he thought.

Interestingly, latter-day capitalists' recuperation of Karl Marx has not extended to his model of historical development. To be sure, the shortcomings of historical materialism are well known and frequently rehearsed. It is flagrantly teleological, hopelessly scientistic, irredeemably historicist and predicated on the West's favourite meta-narrative of perpetual progress. Most significantly perhaps, it has been disproved by subsequent events. Despite Engels' graveside oration and the 'actually existing' experiments in Eastern Europe and elsewhere, Marxian-style communism has signally failed to come to pass. Consumerism, on the other hand, has swept all before it. The proletariat, so it seems, haven't actually *overcome* the bourgeoisie, they have *become* the bourgeoisie. Retailienation rather than alienation is the order of the day. And fashion consciousness has taken over from false consciousness in the cartulary of radical chic. In fact, it is apparent in retrospect that focusing on modes of production, instead of modes of consumption, was historical materialism's fatal mistake (Ritzer 1999). While some thinkers have sought to introduce a consumer dimension to Marxism (e.g. Baudrillard 1998; Burrows and Marsh 1992; Fine and Leopold 1993), none has taken historical materialism as a starting-point and interpreted 'materialism' in terms of its late-twentieth-century meaning.[4]

In the belief that historicism repeats itself – the first time as tragedy, the second time as farce – and in light of both capitalism's appropriation of Marxism and Karl's hitherto unrecognised marketing credentials, it is incumbent upon the present generation of critically minded marketers to identify changing modes of consumption (albeit in an appropriately farcical manner). To be sure, the birth of consumer society has generated much academic discussion of late (e.g. Glennie 1995; McCracken 1988; Miller 1995) and, paraphrasing a tad, five modes of consumption can be tentatively hypothesised. Excepting the unattainable utopian states of Primitive Consumption and Advanced Consumption, we can distinguish between: *proto-modern consumption* of herding, hunting, gathering and subsistence agriculture; *premodern consumption* of barter, periodic markets and extended, if unreliable, trade routes; *modern consumption* of mass production, mass promotion and mass distribution to mass markets, or substantial segments thereof; *postmodern consumption* of globalisation, E-tailing and segment-of-one micro-marketing; and, if the latter-day marketing literature is anything to go by, *meta-modern consumption*, where there is nothing left to consume but consumption itself (Firat 1995; Firat and Dholakia 1998).

Obviously, such stage-type schemata are unacceptable in today's intellectual climate and, for those who can't digest rehashed historicism, Raymond Williams's conceptual garnish of *dominant*, *emergent* and *residual* modes of consumption is available at no extra cost (interlarded, on request, with the 'leaders' to 'laggards' innovation-diffusion typology). Be that as it may, our hypothesised modes of consumption are made up, as per Marx, of *forces of consumption* (department stores, credit cards, World Wide Web, etc.) and *relations of consumption* (buyer–seller, borrower–lender, customer–consumer). Forces of consumption are controlled, not by their owners or regulatory bodies, but by the consuming public at large, who extract surplus meaning from the goods and services of customer-orientated marketing organisations. According to this 'customer theory of value', surplus meaning derives from the difference between *exchange value*, the price consumers pay for the product or service, and *use value*, the social cachet that accompanies its ownership – that is to say, the 'use' to which it is put.[5] However, the intensely competitive nature of consumption, in so far as emulation breeds ubiquity, avoidance and innovation, inevitably precipitates periodic changes in the forces and relations of consumption, whereby marketers desperately attempt to hold on to fickle, fashion-conscious consumers by means of technological developments like loyalty schemes, just-in-time distribution and the cybersouk. A déclassé struggle ensues, but because marketers can't possibly keep up with red-in-tooth-and-claw consumers, where survival of the fitness-suite obtains, a crisis in consumption eventually transpires. This can be circumvented to some extent by the colonisation of space and time (theme restaurants, retro-marketing, etc.), but crisis is unavoidable, consumer orientation is abandoned and marketing is history. You read it here first.

Complete nonsense, some might say, but then so was Marx's original formulation. At approximately 250 words, moreover, Karl's much-vaunted conceptualisation is no longer than the above exercise in pseudo-historicist materialism (Marx 1978). Yet, regardless of its veracity or otherwise, perhaps the most striking thing about such an admittedly absurd inversion of Marxism is its striking similarity to the 'conspicuous' forms of consumption identified by one of the strangest ever incumbents of the scholarly asylum, Thorstein Veblen. Indeed, as academic eccentrics go, Veblen was much further gone than most (Diggins 1999; Hobson 1971; Jorgensen and Jorgensen 1998). By all accounts, he was a hapless lecturer who muttered monotonously for his country; a taciturn verging on incommunicado conversationalist; a less than dedicated follower of fashion whose personal hygiene left a lot to be desired; a campus Casanova so committed to gross moral turpitude that his amorous escapades cost him several prestigious academic appointments; an academic whose idea of pastoral duties involved making himself available from 10.00 to 10.05 every Monday morning and giving all class assignments a 'C', irrespective of their merits (when challenged by a disgruntled high achiever, he observed that 'my grades are like lightning, they can strike anywhere'); a national celebrity in the aftermath of the First World War who famously spurned the proffered presidency of the American Economic Association and when collared by an over-enthusiastic admirer who inquired what the preface of his book was about, promptly replied, 'About four and a half pages, I guess'; and, not least, the coiner of the phrase 'conspicuous consumption' whose own consumption behaviour was inconspicuous to the point of invisibility (he lived in a remote cabin in California, surrounded by boxes of unpacked books and tottering piles of dirty dishes, which were lightly sprayed with the garden hose when a clean-up was unavoidable). Compared to Thorstein, I'm sure you agree, Karl's bum boils were a mere bagatelle.

At the same time, Veblen's voluminous writings were brilliantly insightful, strikingly original and scathingly satirical. Although this ironist of the Progressive Era wrote eleven books and 150 scholarly articles, including a root-and-branch critique of Marx's theory of labour value, he is best remembered for his 1899 tour de force, *The Theory of the Leisure Class* (Veblen 1970). A bitingly sardonic dissection of the East Coast establishment, who flaunted their status by means of offensively ostentatious exhibitions of wealth – houses, yachts, artworks, furnishings, extravagant balls and parties, etc. – the book can still be read with profit. For Veblen, consumption, not production, is the essence of capitalism, and a combination of envy, emulation and evasion is its principal driving force. The roots of this para-primordial activity, he maintained, are found in potlatch, kula and the periodic seizure of property by marauding tribesmen. Nevertheless, it remains very much alive and well, and since the elite classes set behavioural standards for society as a whole, variants of conspicuous consumption are apparent in every social strata, down to and including the most indigent. Emulation, furthermore, unfailingly gives rise to fraud, chicanery, predation, self-aggrandisement and the tantalising obscenities of the marketing system. Against Marx, then, Veblen maintained that social revolution is unlikely to occur, since the labouring classes are envious of and aspire to the behavioural norms of the consuming elite. And, while his emulatory mechanism has since been heavily criticised (see Campbell 1987, 1995), few would deny that the so-called Bard of Savagery succeeded in capturing much of the character of contemporary consumer society. According to Ritzer (1999), indeed, conspicuous consumption is still readily apparent, alongside conspicuous leisure, conspicuous shopping and conspicuous inconspicuousness.

Don't ask!

Unlike Victoria Woodhull, Thorstein Veblen can hardly be described as sadly neglected.[6] Yet comparatively few people seem to be aware of his long-forgotten writings on feminism. The penultimate chapter of *The Theory of the Leisure Class* actually includes a discussion of the 'new woman' and, in the same year as his masterpiece, our friendly neighbourhood curmudgeon published a paper entitled 'The barbarian status of women'. In essence, Veblen argues that it is women – or, rather, the capture of women by invading nomadic hordes – that transforms traditional tribal societies from egalitarianism, ecumenism and approximate gender equality, into the competitive, status-conscious and patriarchal societies that typify the modern world. Women, in effect, represent the first recorded chattel, who primarily serve to enhance the reputation of their owner, the dominant male. Despite appearances to the contrary, furthermore, and the laudable endeavours of feminist activists, the situation hasn't really changed since primitive times. Along with expensive houses, show horses and liveried flunkeys, the 'new' woman comprises just another form of conspicuous consumption. Their barbarian status, Veblen contended, is evident in the fact that women are not permitted to undertake gainful employment or engage in menial tasks. Female fashions (bodices, bustles), patterns of behaviour (needlepoint, good works) and even physical appearance (petite, pretty) contrive to confirm their status as objects of display. The sole function of such trophy wives is to consume incessantly and thereby demonstrate the wealth, power and accomplishments of their heroic husband, the modern barbarian, Conan the Bostonian. These, remember, are the people who set behavioural standards for the rest of society and who are emulated, after a fashion, by the lower orders and aspirant middle classes. Women's oppression, Veblen concluded, is not only endemic and institutionalised but an archaic throwback that is unlikely to be overthrown by *enfranchisement* (as John Stuart Mill suggested), *employment* (as Marx and Engels maintained), *eroticism* (as Victoria Woodhull and the 'free love' movement intimated) or even *ensembles*, as the dress code and bicycling campaigners of the late nineteenth century optimistically anticipated (Wilson and Taylor 1989).

Despite his undoubted prescience, it is fair to say that Veblen's reflections have attracted very little attention from the woman's movement. This neglect may well be due to his reputation as an unreconstructed libertine, who treated his wives abominably. It may be related to the tone of his writings, in so far as irony is very easily misread. Like the supermodels who drape themselves over the latest motor cars in purported 'parodies' of the industry's chauvinistic heritage, the playfulness behind Veblen's 'barbarian status' remarks is sometimes difficult to discern. The debate, moreover, has moved on, in as much as his essentialist assumptions and belief in historical continuity are out of fashion in today's post-structuralist intellectual milieu, albeit historicism is making a comeback (Hamilton 1996). The most likely reason for Veblen's barbarian status, however, is that he failed to offer an actionable alternative and remained content to condemn, rather than change, the existing situation. Thorstein Veblen, as Diggins (1999) ruefully observes, hardly receives a passing mention in contemporary feminist studies. And none other than Theodor Adorno (1941: 396) rightly described him as 'one of the last significant philosophers who dares to take the women question seriously'. But by failing to suggest ways in which female oppression can be alleviated, Thorstein Veblen signally failed to secure his (rightful?) place as a feminist favourite.

Of course, it remains to be seen whether Veblen will be recuperated, like Karl Marx, or whether he will continue to languish in the historical footnote category, like Victoria Woodhull. Several tentative lessons, nevertheless, can be derived from the foregoing escapades of our feminised marketing triumvirate. These pertain to the three Ts of *topics*, *techniques* and *treatments*; or, if you are allergic to academic alliteration, to *subject matter*, *research methods* and *writing style*. The very fact that we are fascinated by subjects like Woodhull and consider Karl's carbuncles a topic worth chewing over, says much about the retro orientation of the late twentieth century. This preoccupation with times past has been variously attributed to the *fin de siècle* effect, the collective mid-life crises of the baby boom generation and our prevailing postmodern aesthetic, which is informed by a remake/remodel/rearrange mentality. Regardless of the causes, retro is readily apparent in marketing matters, in gender matters and in the interstices between the two. Marketing, as I have elsewhere intimated, is awash with retro products, retro services, retro promotions and retro reflections by angst-ridden academics (Brown 1999). The same is true of the gender agenda, where the publication of self-help guidebooks such as *The Rules* or *Men are from Mars*; the celebrity of contemporary stereotypes like *Ally McBeal* or *Brigit Jones*; the renaissance of former feminist hate-figures, be it Miss World or Barbie; and the recent ruminations of 'new wave' – well-nigh recidivist – activists like Susan Faludi (1999) or Natasha Walter (1998), clearly indicate that retro-feminism is very big business. Marketing, moreover, is manifestly implicated in these developments, all the way from the 'girl power' phenomenon to Martha Stewart, America's earth mother manqué. But what do our field's feminists have to say on such retro-marketing matters? Not a lot.

The second lesson of the above essay is methodological. Despite its surface discursiveness and apparent inability to get to the point, it is an example of the New Historicism (Brown, Hirschman and Maclaran 1999). Historicism, admittedly, is a dirty word for many marketing and consumer researchers. Forty-something years on from Popper's (1957) notorious philippic, *The Poverty of Historicism*, the term is still tarred with connotations of communism, fascism and the manipulation of historical facts for nefarious political purposes. Within the humanities, however, 'new' historicism is the research procedure *du jour*. According to M. H. Abrams (1993: 252), indeed, it 'has displaced deconstruction as the reigning form of avant-garde critical theory and practice'. Although there are many versions of the New Historicism (see Brannigan 1998; Hamilton 1996), they are all characterised by attempts to bring the past into the present; by a belief in the essential textuality of historical knowledge; by fondness for historical accidents, incongruous juxtapositions, speculative inversions, telling anecdotes and flights of historical fancy; by a discursive mode of discourse that eschews detailed textual analysis for broad narrative sweep; and, not least, by an aghast fascination with the machinations of the marketplace. New Historicist texts, for example, are littered with terms like 'exchange', 'negotiation', 'transaction', 'circulation' and marketing-suffused allusions generally. They are preoccupied, almost to the point of obsession, with the positioning of New Historicism in the intellectual agora. And Stephen Greenblatt, the movement's leading light and coiner of the terminology, has described New Historicism as nothing less than an intellectual branding exercise.

New Historicism, admittedly, may represent little more than another methodological arrow in the quiver of marketing scholarship, to be selected and fired at will. Nevertheless, its typically tangential tone, digressive drift, peripatetic prosody and seemingly superficial style have implications for the way in which marketing research is written. It is often said that feminine writing – *l'écriture féminine* – is different from the kind of writing that characterises the Western patriarchal tradition (Cixous 1975). Whereas masculine writing is rational, logical, hierarchical and linear, feminine writing is non-rational, anti-logical, contra-hierarchical and essentially circular (Warhol and Herndl 1997). This may well be the case in literary, cultural and women's studies, albeit even there the *écriture* debate has waged back and forth, but it is most definitely *not* the case in marketing and management studies. Notwithstanding the recent rapid rise of interpretive research, with its commitment to humanistic rather than scientific modes of expression, there is very little evidence of experimental writing – let alone *l'écriture féminine* – in the mainstream marketing journals. Unembellished, no-nonsense, straight-to-the-point prose remains the order of the academic day.[7]

Indeed, even in books such as this, it is noteworthy that masculine modes of writing predominate. If ever, surely, an opportunity existed for freedom of academic expression it is in *Marketing and Feminism*, a text written by, for and about feminists, not to mention edited by feminists as part of a series sympathetic to the feminist cause. The traditional escape clause of feminine writing – that it would never survive the review process – clearly doesn't apply in the present circumstances. What continues to apply, nevertheless, is the approval, the endorsement and the legitimising function of the andocentric marketing mainstream. Regrettably, feminist marketers are still required to be more scholarly, more rigorous, more well read than their masculine marketing counterparts. What, after all, could be worse than being dismissed by reviewers as un-academic, as irrational, as the proverbial madwomen in the marketing attic? While the publication of *Marketing and Feminism* is to be welcomed and represents a triumph of sorts, a lot of wrongs remain to be righted and indeed written about in a suitably feminine manner. Then and only then will Victoria Woodhull, the Marketing Medusa, have the long last laugh.

NOTES

1 In marketing, the term 'consumerism' is usually taken to mean consumer dissatisfaction with marketing offerings and any associated protests (Ralph Nader, the WTO riots in Seattle, etc.). Sociologists and other social scientists, by contrast, take 'consumerism' to pertain to today's consumption-orientated society. The latter interpretation is employed herein.

2 This statement, of course, begs the question of whether Barnum was a marketing man. I have elsewhere argued that Barnum is the Ur-marketer (Brown 1998) and, for the purposes of the present discussion, his marketing credentials will be taken as read.

3 The term 'free love' does not mean what those of you who remember the 1960s think it means! In the nineteenth century, 'free love' referred to women's freedom to have a relationship with, marry or indeed divorce, whomsoever they wished.

4 Materialism, in philosophy, alludes to things that are material or real – as opposed, that is, to Idealism – and Marx employed it in that sense. Today, of course, it is taken to refer to consumers' urge to buy or acquire goods and possessions (see Belk 1985). With regard, moreover, to consumption-based readings of Marx, the great man himself used the phrase 'means of consumption', as Ritzer (1999) explains. However, Ritzer's recent consumerist reinterpretation – which, in my defence, I only came across after writing the first draft of this chapter – still relies on the old exploited consumers, pesky marketing people cliché. He doesn't seem to realise that it is consumers who are doing the exploiting these days (actually, he notes this point on p. 75, but fails to make any theoretical capital from the observation).

5 Use value, for Marx, refers to the amount of physical labour that is embodied in a product and which is considerably less than the monetary value it is exchanged for (hence the surplus value that accrues to capitalists, the owners of the forces of production). Use value means something completely different in the present essay, insofar as it is consumers who expropriate products' surplus meaning.

6 As all of Veblen's papers were destroyed after his death, it is not known if he had any direct connection with Victoria Woodhull. Certainly he was in Chicago when she announced her decision, in the city's Auditorium Theatre on 5 May 1892, to run for the presidency. What's more, he was very interested in the women's movement at this stage of his career and, of course, Victoria was a veritable exemplar of 'conspicuous consumption', though she can hardly be described as a trophy wife. Still, it's nice to think that she had some kind of connection to Thorstein Veblen, the 'Victorian Firebrand' (Jorgensen and Jorgensen 1998).

7 It is striking, however, that Marx, Barnum, Woodhull and Veblen were all arrestingly brilliant literary stylists. There must be a lesson there somewhere!

REFERENCES

Abrams, M. H. (1993) 'New historicism', in M. H. Abrams, *A Glossary of Literary Terms*, Fort Worth, TX: Harcourt Brace, 248–55.

Adorno, T. (1941) 'Veblen's attack on culture', *Studies in Philosophy and Social Science* 9, 3: 389–413.

Aronson, R. (1995) *After Marxism*, New York: Guilford Press.

Baudrillard, J. (1998 [1970]) *The Consumer Society: Myths and Structures*, trans. C. Turner, London: Sage.
Beasley, C. (1999) *What is Feminism? An Introduction to Feminist Theory*, London: Sage.
Belk, R. W. (1985) 'Materialism: trait aspects of living in the material world', *Journal of Consumer Research* 12, 3: 265–80.
Berman, M. (1999) *Adventures in Marxism*, Oxford: Verso.
Brannigan, J. (1998) *New Historicism and Cultural Materialism*, Basingstoke: Macmillan.
Brown, S. (1995) *Postmodern Marketing*, London: Routledge.
—— (1998) 'The unbearable lightness of marketing: a neo-romantic, counter-revolutionary recapitulation', in S. Brown *et al.* (eds) *Romancing the Market*, London: Routledge, 255–77.
—— (1999) 'Retro-marketing: yesterday's tomorrows, today!', in S. Brown and A. Patterson (eds) *Proceedings of the Marketing Paradiso Conclave*, Belfast: University of Ulster, 312–28.
—— (2000) *Marketing: The Retro Revolution*, manuscript in preparation.
Brown, S., Hirschman, E. C. and Maclaran, P. (1999) 'Historizing consumption: the Scots-Irish in Ireland and America', unpublished manuscript.
Burrows, R. and Marsh, C. (1992) *Consumption and Class: Divisions and Change*, London: Macmillan.
Campbell, C. (1987) *The Romantic Ethic and the Spirit of Modern Consumerism*, Oxford: Blackwell.
—— (1995) 'The sociology of consumption', in D. Miller (ed.) *Acknowledging Consumption: A Review of New Studies*, London: Routledge, 96–126.
Cassidy, J. (1997) 'The return of Karl Marx', *New Yorker*, 20 October: 248–59.
Cixous, H. (1975) 'The laugh of the Medusa', reprinted in R. R. Warhol and D. P. Herndl (eds) *Feminisms: An Anthology of Literary Theory and Criticism*, Basingstoke: Macmillan, 347–62.
Cohen, G. A. (1979) *Karl Marx's Theory of History: A Defence*, Oxford: Oxford University Press.
Diggins, J. P. (1999) *Thorstein Veblen: Theorist of the Leisure Class*, Princeton, NJ: Princeton University Press.
Diski, J. (1999) 'A human being', *London Review of Books* 21, 23: 34–5.
Durschmied, E. (1999) *The Hinge Factor: How Chance and Stupidity have Changed History*, London: Hodder & Stoughton.
Ebert, T. L. (1996) *Ludic Feminism and After: Postmodernism, Desire and Labor in Late Capitalism*, Ann Arbor: University of Michigan Press.
Faludi, S. (1999) *Stiffed: The Betrayal of the Modern Man*, London: Chatto & Windus.
Ferguson, N. (1998) *Virtual History: Alternatives and Counterfactuals*, London: Papermac.
Fine, B. and Leopold, E. (1993) *The World of Consumption*, London: Routledge.
Firat, A. F. (1995), 'Consumer culture or culture consumed?', in J. A. Costa and G. J. Bamossy (eds) *Marketing in a Multicultural World: Ethnicity, Nationalism and Cultural Identity*, Thousand Oaks, CA: Sage, 105–25.
Firat, A. F. and Dholakia, N. (1998) *Consuming People: From Political Economy to Theaters of Consumption*, London: Routledge.
Gill, G. (1998) *Mary Baker Eddy*, Reading, MA: Perseus Books.
Glennie, P. (1995) 'Consumption within historical studies', in D. Miller (ed.) *Acknowledging Consumption: A Review of New Studies*, London: Routledge, 164–203.
Goldsmith, B. (1998) *Other Powers: The Age of Suffrage, Spiritualism, and the Scandalous Victoria Woodhull*, London: Granta.
Gottlieb, R. S. (1992) *Marxism, 1844–1990: Origins, Betrayal, Rebirth*, New York: Routledge.
Hamilton, P. (1996) *Historicism*, London: Routledge.

Harvey, D. (1999) 'Introduction to the Verso edition', in D. Harvey, *The Limits to Capital*, 2nd edn, London: Verso, xiii–xxviii.

Hirschman, E. C. (1993) 'Ideology in consumer research, 1980 and 1990: a Marxist and feminist critique', *Journal of Consumer Research* 19, March: 537–55.

Hobson, J. A. (1971) *Veblen*, New York: Augustus M. Kelley.

Jorgensen, E. W. and Jorgensen, H. I. (1998) *Thorstein Veblen: Victorian Firebrand*, Armonk, NY: M. E. Sharpe.

McCracken, G. (1988) *Culture and Consumption*, Bloomington: Indiana University Press.

Marx, K. (1978 [1859]) 'Preface to *A Contribution to the Critique of Political Economy*', in R. C. Tucker (ed.) *The Marx–Engels Reader*, New York: Norton, 3–6.

Miller, D. (1995) 'Consumption as the vanguard of history: a polemic by way of an introduction', in D. Miller (ed.) *Acknowledging Consumption: A Review of New Studies*, London: Routledge, 1–57.

Popper, K. (1957) *The Poverty of Historicism*, London: Ark.

Ritzer, G. (1999) *Enchanting a Disenchanted World: Revolutionizing the Means of Consumption*, Thousand Oaks, CA: Pine Forge.

Sakwa, R. (1999) *Postcommunism*, Milton Keynes: Open University Press.

Singer, P. (1980) *Marx*, Oxford: Oxford University Press.

Stern, B. B. (1993) 'Feminist literary criticism and the deconstruction of ads: a postmodern view of advertising and consumer responses', *Journal of Consumer Research* 19, March: 556–66.

Tong, R. (1989) *Feminist Thought: A Comprehensive Introduction*, London: Routledge.

Veblen, T. (1970 [1899]) *The Theory of the Leisure Class: An Economic Study of Institutions*, London: Unwin Books.

Walter, N. (1998) *The New Feminism*, London: Virago.

Warhol, R. R. and Herndl, D. P. (1997) 'Body', in R. R. Warhol and D. P. Herndl (eds) *Feminisms: An Anthology of Literary Theory and Criticism*, Basingstoke: Macmillan, 343–6.

Washington, P. (1993) *Madame Blavatsky's Baboon: Theosophy and the Emergence of the Western Guru*, London: Secker & Warburg.

Watkins, S. A., Rueda, M. and Rodriguez, M. (1992) *Feminism for Beginners*, Cambridge: Icon.

Wheen, F. (1999) *Karl Marx*, London: Fourth Estate.

Wilson, E. and Taylor, L. (1989) 'Down with frou-frou: aesthetes, reformers and emancipated women, 1890–1920', in E. Wilson and L. Taylor, *Through the Looking Glass: A History of Dress from 1860 to the Present Day*, London: BBC Books, 43–73.

Winter, A. (1998) *Mesmerized: Powers of Mind in Victorian Britain*, Chicago: University of Chicago Press.

9 The cultural contexts of advertising to women consumers: the examples of Malaysia and Romania

Len Tiu Wright and Mihaela Kelemen

INTRODUCTION

Advertising is a potent force symbolised by the presence of 'globetrotting global brands'. Their images have been established by successful advertisements across the world's markets. The international advertising industry is a success story growing into a multi-billion dollar global industry at the dawn of the twenty-first century. In the year 2000 global advertising expenditure was estimated at US $339 billion compared to US $303 billion for 1999 (*Financial Times* 1999a), and further growth was projected. The industry has created countless images and phrases to sell millions of products around the globe, from remote villages to towns and cities.

The growth of the global advertising industry is being supported and revolutionised by the convergence and expansion of multimedia technologies, as in cable, satellite and other telecommunications advances and the computerised progress exhibited by, for example, the development of mobile phones, computers and Internet use. Moreover, the breakdown of communications barriers has led to the increasing domination of large media groups espousing Western social and cultural values (see for example, the Australian BSkyB Corporation) through satellite transmission and through companies, mostly American, which control the production and distribution of television, video, music and current affairs programmes. All these have helped to foster the image of the 'global village', a term to explain that individuals and communities suitably equipped with television and computerised facilities can both communicate and have access to international programmes and advertising without the restraints of national boundaries or geographical distances.

One consequence which can be seen within the increasingly competitive and sophisticated global environment is that not only have host governments and local firms become sensitive to the erosion of national controls, but so have local communities and individuals who are the main recipients of advertising. All these stakeholders, in the sense of being part of the community they operate in, become wary of the loss of indigenous cultural norms and ideals. As Czinkota and Ronkainen (1998: 65) have noted, 'if culture-specific adaptations are not made in the marketing approach the charge of "cultural imperialism" could be made against the international marketer'. Jeannet and Hennessey (1998: 509–10) have also pointed out that probably no other aspect of international marketing has had as much attention as global advertising, but that a major cause of 'global advertising mistakes' was the 'neglect of cultural attitudes of consumers in foreign countries'. The offence caused by Benetton's highly controversial and high profile advertising campaigns is a good illustration of how cultural differences influence the effect of global advertising.

It is recognised in this chapter that advertising is an important force in the global economy and that, while there are positive aspects to its growth and development, there has been scant attention paid in the literature to its effects on or appropriateness for non-Westernised markets such as the Far East and Eastern Europe. The focus of this chapter is to assess two such markets, Romania and Malaysia, and specifically to examine how global advertisers portray women and their needs. The Romanian and Malaysian markets are taken to illustrate the global nature of gender as conceptualised by the West, and some of the problems inherent in this when seen in the context of cultural differences. Conclusions are then drawn and recommendations made as to how global advertisers might improve their understanding and sensitivity to national cultures, with specific reference to how they advertise to women as consumers in other, less Westernised countries.

In this chapter we explore the imagery of womanhood as employed by local advertising campaigns in the Far East and Eastern Europe. More specifically, we argue that the local adaptation of advertising campaigns for global brands is simplistic, consisting of the use of local languages and indigenous actresses and role models. The style and imagery continue to bear close resemblance to those of similar advertising campaigns conducted in the West, and fail to take account of the social and cultural differences in these countries as they impact on women consumers.

Although economic explanations can be invoked regarding the simplicity of local adaptation of Western standardised advertising campaigns in Eastern Europe and the Far East, it is important to go beyond these economic considerations and look at the way in which such campaigns seek to organise the 'private' space of the home along a Western patriarchal model, and the implications this might have upon the role of women, not only as consumers but as rightful members of the society. In reviewing some of the economic rationale for the prevalence of Western advertising in the rest of the world, we remain wary of the fact that advertising is a powerful ritual which emphasises male domination and the subordination of women (Goffman 1976).

From an economic point of view, it is argued that there is a need for advertising campaigns to boost immediate sales along with the concomitant pressures to show large returns on capital investment and increases in production. Concentration on this has occupied greater attention than that of paying 'closer scrutiny to indigenous population concerns'. Delegation for such scrutiny is passed to others when specialised agency networks are employed to undertake advertising campaigns for the global brands of Western firms in overseas markets. Moreover, as organisations fight for market shares in mature and declining markets in the name of profit, they intensify their research and development for new products and new markets. These require significant levels of financial capital that lead to the diversion of extra resources from market research into local cultures, habits and traditions.

Second, global competition has led the world's large agency advertising networks to offer a wider range of services to their multinational clientele with a global reach. Diversification between markets and amongst the new media technologies has signalled changes in the way both the advertising and the research agencies fight to maintain their global presence. Such concerns have sustained orientations to standardisation in advertising. To remain up-to-date about modern-day mass communications, advertising agencies have created mergers or taken part in acquisitions to acquire expertise in the new information technologies in order to sustain their service offerings and global reach across both forms of conventional and new media. Moreover, economies of scale are achieved when a single agency can be used by a company to consolidate its purchasing power and its advertising campaigns, to streamline its decision-making and to grow its range of businesses on a global basis. In 1998 Pepsico had BBDO for its media buying world-wide, IBM used Ogilvy & Mather, Proctor & Gamble and Heinz employed the Leo Burnett agency (*Financial Times* 1999a).

Third, the vision of optimising the potential of global brands in an integrated co-ordinated way might prove to be a more difficult task given the introduction of commercial advertising beaming down from satellites to the world's TV and radio channels (*The Economist* 1998), rising media costs and media fragmentation. In Western markets consumers have more choices and control over what they want to watch with the new pay channels, but this is not the case for poorer sections of the population in the less well-off economies of the world who do not have ownership and for whom cinemas represent the usual form of screen accessibility.

Resources have also been diverted when advertisers, concerned that the era of micro-marketing has dawned, with consumers switching from channel to channel and supplier to supplier, give increasing or undue emphasis to direct marketing methods. By downloading information from web sites and their home televisions via advertisers' direct mail and telephone ordering, consumers are encouraged to 'buy' without leaving their homes. The transformation of this 'shopping landscape' is also eroding the conventional view of advertising, which posits that the function of advertising is to 'pull' in order to bring people into the shops where they could be served by sales staff who would then 'push' products for the consumers to buy.

Eastern markets are not similar to Western ones. Malaysia has maintained its diversity of ethnic mix and thus the tradition of outdoor eating at hawkers' stalls, patronage of restaurants and outdoor markets coexists with the sophistication of its large stores and hotels. Romania, emerging from the ravages of a communist regime, is still struggling to develop its economy and to raise the living standards of the working population to levels taken for granted in the West. Local cultures within the two countries, for example, are not normally used in global brand advertising.

The available research on gender roles in advertising and the different portrayal of men and women in advertisements on televisions have come from predominantly North American sources, while in Britain limited research has been conducted into gender stereotyping (for useful sources see Siu and Au 1997). The key idea here is that managers need to understand the forces of traditional cultural values and their impact on advertising (Siu and Au 1997). Since advertising in a sense reflects or mirrors society these authors contended that it should be reflective of a culture's gender-role norms. Interestingly, Siu and Au comment on the way in which the role of women is wholly defined by their relation to men, e.g. from the Confucian tradition and 'Book of Rites'which list three obediences for women: obey father before marriage, husband after marriage, and eldest son upon being a widow. In their study of television commercials from Singapore and China these authors found that they generally reflected stereotypical male and female roles, with women being inferior and dependent, e.g. as recipients of help, with men portrayed as givers of advice. The greater tolerance of nudity and erotic imagery in Western advertisements was also commented upon. This imbalance in television commercials reflects the imbalance of marketing in general, whereby there is a clear division between producers and consumers, a division with significant gender connotations, and one whereby men are positioned as central to the act of production while women are relegated to the private world of consumption, which is usually considered profane and marginal (Desmond 1997).

IMPROVING THE RELEVANCE OF MARKETING TO WOMEN AS CONSUMERS

We have chosen to take two examples of cultures from the East, Malaysia in the Far East and Romania in Eastern Europe, to observe the effects of global advertising emanating from the West for such fast-moving consumer goods as perfumes, toiletries and fashion. There are some similarities in the marketing environments of these two countries, which are dealt with in the later section entitled 'The workings of advertising in Malaysia and Romania'. It is relevant here to note Venkatesh's (1995) explanation as to why the cultural grouping rather than the individual should be used at the level of analysis. Consumer behaviour makes more intuitive sense at a collective level, since individuals are products of their cultures and their social groupings, being conditioned by and in turn conditioning their socio-cultural environments in numerous and unpredictable ways.

Thus, it becomes crucial for advertisers to pay close attention to the needs of their national markets and the make-up of the various target market groups, including the female market segment. From all the marketing communications methods – personal selling, sales promotions, publicity and public relations, direct mail, telemarketing, use of web sites, outdoor posters and sponsorship – advertising, especially on television and in film, represents a very important medium. These advertisers may, however, differ in their use of quantitative and qualitative techniques to measure customer responses. They may, for example, measure and forecast the shifts in sales or make use of focus groups to illustrate shifting changes in attitudes (Wright and Crimp 2000a). In Malaysia and Romania the development of these methods to measure women's responses or to assess women as a market segment are not as fully developed as in the USA and Western Europe. For media planning purposes in Western markets, for example, psychographic (lifestyle) and product-use classifications are translated into demographic terms, that is, how many female consumers would buy, what quantities they would require and how much they would spend.

A market segment is viable when it is accessible and in consumer markets the media channels create this accessibility. For example, if the product has a demonstrable benefit, advertising on television could be more effective than other promotional methods. However, advertising may colonise the home and actively organise the choices of women consumers. Television is a 'natural', for example, in demonstrating cooking appliances or 'glamorising' the use of beauty products and associated lifestyles by actresses and other well-known personalities. An organisation marketing baby food might well be particularly interested in reaching women aged 15–34 years through television advertising, but older women who have had babies and are experienced as mothers could also influence the decisions of younger women in the extended family context. Little has been written, however, in Western academic literature about 'maternal hierarchies' or the influence of older women on younger female members with regard to consumption and purchasing within, say, Malaysia and Romania.

Furthermore, in the field of consumer research, observations into the decision-making processes of family members via self-reports or self-designating scales by the male and female members tend to be unreliable since they do not reflect actual influence among family members (Lee and Marshall 1998). Using video-taped evidence of eighty-nine New Zealand families of European origin and twenty-four Singaporean Chinese families (father, mother and two children, in the 12–19 age range) in their homes and in such purchasing situations as restaurants, Lee and Marshall (1998) observed that New Zealand mothers exercised significantly more influence during the negotiation stage and had more influence with family members than the Singaporean mothers. Singaporean fathers had significantly more power than their male counterparts in New Zealand in the final outcome of the decision-making process. While the extended family is a declining unit in the West, in Malaysia and Romania many parents still live with their married children and assist them with the running of their households. This chapter suggests that one way in which the dual roles of women as family carers and as organisational employees could be reformed is via processes of consumption that challenge societal expectations with respect to the traditional role of women. Western advertisers could play a key part in helping to enhance the role of women in society, given that women make many purchases on behalf of their families.

In the United States and Western European countries regional differences may appear less important in advertising terms because of the modern advances in transport and telecommunications. On the other hand, regional differences can remain important when there are distinctive local traits, for example in the spoken languages or dialects and the ways in which people live. It is also recognised that there are many ethnic groups who are culturally different, particularly as a result of immigrant populations who were not born and brought up in these countries and who represent different market segments for food, toiletries, cosmetics, air travel and package holidays. Operating in a different market overseas poses challenges with respect to understanding and accommodating cultural differences. Different languages, religions, races and social behaviours remain key factors for the understanding of overseas markets. The past histories, traditions and political constraints within overseas markets add to this complex mix. The markets in overseas countries are culturally distinct, and Western companies need to be sensitive to needs and expectations in these different environments, for example in their observations of national customs, dress and business etiquette, as well as the role of women in the society.

Within the last two decades there have been dramatic changes in the global marketing environment. For example, we have witnessed the destruction of the Berlin Wall and the reunification of Germany, with the fall of communism and the break-up of the former Soviet Union contributing to the downfall of the communist regime in Romania. Malaysia is recovering from the destabilisation of the financial economies in the Far East. Political instability in the Balkans, political conflicts in parts of Africa, the Middle East and Latin America, the slowdown of economic growth in Western Europe and the USA have also affected global trading patterns. Uncertainties in the global marketing environment have led to changes in individual and national expectations, e.g. there is less long-term job security and in some cases there has been a redefinition of the roles men and women play in society as disposable incomes change and consumption patterns are affected. In the West, marketing research has been and remains an essential element, frequently used to help advertisers approach their target markets, for instance through the use of women consumer focus groups. Such techniques could also be of value in Malaysia and Romania and could help shed light on the differences in the indigenous factors affecting women's consumption. By taking account of such differences advertisers could provide advertisements which were more appropriate to women consumers in these countries. A greater awareness of the diversity of women's experiences in their social and cultural context might enable advertisers more fully to acknowledge the opportunities women have, in all cultures, increasingly to assign their own meanings by deconstructing, reconstructing and playing with advertising images in the formation of their own gender identity (Firat 1994). In short, advertisers must situate their messages within a broader, macro context.

THE EXAMPLES OF MALAYSIA AND ROMANIA

In this chapter we explore the view that both the standardisation and the adaptation of the advertising of global brands by Western companies aim explicitly and implicitly to construct and reflect Western social values. We explore this view in two non-Western settings, Malaysia and Romania. In the cultural context of Romania, according to Hofstede (1996), collectivist and feminine values are espoused. The question is whether advertising builds upon and reflects such collectivist and feminine values or whether it attempts to construct values aligned to Western individualism.

There have been many debates about how advertising works and these are discussed by Jobber (1998) in considering the strong and weak theories of advertising. The AIDA model (Attention, Interest, Desire or Conviction, Action) is perceived to be strong and the ATR model (Awareness, Trial, Reinforcement) to be weak. There are limitations in the AIDA approach. In theory, an individual is expected to pass through each stage, but in reality the models ignore the fact that consumers can routinely buy brands and not in fact make these brand purchases on the bases of strong desire or conviction. Neither do advertising models explain why some consumers are persuaded to buy while others do not make purchases.

Advertisers tend to take the view that each individual is a coherent, autonomous and rational entity who is able to make informed choices. They reduce the individual to what he or she consumes and therefore any knowledge regarding consumption choice becomes paramount for the advertiser in controlling and guiding human behaviour. After collection, this knowledge is interpreted and put back in the service of the individual and society at large, but not all individuals benefit equally from this 'service', because in the West marketing and advertising are circumscribed in line with social standards which emphasise whiteness, maleness and individualism. Consequently, they position other categories of people as out of place, as mere 'travellers' in a foreign world (Marshall 1984).

The question that arises is whether the workings of marketing via advertising in non-Western collective cultures follows a Western model or whether they are circumscribed to a local, collective model. Collective values emphasise feelings for each other, the importance of group life and family – values typically associated with femininity. Furthermore, some of these collective cultures are ethnically and racially heterogeneous, as is the case with Malaysia, and therefore whiteness is not a central category but possibly a peripheral one. The question is whether advertising of global brands by Western companies capitalises upon the cultural values that prevail in Malaysia and Romania or whether such advertising is 'ethnocentrically inclined', seeking to reform these cultures and the identity of women consumers in line with Western values.

REFRAMING THE INDIVIDUALISM/COLLECTIVISM DEBATE

In the examination of individualism versus collectivism and its impact on women as consumers Hofstede's four-dimensional framework: Power Distance, Uncertainty Avoidance, Individualism and Masculinity, is a helpful starting-point and one which has been used by other scholars (e.g. Kale and McIntyre 1991) for its 'quantitative rigour and intuitive appeal' (Kale 1995). Culture is described as the 'collective programming of the mind which distinguishes the members of one group or category of people from another', so culture is 'learned' from the social environment and is not genetically inherited (Hofstede 1991).

Hofstede (1980) conducted a survey with 116,000 questionnaires, mainly about work-related values in sixty-six countries. His assertion was that cultural data could be usefully gathered at the national level since nation-states exert strong unifying influences on their citizens, e.g. through control of the domestic media, education and the armed forces. Using factor analysis on the responses obtained, Hofstede produced factor scores. For Power Distance Inequality (PDI), Hofstede ranked Malaysia highest, with a score of 104, and Austria ranked lowest, with a score of 11. Hofstede's PDI measured the way societies in different countries control and handle human inequality. Large-PDI societies also have large disparities in income, wealth and status amongst their citizens. Small-PDI societies believe in minimising these disparities.

Hofstede's Uncertainty Avoidance Index (UAI) reflects the way a given society deals with the ambiguities and uncertainties of daily life. Strong-UAI cultures, e.g. such collectivist cultures as Romania, exhibited central planning and control, risk aversion and dogma. Weak-UAI cultures socialise their members to accept uncertainties and risks, and to handle each day as it comes with relative ease.

The United States had the highest score of 91 for Individualism (IDV) while Guatemala scored lowest with 6. High-IDV societies have a larger degree of freedom between their inhabitants while low IDV countries exhibit greater conformity and strong ties between in-group members. Stereotypical male and female values are specified in the Masculinity (MAS) score. In high-MAS countries societies exhibit manliness, success, achievements and making money in a visible manner. Japan, with a score of 95, ranked highest as the most masculine country, and Sweden, with a score of 5, ranked as the most feminine nation. Low-MAS countries showed values associated with femininity, for example nurture and interest in the personal development of others.

Hofstede's cultural framework throws light on societies' concerns with human characteristics and manifestations, though his research was done at the nation-state level. Examination at the 'individual' level is ignored, since the framework does not include the study of the attitudes, motivations and values of individuals between groups or within small sub-groups. The value of his work lies in the fact that knowledge of a target market's position along the four dimensions helps the marketer to design a strategy for optimum results and develop marketing mixes to 'exploit the commonalities within the targeted market segments', segmented along these cultural dimensions (Czinkota and Ronkainen 1998).

In what follows we attempt to look more critically at the divisions between individualism and collectivism and between masculinity and femininity. These categories should not be seen as exclusive or as existing in a dichotomous relationship. They are ideal types that allow us to think about various forms of sociality that exist around us but which in their pure form cannot be found in any contemporary context. Thus, national cultures may be constituted of a mixture of individualistic and collectivist practices, and at various points in time and within various social settings certain practices may indeed prevail.

Individualism is seen to lie at the basis of Western society and progress. It is suggested that only a free individual, who has broken away from communal duties in pursuit of self-actualisation, can contribute to the progress of society (Gusfeld 1975). Rational exchanges between the individual and the society thus ensure the survival and coherence of social relationships. Consequently, one should view the death of communal life that has taken place in the West as the main contributor to progress and civilisation. This is not to say that traditional family values and community bonds that remain quite strong in other parts of the world cannot contribute to certain forms of progress and civilisation. In collective cultures the individual is bound to his or her community to the extent that his or her identity cannot be negotiated within a private space; it exists prior to and independently of individual desires and interests. Furthermore, relationships between individuals are thought to be more emotional, less interest-driven and therefore more fulfilling than in the case of individualistic relationships. The performance of communal duties is seen to be the source of social harmony and progress (Sennett 1978).

Although Romania has been described as collectivist in Hofstede's framework, it is clear that individualistic practices are also present. For example, at the end of 1996 there were more than 540,000 small- and medium-sized enterprises registered in Romania (Government of Romania 1997), which suggests that individualism, at least within the economic sector, may be on the rise. Similarly, the urbanisation process that has taken place in the last five decades in Romania has led to the weakening of traditional values and a decrease in the importance of village life. Entrepreneurship has also been a traditional feature of Malaysian society, with many family-owned businesses particularly in the food and retail store sectors.

In Western societies communal feeling and rhetoric have not completely disappeared. Thus, family life in the West may reinforce many of the values associated with community, such as moral duty. Furthermore, communal values have been revived within the social domain in that 'the community' has been deployed to govern individuals and their collective existences (Rose 1996).

REFRAMING THE FEMININITY/MASCULINITY DEBATE

The differences between femininity and masculinity have received a great deal of attention within the 'gender and organisation' literature (Green and Cassell 1996) and some attention in the marketing literature (Catterall, Maclaran and Stevens 1997). Some of the literature supports the 'difference thesis', which purports that men and women are different in their constitution and behaviour. The biological approach to gender (Browne 1998), for example, explains differences in women's behaviour in relation to their biological characteristics. It is argued that these biologically driven characteristics lead women to value motherhood and other nurturing-type roles rather than managerial, organisational roles which are deemed more suitable for men. Differences between men and women are seen to be enhanced further by the different socialisation processes to which each of them is subjected. Socialisation processes can be supported by various consumption practices: so, for example, little girls are encouraged to play with dolls and are socialised into a motherhood role. Boys, on the other hand, are encouraged to play with cars, guns or Lego toys, to acquire skills deemed necessary in the organisational world. This is not to say that women and men acquire only those resources that support their traditional role, but it shows that differences between men and women could indeed be played out and maintained via consumption. Thus, advertisers can frame messages relevant to each particular group in order to maximise the attractiveness of their offerings.

Numerous authors have criticised the dichotomous positioning of female and male behaviour, suggesting that it presents only the essence of and therefore simplifies the notions of manhood and womanhood (Gilligan 1982; Butler 1990). These authors suggest that society has tended to value qualities associated with 'maleness' to a higher degree than female qualities. Thus, the ideal organisational actor is constructed in terms of rationality, aggressiveness and self-restraint (characteristics associated with maleness), while women are discussed in terms of emotions, caring and bodily functions (female stroking characteristics). Recent organisational discourses have 'rediscovered' female qualities only to circumscribe them to traditional male structures of power (Wajcman 1998). Indeed, the new organisation is seen to require more humanistic and caring approaches for the management of people. Yet, this apparent valuing of women's characteristics is dangerous, as it creates the illusion of equality while at the same time obstructing the critical examination of day-to-day practices and their underpinning theoretical assumptions (Calas and Smircich 1993).

However, one should not view gender as a fixed category. Gender is a process constantly performed in both acts of production and consumption. Gherardi (1995), for example, suggests that gender is performed in human interactions through both 'ceremonial' and 'remedial' work. 'Ceremonial' work is represented by those 'institutional' activities which reinforce traditional differences between maleness and femaleness, while 'remedial' work contextualises and confines gender to its locality, to specific practices and immediate experiences. We would suggest that advertising campaigns perform some sort of ceremonial work in that they delineate and reinforce clear boundaries between masculinity and femininity, whereby feminine values are pushed to the margin. When such boundaries are challenged – for example, when a parent buys a doll for his/her son – remedial work is called upon in order to naturalise and explain in one way or another why the status quo of the sexes was broken. In time such explanations become the new status quo and are no longer questioned. It is quite common in the UK for working men to do the weekly shopping or for women to buy cars on their own. In more traditional countries such as Romania and Malaysia such instances are relatively rare and require remedial work to be performed. In what follows we shed some light on the workings of advertising in Malaysia and Romania.

THE WORKINGS OF ADVERTISING IN MALAYSIA AND ROMANIA

Malaysia and Romania are marketing environments characterised by a host of similarities. There are 23 million people in Romania living in an area of 230,000 sq. km. The country is home to many nationalities, not just Romanians, the most significant being Hungarians and Germans in Transylvania and Banat, the Serbians in Banat and the gypsies spread across the whole country. Malaysia is a country of similar population size with 21 million people inhabiting 329,000 sq. km (World Bank 1998). Malaysia is ethnically and racially mixed, the largest groups being Malays, followed by the Chinese, Indians and a host of indigenous native groups. Malaysia, however, is more developed in economic terms: its GNP in 1996 was US $89.8 billion as compared to US $36.2 billion in Romania. This ensured that Malaysia was ranked thirty-second in the world with Romania being placed in the sixty-second position (World Bank 1998). Interestingly enough, in 1996, Romania had almost twice as many daily newspapers as Malaysia (297 as compared to 124) and as many TV sets as Malaysia did. Advertising expenditure on television in 1994 was US $201.3 million in Malaysia and US $47.9 million in Romania. This increased in 1997 to US $277.3 million in Malaysia and US $73.5 million in Romania (Adspend 1999). More recent evidence suggests that the numbers of personal computers and Internet hosts, mobile phones and the provision of main telephone lines are on the rise in both countries. In 1997, for example, for every 1,000 people Malaysia had approximately 170 main telephone lines, slightly less than Russia, which had 180 (*The Economist* 1997).

In respect of race, geography, ethnic cultures and urbanisation, Malaysia is politically a federation where local emotional loyalties apply to both the state and the nation. For example, the differences inherent in saying 'I come from Johore Bahru' or 'I come from Malaysia' are as significant as those found in the statements 'I come from Texas' and 'I come from the USA'. Geographically, the states of Sabah and Sarawak are hundreds of miles away from mainland Malaya. In these states in particular local nationality is important.

Mainland Malaya is a mix of industrial and commercial urbanisation and kampong (village) life. The activities of either local or national government agencies to regulate, or large business organisations to provide employment to both males and females, have an impact on the economic life of the kampong. Thus, village life is economically subject to urban constraints. Access to television is normally available in the hinterland and even in the mountainous regions of Sabah. Malaysian television coverage is complete on mainland Malaya and across the sea. It is fairly pervasive in Sabah and Sarawak on the island of Borneo. It is a feature of Malaysian television and press advertising that they seem to be significantly aimed at two cultures. The city cultures of Kuala Lumpur and Penang demonstrate considerable spending power for expensive discretionary products, e.g. Mercedes or BMW cars, electrically operated garage doors, and so on. At the other extreme there is the extended family kampong culture of the villages, where substantial elements of traditions are still preserved in the simple life. Between these two lies the urban working population of the larger towns, which is another target for the day-to-day products of ordinary consumption within the limits of relatively basic incomes. Projected media values tend to dwell on improving lifestyles, a better future and what is on offer to achieve these ends. There is receptivity, therefore, to images that reflect stylised adaptations of Western cultures, lifestyles and products. However, Malaysian advertisements have a Malaysian flavour in line with government objectives that Malaysia should stand up as a nation amongst nations. Kuala Lumpur, its capital city, has its own consumer research agencies, and carefully targeted advertisements portray its success and importance as the capital city of the nation. In Malaysia both press and television advertisements can be locally designed, since the country has its own local organisations for this purpose.

By the standards of the West, localised portrayals of goods by commercial organisations, when directed at less-educated and less-critical markets, are elementary when the messages do not possess the entertainment gimmicks that are sought by Western viewers. In addition, it should be realised that Malaysian advertising is presented alongside continual messages from government agencies about the general improvement and Westernisation of living standards which are a longstanding feature of social and economic policy.

However, media treatment of women has not evolved much beyond stereotypical views of women, with a heavy emphasis on their roles as good wives and mothers. As Ariffin has indicated:

> In Malaysia some key issues fought by women are: violence against women; advocacy for equal rights under the law; reduction of the negative and stereotyped images of women in the media; a more sympathetic treatment for single parents especially unwed mothers and abandoned babies; . . . a higher representation of women in decision making, particularly in politics; and the rights of women in Islam (and under Syariah laws).
>
> (Ariffin 1999: 419–20)

Before becoming a communist country in 1947, Romania was a rural country with a strong peasant culture. In order to understand women's position in

Romania today one has to take into account the deeply entrenched peasant culture which, at one time, provided the traditions, values and moral standards for the whole country. This culture combined with the values brought about by the communist regime explain the marginalised position and limited role of women in the Romanian society today (Harsanyi 1993). Both peasant and the communist cultures are collective in that they emphasise togetherness and shared goals. However, the peasant culture is patriarchal in nature, thus constituting women as subordinate to men. The communist culture, on the other hand, claimed to have redressed the inequality between genders in that both women and men had equal access to work since the care of the children was to be placed with state institutions.

In reality, however, women's lives were even more controlled than before. Hausleitner (1993) argues that women's bodies were brutally instrumentalised for the sake of population policy and that they were doubly exploited: every woman was expected to work and at the same time to take full responsibility for the family. The collapse of communism in December 1989 brought with it some changes to the life of women (e.g., the legalisation of abortions). However, these changes have not been substantial enough to affect significantly women's day-to-day experiences or to change the role women play in Romania. Romanian society is still patriarchal, as most organisations and state institutions are run by men for men, with women's issues not forming part of the agenda. While we may be tempted to agree with Hofstede that Romania is a collective culture, we are more cautious in stating that it is also a feminine one.

The transition to a market economy for Romania has given birth to a new set of values: individual rights, achievement and personal fulfilment are now at a premium in certain sectors of public and private life. The new emphasis on individualism is, however, in open contradiction to the collectivist values retained from the peasant and communist cultures. Western advertising techniques need to be tuned in to the new values of individualism and the existence of collective values so that society's traditional expectations of women as passive consumers capable of soaking up a daily diet of Western-oriented advertisements could give way to a healthier situation where women are given a voice that may be used to challenge the status quo. To what extent do global advertisers take the social and cultural characteristics of individual, non-Western countries into account when advertising to them? More specifically, to what extent do they take into account women consumers' values and experiences when targeting them with their products?

An analysis of national television advertisements in Malaysia and Romania carried out for three weeks in April 1999 revealed that both domestic and foreign advertisements promoted Western values. The authors have taped fifty adverts that were played on the national channels. Rather than emphasising local values and traditions, the focus of most adverts was found to be the individual (for example, in 69 per cent of Malaysian television advertisements and 91 per cent of Romanian television advertisements). Furthermore, in Romania, more than 80 per cent of the 200 advertisements recorded and analysed were foreign adverts translated into Romanian.

The message of most adverts is that the individual can improve him/herself via consumption. He (sic!) is told and reassured that he can become the best by driving the best car, drinking the most refreshing beer, using the whitest toothpaste, and so on. In both Romanian and Malaysian local adverts, women tend to be portrayed as washing clothes with 'the best detergent', washing dishes with 'the most effective liquid' or feeding their children with 'the most nourishing food on the market'. These ideas are reinforced via the imagery of women as carers and homemakers. In Romania, women are also presented as seductive and sexy: cosmetics and some car advertisements in particular dwell on such feminine attributes. In the Romanian case, the woman's body seems to an easy target. On the one hand, the woman consumer is told that it is acceptable to indulge in gastronomical pursuits while, on the other hand, the women featured on adverts are slim, slick and fit, a model to be emulated by the rest of the women consumers. It could be suggested that local advertising in Romania attempts to build upon and reinforce masculine values that construe women in terms of flesh and biology, positioning them as subordinate and fulfilling only a secondary role in society.

CONCLUSIONS

Advertising strategies of Western companies in Malaysia and Romania do not seem to take account of the ways in which individuals make sense of the world and the processes by which the identities of women and men are constituted in particular social and cultural settings. Western companies do not appear to position their brands strategically in relation to local competitors' brands. Little attention is paid to the requirements of the different religions within these cultures, to the demographic and occupational needs of the indigenous cultures or to how these impact on women's roles.

The importance of the 'family' and the social contexts of living under democratic regimes combined with authoritarian controls or stricter religious codes have the effect of defining the expectations and aspirations of women living and working in an Islamic society, such as Malaysia. The assumption that what works or is attractive in Western advertisements will work elsewhere belies certain localised truths. Standardisation of advertising campaigns might be preferable for global brands in the interest of economies of scale, might usefully exploit the creativity of one good advertising idea and might promote consistency in treating the world as one global market. However, even well-known brands can suffer from overseas competition, as illustrated by Levi's in the 1990s, British Airways (*Financial Times* 1999b) and the demise of the global name Hoover in the 1980s, which at one time was synonymous with vacuum cleaning.

There is much gathering and analysis of market research data about the habits, attitudes and needs of women consumers in Western markets. To guard against competition most Western companies rely on market research and product testing before designing their advertising commercials, particularly for domestic consumption. This is supported by the fact that the market research industries in the

West have seen the growth of both qualitative and quantitative research activities (Wright and Crimp 2000b). Yet this attention to market research does not seem to be applied when entering other diverse markets such as Malaysia and Romania.

By failing to undertake significant market research in other markets Western advertisers do not consider the requirements of women consumers in these countries. This is clearly a golden opportunity which global advertising, perhaps because of its very nature, fails to recognise. Instead it assumes that women consumers are a homogeneous group, and a Western model of womanhood is taken to represent women everywhere. Of course, this marketing approach fails to take into account that women consumers' aspirations need to be seen in the context of their social and cultural environments, environments which continue to be socially constructed and controlled by men.

To understand national habits requires more than the application of theoretical frameworks developed in the West. It is quite clear from our analysis that Malaysian and Romanian national cultures cannot be understood, measured and targeted on the basis of the four-dimensional framework suggested by Hofstede (1996), where collective values and risk aversion are interpreted as particularly feminine. It is also clear that the meanings of collectivism and femininity are not fixed but change as a result of the economic, political and social developments taking place in each society. Hofstede's framework also fails to account for contrasts between different religions and their impact on men and women in society.

In Malaysian society women who are employed are quite independent from an economic point of view, and the role of women in society has become increasingly prominent. In a study of the psychographic dimensions of Chinese female consumers in China, Taiwan and Hong Kong, Tai and Tam (1996) observed that as women achieve higher levels of education and higher positions at work they do not want to be portrayed in the home as cooks, cleaners and carers for their families, but as mature, intelligent and independent individuals. The Chinese make up a large ethnic group, the second-largest in size after the Malays in Malaysia, and here too education has reinforced the aspirations of younger Chinese female members to be depicted as successful in the workplace.

In Romania women are more 'exploited' than their Western counterparts due not only to the traditional patriarchal culture but also because the workings of the market are not yet efficient. Furthermore, advertising techniques attempt to reinforce the marginal status of women in the society by portraying them as homemakers or sex objects. Given that women have not achieved economic freedom and continue to be employed in the marginal sectors of the economy, it is more difficult for them to challenge some of these images and the expectations they construct with respect to their role and position in society.

In the West, however, women are in a better economic position to construct spaces of resistance against the dominant masculine discourse, given that Western values have become more diverse and more gender-sensitive then before. Advertising could play a significant role in changing some of the gender stereotypes. Yet we believe there still is a long way to go until womanhood will be defined in its own terms rather than against the male benchmark. What is needed is a greater consideration by marketers of the particular social contexts of their new markets and the changing roles of women within them.

REFERENCES

Adspend (1999) Adspend Databank (NTC Publications) at http://www.warc.com/scripts/WAD_res.asp'.

Ariffin, R. (1999) 'Feminism in Malaysia: a historical and present perspective of women's struggles in Malaysia', *Women's Studies International Forum* 22, 4: 417–23.

Browne, K. (1998) *Divided Labours: An Evolutionary View of Women at Work*, Weidenfeld & Nicolson: London.

Butler, J. (1990) 'Gender trouble, feminist theory and psychoanalytic discourse', in L. Nicholson (ed.) *Feminism/Postmodernism*, New York: Routledge, 324–40.

Calas, M. B. and Smircich, L. (1993) 'Dangerous liaisons: the "feminine-in-management" meets "globalization"', *Business Horizons Special Issue on Women and Work* 36, 2: 223–8.

Catterall, M., Maclaran, P. and Stevens, L. (1997) 'Marketing and feminism: a bibliography and suggestions for further research', *Marketing Intelligence and Planning* 15, 7: 369–76.

Czinkota, M. and Ronkainen, I. (1998) *International Marketing*, USA: Dryden Press.

Desmond, J. (1997) 'Marketing and the war machine', *Marketing Intelligence and Planning* 15, 7: 338–51.

The Economist (1997) 'Emerging market indicators,' 24 May: 156.

—— (1998) 'Britain's media giants', 12 December: 19.

Financial Times (1999a) 'The advertising industry', 11 November, survey: 1–2.

—— (1999b) 'Ayling searches for clear skies after a turbulent flight': 20.

Firat, A. F. (1994) 'Gender and consumption: transcending the feminine?', in J. A. Costa (ed.) *Gender Issues and Consumer Behaviour*, Thousand Oaks, CA/London: Sage.

Gherardi, S. (1995) *Gender, Symbolism and Organizational Cultures*, London: Sage.

Gilligan, C. (1982) *In a Different Voice*, Cambridge, MA: Harvard University Press.

Goffman, E. (1976) *Gender Advertisements*, New York: Harper Torchbooks.

Government of Romania (1997) *Adevarol* (The Truth), 8 February: 12.

Green, A. and Cassell, C. (1996) 'Women managers, gendered cultural processes and organisational change', *Gender, Work, Organization* 3, 3: 168–78.

Gusfeld, J. (1975) *Community: A Critical Response*, Oxford: Blackwell.

Harsanyi, D. P. (1993) 'Women in Romania', in N. Funk and M. Mueller (eds) *Gender, Politics and Post-communism*, London: Routledge, 39–52.

Hausleitner, M. (1993) 'Women in Romania: before and after the collapse', in N. Funk and M. Mueller (eds) *Gender Politics and Post-communism*, London: Routledge, 53–61.

Hofstede, G. (1980). 'Motivation, leadership and organization: do American theories apply abroad?', *Organizational Dynamics* 9: 42–63.

—— (1991) *Cultures and Organizations*, New York: McGraw-Hill.

—— (1996) 'Images of Europe: past present and future', in P. Joynt and M. Warner (eds) *Managing Across Cultures: Issues and Perspectives*, London: International Thompson Business Press, 147–65.

Jeannet, J. and Hennessey, D. (1998) *Global Marketing Strategies*, USA: Houghton Mifflin.

Jobber, D. (1998) *Principles and Practice of Marketing*, London: McGraw-Hill.

Kale, S. (1995) 'Grouping euroconsumers: a culture-based clustering approach', *Journal of International Marketing* 3, 3: 35–48.

Kale, S. and McIntyre, R. (1991) 'Distribution channel relationships in diverse cultures', *International Marketing Review* 8, 3: 60–70.

Lee, C. and Marshall, R. (1998) 'Measuring influence in the family decision making process using an observational method', *Qualitative Market Research: An International Journal* 1, 2: 88–98.

Marshall, J. (1984) *Women Managers: Travellers in a Male World*, Chichester: Wiley.

Peñaloza, L. and Gilly. M. (1999) 'Marketer acculturation: the changer and the changed', *Journal of Marketing* 63, July: 84–104.

Rose, N. (1996) 'The death of the social? Re-figuring the territory of government', *Economy and Society* 25, 3: 327–33.

Sennett, R. (1978) *The Fall of the Public Man*, New York: Alfred A. Knopf.

Siu, W.-S. and Au, A. K.-M. (1997) 'Women in advertising: a comparison of television advertisements in China and Singapore', *Marketing Intelligence and Planning* 15, 5: 235–43.

Tai, H. C. and Tam, L. M. (1996) 'A comparative study of Chinese consumers in Asian markets: a lifestyle analysis', *Journal of International Consumer Marketing* 9, 1: 25–41.

Venkatesh, A. (1995) 'Ethnoconsumerism: a new paradigm to study cultural and cross-cultural consumer behaviour', in J. Costa and G. Bamossy (eds) *Marketing in a Multicultural World*, New York: Sage, 27–67.

Wajcman, J. (1998) *Managing Like a Man: Women and Men in Corporate Management*, Oxford: Polity Press in association with Blackwell.

Wright, L. and Crimp, M. (2000a) *The Marketing Research Process*, Hemel Hempstead, Herts: Prentice-Hall, ch. 13.

—— (2000b) *The Marketing Research Process*, Hemel Hempstead, Herts: Prentice-Hall, ch. 1.

World Bank (1998) *World Development Indicators 1998*, CDROM, World Bank.

10 Reading *Rabotnitsa*: fifty years of creating gender identity in a socialist economy[1]

Natasha Tolstikova

INTRODUCTION

American women's magazines have consistently been charged with playing a central role in the oppression of women. The history of these magazines is closely tied to the rise of modern capitalism, and their success as national media was clearly made possible by their reliance on national advertising. Feminist historians have identified several ideological propositions, attributed to the social requirements of capitalism, which have circumscribed the roles available to women in the United States (see for example Winship 1978; McCracken 1993). These feminists typically argue that women's magazines have articulated these tightly prescribed roles for over a hundred years. These role restrictions are said to infect many domains, specifying gender role requirements from motherhood to consumer behaviour. To most feminists the role of the women's magazines in the oppression of women under capitalism appears congenial (Friedan 1963). To them, the political necessity to overthrow both capitalism and its powerful ideological apparatus, in this case, women's magazines, seems unambiguous.

Like many critical feminist pronouncements, this one lacks empirical grounding. While asserting the advancement of modernity and market capitalism as the proximal cause of this oppression, nowhere is directly relevant data offered. One possible source of such data would be comparative analysis. If capitalism is the problem, then one should not see the same or similar oppression in the magazines of centrally planned socialist economies.

To this end, I offer a comparative analysis. The purpose of this chapter is to fill the need for an analysis of women's magazines under a socialist system by documenting the history of *Rabotnitsa*, the longest-running and most widely read women's magazine under the Soviet regime in Russia.[2] Though the specific agency administering *Rabotnitsa* has changed from time to time, the magazine has always been the official women's magazine of the Communist Party. Besides delivering political propaganda in the form of editorials, *Rabotnitsa* covered a variety of other topics. Depending on the particular historical period, it addressed family, child rearing, cooking, fashion and general education topics. Perhaps most importantly, *Rabotnitsa* emphasised the characteristics of the model woman worker by transmitting 'exemplary experience and codes of behaviour, in somewhat the same way as American women's magazines cumulatively portray a model of the ideal American family and the woman's role' (Hopkins 1970: 231). By examining a fifty-year run of *Rabotnitsa* under the rule of Lenin, Stalin and Khrushchev, I hope to illuminate not only the role of gender-specific magazines in foisting social limitations on women, but also to raise questions about the 'woman-friendliness' of a socialist economy as compared to a capitalist one.

By doing a close reading of every fourth issue from 1914 to 1964, I tried to identify the manner in which women were presented, the prescribed social practices and gender roles, and attitudes towards such traditional Western female features as femininity, sexuality, women's family roles, consumption and work outside the home. However, I realised the incompleteness of this form of analysis since the text of *Rabotnitsa* was carefully crafted by politically informed correspondents and censored by the editors according to the ideological needs of the moment. So, although a close reading would reveal official attitudes and desirable cultural values, it might not reveal the readers' day-to-day struggles and conflicts. Indeed, since one of the key attributes of ideology is its tendency to contradict reality, I would expect that the daily lives of Soviet women were substantially different from the depictions in this magazine. Therefore, I also made an effort to compare the magazine with historical data. By contextualising my reading of the magazine with larger economic and political forces, I hoped to infer what role *Rabotnitsa* played in different historical periods and how it attempted to shape the perceived reality of its female audience. In short, I define my method as textualised historical analysis, or historicised close reading.

My third level of analysis was a comparison of the Soviet women's magazine with the reported characteristics of the American women's magazines. I try to suggest how the role of *Rabotnitsa* differed from that of the American women's magazines and also how it was the same. My working hypothesis is that women were co-opted by both capitalist and socialist governments to play roles that were convenient for the corresponding historical needs, and that the popular women's press played an instrumental part in this process. Trends in the status of women are connected with the political system, but they are not as dependent on it as criticism of American women's magazines suggests. By choosing to study the ideological extremes – socialism and capitalism – I hope to build a convincing argument in support of this thesis.

THE WESTERN WOMEN'S MAGAZINES

There is an extensive literature on gender and mass media in the United States. This literature reveals recurrent themes which, as mentioned above, will form the organisation for my own analysis. Frank Luther Mott (1939), followed by Theodore Peterson (1964) and John Tebbel (1969) first documented the development of

American women's magazines. Mott writes about the rise of magazines in the 'Golden Age' (1865–80), when literacy among upper-class women became widespread. Peterson documents the history of women's magazines in the twentieth century when literacy diffused into the lower strata of society. He sees a commonality of women's periodicals in helping their readers to manage households by relying on the same formula of fashion, food and family (1964: 165). All these authors acknowledge the importance of women's magazines as vehicles for delivering audiences and for developing women's culture. The further connection between women's magazines and capitalism is said to have happened when marketers and advertisers discovered women as consumers. Tebbel (1969) attributes the rapid rise of women's magazines in the middle of the nineteenth century to the realisation that women constituted a lucrative market. Thus, even the earliest magazine histories connect the rise of magazines with the rise of capitalism.

Feminist history, beginning in the early years of the Second Wave, elaborates on this theme. Betty Friedan, for instance, makes the connection between women's magazines and the imperatives of post-war capitalism, and this theme constitutes a central building block of the *Feminine Mystique* (1963). Nancy Cott in her landmark book, *Bonds of Womanhood* (1977), argues that the 'separate spheres' ideology of the early industrial era supported a family structure that was necessary to capitalism. This family system required that women stay at home, in the 'private sphere', while men went out to work in the 'public sphere'. Cott, along with several other feminist historians covering the same period, argues that Sarah Hale, the editor of the first widely circulated women's magazine, *Godey's Ladies' Book*, was a primary inventor, elaborator and promoter of the separate spheres ideology. Many years later, Gloria Steinem (1990) used Hale as a scapegoat for the demise of *Ms.* magazine, arguing that the long-established link between advertising and women's magazines had resulted in advertisers playing a censorship role in the women's press, silencing attempts to give a feminist voice to the mass media.

The earliest women's magazine in the United States reportedly started in 1792 (Okker 1995: 7). Aimed at upper-class women, the first magazines for female readers focused on teaching women how to be ladies (Mott 1939). By the nineteenth century, with the growing social changes brought by industrialisation and urbanisation, some progressive women's periodicals systematically promoted women's intellectual development and their personal fulfilment. But most women's magazines held on to Victorian values, particularly to the separation of the gender spheres. Domesticity and family thus became the staple content of women's magazines early in their history. Women's magazines have continued to give a special emphasis to family and maternity. Bettering the home was seen as the purpose of womanhood, but the women's magazines maintained the new modern attitude that women are not born homemakers but require special education to become competent (McCracken 1993: 191). In the early 1920s, some of the home economic specialists proposed that homemaking was a synthesis of all the sciences in an effort to solve problems at home (Cott 1977: 64). Popular periodicals for women offered not only food recipes but also family advice and child rearing recommendations. The popular women's press assumed that a woman was not truly fulfilled until she found the right man. It was a woman who was responsible for making the family work and she should be flexible enough to change herself within the traditional framework so her partner would be satisfied but not threatened (Scanlon 1995: 25). Thus, the roles of wife and mother remained paramount despite historic challenges and new social developments. The rhetoric of the separate spheres resulted over time in a general idealisation of 'the domestic arena as a place of nurture and comfort' (Bordo 1993: 118).

The literature on women's magazines often explores how women's periodicals helped elaborate and continue this process. A key element is the magazines' continuous attempts to define femininity, a theme explored by feminist critics from Susan Brownmiller (1984) to Susan Bordo (1993). For instance, Marjorie Ferguson (1983: 1), the author of *Women's Magazines and the Cult of Femininity*, considers women's magazines one of the most significant contemporary social institutions: 'Alongside other social institutions such as family, the school, the church and other media . . . they help to shape both a woman's view of herself, and society's view of her'. Her main interest is how women's magazines define femininity and her study is concerned with the messages that the post-war women's books transmitted to women. Ferguson (1983: x) analyses how those messages reflected the impact of 'social, cultural and economic change upon their female audience'. The central argument of her work is that the institution of women's magazines served to foster and maintain the culture of femininity. These magazines not only reflect the female role in society but also define and offer ways to socialise into that role.

Until the 1950s, women's sexuality was largely subsumed under the topics of domesticity and maternity in the women's magazines (Ballaster *et al.* 1991). As Betty Friedan (1963) noted, however, a growing emphasis on being sexually desired appears in the magazines of the early post-war period. She highlights the shift in the fiction of women's books from stories of empowerment to romantic fiction. Since that time, the depiction of women as 'sex objects' has been a central focus of feminist history and criticism. The pleasurable subjects of love, beauty and sex are turned against the female reader and used to bring her into line with social objectives. For instance, Ellen McCracken (1993: 3) asserts in her book *Decoding Women's Magazines* that advertising, editorial content and 'covert' ads in women's magazines 'exert a cultural leadership to shape consensus in which highly pleasurable codes work to naturalise social relations of power'. Janice Winship (1978) also claims that women's magazines are a primary source of ideological production, reflecting dominant ideologies but also reinforcing and even actively generating oppressive beliefs.

Because women's magazines became heavily dependent on advertising revenues, many argue that women were linked more closely to the growing consumer culture than men. Stuart Ewen (1976) says women's role as primary consumers of household goods has been both a source and a symptom of their powerlessness in capitalist society. Because, he argues, capitalism depends upon an insatiable demand for consumer goods, women had to be enculturated into a privatised way of life in which the pursuit of goods was the ultimate end. The mass media, particularly advertising in the women's magazines, were said to seduce and mollify women by offering them labour-saving devices and frivolous luxuries, while always increasing standards of acceptance in both housekeeping and grooming. This emphasis on consumption also allegedly excluded women from productive work (Tiano 1984).

Helen Damon-Moore (1994), who wrote her book on the history of the *Ladies' Home Journal* (*LHJ*), also sees a connection between gender and commerce under capitalism. She argues that gendering audiences was the first attempt at 'targeted marketing'. The author claims that the connection between commerce and gender reveals a historical configuration of gender construction, and that understanding this helps us to approach questions of gender in contemporary culture: 'Women's role as consumers meant not only that consumers were women, but also that women were consumers' (Damon-Moore 1994: 12). Thus, consumer culture succeeded both in bolstering capitalism and nurturing patriarchy. In exchange for promised satisfaction through consumer goods, women had to accept the limited definition of womanhood presented by the women's magazines, according to Jennifer Scanlon, author of *Inarticulate Longings: The* Ladies' Home Journal, *Gender and the Promises of Consumer Culture* (1995: 230). Scanlon explores the relationship between popular culture and consumption in the period 1910–30. She finds that dominant social groups influenced the ideology of the *Ladies' Home Journal*: the 'average' *LHJ* reader was assumed to be white, married and middle class. This reader purchased the latest appliances and served canned food to her families. The *LHJ* urged readers to expand their roles as consumers rather than as producers. Editorials, advertising and fiction reinforced this position, creating the appearance of consensus.

Indeed, American feminist activists often seem to view women's magazines, particularly the advertisements in them, as being almost single-handedly responsible for women's oppression. Not only do they claim this in their writings, but also feminists have led physical action against women's periodicals. For instance, in the 1968 demonstration, women tossed things they considered to contribute to their oppression into the 'Freedom Trash Can', including not only girdles and copies of *Playboy*, but issues of *Vogue, Cosmopolitan* and the *Ladies' Home Journal* (Cohen 1988: 151). Marcia Cohen (1988: 184–96) in her *Sisterhood* also reports the sit-in demonstration in the office of the editor-in-chief of the *Ladies' Home Journal* in 1970. For many American feminists, writes Cohen, the *LHJ* was an embodiment of everything ideologically oppressive in a glossy, glamorous women's magazine. Among their demands were the elimination of ads that degrade and exploit women, the exclusion of articles on home and romance, and instead the inclusion of articles that portrayed different lifestyle alternatives to family and marriage. The American women's magazines have, therefore, not only played a key role in the production of gender prejudice and the dissemination of capitalist consumer culture, but they have also been a frequent target of feminist critique and action.

THE SOVIET CASE

Rabotnitsa has a long history. First published in 1914 during the tsarist regime, this revolutionary magazine for women has had a nearly continuous run until the present day. From the moment of the Revolution of 1917, it has been the official publication for women under the Communist Party in Russia. Thus, while *Rabotnitsa*'s mission differed from those of the American women's magazines in its particulars, it served the broader socio-economic purpose attributed to the women's press in the West: *Rabotnitsa* was primarily concerned with the indoctrination of women according to the political needs of the existing system.

According to the Soviet 'hagiography', *Rabotnitsa,* which means 'Woman Worker', was initiated by Nadezhda Krupskaya in 1914, when Russia was still ruled by the tsar. In fact, it was started by a group of distinguished revolutionary women who came from the middle and upper classes and had had a higher education. Krupskaya was only one of them. The editors were linked to important men in the revolutionary movement (Krupskaya was Lenin's wife; Inessa Armand was his close friend, Anna Elizarova was his sister) (Wood 1997: 34). The magazine started as a revolutionary medium that called to women for unification with men under a single goal of overthrowing the regime. In the ideology of the magazine, the rights of women were subsumed under the rights of workers. The tsarist government quickly closed *Rabotnitsa* and all members of its editorial board were jailed. It resumed publication after the October Revolution, in 1917, as an organ of the Russian Social Democratic Workers' Party. The magazine helped Bolsheviks to achieve a victory in the political struggle with other socialist parties for a lead in the socialist Revolution of 1917. The circulation of *Rabotnitsa* grew at an astonishing rate and it became the most popular women's magazine in the country. From a dry, bi-weekly pamphlet, it became a popularly written illustrated weekly and later monthly, which was circulated nation-wide.

The Soviet state was officially dedicated to the equality of the sexes from the beginning. During its first fifty years, Soviet history was associated with profound and dramatic change. Severe political struggle and deep economic hardships marked the revolutionary period (1914–20). The Bolsheviks who led the country in the Revolution had a mission to destroy the old world and to build a dazzling world of communism. However, factors such as revolutionary struggle, the Civil War, nationalisation and the state monopoly on trade by the end of the 1920s reduced gross output of all industries to less than a third compared to 1913 (Nove 1969: 68). The New Economic Policy (1921–9) was initiated by Lenin to help the country's destroyed economy. It temporarily improved people's daily lives and brightened their existence (Ball 1991). When Stalin came to power in the 1930s, he acquired an absolute power, which spread out over all aspects of life. This long and dark period was characterised by fear and suspicion, hard labour and life struggle (Randall 1965). The Khrushchev period is often called a 'thaw' because he gave new hope to Soviet citizens, restored communist ideals and opened the country for foreign contacts. Perhaps most importantly for this proposal,

Khrushchev sought to improve living standards by making more consumer goods available (Breslauer 1982).

The official belief system of the Soviet Union was Marxism-Leninism, mainly an idealistic concept. The Party relied on this ideology not only for building a strong political system but also to intervene in and influence the citizen's daily lives, thus creating a totalitarian society. As Althusserian ideology, therefore, Soviet dogma intended to affect all spheres of life and guide people's actions. However, Marxism-Leninism was also constantly revised by the Party, according to political and economic needs, as well as historical events, social values, demographics and theoretical considerations (Buckley 1988: 159). Thus, Marxism-Leninism was itself put into the flexible service of the Party rather than being a static, abstract body of thought to which the government was bound.

In the Soviet case, the forced change of the social system pledged new social relationships. According to the official ideology, women gained equality with men after the Revolution of 1917. Moreover, this right was embedded in the Soviet Constitution. Given the strength of the more traditional, organic ideology of gender, however, a wide gap appeared between what was prescribed and what was happening in reality. Shlapentokh (1986) argues that Soviet people were aware of such distinctions, which helped to create a complex ideological mentality in which opposite ideas were sometimes combined and made into sense. For instance, the lack of clear definition of gender – a woman was regarded as most backward yet was hailed as most progressive – during the early post-revolutionary times contributed to the strength of the Party (Wood 1997).

Shlapentokh (1986) also separates public ideology ('ideology for the masses') from the Party ideology ('ideology for insiders'), suggesting the potential for contradiction between the messages in the mass media and the beliefs of those producing these messages. This author argues that the Soviet ideology was actually a dogma of domination, which sought to legitimise the existence of the political regime by offering a class interpretation of reality. Thus, the rights of women were not only secondary to those of workers, they were also subject to domination by 'insider' interests.

The Soviet press served ideology in the official sense because it was structurally bound to the Communist Party and the government. Functionally, according to Lenin, the press was the 'collective propagandist, agitator, and organiser,' thus constituting the most significant tool in ideological work (Lenin 1959). With time, functions of the Soviet media were further expanded to include roles as mass mobiliser, keeper of morals, public forum, social critic, educator and reporter. Its tasks were not only to judge events from an ideological or class point of view but also to conceal information (Hopkins 1970: 19–52). The Soviet editor had to balance Party orders, ideological considerations, personal beliefs, personal integrity and, *lastly*, the interests of the readers, to create the final product.

Because the Soviet press was owned by the state, publishers were driven not by profit, as in the American situation, but were impelled first and foremost to satisfying the Party's immediate ideological goals. Magazines were normally distributed by subscription; retail sales of Soviet periodicals were not significant. Because of the limited variety of magazines and newspapers, most titles had a long-established readership with entrenched habits. Therefore, Soviet journalists did not have to worry about satisfying audience tastes and demands. Although the Soviet press was always preoccupied with shaping public opinion, audience research began only in the 1960s, under Khrushchev. Not until the demise of the Soviet Union did the press start to collect significant revenue from advertising. Thus, the link between capitalism and the ideologies of gender found in the American experience (such as the 'separate spheres' notion, the double standard, the emphasis on beauty) are absent until *perestroika.*

THE EARLY REVOLUTIONARY PERIOD (1914–28)

The first issue of *Rabotnitsa* grew out of *Pravda*, an official newspaper of the Bolshevik party. *Pravda* was not able to publish enough letters from women workers since these were too abundant (Stal 1959: 109). Besides, *Rabotnitsa* was a legal outlet and would not only satisfy the immediate needs of the women workers of St Petersburg but also would raise class-consciousness among women of Russia as a whole (Elwood 1992: 105–7). The editorial of the first issue stated: '[*Rabotnitsa*] will educate women workers with low [political] conscious. [It] will point out their common interests with the rest of the working class not only in Russia but all around the world' (*Rabotnitsa* 23 February 1914: 1). *Rabotnitsa* assumed that women workers were the most backward and exploited part of proletariat and needed the special assistance of the Bolshevik Party. With political propaganda, it was clear to them that the only way to improve their conditions was by getting the same rights as those enjoyed by the well-off classes.

This first issue covered mostly current events in the workers' movement, with particular attention to the participation of female workers. Women's working conditions at different locations were also reported, along with stories on revolutionary struggle abroad. In 1914 *Rabotnitsa* did not have a cover, any illustrations or even an issuing body. There were almost no discussions of family, femininity or other issues with particular importance to the subjugation of women. If these topics were used, they were presented under a political angle. Thus, in the second issue the article entitled 'Working woman, family, and prostitution' appeared. It argued that the extensive use of female labour overthrew the existing family relations. As a result, a woman doesn't have time to make something at home, to cook and look after kids. Her wages were so low that often she had to sell her body just to survive. The only option that the author identified was a united struggle for improvement of her conditions.

A handful of advertisements that appeared on the last page of this issue reflected the ascetic revolutionary spirit, being text-only, sober in tone and announcement-orienated in content. The ads promoted new books and magazines aimed at the improvement of working environments. These ads did not tout household goods or grooming products as their American or British counterparts did, rather they reflected the ideology of the worker's movement and advanced the interests of Lenin and his Bolshevik Party.

Inside Russia in 1914, many revolutionary subgroups struggled to capture the loyalties of the Russian people. The Bolsheviks were careful to separate themselves from other movements, especially from feminists and Mensheviks. Bolsheviks thought Russian feminists, who were 'bourgeois women' and nicknamed '*ravnopravki*' [equal rights' women], and the Mensheviks were trying to divert working women from the revolutionary struggle by emphasising the relative inferiority of women' position compared to men's. The Bolsheviks believed that women workers must instead unite with male workers – because they had more in common with proletariat men than with bourgeois women (Vavilina 1964). *Rabotnitsa*, therefore, addressed women only as workers and only for the purpose of recruiting them to the workers' revolutionary struggle. Though other topics eventually appeared in its pages, this overriding emphasis on women as members of the labour force would be characteristic of *Rabotnitsa* until the fall of the Soviet Union.

In 1914 only seven issues of *Rabotnitsa* were published; the magazine ceased its publication due to the hardships of the First World War. It picked up again only in 1917. Its cover boldly announced that it was an organ of the central Committee of the Russian Social Democratic Workers' Party. The double issue dated January/February 1917 celebrated the victory of the February (Bourgeois) Revolution which had just taken place. The first step, effected by the intelligentsia, forced the tsar to abdicate and replaced him with a parliamentary government. With the February Revolution, the women of Russia gained voting rights, and many women who had been incarcerated were released. In spite of the expressed approval for the recent success of the bourgeois effort, the Bolshevik sympathies of *Rabotnitsa* were still evident in its calls for unification of the working class for the goal of building socialism: 'In organisation is all our might and all our hope! Let us work toward unity and solidarity of the workers of the world' (*Rabotnitsa* January/February 1917: 4).

The October Revolution of 1917, the event best known in the West, ultimately resulted in the execution of the tsar and brought the Bolsheviks to power. From here on, *Rabotnitsa* reflects Lenin's position toward the liberation of women. He considered the 'domestic slavery' of the family to be an obstacle in the path to communism. Petty housework 'crushes, strangles, stultifies and degrades' a woman (Lenin 1966: 64). It was a waste of her labour on barbarously unproductive drudgery. Traditional female chores were to be taken over by communal organisations, freeing women for political work as well as for industrial labour.

The new order considered a desire for material goods to be individualist and, thus, anti-collective and anti-revolutionary. Conveniently, this ideological position could be used also to dismiss any complaints about the everyday hardships endured by Russian families during the severe scarcity that characterised the first five years of the new order. Just as Western pro-consumption ideology shored up the capitalist system, the Soviet anti-consumption ideology helped strengthen the new government by glossing over its difficulties.

Labour-saving devices and convenience foods practically did not exist in working families, and Russian women found themselves saddled with difficult, time-consuming household chores, which left them little or no time for political participation. Their male comrades did not come forward to help with the housework so that their wives and sisters could be full revolutionary citizens. Instead, even most radical revolutionary organisations continued to see women as inferior to men and channelled what little energy they had for political action into such activities as serving refreshments and mending clothing (Gorsuch 1996). The frustration women felt at being excluded from the organisations that had promised them so much did not emerge in the reports and editorials of *Rabotnitsa*, which continued to focus exclusively on women as workers *outside* the home.

The same contradiction occurred in sexual relations. A sexual revolution had been declared, which aimed at achieving equality in love as well as equality in economics (Gorsuch 1996). Russian-style 'free love,' the exercise of choice, civil marriage and a withering of the family became more and more popular among progressive revolutionaries. Marriage, divorce and abortion were granted on an almost casual basis – practices that also aimed at women's emancipation (Brown 1968). At the grassroots level, however, women who tried to exercise the same sexual freedom as men were branded as whores and were excluded from the revolutionary organisations. This situation must have caused women pain, but *Rabotnitsa* did not address the problem.

Naiman argues that the discourse of the time was marked by 'an obsessive stigmatisation of femininity' (1997: 290). A female soldier of the Revolution was to show everyone that she was a communist by 'dressing like a slob' in militarised clothing, sporting a Browning on her hip and affecting a harsh manner of speech. Moore writes: 'Personal attractiveness in the socialist state was not supposed to lie in physical charms, suggestive clothing, and appropriate body odours stressed by American advertising copy, but in heroic attributions to the victory of socialism' (1966: 205). However, changes in female appearances did not affect deeply ingrained traditional attitudes toward women. The sources of resistance, therefore, seemed rooted in longstanding beliefs and practices – those with deeper roots than industrial capitalism could claim.

New Economic Policy (1921–8)

The New Economic Policy (NEP) initiated by Lenin in 1921 was intended to restore the state's economy that had been seriously damaged by the hardships of the World War, the Revolution and the Civil War. In practice, however, it was a return to capitalism, a 'strategic retreat' that reinstated private trade. High-quality goods in every variety suddenly reappeared for purchase. Retail trade and food sales supplied the population with forgotten or never known luxuries. Under the NEP, standards of living rose, trade boomed, and the overstrained population experienced a break in rationing and famines (Ball 1991).

Rabotnitsa re-emerged in 1923, having been closed by Civil War shortages since 1918. The new *Rabotnitsa* was issued under the aegis of the Women's Department

Figure 10.1 One of the earliest images in *Rabotnitsa*: photograph of women heroes of war and work
Source: *Rabotnitsa*, January 1923

of the Central Committee of the Russian Communist Party with a familiar slogan on the cover: 'Workers of the world, unite!' Consistent with its revolutionary tradition, *Rabotnitsa* expressed fears about restoring a capitalist system, by satirising NEP (1923, issue 2). It continued to emphasise the importance of communal institutions – day care facilities and canteens – that emancipate a woman from housework.

In the first issue of 1923, a photograph of women heroes of both war and work appears – one of the first images to be shown in *Rabotnitsa* (Figure 10.1). The women stand in front of a building with a revolutionary banner and what appears to be a broken trade sign. It might also be another banner, which is possibly lifted by a wind. The poor quality of the print does not allow us to see all the details. The women are dressed in short overcoats and dark skirts. All but three wear kerchiefs 'babushka'-style. To a contemporary viewer, the image shows a cold, poorly equipped, semi-destroyed life, in which this small group of serious women intends to build socialism. They do not seem upset with deteriorating conditions and the absence of material well-being.

By the end of the decade, images became more prominent, but most differed little from this early one. The cover of the December 1927 issue (Figure 10.2), for instance, depicts a typical woman of the era. She is writing with an open ink steel pen. She does not smile. Her hair, very short, resembles a man's haircut and she wears a dark military service jacket. The absence of any embellishment such as jewellery, cosmetics, or a manicure shows her seriousness and determination. In fact, one could easily mistake her for a man. Though the cover of this issue seems right on target for communist ideology, a surprisingly different image appears on the last page of the same issue. Here we find, of all things, a dress pattern showing women how to make the very flapper-style against which the 'true' revolutionary raged the most (Figure 10.3). Everything here speaks of femininity: the short skirt of the dress, the delicate pointy shoes, the chic bob and arty illustration style. It resembles a typical image of an American flapper with her slim figure which 'seemed designed for play and pleasure' (Ryan 1983: 220). Although the Soviet flapper image clearly refers to a working girl (a necktie and rolled-up sleeves), the two different female images in *Rabotnitsa* illustrate the duality in attitudes towards women.

By the end of the NEP, therefore, the magazine had relaxed from the earlier rigidness. There were a wider variety of topics, from poetry to educational treatises on Darwin to travelogues. Importantly, articles appeared that advised women on consumption choices ranging from children's toys to contraceptives. Even romantic fiction made its way into the pages of *Rabotnitsa*. Thus, despite its determined loyalty to revolutionary purity, *Rabotnitsa's* editorial content and tone clearly shows the influence of NEP 'gentleness' over the course of the decade.

Under the NEP, standards of living rose, trade boomed and the overstrained population experienced a break in rationing and famines (Kort 1996). Newly privatised shops offered a variety of quality goods. However, 'to many communists, NEP essentially meant Utopia Postponed' (Naiman 1997: 12). So, in spite of the relief NEP brought to daily life, the society was ambivalent over the change in

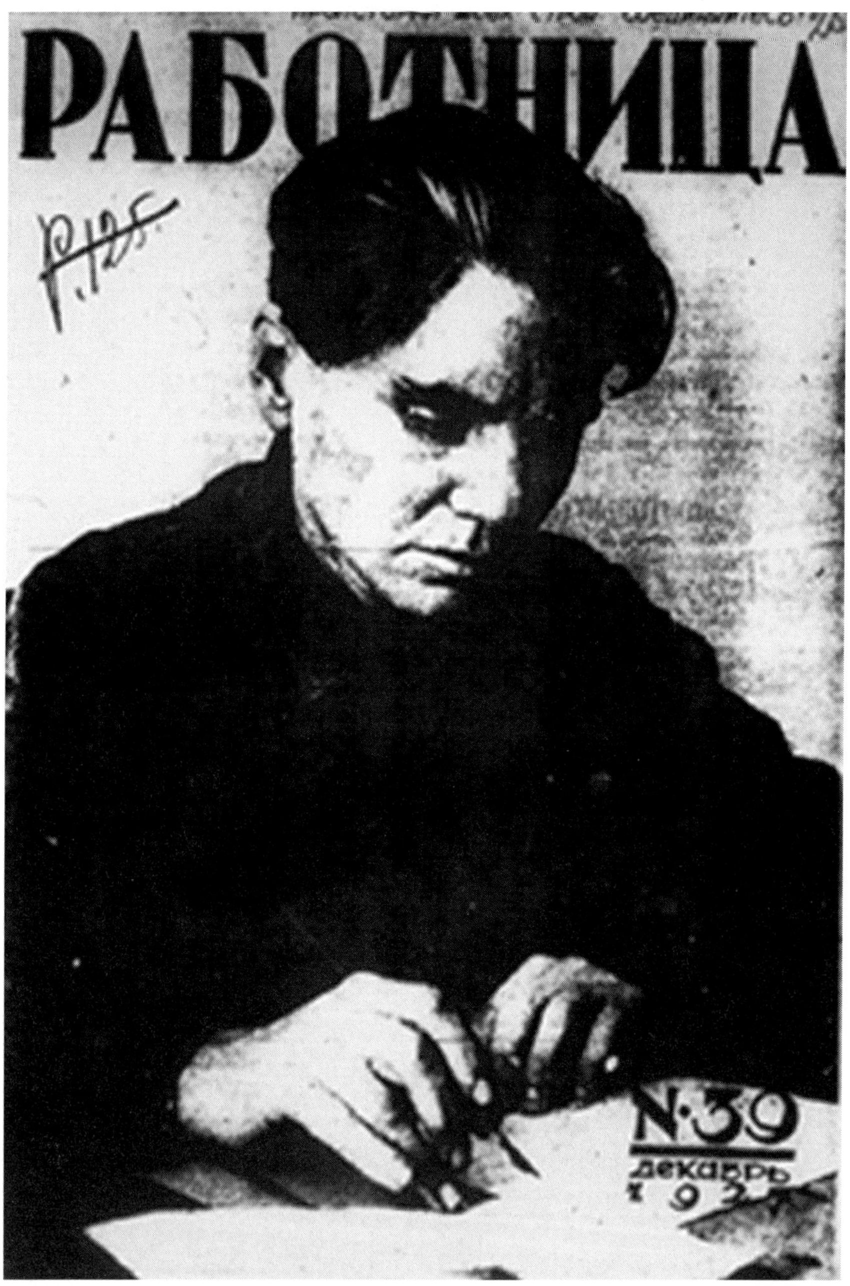

Figure 10.2 A typical Bolshevik woman
Source: *Rabotnitsa*, December 1927

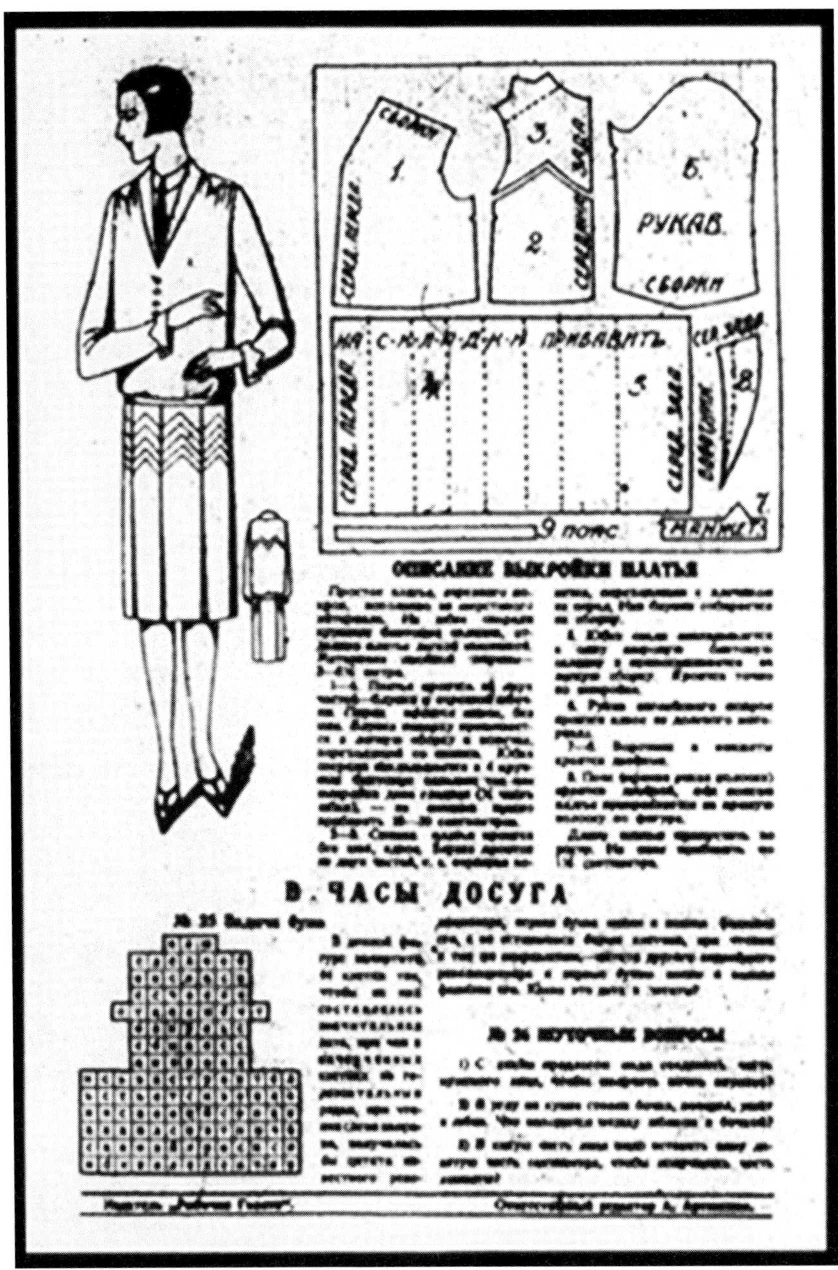

ОПИСАНИЕ ВЫКРОЙКИ ПЛАТЬЯ

В. ЧАСЫ ДОСУГА

Figure 10.3 A pattern for a flapper-style dress
Source: *Rabotnitsa*, December 1927

policy. When Joseph Stalin rose to power in 1929, bringing back with him the old communist rigidness, NEP ended.

THE STALIN GOVERNMENT (1929–53)

Stalin saw his mission in restoring the government to a true communist regime. Unfortunately, his notion of the 'true' communist state included very traditional ideas about women. Stalin had little respect for women, believing that, on the one hand, they should model themselves after men in the old revolutionary style, but on the other, that their only rightful place was in the home. The relative strength of the latter view was evident in his actions. Upon acquiring power, he immediately abolished the Women's Section of the Central Committee of the Party, which had been in operation since 1918 and was responsible for the publication of *Rabotnitsa* (Randall 1965).

Under Stalin, the institution of family began to be important for the state – rather than being the target for the revolutionary destruction. Because family stability also meant labour stability, the laws on divorce and abortion were tightened. The Decree of 1936 officially rehabilitated marriage as an institution, while the Decree of 1944 declared the importance of motherhood – both paved the way back to tradition for Russian women (Meek 1957). Under Stalin, private life came under intense scrutiny and state power was expanded to almost all spheres. As sexuality became a forbidden topic, a prudishness that pervaded official Soviet life for the next fifty years emerged (Moore 1966).

In the early 1930s, Stalin's goal of making Russia into a world player resulted in massive forced industrialisation. His attempt at modernising the economy overstrained individual workers, particularly women, who continued to shoulder the burden of housework. Women's participation in the labour force had been substantial since the early post-revolutionary days (Dallin 1977). Unlike the United States, the Soviet economy was dependent on women for a large portion of the labour force, as opposed to principally relying on their activity as consumers. However, the rule of Stalin inadvertently added further impetus to the feminisation of labour. Over the course of Stalin's rule, 20 million men died either in his jails and concentration camps or in the Second World War. His murderousness not only produced a culture of fear, it also created a significant labour shortage.

At the same time, by 1939 Stalin wanted to balance the economy and to show the overstrained population that there was substance behind his often quoted phrase: 'Life is getting ever better and ever merrier!' Statistics show that he planned to improve living standards and increase production of consumer goods. So once again, the old revolutionary asceticism was in retreat (Dunham 1990).

Rabotnitsa became the 'Magazine for Working Women and Wives of Workers', still remaining the organ of the Central Committee. In the early days of Stalin's regime, therefore, *Rabotnitsa* emphasised the public side of women's lives. There were no pictures of women at home – only work was regarded as worthwhile. As Stalin's strategy changed, an emphasis on the family became apparent on the pages of *Rabotnitsa*. For example, an article in issue 18 (1935) insists that a healthy woman must become a happy mother and that motherhood is real happiness, not a burden. An article in issue 3 (January 1936) praised the new achievements in Soviet medical science that offered to ease labour pain with narcotics. Increasingly, a Soviet woman was seen as means of reproduction.

Stalin's avowed intentions to create a 'merrier' economy were destroyed by the war with Germany. During this time, *Rabotnitsa* underscored two major roles of women: as soldiers and as defence workers. As in the American women's magazines of the period, the content evolved around the war effort. Peacetime brought back other roles to the Soviet women. Thus, a front cover of issue 3 (March 1946) shows a drawing of a woman who tries on a large piece of a new fabric. After the war, Stalin decided that material interest would work alongside ideological condemnation to create a political support system (Dunham 1990). Stalin thus focused on stimulating material demand, particularly among women: 'Material cravings engulfed post-war society from top to bottom. Coiffures, cosmetics, perfume, clothes – the trappings of enchanted femininity – gained social significance' (Dunham 1990: 43). In Stalin's Russia, then, the consumption that created femininity was harnessed to support the system – just as it was in the US. In 1952, a year before Stalin's death, issue 2 has an article on a young couple buying furniture. Recently married, they have moved into a new apartment and are ready to start a new life. The article is illustrated with the patterns of furniture that are offered by a furniture factory. In short, this little bit of 'news' is really an advertisement – and it differs little from the advertising aimed at the soon-to-be-parents of the new Baby Boom, as they too began nesting. In the November 1953 issue, models present dresses not unlike the fashions in the United States during the same period (Figure 10.4). We find similar to what Lois Banner (1983) called a return to Victorian period in dress: skirts became longer and fuller and waists became tighter. This is most notable if we recall that the country was in a cold war with the West and the 'iron curtain' was already in place.

'Feminisation' of women on the pages of *Rabotnitsa* became increasingly apparent. Dress patterns and embroidery appeared in almost every issue. Women were expected to please the eye and to look pretty. So, though women under Stalin were expected to be feminine in an almost Western sense, they were also expected to work in the factories and to produce as many babies (future workers) as possible.

THE KHRUSHCHEV GOVERNMENT (1954–64)

Nikita Khrushchev was committed to ending the material shortages that had plagued the Soviet Union since the days of Lenin (Breslauer 1982). Khrushchev's vision of a communist society was characterised by abundance. Though his vision of communism included plenty of food and consumer goods, Khrushchev was also dedicated to reviving Leninist ideology. He seriously believed that a communist society would be achieved in the Soviet Union within twenty years.

Figure 10.4 A fragment of a fashion page
Source: *Rabotnitsa*, November 1953

Nevertheless, he retained a down-to-earth mentality throughout his life. He once said that 'it was no use for everyone having the correct ideology if they have to walk around without any trousers on' (Keep 1995: 47).

Khrushchev's liberal times brought yet different ideals of femininity. Female images on the pages of *Rabotnitsa* became young, fit and attractive. Editorials insisted on the importance of appearance. The new socialist femininity became not only acceptable but also desirable and was seen as being worth the extra work of exercise or cosmetic manipulations. The new builders of communism must look nice. But it was a special 'socialist' appearance that went along with the moral Code of the Builder of Communism – modest, pure and simple (Field 1996: 29). *Rabotnitsa* took part in 'beautifying' Russian women. In issue 5 (1961: 29), they were urged to 'take care of themselves'. Home concoctions like water and carrot juice were promoted as good cosmetics: 'Your skin will be elastic, fresh and of a very nice colour.'

Under Khrushchev, *Rabotnitsa* acknowledged the existence of romantic love. Numerous short stories celebrated romantic involvement of young couples. Norms in fashion also supported the sensualisation of women. During the workday, a woman was supposed to dress modestly and simply. However, at night, she was transformed: 'A soft blurred silhouette, folds, flowers, glittering embroidery' (1963, issue 8). A woman in the 1960s was almost expected to play the role of seductress outside her place of work. During this same period, as Betty Friedan noted in 1963, the stories in the American women's magazines also became more romantic. Yet the political implications of work and sex were quite different in the Soviet Union, where women had not been excluded from work, and had been accorded sex only as a way of producing babies for the state's factories and armies.

Romantic and lyrical images became common on the pages of *Rabotnitsa*. The photograph on the cover of issue 7 from 1960 (Figure 10.5) presents a young woman in a forest picking wild strawberries. She seems to be absorbed in deep thoughts, and in the background is a mysterious fog that helps create a romantic mood. The picture is unusual because the girl is not identified as a worker and a viewer can see her in leisure pursuit. The composition is called 'Wild strawberries are ripe'! To some contemporary American readers it might be full of symbolism, where strawberries might be associated with sexual maturity. We can only guess how the Soviet reader perceived this image, but one thing is certain: the woman is unmistakably feminine, especially compared to the woman in Figure 10.2.

CONCLUSION

Although the Soviet Union created an economic system and ideology vastly different from that of the West, many of the issues that women experienced in both types of societies were very similar. Some of these, the roles of motherhood and family and the sexual double standard, for instance, were deeply ingrained in the

Figure 10.5 Cover composition entitled 'Wild strawberries are ripe'
Source: *Rabotnitsa*, 1960, issue 7

traditions of both societies prior to industrialisation and are observable in many – in fact, most – pre-industrial societies. These issues seem centrally related to the oppression of women, but not perhaps uniquely a function of either capitalism or industrialisation.

Despite the fact that the Soviet system promoted a producer society where collective production for the good of the nation was a cornerstone (as opposed to a consumer society where consumption is the centre of the system), the Soviet people's desires, especially the women's desires for goods, were strong. Beauty, grooming and the consumer behaviours of feminine appearance seem to enter in the service of both nations' ideologies. However, in the Soviet Union, the feminine aesthetic comes and goes from the official Party line. It appears in both hard line regimes like Stalinism, but also in more liberal times such as the Khrushchev years.

The emphasis on work versus consumption in the Soviet Union is clearly quite different from the situation in the West, particularly in the United States. The question, however, is whether the workforce participation of Soviet women – and the simultaneous denial of their material needs – has improved their lot or increased their power. As surely as the West needs women to consume, the Soviets needed women's hard labour, both at home and in the factories.

The role of consumer culture is more ambiguous than many writers have suggested. While the growth in consumer goods may have lulled Western women into inactivity, according to many critics, the lack of consumer goods in Soviet culture often forced Soviet women to work harder. Thus, in Russia, perhaps even more than in the US, the desire for consumer goods became a tool for domination. In this case, it was the shortages, rather than the excess, of consumer goods that made this phenomenon possible.

Soviet society tried to create a utopia. Its militarised economy did not allow for marketing – a parasite service from the Marxist point of view. Instead its role was performed by the central planning system with its many problems and faults. However, the market still existed in the Soviet Union in a form of illegal black economy. It was a response to the excruciating need of people for consumer goods. Surprisingly, there are some similarities between the Soviet system and contemporary Western marketing. Stephen Brown and his co-authors (Brown, Maclaran and Stevens 1996) argue that the late twentieth-century marketing is really a social utopia. It attempts to create a shiny glitter of consumer paradise by the inflation of buyers' expectations. They define the field as 'the production, distribution and consumption of utopias' (ibid.: 680) – exactly the same things that the Soviet ideology was engaged in.

In a private letter Stanley Hollander (Jones and Monieson 1990: 275) noted that it is important to have different perspectives on marketing and not just that of the 'male professors of marketing in the United States'. The above study presents an alternative historical view from a Russian feminist researcher who has experienced the Soviet system firsthand.[3] It is important to untangle the threads of Soviet women's oppression by the use of media and ideology and to show the similarities with women's oppression in the West. By taking into account the traditional ideologies that characterised both these systems prior to industrialisation, by taking a more subtle and sophisticated view of women's lives under a Marxist regime, and by resisting the temptation to attribute complex historical gender phenomena to simple categories of economic ideology, I hope to enrich our understanding of the factors that support the oppression of women and to illuminate the path toward liberation.

NOTES

1 This is a work in progress. An earlier version of this paper was presented at the 1998 Association for Consumer Research Gender Conference
2 By the 1960s, its circulation reached 10 million (Hopkins 1970).
3 The future research will concentrate on the consumer culture as *Rabotnitsa* presented it. I believe consumption has been the important element of the Soviet system through which both oppression and liberation were manifested.

REFERENCES

Ball, A. (1991) 'Private trade and traders during NEP', in S. Fitzpatrick (ed.) *Russia in the Era of NEP: Exploration on Soviet Society and Culture*, Bloomington and Indianapolis: Indiana University Press.

Ballaster, R., Beetham, F. E. and Hebron, S. (1991) *Women's Worlds: Ideology, Femininity and the Woman's Magazines*, Basingstoke: Macmillan.

Banner, L. (1983) *American Beauty*, New York: Knopf.

Bordo, S. (1993) *Unbearable Weight: Feminism, Western Culture and the Body*, Berkeley: University of California Press.

Breslauer, G. (1982) *Khrushchev and Brezhnev as Leaders*, London and Boston, MA: George Allen & Unwin.

Brown, D. (1968) *The Role and the Status of Women in the Soviet Union*, New York: Teachers' College Press.

Brown, S., Maclaran, P. and Stevens, L. (1996) 'Marcadia postponed: marketing, utopia and the millennium', *Journal of Marketing Management* 12: 671–83.

Brownmiller, S. (1984) *Femininity*, New York: Linden Press.

Buckley, M. (1988) 'Soviet ideology and female roles', in S. White and A. Pravda (eds) *Ideology and Soviet Politics*, Basingstoke: Macmillan.

Cohen, M. (1988) *The Sisterhood: The True Story of the Women Who Changed the World*, New York: Simon & Schuster.

Cott, N. (1977) *The Bonds of Womanhood: Woman's Sphere in New England, 1780–1853*, New Haven, CT: Yale University Press.

Dallin, A. (1977) 'Conclusion', in D. Atkinson, A. Dallin and G. Warshofsky (eds) *Women in Russia*, Stanford, CA: Stanford University Press.

Damon-Moore, H. (1994) *Magazines for Millions: Gender and Commerce in the* Ladies' Home Journal *and the* Saturday Evening Post, *1880–1910*, Albany: State University of New York.

Dunham, V. (1990) *In Stalin's Time: Middle-class Values in Soviet Fiction*, Durham, NC: Duke University Press.

Elwood, R. (1992) *Inessa Armand: Revolutionary and Feminist*, Cambridge: Cambridge University Press.

Ewen, S. (1976) *Captains of Consciousness: Advertising and the Social Roots of Consumer Culture*, New York: McGraw-Hill.

Ferguson, M. (1983) *Women's Magazines and the Cult of Femininity*, London: Heinemann.

Field, D. (1996) 'Communist morality and meaning of private life in post-Stalinist Russia, 1953–1964', doctoral dissertation, University of Michigan.

Friedan, B. (1963) *The Feminine Mystique*, New York: Norton.

Gorsuch, A. (1996) 'A woman is not a man: the culture of gender and generation in Soviet Russia, 1921–1928', *Slavic Review* 55, 3: 636–60.

Hopkins, M. (1970) *Mass Media in the Soviet Union*, New York: Pegasus.

Jones, B. and D. Monieson (1990) 'Historical research in marketing: retrospect and prospect', *Journal of the Academy of Marketing Science* 18, 4: 268–78.

Keep, J. (1995) *The Last of the Empires: A History of the Soviet Union, 1945–1991*, New York: Oxford University Press.

Kort, M. (1996) *The Soviet Colossus: History and Aftermath*, New York: M. E. Sharpe.

Lenin, V. (1959) *Lenin o pechati* [Lenin on Press], Moscow: Gosudar Stvennoe 12 Datelstvo Politicheskoi, Literatury.

—— (1966) *The Emancipation of Women: From the Writings of V. I. Lenin*, New York: International Publishers.

McCracken, E. (1993) *Decoding Women's Magazines: From* Mademoiselle *to* Ms., New York: St Martin's Press.

Meek, D. (1957) *Soviet Youth*, New York: Routledge.

Moore, B. (1966) *Terror and Progress – USSR: Some Sources of Chance and Stability in the Soviet Dictatorship*, New York: Harper & Row.

Mott, F. (1939) *A History of American Magazines 1741–1850*, Vol. 1, Cambridge, MA: Harvard University Press.

Naiman, E. (1997) *Sex in Public: The Incarnation of the Early Soviet Ideology*, Princeton, NJ: Princeton University Press.

Nove, A. (1969) *An Economic History of the USSR*, London: Penguin.

Okker, P. (1995) *Our Sisters Editors: Sarah J. Hale and the Tradition of Nineteenth Century Women Editors*, Athens: University of Georgia Press.

Peterson, T. (1964) *Magazines in the Twentieth Century*, Urbana: University of Illinois Press.

Randall, F. (1965) *Stalin's Russia: A Historical Reconsideration*, New York: The Free Press.

Ryan, M. P. (1983) *Womanhood in America: From Colonial Times to the Present*, New York: Franklin Watts.

Scanlon, J. (1995) *Inarticulate Longings: The* Ladies' Home Journal, *Gender and the Promises of Consumer Culture*, New York: Routledge.

Shlapentokh, V. (1986) *Soviet Public Opinion and Ideology: Mythology and Pragmatism in Interaction*, New York: Praeger.

Stal, L. (1959) 'Iz istorii zhurnala *Rabotnitsa* [From the history of *Rabotnitsa*]', in A. V. Artiukhina (ed.) *Zhenshchiny v revoliutsii* [Women in Revolution], Moscow: Gosudarstvennoe izdatel'stvo Politicheskoi Literatury, 108–11.

Steinem, G. (1990) 'Sex, lies and advertising', *Ms.*, July/August: 18–28.

Tebbel, J. (1969) *The American Magazine: A Compact History*, New York: Hawthorn Books.

Tiano, S. (1984) 'The public–private dichotomy: theoretical perspectives on "Women in Development"', *Social Science Journal* 21, 4: 11–28.

Vavilina, V. (ed.) (1964) *Vsegda s vami: sbornik posviashchennyi 50-letiiu zhurnala* Rabotnitsa [Always with You: Collection in Honour of the 50th Anniversary of *Rabotnitsa*], Moscow: Pravda.

Whitney, J. (1954) 'Women: Russia's second-class citizens', *Look*, November: 30–5.
Winship, J. (1978) 'A woman's world: *Woman* – an ideology of femininity', in University of Birmingham Centre for Contemporary Cultural Studies, Women's Group, *Women Take Issue: Aspects of Women's Subordination*, London: Hutchinson.
Wood, E. (1997) *The Baba and the Comrade: Gender and Politics in Revolutionary Russia*, Bloomington: Indiana University Press.

11 Off to the shops: why do we *really* go shopping?

Sue Eccles and Helen Woodruffe-Burton

INTRODUCTION

Recent studies into shopping behaviour and associated phenomena such as the study of 'shopaholics' (e.g. Elliott 1994) have thrust shopping (and the role of shopping) into the popular spotlight with a rush of articles appearing in the press. When one of the most widely read women's magazines in the UK asks its readers 'Which do you think is better, shopping or sex?' (*Prima* reader survey, February 1997), the time must be ripe for serious consideration of the role of shopping in our lives today. This chapter poses the question 'Why do we *really* go shopping?' and examines the history of shopping and its role in women's lives. Comfort shopping, or 'retail therapy', is explored under the broader concept of compensatory consumption and the focus then moves to a detailed discussion of shopping addiction, with examples and illustrations from our ongoing research into women's lived experience of consumption.

THE HISTORY OF SHOPPING AS A GENDERED ACTIVITY

The development of the consumer society in the Western capitalistic system of exchange can be traced back centuries. However, it has been the major economic and political revolutions that have made the most marked impression on developing consumption as we understand it today. As Jones (1996) explains, in the period between 1650 and the French Revolution Western Europe experienced a 'consumer revolution' whereby the urban middle and lower classes began to enjoy some of the material goods, trinkets and luxuries only previously available to the aristocracy. Even so, except for visits to local markets for day-to-day necessities by the lower- and middle-class women, men undertook most other shopping activities until the end of the nineteenth century. Indeed, shops, such as they were, 'spatially linked licit and illicit pleasures; spaces for consumption of luxury goods flowed directly into spaces for drinking coffee, gambling, examining curiosities and puppet shows . . . hardly a place appropriate for virtuous bourgeois wives and mothers' (Jones 1996: 31). There was a distinct difference in consumption habits according to class. The aristocracy traditionally had the money, time and desire to express themselves through opulent consumption. More often than not, aristocratic women would be visited by merchants (such as dressmakers and jewellers) in their own homes, and there was often more scope for expression of personal and family values through their possessions. Working-class women rarely had the money, time or domestic space for anything other than necessities. Due to the effects of such major political and economic change as the French Revolution and the Industrial Revolution, it was the middle-class women who, as part of their role as wife and mother, defined and maintained their family and class status through acquisition of material goods for the home. By the mid-nineteenth century, then, the emphasis of 'popular' consumption had shifted from the aristocracy to the middle classes. Journals, texts and pamphlets urged middle-class women to buy and display goods appropriate to their station. Overt and excessive opulence was discouraged. Functionality and modesty in every aspect of consumption was all-important, embracing political, social and economic dictates (Jones 1996).

The importance of shopping in the UK as part of women's everyday experience was developed towards the end of the nineteenth century primarily through the introduction and expansion of department stores (Nava 1996). This was one of the first major opportunities for women to enter the public sphere in a relatively safe, socially acceptable and women-orientated environment. As Nava (1996: 46) explains, 'the pleasurable social activity [of shopping] was already established among the upper classes prior to this period'. However, the growth in the economy, together with developments in public transport and new forms of mass production, all contributed to the expansion of shops and shopping during the end of the nineteenth and beginning of the twentieth century. Of equal importance was the growing demand from an increasingly affluent and socially and geographically mobile urban population. For the first time, women were able to enjoy, through the development of the department store, their own purpose-built public space for activities that satisfied their functional, social and aspirational needs.

At this time, shopping went beyond the consideration or acquisition of goods that conveyed some kind of symbolic meaning about the owner, her family and her status. Many department stores at this period became luxurious, purpose-built 'fantasy palaces' (Nava 1996: 48) which provided a range of entertainment – musical, visual, theatrical and oriental. Further facilities for the comfort and convenience of the department store shopper included 'supervised children's areas, toilets and powder rooms, hairdressing courts, ladies' and gentlemen's clubs and writing rooms, restaurants and tea-rooms, roof gardens with pergolas, zoos and ice rinks, picture galleries, banks, ticket and travel agencies, grocery provision and delivery service' (Nava 1996: 50). For many women, and especially those from the burgeoning middle classes, this was their first opportunity to experience a range of activities and social encounters without the need for a male escort. Social niceties could be observed beyond the drawing room, providing a greater freedom for women, many of whom had previously only been able to enter the public sphere through their philanthropic or charitable activities.

It is questionable whether the emergence of department stores provided merely an extension of the domestic sphere – a continuation, if on a far more public scale, of the opportunity for social interaction of women via a respectable, purpose-designed environment – or whether it was indeed the first, albeit tentative, opportunity for women in their own right to enter the wider outside world. Either way 'as institutions, the stores made a major contribution to the twentieth century consolidation of women as consumers, and to consumption and consumer expertise as activities that were as gendered as production' (Nava 1996: 48). Some writers took this a stage further: developments in shopping such as the introduction of the department store actually went towards the 'feminisation' of shopping, according to Laermans (1993), who describes the early department stores as 'female leisure centres'. Certainly, many traditional leisure pursuits were more or less exclusively the realm of men – drinking in pubs and bars, many sports, gambling and betting – and even today there are social and cultural barriers to certain activities for many women who would still feel uncomfortable, for example, visiting pubs or bars alone.

Shopping is an activity seen as complementary to female roles (Kelly 1991) which themselves are changing; the traditional woman's role (as wife, mother, carer) has undergone change due to the revolution in shopping heralded by the development of the department store, as discussed elsewhere in this chapter. It was primarily women who orchestrated domestic consumption and who found an opportunity for social expression through shopping (Cross 1993). According to Laermans (1993) women's performance of their traditional roles was redefined in terms of commodities and women were seen to be professional shoppers or consumers.

There is evidence that women take their role as shoppers seriously; in their study of gender roles and Christmas gift shopping, Fischer and Arnold (1990) noted that women appeared to take it quite seriously as real and important work, unlike men who saw Christmas gift shopping as 'play'. Nava (1996: 57) refers to the substantial levels of skill and expertise required by the work women were doing as consumers and notes 'the ambiguous position of shopping as an activity which was clearly neither work nor leisure'.

Shopping is increasingly seen as a leisure activity (Martin and Mason 1987; Jansen-Verbeke 1987) and, as such, fulfils a role in family and social life which goes beyond the traditional shopping activities (the American term 'marketing') of buying in provisions and other goods when required.

Jansen-Verbeke (1987) issues a caveat to researchers, however, that 'shopping as a leisure activity for women could very well be an imposed and perhaps biased view on the part of the research worker on the actual experience of shopping', because shopping is often seen by women as a legitimate activity, belonging to their gender role and therefore not necessarily experienced as a leisure activity.

This, in the authors' view, may be one of the reasons why shopping behaviour is often found to be a manifestation of compensatory, even addictive, consumption behaviour, as will be explored later. Shopping can always be justified. A busy woman, experiencing pressure on all sides from family and work, and faced with increasing competition for her time, may find it more easy to justify (to herself and important others, such as her family and partner) using resources such as time, money and effort on shopping rather than alternative activities. Furthermore, her social image is not at risk and may well be enhanced if she is perceived as being a good shopper, whereas if she frequently uses resources to pursue some other activity – sport, art, a college course, for example – she could be open to criticism of neglecting her role, that is to say her duty to family and others. Elliott's (1994) work bears this out as he suggests that 'for women, shopping provides a socially acceptable alternative to alcohol for mood repair'; he also suggests that it is less problematic than the use of tranquillisers.

It is generally accepted that women at the start of the twentieth century made 80 per cent of purchasing decisions (Nava 1996: 71). Over the past century, the importance of shopping and the shopping environment has continued to impact upon women. There have, of course, been phenomenal social and economic changes which have allowed women's roles, responsibilities and status in society to develop, such as two world wars, the emancipation of women, the rise of the feminist movement, the introduction of the National Health Service, and child and other benefits. Within the past few decades, moreover, technological advances have dramatically affected domestic, commercial and industrial life. Among the many things that have stayed constant is the proportion of 8 : 2 of women shoppers to men (Nava 1996: 71), although this excludes household shopping. In this case, the responsibility falls to just under 50 per cent of women, and nearly half the household shopping is now a shared activity (Central Statistical Office 1995: 14). Times may have changed, and consumption patterns with them, but shopping in the UK is still very much an activity carried out by women.

RETAIL THERAPY – SHOPPING AS COMPENSATORY CONSUMPTION

Compensatory consumption can be defined as follows:

> Compensatory consumption is engaged in whenever an individual feels a need, lack or desire which they cannot satisfy with a primary fulfilment so they seek and use an alternative means of fulfilment in its place.

Various studies have examined the concept of compensatory consumption (e.g. Gronmo 1988; Grunert 1993) but the link between shopping and compensation, *retail therapy*, has only been examined more recently (e.g. Woodruffe 1996, 1997). Previous studies of other associated phenomena lend support to this focus on the role of shopping as compensation. Babin, Darden and Griffin's (1994) study of hedonistic and utilitarian shopping also reveals qualities or values in shopping which are compensatory in nature. As one respondent in their study is reported to have said: 'I enjoy shopping when it helps me forget my problems'. Another stated: 'It's a high. It occurred to me that when I get depressed then I want to go shopping. It's too bad it's expensive. It's a thrill. It gives you a lift to buy something.' Shopping offers a means of compensating which is generally accessible and available. As Langrehr (1991: 428) put it: 'people buy so they can shop, not shop so they can buy'. Hope is closely linked to imaginary ideals in consumption as in McCracken's (1990) view that there is an intimate connection between consumer goods and hope in consumer societies, and that goods can act as bridges to displaced meaning (in other words, objects can tell us not who we are but who we wish we were). Nava (1996: 53) comments on the exciting role that shopping can play in this respect: 'It [the department store] offered a language to imagine a different and better future, one in which the injuries and wants of everyday existence could be soothed and family lives enhanced.'

In the authors' view, compulsive buying and shopping addiction, which are the focus of the next section of this chapter, are chronic forms of compensatory consumption behaviour. Facets of the phenomenon mentioned by O'Guinn and Faber (1989) also add weight to this proposition. For example, they highlight the fact that for many people compulsive buying seems to be strongly tied to their need for affection and support from others. In other words, the authors believe this can be interpreted as meaning that they are responding to a perceived 'lack' (suggested by the author in italics). Informants in their study spoke of their need to lead more exciting lives (a lack of excitement?), 'feel alive' (a lack of life? As in 'get a life!', to coin a highly illustrative phrase) and to be stimulated by their surroundings (a lack of stimulation; boredom?).

Motivational explanations for addictive consumption cited by Elliott (1994) include coping with anxiety states and stress (a lack of calm, inner peace, well-being?), links with self-esteem (a lack of self-esteem?) and construction of a 'self' (lack of self?). The findings of Elliott's study showed that respondents were engaging in various compensatory behaviours to make up for perceived inadequacies or emotional deficits through their descriptions of their own addictive consumption tendencies in relation to insecurities, childhood problems, feelings of being unattractive, depression and lack of emotional support from partner and relationships. Because, as Elliott, Eccles and Gournay (1995) suggest in later work, this addictive consumption behaviour is an extension of 'normal' behaviour, this also adds weight to the notion that compensatory consumption is 'normal' and hence widespread, occurring on a continuum basis with an addiction to such behaviour representing an extreme form. In this subsequent research, Elliott, Eccles and Gournay (1995) found that some addictive consumers were not trying to compensate for negative feelings. Rather they used the shopping experience not only as a form of self-expression but also as a means of having some control over a part of their lives or, to some extent, over their partner. This again could be an illustration of a form of compensatory consumption to regain control or exercise some power (as a response to a perceived lack of control or power).

THE REALITY OF SHOPPING – ITS ROLE IN WOMEN'S LIVES

The following examples from our research highlight facets of the role of shopping in women's lives; its compensatory nature, where it can be used to overcome life's shortcomings, and accounts of what it feels like when this behaviour turns into an addiction. The initial research has been conducted in the form of phenomenological interviews with women shoppers, adopting the format and context outlined by Thompson, Locander and Pollio (1989). It is argued that the interview is the most powerful means for attaining in-depth understanding of another person's experience (Kvale 1983). Existential-phenomenological understanding is attained by describing lived experiences and the meanings that emerge from them (Thompson, Locander and Pollio 1989) and this is the means by which it is hoped that an understanding of these aspects of shopping behaviour may begin to be developed. Phenomenological descriptions were interpreted in line with the criteria noted by Thompson, Locander and Pollio (1989).

When studying shopping as compensatory behaviour or 'retail therapy', a key factor that emerged was the contrast between the act of shopping itself, the shopping experience, as the most important aspect, and the act of buying things as the essential, almost urgent, goal when shopping for these women (the initial and age of the respondent is indicated in brackets in each case):

> 'It's mainly shopping that does it for me – it can just cheer me up so much . . . I don't think "Oh, I'm depressed, I'm going to go shopping." I must just do it automatically or something.'
>
> (L 20)

> 'I sometimes go shopping because I haven't got much else to do in my life, so I go shopping for something to do rather than to buy things.'
>
> (S 29)

> 'If I have been a bit depressed and I go and have a look round the shops and I do see something that I want then it becomes an obsession that I have to get it and if I don't get it there and then it will just play on my mind all the time.'
>
> (J 19)

Sometimes they described a feeling that they needed to buy something, no matter how small, to make them feel better:

> 'Even little things, you can have a stressful morning and you go and buy something from Bodyshop . . . just go and buy a little bottle of £1.19 something or other and it is going to cheer you up a lot.'
>
> (L 20)

> 'If I've got some new clothes it's like having a reason to cheer up. If I just have a bath or go for a walk I don't have anything to show for it so it's less of a reason to be happy.'
>
> (M 20)

The importance of the role played by shopping in some respondents' lives came through in various ways, for example a widow used shopping as a means of coping with her bereavement:

> 'I had to go to shops to feel comfortable again and in an environment I was used to being in on my own . . . I meet people in there and I say "hello" and it's comforting to be somewhere you know.'
>
> (S 60)

To S shopping was the only time she felt really independent:

> 'It's the thought that shopping is independent and I can do that if I want to and I can do that and I don't have to consult anybody else and I'm free to do that whenever I want and how I want and I can spend whatever I wanted like £100 or I could just go and have a look, that's totally up to me.'
>
> (S 29)

The idea of shopping being a solitary and personal activity was very important to several respondents:

> 'Going out is for when you want to have a really good time and you feel that if you don't go out you'll snap. But shopping is for when you want to be on your own.'
>
> (S 19)

> 'I can't shop with anybody else, it's no fun with somebody else about (pause) it's a very private pleasure.'
>
> (M 28)

The idea of escaping, or getting away from everything, also cropped up frequently:

> 'I just like the way you can escape reality – it's like you are completely on your own, even though there are lots of people around you, you can get lost . . . be alone with your thoughts and you can, I don't know, it's like you're interacting with other people but you're not.'
>
> (S 19)

Several respondents discussed their own feelings of low self-esteem and lack of self-confidence and expressed the view that buying good clothes (especially designer labels) helped them to overcome their feelings of inadequacy. Clothes and other material possessions became props used to construct a more positive self-image. These respondents seemed inclined to frequent or even chronic compensatory consumption behaviour. Other respondents did not feel themselves to be lacking in self-confidence but used shopping as a compensatory mechanism in response to particular instances which had annoyed or upset them in some way, for example, a relationship breakdown or stress at work. In these cases, the instances of compensatory consumption were more episodic in nature. Many of the respondents had also engaged in other forms of compensatory behaviour, such as comfort eating, getting drunk, buying chocolate and sweets or smoking and socialising.

In further, more detailed, case studies of female consumers (Woodruffe-Burton 1998), the role of consumption – most specifically shopping – in their lives emerges as a highly complex series of inter-related activities which exemplify Firat and Dholakia's (1998) assertion that 'Life is to be produced and created, in effect constructed through multiple experiences in which the consumer immerses . . .'.

There is evidence, for instance, which suggests examples of consumers who use consumption as mood repair (Gardner 1985; Luomala 1998), such as this account of E going out to buy a new suit because she was 'cross' with herself.

> 'Then I realised that half the stuff he had asked for we couldn't use and I should have checked it before whatever, so I was quite cross with myself and quite cross with him [her boss]. Then I went and bought this red suit which turned out to be very useful.'
>
> (E 34)

Others see the shopping trip as an escape from family or work responsibilities:

> 'I think I went shopping basically because with having the kids 24 hours a day . . . I work from home . . . it was like a day out just for me.'
>
> (J 32)

> 'I use shopping a lot of the time to escape, because it's so different from what I do, sort of most of the time and it gives me a break from sitting at the computer and being serious . . .'
>
> (M 44)

The importance J attaches to shopping trips and the anticipation beforehand can sometimes lead to feelings of being let down, as she reflects here on such a shopping trip:

> 'I think you build yourself up, you think "ooh, well, I might find something really exciting today", and you get like this, bit of a high, don't you? And sometimes, I mean when I've done the shopping – like I've had a day out and it's when you come home and the buzz has gone and you're slightly,

> slightly sad inside . . . I think you build yourself up to have this fantastic day and you go and find this brilliant thing, this . . . this dress that's going to make you feel fantastic, and it'll make you feel good and it doesn't happen and it's all an imaginary dress and there's no bloody dress out there like the dress you've got in your head and that's disappointing.'
>
> (J 32)

These incidents can be examined from a compensatory perspective (Grunert 1993; Woodruffe 1997) as they reflect a lack of satisfaction and the need to escape, or a lack of power or control (in work situations). In the case of E, her attitude to fashion, and, in particular, repeated accounts of selecting and wearing the 'right' clothes, the 'right' suit (Woodruffe 1998) could be explored via, for instance, the literature on self and identity creation (e.g. Giddens 1991; Thompson 1995) and the notion of an idealised self (Ferguson 1992), which also relates to J's account of searching for the right dress.

E uses shopping creatively; she devised a game out of shopping to make up for problems on her honeymoon, for example, and scours charity shops strategically (with predetermined objectives and a route plan) as a 'hobby'. This behaviour could be looked at from the perspective of the vast literature on shopping behaviour, bargain hunting, shopping as leisure (cf. Woodruffe 1997) and so on but, on reading the story closely, it can be seen that this is a coping strategy which she uses to maintain balance in her relationship with her husband (it gives him time to go horse-riding, for example; it made the honeymoon viable).

ADDICTIVE CONSUMPTION

For some consumers, shopping habits are developed and maintained over a long period of time to such an extent that the behaviour can be classified as addictive. Typical addictive consumption manifests itself through a short-term cycle of anticipation, excitement and craving for a shopping experience, then careful selection of products (often clothing and fashion accessories) during which time the consumer experiences a 'high' or 'buzz'. Having paid for the goods and left the shopping environment, feelings of guilt and remorse set in. Rather than return the goods, or even wear them, addictive consumers hide away their purchases in wardrobes, attics or cupboards where they remain unused and unopened. In the longer term, this behaviour leads to secretive, excessive and unmanageable debt, relationship problems and personal conflict. Instead of being able to control their consumption, *it* controls *them* (see, for example, O'Guinn and Faber 1989; Elliott 1994; Eccles, Hamilton and Elliott 1999).

As much as there has been interest in the behaviour of the addictive consumer in recent years, there has been some debate as to the appropriate terminology for this form of aberrant and excessive behaviour. Described variously as 'compulsive buying' (e.g. Valence, d'Astous and Fortier 1988 and O'Guinn and Faber 1989), 'compulsive consumption' (Shoaf *et al.* 1995) and 'addictive buying'

(Scherhorn, Reisch and Raab 1990), there appears to be little acceptance of one term that can be used universally. This is important, because evidence to date would suggest that researchers are actually investigating a similar sort of behaviour, and developing and exploring similar issues, yet apparently fail to agree on one of the most fundamental issues – the term for describing the behaviour. This difference in opinion is important, not only from a conceptual point of view but also because of the differences in the ways of measuring and treating compulsive as opposed to addictive behaviours. There is increasing concern regarding the personal, social, physical and financial implications of addictive behaviours generally, and a recognition in medical and counselling fields that addictive behaviour may require very different and specialised treatment (see, for example, Concar 1994).

ADDICTIVE CONSUMPTION AS A GENDERED ACTIVITY

One of the commonly explored areas for discussion during radio, television and magazine interviews on addictive consumption is why it is predominantly *women* who become addicted, and why it is the *shopping experience* that they become addicted to, as opposed to, for example, alcohol, gambling or drugs. Indeed, previous research has shown that addictive consumers are predominantly women (e.g. Scherhorn, Reisch and Raab (1990) state that twenty-two out of twenty-six in their sample were women; O'Guinn and Faber (1989) had a sample comprising 92 per cent women). An understanding of the history, role and significance of shopping for women in general terms as outlined in the opening sections of this chapter may assist us in the examination of the effect of gender on the development and maintenance of addictive consumption behaviour amongst women.

THE EFFECT OF GENDER ON ADDICTIVE CONSUMPTION

As Barker (1997: 292) points out 'gender influences our lives from the moment we are born'. Women are traditionally treated as more passive, caring and dependent, whilst men are seen as more aggressive, self-reliant and protective. Thus, women are given the roles of mothers, homemakers, sex objects and assistants, and social training (in, for example, dress, physical features, behaviour and activities) which will encourage these limited roles. Barker (1997: 294) continues that 'in some areas, women have greater and more persistent [mental health] problems than men: certain anxiety states, depression . . . and aspects of social relationships figure strongly in this respect'. He acknowledges that this is due, in many cases, more to the social upbringing and position of the individual rather than being a function of biological or personality sex differences.

So it would seem that because of social pressure and upbringing, some women who develop aberrant behaviour over a period of time will do so within the confines and restrictions of activities that are deemed to be 'acceptably feminine'.

Even excessive behaviour is gendered, in that it is more socially acceptable for men to become dependent on drink, gambling or even sex, whilst women will turn to tranquillisers or anti-depressants (passive; dependent), develop eating disorders (physical attractiveness) or become addictive consumers (mother, homemaker). This is especially obvious amongst older adults, whose lifestyles have become more gendered in the course of their lives than young people and teenagers where, for example, drug and alcohol abuse appear to be less gendered.

THE VOICES OF ADDICTIVE CONSUMERS

Forty-seven phenomenological interviews with women were carried out throughout the UK, which provided a rich first-person description of the lives, beliefs and experiences of these addictive consumers. What emerged was a range of similarities and differences within the group. The lived experiences of the shopping episodes, the personal feelings and the consequences of the behaviour were almost identical in each case. The differences emerged in the proximal and distal precursors to the development of addictive shopping. In broad terms, it is possible to identify four groups of women, who develop and maintain this addictive behaviour for very different reasons.

The four groups can be termed the 'existentialists', the 'revenge-seekers', the 'profoundly unhappy' and the 'mood-repairers', and were detailed by the research leader, Richard Elliott, in his report to the Economic and Social Research Council (1996).[1]

The following section of this chapter will explore these groups in more detail, and seek a greater understanding of their own experiences. Inevitably, individual quotes presented in isolation from the rest of the interview risk interpretation out of context. However, the aim here is to provide some insight into their feelings and behaviour, in various parts of their lives.

The existentialists

The existential addicts are creating a sense of meaning in their lives through their consumer choices, which for them involve the experience of 'flow' (Csikszentmihalyi 1992). When making choices in the shop, they are matching their skills as a consumer with the challenge of achieving the 'best' possible purchase, which takes them into the autotelic state described by Csikszentmihalyi (1992: 67). This is not mere pursuit of pleasure, however, but part of a conscious process of self-development whereby the individual is seeking to create and maintain an identity that is founded upon skilful shopping behaviour. This is reasoned behaviour described in the 'normal' population by Fischer and Gainer (1991) as being an integral part of the social construction of women's identity. Thus, addictive consumption is not qualitatively different from 'normal' consumption but involves a more intensive behaviour carried out more frequently and with increased negative long-term consequences. However, the biphasic reinforcement effect that is characteristic of many addictions means the short-term benefits of the behaviour influence the 'existentialist' much more powerfully than the long-term negative consequences. The positive reinforcement provided by the achievement of flow and the construction of existential meaning suggests that this behaviour pattern will be very resistant to change.

Mary is typical of this group of addictive consumers. She is 58 years old, twice divorced and now married to Mark, who is fifteen years her junior. Her son committed suicide some thirteen years ago, but she has a married daughter and grandson. She lives in a spacious modern house. She works full-time as an administrator, but is due to retire soon. She is not in debt, but has spent several thousand pounds of her own savings over the past few years to pay off credit cards and loans. She tends to buy goods in phases – a week buying handbags, a few days buying blouses, and so on. Mary is extremely energetic and she does not appear to need (or get) much sleep. She is very smartly dressed and well presented, and her house is tastefully decorated and furnished. She describes herself as:

> '. . . a very, very fussy shopper. I go into the shop and I've got to have a sweater. I weigh them all up; I measure them all out; I can't make up my mind about three of the same colour. I bring them all home and try them on until 2 a.m. or 3 a.m. in the morning, until I find the one that is just right. Then, when I've found the right one, I have to go back the next morning and buy one of every colour in that. Then, they are forgotten. Probably just hung up in the wardrobe and never worn.'

She describes these phases of buying particular items as 'missions':

> 'When I knew I was going to retire, I went off sick for a couple of days. My next mission was something to wear in the house. So I bought track suits (indoor and outdoor), Reebok trainers (lightweight and silky), polo shirts in every colour. I know I'll be like a tramp in the house and just wear old jeans, but they are there, so at least I can think about what I could put on.'

Apart from the purchases themselves, Mary finds the whole experience of going to the shops exciting and describes the experience of flow:

> 'I just love the feeling of excitement and wonderment as I go into the shopping mall. I love the buzz of people; the colour and displays; the whole atmosphere. I can just soak up that feeling at the beginning of my shopping trip – it's almost as if I say to myself, "OK, you're at home now, you can relax and enjoy yourself".'

Mary considers herself to be a very discerning shopper ('I do surveys on things, like which will wash the best') and will check each item to make sure it is perfect (i.e., has no snags or marks) and that the fit and cut are just right. She has a real 'eye' for colour and design, and can tell almost at a glance whether an item will match up with other clothes in her wardrobe. She admits:

> 'I will spend hours both in the shops and at home considering and comparing different items – invariably, buying more than one and, on many occasions, worrying at night about something I have seen that day in the shops but not bought.'

On these occasions, she will arrive late for work in order to go back to the shop as soon as it opens the next day. Mary is not as secretive about her shopping behaviour as some of the other informants:

> 'I don't think I necessarily boast about my purchases, but I do feel a great pride when I find that "perfect outfit" – even though I may have spent several days searching for it and it ends up, along with most of my other purchases, either in the loft or hanging unworn in one of my four double wardrobes!'

She feels she is seen by others as a 'canny shopper' (similar to the 'market maven' described by Feick and Price (1985)) and friends often turn to her for advice on where to shop or how to co-ordinate an outfit. However, she goes shopping virtually daily:

> 'I get withdrawal symptoms and feel depressed if I don't go to the shops. I tried staying in on a Saturday last week and went for a long walk with Mark. We got back at 4.20 p.m. and I was sweating. I thought, "I have to go in to town", and I thought, "Well, what am I looking for? I don't need anything", but I can always see something.'

About shopping generally, Mary is quite adamant about its importance in her life:

> 'If ever there was anyone born to shop, it must be me! I have to say it's the most important thing in my life and gives me a real sense of purpose. Although I hate the fact that I can't break the habit, if I'm really honest, I don't want to – what else could I do that would give me so much pleasure and satisfaction?'

The revenge-seekers

Julie is 36 years old, married and with three children (all females) under 12 years old. She lives in a large and elegant Victorian house. She was very spoilt as the youngest of four and admits that she was her 'father's favourite'. Her husband David is aged 43 and is a medical practitioner working long and irregular hours. Julie works part-time at the local radio station. She is not in debt, as her husband pays off the credit cards regularly and she has a small inheritance of her own. She buys clothes and accessories and is particularly interested in attending fine arts auctions. Julie and her husband appear to have a fairly stable and loving relationship, but she feels that he has taken over from her father as an indulgent father-figure:

> 'He says: "Well, you were spoilt as a child and I suppose I will have to continue the tradition." '

About her husband she says:

> 'He loves to work and, in the early days when the children were very small and I was bringing them up practically single-handed, he would work Saturdays and Sundays. I would resent that so I would think, "Right, if he's working, then I'm spending". Now we're in a vicious circle – I'm spending and he's working. He says, "How can I cut down on work? I have to work to pay the bills". In the early years we would have big rows about it.'

She feels her husband treats her as frivolous and incompetent with regard to money:

> 'Sometimes I get the Spanish Inquisition . . . until recently, it would have been, "Show me your chequebook and explain where this money has gone", and I, trembling, would have to give him my cheque stubs. I've put a stop to that now but I still feel that he has control over me – at least, he thinks he has.'

Julie herself seems to be in conflict between the child in her that wants to 'get back' at her husband, and the adult who has responsibilities as a mother and worker. About her shopping behaviour she says:

> 'The sensible side of me says, "stop it – grow up!", whilst another little voice is saying at the same time, "I deserve it, and I want it, so it's mine".'

Julie considers herself to be generally happy and fortunate. She doesn't feel she shops to bolster low self-esteem or depression, but acknowledges it may sometimes be through boredom and is often a way of getting back at her husband (even though she acknowledges that he has no idea of the extent of her shopping and spending):

> 'Sometimes when I'm shopping, I see something I like and it's as if I think: "Right, I'll show him!" Even though he doesn't know how much I'm spending, I feel that I am getting revenge on David for all the times he ignores what I want or isn't there when I need him. I don't think I could confront him anymore, but I really can get back at him through shopping.'

She and her husband rarely spend any time together, and he leaves the running of the household and bringing up the children mainly to her – which she generally enjoys but sometimes finds it lonely and boring. She has no other close confidantes.

Addictive consumption and the revenge addict

Julie and other informants who showed elements of revenge in their addictive shopping behaviour all appeared to have feelings of lack of control in their relationship with their partner (and often, previously, their father). They felt undermined and patronised, and that their only responsibility was for 'mundane' tasks such as housekeeping and cooking. Comments such as 'he still treats me like a child' were common, even though the respondents themselves feel they have 'grown up' because of family or professional responsibilities. It appears therefore that they developed and maintain their shopping behaviour in order to have some kind of 'exciting' or even slightly dangerous control over a part of their personal lives and their finances. This in turn suggests some feeling of power (albeit secretive) over their partner. The fact that many partners appear to tolerate what they know or suspect about the shopping activities seems, if anything, to encourage the informants to take even greater risks and be even more outrageous in their activities.

To build upon Duck's (1994) Model of Relational Challenges, some consumers perceive themselves as victims of betrayal in a relationship, in that the partner has not fulfilled previously suggested or stated requests for the dynamics of the relationship to adapt to changes in external or family circumstances. Having taken overt action in the past to address the situation and found it unsuccessful, they adopt a more subversive, less overt method of 'getting back' at their partner by developing and maintaining an addiction to consumption.

The profoundly unhappy

This group of respondents showed evidence of deep-rooted unhappiness. They either were or had been addicted to other behaviours or substances (e.g. alcohol or eating disorders) or were currently being treated for clinical depression. Their consumption behaviour tended to be more spasmodic and manic.

Janet is aged 41, with a husband and two teenage children, as well as two older children from her previous marriage. She works full time as a researcher and uses her own salary to pay for her excessive consumption. She has some debt at present, which she is desperately trying to control. Her story is as follows:

> 'Well, I'm an alcoholic, and I've been sober for coming up to fifteen years. I still go to Alcoholics Anonymous, but they only talk about the alcohol bit, not other things. Since then, I've got hooked on spending and eating. When I got myself into difficulties with the spending, I recognised what I was doing and it seemed to be that I put on weight because I suppose I was comfort eating, and then the slimming seemed to become an obsession. I have been

> to Over-eaters too. Like, I'll go from one crutch to the next. It must be something in my make-up. I had quite a deprived childhood. My father was a heavy drinker so the money really went on him drinking. My mother was the one that, kind of, kept us all together type of thing. Like, I suppose she made sure we had everything. But I went to Dysfunctional Families at one point to find out what made me do the things that I did, because in saying that, I didn't want to make the same mistakes with my kids that I thought my parents did with me. I would say that my husband is really good to me, nice kids, nice family – no worries there. But I just seem to always be unhappy.'

Although Janet has attended several different types of self-help group over the years, she refuses to talk to the doctor about her deep-rooted unhappiness and various addictions 'in case they think I need to see a psychiatrist or something'.

The mood-repairers

The final group identified appeared to be generally more content and able to cope with their lives, but were addicted to the consumption experience in order to aid mood-repair.

Jean is a nurse, in her late fifties. She was divorced from her husband several years ago, and now lives alone. She has one daughter, aged 28, who lives nearby. Overall, Jean is typical of other 'mood-repair' addictive consumers. She has a higher level of control over her consumption behaviour most of the time, and finds it easier to stick to a pre-set financial limit. She feels she 'inherited' her use of shopping as a means of treating herself or cheering herself up from her mother:

> 'Some of my dearest memories are with my mother, being taken shopping at a very young age. She didn't have a terribly happy marriage. She often argued with my father, and she used to go to the shops a lot. She loved them. She'd have a row with my Dad perhaps, and she would say, "Come on, let's go to town". And her mood would lift. She'd say, "Oh, come on, let's go and have a cup of tea", and just the whole thing. I have such fond and safe memories of that.'

Although very unhappy for a period of time before and after her divorce, Jean now feels generally content most of the time, and can analyse many of her previous negative behaviours and feelings. But even now, she still feels the need to regularly go shopping – she may not necessarily need to spend money, but 'drinks in' the atmosphere and ambience:

> 'It is an unbelievable high [when I am in the shops], cleanliness. I'm talking about nice shops. I'm quite selective. I don't get the same feeling if I go into the market, for example. So there is something about the whole shop that lifts my mood immediately, and if I'm fed up I will go into town. It's as therapeutic to me as taking a tablet. I don't drink, I don't smoke, I don't take

drugs, and I don't do anything expensive. I don't run a car, so I think, "Well, why not if it keeps me sane? If this keeps me going, and together and happy, what's wrong with it?" '

CONCLUSION

The case studies above demonstrate factors within the addictive behaviour which suggest that, for a number of addictive consumers, the terms 'addictive' or 'pathological' are not in themselves sufficient to explain the totality of the complex behaviour. Whilst the behaviour before, during and after the shopping experience itself may be common to most addictive consumers, additional reasons for the development and maintenance of the behaviour over a prolonged period can and do differ.

Viewed in the light of the earlier section on compensatory consumption, it can be seen that the reasons why women *really* go shopping can be as complex and diverse as the lived experiences and histories of individual female consumers.

NOTE

1 The study 'Addictive consumption in the UK' was funded by an Economic and Social Research Council grant awarded to Professor Richard Elliott.

REFERENCES

Babin, B. J., Darden, W. R. and Griffin, M. (1994) 'Work and/or fun: measuring hedonic and utilitarian shopping value', *Journal of Consumer Research* 20, 4: 644–56.

Barker, P. J. (1997) *Assessment of Psychiatric and Mental Health Nursing*, Cheltenham: Stanley Thornes.

Central Statistical Office (1995) *Social Focus on Women*, London: HMSO.

Concar, D. (1994) 'The roots of addiction', *New Scientist*, 1 October: 26–36.

Cross, G. (1993) *Time and Money: The Making of Consumer Culture*, London and New York: Routledge.

Csikszentmihalyi, M. (1992) *Flow: The Psychology of Happiness*, London: Rider.

Duck, S. W. (1994) 'Stratagems, spoils and a serpent's tooth: on the delights and dilemmas of personal relationships', in W. R. Cupach and B. H. Spitzloery (eds) *The Dark Side of Interpersonal Communication*, Hillsdale, NJ: Lawrence Erlbaum Associates.

Eccles, S., Hamilton, E. and Elliott, R. (1999) 'Voices of control: researching the lived experiences of addictive consumers', *Proceedings of the International Conference on Critical Management Studies*, July, UMIST.

Elliott, R. (1994) 'Addictive consumption: function and fragmentation in postmodernity', *Journal of Consumer Policy* 17, 2.

—— (1996) *Addictive Shopping in the UK*, Report to ESRC, London, no. R0002358101.

Elliott, R., Eccles, S. and Gournay, K. (1996) 'Revenge, existential choice and addictive consumption', *Psychology and Marketing* 13, 8: 753–68.

Faber, R. J. and O'Guinn, T. C. (1992) 'A clinical screener for compulsive buying', *Journal of Consumer Research* 19: 459–69.

Feick, L. F. and Price, L. L. (1985) 'The market maven', *Managing*, July: 10.

Ferguson, H. (1992) 'Watching the world go round', in R. Shields (ed.) *Lifestyle Shopping: The Subject of Consumption*, London: Routledge, 28.

Firat, A. F. and Dholakia, N. (1998) *Consuming People*, London: Routledge.

Fischer, E. and Arnold, S. J. (1990) 'More than a labor of love: gender roles in Christmas gift shopping', *Journal of Consumer Research* 17, 3: 333–45.

Fischer, E. and Gainer, B. (1991) 'I shop therefore I am: the role of shopping in the social construction of women's identities', in J. A. Costa (ed.) *Proceedings of the First Conference on Gender and Consumer Behavior*, Salt Lake City: University of Utah Printing Press.

Gardner, M. P. (1985) 'Mood states and consumer behaviour', *Journal of Consumer Research* 12: 281–300, cited in Elliott (1994).

Giddens, A. (1991) *Modernity and Self-Identity: Self and Society in the Late Modern Age*, Cambridge: Polity Press.

Gronmo, S. (1988) 'Compensatory consumer behaviour: elements of a critical sociology of consumption', in P. Otnes (ed.) *The Sociology of Consumption*, Norway: Solum Forag; New York: Humanities Press.

Grunert, S. (1993) 'On gender differences in eating behaviour as compensatory consumption', in J. A. Costa (ed.) *Proceedings of the Second Conference on Gender and Consumer Behaviour*, Salt Lake City: University of Utah Printing Press, 74–86.

Jansen-Verbeke, M. (1987) 'Women, shopping and leisure', *Leisure Studies* 6: 71–86.

Jones, J. (1996) 'Coquettes and grisettes: women buying and selling in Ancien Regime Paris', in V. de Grazia (ed.) *The Sex of Things*, Los Angeles: University of California Press, 25–53.

Kelly, J. R. (1991) 'Commodification and consciousness: an initial study', *Leisure Studies* l, 10: 7–18.

Kvale, S. (1983) 'The qualitative research interview: a phenomenological and hermeneutical mode of understanding', *Journal of Phenomenological Psychology* 14, Fall: 171–96.

Laermans, R. (1993) 'Learning to consume: early department stores and the shaping of the modern consumer culture (1860–1914)', *Theory, Culture and Society* 10: 79–102.

Langrehr, F. W. (1991) 'Retail shopping mall semiotics and hedonic consumption', in R. H. Holman and M. R. Solomon (eds) *Advances in Consumer Research* 18, Provo, UT: Association for Consumer Research, 428–33.

Luomala, H. T. (1998) 'A mood-alleviative perspective on self-gift behaviours: stimulating consumer behaviour theory development', *Journal of Marketing Management* 14: 109–32.

McCracken, G. (1990) *Culture and Consumption*, Bloomington: Indiana University Press.

Martin, B. and Mason, S. (1987) 'Current trends in leisure', *Leisure Studies* 6: 93–7.

Nava, M. (1996) 'Modernity's disavowal: women and the department store', in M. Nava and A. O'Shea (eds) *Modern Times: Reflections on a Century of English Modernity*, London: Routledge.

Nava, M. and O'Shea, A. (eds) (1996) *Modern Times: Reflections on a Century of English Modernity*, London: Routledge.

O'Guinn, T. C. and Faber, R. J. (1989) 'Compulsive buying: a phenomenological exploration', *Journal of Consumer Research* 16, 2: 147–57.

Scherhorn, G., Reisch, L. A. and Raab, G. (1990) 'Addictive buying in West Germany: an empirical study', *Journal of Consumer Policy* 13: 355–87.

Shoaf, F. R., Scattone, J., Morrin, M. and Maheswaran, D. (1995) 'Gender differences in adolescent compulsive consumption', *Advances in Consumer Research* 22: 500–4.

Thompson, C. J., Locander, W. B. and Pollio, H. R. (1989) 'Putting consumer research back into consumer research: the philosophy and method of existential phenomenology', *Journal of Consumer Research* 16: 133–46.

—— (1990) 'The lived meaning of free choice: an existential description of everyday consumer experiences of contemporary married women', *Journal of Consumer Research* 17, 3: 346–61.

Thompson, J. B. (1995) *The Media and Modernity: A Social Theory of the Media*, Cambridge: Polity Press.

Valence, G., d'Astous, A., and Fortier, L. (1988) 'Compulsive buying: concept and measurement', *Journal of Consumer Policy* 11: 419–33.

Woodruffe, H. R. (1996) 'Methodological issues in consumer research: towards a feminist perspective', *Marketing Intelligence and Planning* 14: 213–18.

—— (1997) 'Compensatory consumption (or: why do women go shopping when they're fed up?) and other stories', *Marketing Intelligence and Planning* 15, 7: 325–34.

Woodruffe-Burton, H. R. (1998) 'True life tales of postmodern consumers: Emily's story', *Irish Marketing Review* 11, 2: 5–15.

12 Women-focused consumption spaces: cafés/bars in Amsterdam

Helene Hill

INTRODUCTION

Services marketing has gained considerable pace in recent years and has highlighted the fact that both the service encounter and the servicescape require careful planning within a service environment. The servicescape has received relatively limited consideration, despite its importance in framing the extent to which customers will be satisfied with a service encounter. An aspect of the servicescape which is only beginning to be explained is that of gender and sexual orientation and how they impact on and influence design and customer satisfaction.

This chapter explores these issues in stages: first by discussing the servicescape, then by examining the impact of gender on the servicescape and, finally, by drawing on a study of three women-focused cafés/bars in Amsterdam it considers the impact of the sexual orientation of women on the servicescape environment.

THE SERVICESCAPE

It is a truism that service is key to a successful retail or leisure experience, but it must be recognised that such interactions are relatively intangible. It is clearly not something that can be observed or tested in advance. To reduce their risk of participating in a service that may turn out to be unsatisfactory, customers may look for other cues or evidence of what they can expect. Whilst part of this may come from other aspects of the service encounter such as dress, considerable cues can be taken from the physical environment or servicescape (Zeithaml and Bitner 1996). These cues can be both internal and external to the venue, for example, the location and state of the street may indicate something about what to expect, or the outside appearance of the café signage and furniture. When inside, the furniture, colour schemes and music will also induce the customer to draw conclusions about what they can expect from this interaction. These cues alone may be a deciding factor as to whether the customer even chooses to partake in the interaction. As noted by Wakefield and Blodgett (1994), the consumption of services is not only driven by such 'functional' motives as the desire for a drink, but also by such 'hedonic' or emotional motives as excitement. The type of music and colour scheme may give strong indications of what to expect in a given venue.

Bitner (1992) defines the servicescape as the 'built environment', and splits it into three components.

1. *Spatial layout and functionality*
   This refers to the functionality of the design and layout of the venue, the arrangement of furniture, and the location of exits, entrances and toilets. It raises issues of both actual layout and the ability to facilitate the performance required.
2. *Signs, symbols and artefacts*
   This refers to signs and signals which communicate with the customer such as labels and logos, company names, directional signs and more implicit signs that may emanate from furniture, artwork, etc. Also included are the textures and materials used in construction. All may consciously or unconsciously affect consumer response, colouring both their reaction to and behaviour in the environment.
3. *Ambient conditions*
   These refer to the 'feel' or background characteristics of the environment and come from such elements as temperature, smell, lighting, music and colour scheme. They may also be imperceptible.

Closely linked to these three elements is the concept of *low load* and *high load* environments which relate to the amount of information customers must process from their environment, and are associated with the mood or emotional state of the customer. Novelty, complexity, bright colours and loud music are associated with high load, whilst low load comes from environments which suggest assurance or simplicity. The choice of servicescape elements therefore strongly impacts on the emotional state of customers and must be closely linked to the needs of the target market. Conversely, and from a less proactive standpoint, the choice of 'loading' will strongly impact on the types of customer that will visit the venue. This relates to the concept of approach or avoidance behaviour: how the customer responds to the environment and the extent to which they will choose to either approach or avoid the venue in the future.

SERVICESCAPE AND GENDER

The specific issue of how gender impacts on the servicescape and how consumers interact with it has been considered in a relatively small number of research studies. Schmidt and Sapsford (1995) explored the pub context from a woman's perspective and found that, in such a traditionally male environment, key barriers to women were found to be wide open spaces on entering the pub and a linear bar which resulted in a line of backs facing one on entering the venue. Fischer,

Gainer and Bristor (1998) also explored the relationship between servicescape and gender when they conducted research within barber shops and hair salons. Their research specifically questioned whether gender-focused servicescapes were socially constructed or embedded within the built environment. Their results pointed to the importance of an awareness and understanding of how environments are socially constructed via wider cultural and gender values, and suggested that these wider frameworks of socialisation have a strong impact on more tangible aspects to built environment design. This questions the ability of managers within an environment to be able to control and manipulate that environment without recognition of the broader societal context. Their study led them to conclude that there was very little difference between the sexes in terms of servicescapes; indeed the biggest variance came from artefacts such as magazines. A significant factor to emerge was that the actual personnel and customer base in these venues were what determined whether they were perceived as male or female. It was also significant that the actual built environment cues were socially constructed by individuals prior to experiencing the environment, and that even very similar built environments would still be perceived as gendered.

A less traditional context, that of women's sex shops, was examined by Malina and Schmidt (1997). By assessing a case study the authors were able to conclude that the servicescape did play a significant role in encouraging customers to enter and linger. The service environment or servicescape in this case was intentionally women-focused. This was acheived by the use of deep pink colours; warm lighting, which merged internal and natural light, softened by pink netting; the physical arrangement of furniture to 'invite a relaxed service encounter'; the use of chairs and the provision of hot drinks. These details reinforced the relaxed nature of the encounter, encouraging customers to interact and explore within the environment, rather than using the shop for a more functional interaction. In addition, the music was varied so as not to alienate specific sub-groups. This management of the servicescape was seen as especially important in an unfamiliar, and potentially 'subversive', context. The research also linked issues of servicescape management to management of the service encounter involving the level and nature of interaction between staff and customers, and highlighted that both played a key role in determining customer interaction and satisfaction. Whilst this venue was clearly women-focused, the findings were less able to clarify issues around gender and sexuality, simply indicating that the venue provided equally for heterosexual and lesbian customers, but recognising that this was an area needing more consideration.

Whilst the issue of gender and servicescape has been developed and explored, the issue of women-focused venues that 'advertise' themselves as being for women has been given very little consideration. Although such venues will be socially framed by consumers as gendered or for women, these women-focused venues have in no manner actually stipulated that they are *solely* for women. This distinction may only have been socially constructed. The issue of explicitly women-focused venues needs exploration. This is especially the case when women-focused venues are strongly associated with sexual orientation as well as gender.

LINKING SERVICESCAPE WITH SEXUAL ORIENTATION

Women-focused leisure facilities are not common, even in the context of cafés and bars. We decided to use the servicescape framework to explore the relationship between women-focused venues and their clientele, and to use personal observations and impressions to reflect on how the servicescape evoked particular responses with regard to interactions, ambience and environmental cues. This link between servicescape and personal impressions was also combined with specific reflections on the identity of the bar and on whether it had an overt or covert gay identity. Sexual orientation was thus introduced to the exercise to assess to what extent this factor adds new dimensions to servicescape design.

Research by Haslop, Hill and Schmidt (1998) indicates that there are considerable cultural issues pertaining to the gay market that highlight the need for specifically 'gay' venues to develop an identity that falls outside the mainstream. In their study pubs and bars were explored specifically to elicit their role in the socialisation process within the gay subculture. Such venues were found to have significant impact, both in terms of 'learning' about the subculture and in showing how the venue's servicescape can create certain responses from customers, including both positive and negative responses to this process. The research indicates, for example, that gay venues were seen as places for gay consumers to explore what the subculture involved, and also as places to feel secure and have a sense of belonging. Importantly, too, the venue servicescape impacted on customer satisfaction; for example, the music was perceived as being very heavily biased towards dance music, and this was perceived by one gay consumer, who was not especially keen on this, as being alienating. This emphasises that gay venues are not chosen solely for being oriented towards a particular sexual group, and that such venues must also provide a service offer which is at least comparable to other non-sexually-oriented venues.

RESEARCH DESIGN

This project covers women-focused cafés/bars in Amsterdam, a location with strong gay associations. It is an extension of earlier research based in gay bars/cafés in Manchester targeting a mixed gay market. The study aimed to make closer links between gay subculture, the development of gay identity and the role of cafés/bars in this process. Issues of gender and sexual orientation are central. These are complemented by exploration of the servicescape and wider socially constructed expectations. The project explores the interrelationships evident between these often agglomerated concepts. An important prerequisite for conducting the research was the ability of the researcher(s) to emerse themselves in the environment and to feel part of it. To add validity to this, both researchers could be described as knowledgeable and broadly acculturated into the gay subculture. This research therefore took an ethnographic standpoint. Alongside this, it was intentionally designed to triangulate this with two other data collection methods: a more formal part consisting of a framework by which to observe and note each aspect of the servicescape, and a personal view of the interrelationship between the observed servicescape and the feelings the environment aroused in us as customers.

For ease of access and focus, gay helpline material, gay magazines and tourist-focused gay maps, were used to locate suitable venues. The gay tourist map listed all gay venues which were 'mainly or only women' venues and also indicated that 'all listed venues are exclusively or almost gay unless mentioned otherwise'. From these sources, three venues were selected which were listed as cafés/bars, and which were still in business. Retrospectively, the decriptors given to the venues proved to be cross-referenced and interrelated, and the lack of clarity between the terms 'women-focused', 'homosexual' and 'lesbian' was evident throughout the research observation. This was further complicated by the variance between the advertised descriptions and labels that would be given to venues based solely on observation and without prior knowledge.

Each venue was visited and all the data collected from the formal and more impressionistic approaches was cross-referenced between the two researchers. All research was undertaken over three days to ensure consistency within the wider city environment in terms of events and so forth.

THE THREE VENUES

Venue A: *Françoise*

The 'offer'

Françoise focused on selling beverages and also offered a basic menu, e.g. salad, soup, roll. The typical order would be a light snack or a soft drink. No alcohol was visible. The café was only open during the day, both in the morning and afternoon.

Location and layout

Françoise was described on the gay tourist map as a café that was both 'mainly or only women' and 'mixed straight/gay'. It was located in the central business area of Amsterdam still within the tourist area of the city, but the street had a secluded, residential feel. The street contained both homes and businesses and was well maintained with a traditional Dutch feel to the house fronts.

The outside of the café had wicker chairs and tables on the street. The sign was subtle and had an 'arty' style to the logo. The words 'coffee breakfast shop-gallery' were used to describe the venue, and windows and glass-fronted doors made the interior visible from the street. Inside, the café consisted of two levels. The lower level was clearly visible from the outside and consisted of wicker chairs and tables, with cream walls. Menus were located on each table. A number of paintings and works of art were on view and for sale. All followed a 'female' theme, featuring women from different races throughout the world. This area had a tiled floor with a rug.

Beyond this area, a small number of steps led to the second level of the café. This area was separated from the front by a banister, was more spacious and consisted of dark oak chairs, tables and benches. Further towards the back, numerous newspapers and magazines were available on a shelf unit which included artistic material, gay papers/magazines, 'wholesome' magazines, advertising for other venues, and a chessboard. A piano was also in the far back corner along with a games table. This area also included the working space: a long bar with a coffee machine, cups, glasses and wooden bar stools. Again, there were menus on every table.

Varying offers within one servicescape

On entering the venue the split between the two areas was evident due to the different levels, but this was reinforced by the changing style of decor and furniture. The spacing was also more relaxed and open on the second level. The result was that the second area induced a more relaxed atmosphere where you felt comfortable to spend time and to emerse yourself in your own world. This was further emphasised by the location of newspapers and magazines in this area. The split within this venue gave the impression of a functional front area where passersby would stop for a drink or snack and then leave relatively quickly, whereas the second level was more akin to one's own living room, where you could have a drink/snack and simply relax and not be rushed.

The use of decor and artefacts did give a feeling of it being women-focused, in that the paintings and pictures were of women and their lives/environment. Beyond the paintings and the pictures, the decor was not perceived as specific to a particular gender. In terms of sexual orientation, the only way in which this was explicitly evident was through the literature available at the back of the venue, a mixture of self-help and self-development materials and gay magazines. This would only become evident to somebody who had chosen to explore the venue more closely, and would be unlikely to have had any impact on the more functional front area.

The atmosphere

The front area was well lit with a lot of natural light and hanging table lights. The second level was slightly darker with a mix of roof lights and suspended lights above the bar. Tapes were played from behind the bar area and consisted of a mix of easy listening and classical music. All music was background music. The style of music and the fact that it was a well-lit venue gave it a low load atmosphere in keeping with its daytime opening hours.

The choice of decor, paintings and literature did give a feeling of a venue that catered for more 'educated' and cultured customers and, possibly as a result of this 'tasteful' environment, it could be perceived as being less focused on younger women customers. The quiet nature of the venue was also noted to the extent that it was observed that when the music stopped, you felt like you should whisper. This too complemented the feeling of personal space and time to oneself, of a sedentary, relaxing nature.

Interaction

Orders were taken from tables in a relatively formal manner by a woman dressed in jeans and a casual top. Food was paid for after the event, before leaving. There was no attempt made to engage customers in conversation, and overall the interaction had a non-intrusive, task-orientated feel to it – it was not part of the experience, merely a facilitating element. This was further illustrated when she was often not visible at all when preparing food, which left the venue apparently with nobody available to serve.

This style of interaction was felt to very much reinforce the atmosphere on the second level of relaxing and emersing oneself in one's own world. The interaction was purely functional, to serve your drink/snack, and then you were left to yourself. Importantly, you never felt that you had to leave, and this added to the feeling of being in your own space rather than in a functional area.

The customers in the venue also were perceived to reflect the dual nature of the servicescape. Passing trade at the first level of the venue seemed to be mixed gender and couples. This was not observed in the second area, where the space tended to be women-only, either alone or in pairs.

Additional issues

This café had been purchased by a man who had widened the clientele beyond the solely women-focused. The extent to which this perceived split in the venue was apparent, from the addition of a more commercial front area, is unclear, but may partly explain this change in policy. This repositioning of the venue is reflected in its two distinct areas, one of which is women-focused while the other endeavours to draw in passing trade. It is also felt to be important to recognise the fact that the researchers knew it was partly classed as women-focused and mixed gender, which may have biased the observation. Whilst the paintings were based on women this in itself would not necessarily lead a customer to think the venue was women-focused or a lesbian venue, though it would potentially make them feel more relaxed in the venue. Clearly, the awareness of a venue's customer base can greatly influence how the servicescape is interpreted.

Venue B: *Vive la Vie*

The 'offer'

The venue was open all day and in the evening and the menu consisted of alcohol and beverages. No food was served.

Location and layout

Vive la Vie was described in the gay tourist map as a bar that was both 'mainly or only women' and 'mixed straight/gay'. It was located on a square in the main business area of Amsterdam within the central tourist area of the city. This is a key tourist area with many bars/cafés nearby.

The bar was on the lower floor of a modern concrete building, in a main square served by trams, etc. The outside consisted of signage: a large rainbow flag on the corner (also known as the freedom flag which represents gay pride and is recognised as a symbol of a gay venue), a small sign with the name of the venue, and a number of old merchandise promotional signs such as one for Heineken. The bar was multi-sided and glass fronted, with the upper portions blocked off with a mural based around pre-Raphaelite women. The remaining glass areas had a large number of posters and advertisements including lesbian party posters. Due to the limited lighting inside there was minimal visibility of the inside of the venue from outside.

The bar had one level of flooring. The area immediately inside the entrance consisted of wicker chairs and tables, with a bar area in the far corner of the bar. This had bar-stooling around it. All areas around the windows had small boxed areas with magazines and papers for reading. A large number of these were gay ones.

The bar was decorated with bright colours and rainbow colours, with a large pre-Raphaelite-style mural of a woman on the corner wall. Two slot machines were also in the bar nearer the side walls, alongside a cigarette machine. The bar area was styled with silver taps and had a large mirrored shelving area filled with glasses and bottles. Ornamentation within the bar was of an older retro style, and had a slightly 'dingy' look. In terms of spatial layout, the venue was quite small, and this combined with the low lighting made it feel relatively cramped.

Varying offers within one servicescape

The style of the venue was felt to complement the general location of the venue in a more 'glitzy' part of Amsterdam, heavy with neon lights. The decor was very 'heavy load', with dark lighting and strong use of colour. This was reinforced by the mirrored and silver/chrome decor. *Vive la Vie* seemed to present a relatively consistent environment or experience, though the split between day and evening venue, it was felt, presented a slight problem. The presence of wicker chairs and tables suggested an area for daytime passing trade who might call in for a drink, whilst the bar area, tucked away in the corner of the venue, was suggestive more of the evening. Whilst these did not clash, they did present a front of two different experiences based on the time of the day.

The decor suggested a focus on women to some extent, for example the mural, but again, it was the overt literature and posters which strongly signalled that the venue had a strong identity based upon sexual orientation rather than gender. This was most strongly emphasised by the rainbow flag flying outside the venue.

The atmosphere

Lighting within the bar was at a low level. It had more of a nightclub level of lighting even during the day, and the murals and posters on the glass windows around the outside of the bar did not facilitate the introduction of much natural light. This gave a feeling of the venue being more evening-orientated and, in combination with the heavy load decor, it gave the impression that this was a more youthful and hedonistic environment.

The music within the bar was self-styled. A modern CD deck and a large CD collection enabled the barstaff to select their own choice of music, which made the environment more personalised to the barperson. The music was in the background but was more modern/upbeat than at *Françoise.* The change of barstaff at 8 p.m. led to a noticeably more upbeat style and the volume of music increased, which helped transform the venue into one designed for an evening experience.

Interaction

During the afternoon a scruffily dressed man with long hair tended the bar. He remained relatively in the background but appeared to be comfortable as he occasionally danced to the music.

The shift changed at 8 p.m. and the woman who took over remained until the end of the evening. She wore smarter casual clothes that could be described as more akin to lesbian attire – jeans, black leather waistcoat and T-shirt – and her more interactive manner with customers was noticeable. It could be said that she was much more a part of the experience. Her style, music choice and chats with customers all reinforced the impression that she was 'part of the furniture' but also an integral part of the experience. Whilst she was interactive and friendly, this was not forced upon customers.

The barperson was felt to be a key to this venue. During the afternoon when a man had been on duty the venue had felt strongly focused around sexual orientation. It was perceived also that the barman did not sit comfortably with the overtly gay materials and flag in terms of being a venue for 'mainly women' with a gay orientation. Despite this venue description in the gay map nothing especially gave the perception of it being women-centred during the day, despite the mural. In the evening, however, the presence of a woman at the bar who was much more interactive around a bar area where women were sitting, made the venue feel more strongly like a lesbian one.

Additional issues

On speaking with the barperson it became evident that she was the owner of the bar. She indicated that Amsterdam had little to offer lesbians in terms of evening discos/parties and said she had taken it upon herself to arrange a lesbian party every three months. This was quite inventive and she told us parties were usually held at another venue that could facilitate as gambling and dancers, for example. That particular month she had arranged a visit by a women's sex shop owner based in Amsterdam, to provide a fashion show.

The interactive nature of this woman may partly be explained by her own identity and presence within the lesbian subculture. It must also be noted that the feeling was that any gay man would detect the heavy presence of women in the venue, as well as noting the female barstaff, and would infer from this that the venue was lesbian-orientated. In addition, we speculate that a gay man, socialised into that subculture, would be inclined to know in advance which venues were orientated to gay men. In terms of the overtly gay flag on the outside and advertising on windows, we would suggest that this would have tended to 'scare off' any heterosexual consumers unhappy with the concept of a gay lifestyle. This may especially be the case in Amsterdam, where sexual orientation is presented in an overt manner, and where society is more likely to be educated on this issue. The sexually orientated focus of the venue was felt to make 'passing traffic' a less likely source of customers, with more customers knowing of the venue before visiting.

Venue 3: *Saarein*

The 'offer'

The bar focused upon selling alcoholic drinks along with some light snacks such as cake and other beverages. This bar was specifically an evening venue.

Location and layout

Saarein was described on the gay tourist map as a bar for 'mainly or only women'. It was located on the west of the central city area down a small residential street. The bar was at the end of the street on a corner. The location was not within the main tourist area per se and walking to the end of the street led one further away from the tourist district. This area was not especially well lit and the height of surrounding buildings made it feel a little unsafe and akin to a 'back alley'. This feeling was emphasised since the bar was evening-focused.

The venue appeared as if it was the ground floor building on a street end/ corner. There was no seating outside except for a city bench. The decor was black and cream with very limited signage or decoration, but it was significant that the external sign stated 'vroumencafé', which indicates it being a women's café. The majority of space was glassed (windows to within one foot of the ground). This area was netted to just above head level with cream netting. The only signage was also in cream and white – a small simple sign stating the name of the bar and the fact that it was a women's café. It was therefore clear to all passersby that this was a bar for women. Overall, the exterior had a feeling of an English pub, compared to the other venues – perhaps more akin to the traditional brown café in Amsterdam.

The bar was on three levels. The entrance was at ground level and customers could either stay at that level, or go upstairs/downstairs. Each area had its own 'domain'.

Varying offers within one servicescape

The ground level was marble-floored and consisted of bar stools around the bar, and fitted benches, chairs and tables around the outside of the bar area. Coat racks were located near the door. It was decorated in dark green. The bar area was the focus of this floor and had a brass tap, with beer kegs and bottles of beer at the back. There was also a music system. The netting was on brass rings and there were also velvet curtains. This area gave the impression of being the focus of the venue where the majority of customers would be located for a friendly and relaxed evening out, unless they chose to explore the venue more closely. The colours and decor gave a 'lush' and rich, even a sensual, impression.

The lower level was a space that did not feel overly easy to enter, to the extent that neither researcher actually entered this environment but simply observed from a distance. There was limited visibility from the ground floor and the lower level was also limited in size. This made the area feel quite private and intimidating. Within this space there was a kitchen space, and a pool table and pinball machine. From a lesbian subcultural perspective, the pool table and games could be interpreted as a domain for the more 'masculine' lesbian – a recognised type within the subculture.

The upper floor allowed one to observe the floor below. It was reasonably spacious, consisting of smaller chairs and tables, and a larger table and chairs in the centre. Thus, varying group sizes were catered for. At the back there were a number of magazines and information was available. The bar also had its own T-shirt design which was on view on the wall. The decor was in art-deco style, and there was a freestyle two dimensional cut-out of a ballerina with a helmet on. It was eclectic and individualistic. The brass rails and velvet curtains theme was continued from the ground floor. As in *Françoise*, there was also a piano. This gave a feeling of an area for social interaction with friends, which was slightly more secluded and 'heavy load' than the main area, which was more hedonistic and active.

This venue therefore seemed to provide spaces for different sub-groups within the lesbian subculture itself, but had the overarching women/lesbian focus. Perhaps related to this subculture was the fact that the bar had a quite traditional feel to it with no 'airs and graces'. It was unpretentious and not gimmicky, and this was reflected in the relaxed postures of customers. The environment induced a relaxed atmosphere for social gatherings of women who could be separate from the rest of the heterosexual or male world. It was very much their own space. It was obviously successful, as it was extremely busy.

The location of this bar meant customers would be unlikely accidentally to stumble across it. It was a destination in itself, and the external sign further stressed that this was a female space. There were no men inside the bar, though there was no opportunity to view what would have happened if a man had actually attempted to enter the bar.

The atmosphere

The ground and upper floor had a certain amount of natural light and the level of lighting was neither particularly bright nor noticeably dark. This induced a relaxed atmosphere. The lower level, whilst having no natural light and feeling a little like a hole, was well lit for the games table, which appeared to be well used.

The music again was in the background and was modern dance. This made the bar feel more of an evening venue but the music was not loud enough to hinder conversation.

This bar had its own distinctiveness. It had a very strong female and lesbian atmosphere and could be perceived as giving an empowering feeling when inside because of this. The lesbian atmosphere again may be questioned, based on whether the women-only clientele implies this or whether it is more acculturated knowledge that leads an individual to draw this conclusion.

Interaction

The barwoman was very much part of the experience on the ground floor, and was very interactive. She was part of the group, and fitted in. She was the focus of attention with the crowd of women who sat around the bar. She was dressed casually and looked part of the lesbian scene. This had many similarities with the *Vive la Vie* barwoman's style of interaction, and strongly suggested that the barwoman was fairly central to the whole experience.

Additional issues

A very significant feature of the bar was the presence of a cat which sat and moved amongst the customers. This was felt to be especially poignant because of the well-known clichéd image of lesbians owning/loving cats, which is heavily reflected in lesbian images and literature. Another noticeable factor was the extent to which the bar had a smoky atmosphere. Whether this was linked to the customer is not clear but it has been observed on other lesbian venues in other cities.

Amongst women's venues it was also quite unusual in that it felt as if it had its own domains within the bar, each catering for different needs and customers. This is relatively unusual as one accusation often aimed at lesbian venues by lesbians is that they tend only to cater for a certain type of lesbian.

DISCUSSION

Varying provision within a subculture

It can be seen from the above descriptions that all three venues had very different consumption experiences to offer, and either actively or accidentally catered for different customers: *Françoise* has a focus on women or was gender-focused, though this did also link to sexuality in a more covert manner. *Vive la Vie*, whilst having a women's focus via its advertising, appeared to have its main focus on sexual orientation, though this did vary slightly between afternoon and evening experiences, taking on a stronger lesbian identity in the evening. *Saarein* was very much women-focused, with a strong emphasis on sexual orientation. The venues were also linked closely to the provision in terms of time of day and ambience. So, for example, *Françoise*'s key message was felt to be the nature of the experience rather than gender or sexual orientation, which therefore brings into question the extent to which experiences and perceptions are drawn from the environment or from prior knowledge about the venue's description. This would suggest, therefore, that any venue wishing to present a certain image or experience can strongly influence this by proactive communication with individuals before they arrive at the venue. The time of day was also perceived to be a key factor that strongly orientated the venues in terms of their servicescape. It was found to be a source of potential confusion when the venue catered for both daytime and evening customers.

Gender versus sexual orientation

One issue emanating from these results must be the extent to which a women-only venue will automatically imply a lesbian venue. The reality of the situation very often reflects this, but another key issue implicit within this debate is the extent to which you can knowingly state that the women within a venue are lesbian or heterosexual: gender is easily identifiable whereas sexual orientation is not so easily determined. Sexual orientation only becomes evident, to a certain extent, by the consumer having been socialised into that subculture and reflecting their identity according to how that subculture may identify itself. Even then, this is only a perception/reading or 'sixth sense' as to whether that person is lesbian. Therefore, evaluation of a venue and its identity is strongly influenced by customers' pre-understanding or preconditioning, or their individual mental frameworks. These may vary according to sexual orientation, but potentially there may be more common ground across the same gender, in the sense that women, because of their gender, may have common experiences and mutual understanding. Once sexual orientation is added to the gender dimension, however, greater diversity may begin to emerge.

Servicescape versus social construction

An important dimension of these impressions is the extent to which they emanated from the servicescape itself rather than being more broadly socially constructed. Alongside this, there is also the question as to whether these perceptions were guided by preconceptions as to the status of the venue. Did we register elements of the servicescape because of prompts as to its status gained before entry? Would independent entry to the venue have led us to register different perceptions?

On consideration of whether perceptions about identity of the venue came specifically from the built environment, it was felt that the actual identity emanated from two factors. The first factor was the clientele: *Saarein*, for example, had only women in it and this was noticeable. Even an independent outsider could enter the venue with no preconceptions and feel that the venue was women-only. It is suggested in such an instance that at that point it would be socially constructed frameworks that would be more likely to lead that individual to link a women-only venue to being unusual and potentially lesbian. This would emerge partly due to the current unavailability of venues for women-only that are not also connected to women's sexual orientation.

The second factor was previous knowledge of the venue's identity. For example, the researchers knew the venue was women-focused and therefore read the servicescape accordingly. In this instance, *Françoise* was recognised for its use of women-focused artefacts, such as pictures, but the extent to which these would give cues to independent customers entering the venue is seriously doubted. It is therefore suggested that the built environment has more of a facilitation role in creating an identity for a venue. If this is explored further, the example of *Françoise* having the clientele as a key cue to its identity could also be linked to the concept of preconceptions. In that instance, previous knowledge of it being woman-focused would tend to limit its appeal on a sexual orientation basis. Lesbians would tend to be socially skilled in recognition of their own subculture and would also have more subtle detection systems to identify that the venue was indeed lesbian. Whilst both lesbians and heterosexual women may infer the lesbian identity of the venue, the lesbian customer differs from a heterosexual customer in that this is based on knowledge of the lesbian culture. The heterosexual woman, in contrast, bases this on a lack of knowledge of the lesbian culture, and more so on wider socially constructed frameworks.

Overt versus covert use of servicescape

It is suggested above that clientele and prior knowledge are key determinants for recognising a venue's identity, and that the servicescape plays more of a facilitation role. If the servicescape is to play a more active role in determining a venue's identity, it is argued, this can only happen through the use of overt symbols and artefacts. This was evident in *Vive la Vie*, which had a rainbow flag outside. Again, all venues had more subtle gay artefacts within the venue, such as gay magazines and newspapers, and cards and posters for services. But these alone, unless in a prominent position, are likely to be missed unless a more active search of the venue ensues. Whilst the suggestion of the servicescape playing a more facilitating role unless used in an overt manner may be true to more standard service experiences, as stated by Malina and Schmidt (1997) in their sex shop case study, a more subversive context for a service experience may lead the servicescape to play a more significant role in gaining customer interaction and satisfaction. Thus, service venue owners need to consider carefully the extent to which customers may feel 'uncomfortable' entering such an environment, and then design the servicescape accordingly.

Gender implications of the servicescape

One question, indicated above, which results from this discussion is whether women's venues actually cater for lesbians only or heterosexual women also, and whether there is a demand from heterosexual women for women-focused venues. Previous research the author has been involved in (Group Commission Project 1998) indicates that there is demand for women-centred consumption spaces for heterosexual women. Those research findings showed that heterosexual women felt uncomfortable in male-dominated bar spaces and had different needs from their male counterparts, such as nicer toilet areas, more relaxed seating, and even the desire for seating, a desire to be able to see inside a venue to assess it before entering, and good lighting for security when in night-time venues. Actual products (drink) were a less important factor in determining the choice of bar/café. Whilst it was suggested that the servicescape can be made to be more woman-focused, a key factor for wanting women-focused venues was to avoid certain types of male client. Heterosexual women expressed a desire to be in venues where they were not hassled by undesirable and sexist males. Therefore, their concept of a woman-friendly or woman-focused venue was not so much to do with the exclusion of men, but the exclusion of predatorial men. Whilst there may be a latent demand for women-driven consumption spaces that would allow women to go beyond the more male-dominated environment, it must also be questioned whether heterosexual women would feel comfortable in women-only venues as, in reality, these often tend to be lesbian venues. There appears to be a subtle difference between preferring a venue to be less male-focused and actually wanting to preclude males. It could be concluded that for heterosexual women the issue relates more to certain types of male needs and behaviours being considered undesirable, whereas for lesbians the more pertinent issue is that of wanting a female-only space as a preferred option. It could be suggested, therefore, that both of these desires may be a direct result of sexuality or sexual preference. It must also be considered, however, that there may be demand for women-only spaces for heterosexual women, but the key issue here seems to be provision of a space which is 'hassle-free'. This might then preclude lesbians in such spaces, if they were in the venue for a sexually orientated reason.

Sexual orientation implications on servicescape

It must be recognised that heterosexual and homosexual women may make subtly different demands in terms of the service environment. Research and experience beyond this particular project suggests that such differences exist. For example, in lesbian spaces there may be more demand for the ability to remain standing at the bar. This reflects the fact that, within the lesbian subculture, a women-only venue revolves around sexual orientation, which needs to be reflected in the more predatory nature of the environment. It must also be noted that this may reflect several issues: the desire to be able to observe others in the venue; the fact that this subculture is closed to sexually predatory males; and that within the lesbian subculture, the different 'types' of lesbians need to be reflected.

Another potentially significant factor is that of anonymity: the lesbian client is more interested in a venue's anonymity. This presents an opposing need between heterosexual and homosexual women. Heterosexual women like to see inside a venue before entering it, whereas a lesbian is more inclined to prefer both their identity and the venue to be anonymous. Such anonymity could be seen in the two venues which were more sexually orientated. This reflects a security issue for both sexual orientations, but the underlying reasons are different. With lesbians, the security issues may be based on social conditioning or awareness of sexual orientation being a source of 'discrimination', whereas heterosexual women are concerned about ensuring visibility so they can see in to a venue to judge the clientele for 'agreeable' customers, namely, whether it contains desirable or 'undesirable' men. In addition to security, lesbians may also prefer a secluded, segregated venue that is invisible on the outside, as a mechanism to ensure that the venue only attracts those who know about it, and not passersby. Therefore, besides the sexual attraction factor for visiting a lesbian venue, another key enjoyment within such venues results from the feeling of being in the majority and 'normal'. This allows lesbians the opportunity to relax and relish their identity rather than keeping it 'under wraps'.

The conclusion must therefore be that whilst there are common preferences between heterosexual and homosexual women in terms of their service environment, there are also some distinct variations. The initial similarities evolve from the gender issue pertaining to service environments and the different desires between men and women, whereas the variations can be seen as driven by sexual orientation. This emphasises that the issues for gender and sexual orientation are not the same, and that both categories should be given separate consideration in relation to the management and design of the servicescape.

When considering the servicescape of women-focused spaces, we have illustrated that it plays a significant role in determining how customers feel towards the venue, and in shaping the type of experience that will result; but servicescape may play a more peripheral role in determining the identity of the venue on the basis of gender or sexual orientation. It is less clear to what extent the servicescape is proactively designed, is simply an instinctive issue or occurs by accident.

CONCLUSION

It is acknowledged that there is confusion between such terms as 'women-focused', 'women-only' and 'lesbian': the first implying a venue which is friendly towards women; the second indicating a venue for women-only but with no explicit indication whether this is heterosexual or homosexual women, or both; and the latter which explicitly indicates that it is for lesbians only. It has also become evident that such descriptors do not stand alone; they are closely linked to prior knowledge and socially constructed frameworks which affect individual interpretations.

Françoise and *Saarein* felt more like specialist niche venues in terms of the atmosphere they induced, whilst *Françoise* and *Vive la Vie*, with their more central tourist locations, were considered to be more likely to collect 'passing trade'. *Françoise* and *Saarein* were felt to have more congruent aligned servicescapes. This was despite *Françoise* collecting passing trade of a varied nature, and was facilitated in part by its service area having two distinctly separate areas, and its offer being distinguished by atmosphere rather than gender or sexual orientation.

From our observations and impressions gathered in relation to gender and sexual orientation issues in venues, it may be concluded that there do appear to be different needs between men and women in terms of servicescape, though these differences tend to emanate from women who express dissatisfaction with existing male-driven environments. Differences also appear to exist between the needs of lesbians and heterosexual women, though some motivations behind these differences do cover such common issues as security. Despite this, differences clearly exist, based on themes of sexual attraction and the need for a majority/ 'normal' space for a traditionally minority grouping. On this basis, such themes may be common across both gay men's and lesbian venues, though this research has not endeavoured to consider this issue.

All three venues could be shown to appeal to all women or lesbians alone, but the dimension of sexual orientation raises a number of fundamental questions relating to gender versus sexuality differences, and the extent to which the servicescape is the key dimension which communicates the identity of a venue. Also incumbent within this debate are the wider societal/cultural issues around social construction of both individual and venue identity, and how this translates into expectations and behaviour from the individuals.

These results must also be set against the commercial backdrop that requires owners to be realistic about the types of customer and/or the service experience that can realistically support a business. As is well recognised in the marketing literature on segmentation, any target market must be big enough to support a business tailored to that level of individuality. This point seems especially pertinent considering the small number of women-only venues in existence. This broadens the debate to a wider economic discussion. Cultural issues over the contrasting identities and behaviours associated with either gay men or lesbians may also partly explain a potentially different need for types of venues within the gay community, and what is seen as both acceptable and desirable. This particular issue requires much more research to gain both cognitive and behavioural understanding of these issues.

The servicescape has been shown to play a considerable role in the types of customer that may be attracted to a venue and the varying experiences they may associate with different venues. Finally, though, any decisions taken at this level must be tempered against a wider perspective that recognises the issues that exist at a gay subcultural level, and broader macroeconomic level.

REFERENCES

Bitner, M. J. (1992) 'Servicescapes: the impact of physical surroundings on customers and employees', *Journal of Marketing* 56: 57–71.

Fischer, E., Gainer, B. and Bristor, J. (1998) 'Beauty salon and barbershop', in J. F. Sherry, Jnr (ed.) *Servicescapes: The Concept of Place in Contemporary Markets*, Chicago: NTC Business Books.

Group Commission Project (GCP) (1998), completed by students on year 4 of their BA in Retail Marketing.

Haslop, C., Hill, H. and Schmidt, R. (1998) 'The gay lifestyle: spaces for a sub-culture of consumption', *Marketing Intelligence and Planning* 16, 5: 318–26.

Malina, D. and Schmidt, R. (1997) 'It's business doing pleasure with you: Sh! a women's sex shop case', *Marketing Intelligence and Planning* 15, 6/7: 352–60.

Rudd, N. A. (1996) 'Appearance and self-perception research in gay consumer cultures: issues and impact', *Journal of Homosexuality* 31, 1/2: 109–34.

Schmidt, R. and Sapsford, R. (1995), 'Issues of gender and servicescape: marketing UK public houses to women', *International Journal of Retail and Distribution Management* 23, 3: 34–40.

Sherry, J. F., Jnr (ed.) (1997) *Servicescapes: The Concept of Place in Contemporary Markets*, Chicago: NTC Business Books.

Wakefield, K. L. and Blodgett, J. G. (1994) 'The importance of servicescapes in leisure service settings', *Journal of Services Marketing* 8, 3: 66–7.

Zeithaml, V. A. and Bitner, M. J. (1996) *Services Marketing*, New York: McGraw-Hill.

13 A postmodern analysis of the implications of the discourse of mass customisation for marginalised and prized consumers

Eileen Fischer

Elton John, *Someone Saved My Life Tonight*

You're a butterfly.
And butterflies are free to fly.
Fly away . . . fly away.

INTRODUCTION

This chapter will explore the implications of discourses associated with emerging, technology-enabled strategies, often called 'mass customisation', for both marginalised and idealised groups. The approach used will be a postmodern one that focuses on the language used to describe and discuss mass customisation. The goal of the chapter is to focus critical attention on how the sometimes postmodern rhetoric of mass customisation may reinforce and uphold patterns of discrimination that both perpetuate certain traditional patterns of privilege and, ironically, privilege the marginalised in some non-market ways.

COLLECTING CONSUMERS: THE MARGINALISED AND THE PRIZED

The hand of the market may be invisible, but the hands of marketing are not always thus. These hands grasp at target groups of customers who are perceived as attractive, as desirable, as worth pursuing; less desirable potential customers may be fingered with greater indifference. As feminists and other critics of the status quo have frequently observed, social structures of privilege and marginalisation are reinforced by marketplace practices: those classes or categories of customers who 'have' get special attention from marketers; those who typically 'have not', or who traditionally had less, are served less attentively (cf. Bristor and Fischer 1993, 1995; Fischer and Bristor 1994). In particular (and not surprisingly given that marketers' jobs are ultimately to enhance the profitability of the firms they work for), the poor – a disproportionate number of whom are women and children – are not particularly desirable as target markets given their limited ability to pay. Though they are free to spend what they have on goods in the marketplace, efforts to determine and meet their needs are simply less intense than those directed at attracting more affluent customers.

An analogy that might usefully be considered here is that of butterfly collecting. Marketers might be likened to the collectors who prize certain types and place less value on those that are perceived as more common. A correspondence might be drawn between segmenting markets and classifying species, between targeting and deciding which species are worth collecting, between positioning and attempting to attract specimens. For the purposes of this chapter, an aspect of the analogy that is of particular interest is the correspondence between the attempts that marketers make to win the loyalty of targeted consumers and the attempts that collectors make to capture desirable specimens. As noted above, marketers have traditionally exerted considerably more effort to win over prized groups than marginalised ones. As new techniques, or at least new rhetoric about techniques, has developed over the last several years, increasing emphasis has been placed on finding ways to increase the likelihood that individual consumers will become and remain 'loyal' to particular marketers. In the collector analogy, these loyal customers can be likened to specimens that the marketer/collector 'owns'.

This chapter will be concerned with exploring some of the implications of the escalating concern for creating customer loyalty. It will focus on one of the latest trends, or at least buzzwords in marketing: mass customisation. Mass customisation has gained attention because it is, allegedly, a new, technology-enabled practice that helps companies to attract and retain customers. The chapter will be concerned with the implications of this new 'butterfly net' both for the categories of customers that yield prized specimens and those categories that, traditionally, do not.

MASS CUSTOMISATION: A NEW OPIATE?

The latest linguistic tidal wave in marketing with sufficient momentum to propel itself onto the pages of graduate-level textbooks is so relatively new that no single label has yet emerged. This new force in the universe, or new buzzword on the marketing block, is variously referred to as 'individual marketing', 'segments of one', 'customised marketing', or 'one-to-one marketing' (Kotler and Turner 1998), but the term that is almost always used alone in combination with one of the others is 'mass customisation'.

Some acknowledge that this multi-named phenomenon is, at one level, simply a logical extension of previous targeted marketing tactics (e.g. Kotler and Turner

1998). But enthusiasts portray it in rather more messianic terms, as both the wording and the capitalisation in the following quotation would suggest '[A] new frontier in business competition, the paradigm of Mass Customization, is at hand. . . . The time has come to shift to Mass Customization' (Pine 1993: 264).

In more prosaic language, it is typically argued that a type of consumer marketing that was practically unfeasible prior to recent technological developments has now become possible (Kotler 1989; Pine, Victor and Boynton 1993; Hart 1996). In business-to-business marketing, where the absolute numbers of customers in a market is smaller and the dollar value of each sale is typically higher, some degree of customisation has often been economically feasible. This customisation has ranged from an individualised pitch from a company salesperson, to a tailored offering of delivery conditions, training and financing, to a fully customised product. But until the concurrent advent of sophisticated customer databases and data mining techniques, flexible manufacturing processes and easily individualised communications, the degree of customisation pursued in consumer markets was relatively modest. Now, in both service- and product-based industries, it is increasingly possible to prepare, on a mass basis, varied and often individually customised products and services at or close to the price of standardised, mass-produced alternatives (Hart 1996; Gilmour and Pine 1997), and companies are being encouraged to investigate the possibility of offering individualised products to individual consumers as a route to building profitable, long-term relationships with these customers (Pine, Peppers and Rogers 1995).

My concern is not (or at least not directly) with the competitive advantage that mass customisation as a basis for individualised marketing may offer (though for an insightful study challenging the strategic advice that mass customisation must replace mass production as Pine (1993) and others suggest, I refer the reader to Kotha (1995)). My interest is, rather, in the rhetoric that surrounds the emerging set of practices. What discursive realities are being reflected and created by the academics and consultants who are making their mark by popularising this discussion of the possibilities of one-to-one marketing? What messages are being conveyed to students of marketing by the writers of popular textbooks?

And, if we can answer the first two questions, what are the implications of this development in marketing discourse for those who have, traditionally, been marginalised (versus those who have been prized) by marketers, based variously or in combination on their gender, race, ethnicity, social class, sexuality, age or income? If the description of mass customisation above is taken at face value, this development might seem to hold out promise both for those who have and those who have not been well-served by marketing in the past. Those who have not had products and services that really met their needs should surely benefit from a tailor-made approach that is not based blindly on assumptions derived from demographics. Those who have been alienated or ill-served by the marketing communications or the means of distribution that have been used should now have hope of being treated as *they* would like to be treated. Even those who simply could not get a decent product for the price they can afford might have some hope of benefiting from the potential inherent in mass customisation.

In order for such institutional changes to occur, however, a rhetorical revolution will be required socially to reconstruct marketing practices. And it is evidence of such a discursive change of direction that I will address in this chapter.

A POSTMODERN EAR LISTENING FOR PREMODERN, MODERN AND POSTMODERN VOICES

To pursue the answers to the questions I have posed, I will adopt a postmodern approach to textual analysis using a feminist filter (cf. Calas and Smircich 1991, 1992; Martin 1990; Mumby and Putnam 1992; Fischer and Bristor 1994). But before I take up the task of torturing texts as I intend, I want to highlight the distinction I am drawing between postmodern approaches (versus modern or premodern ones) and postmodern analysis which can help to look both at postmodern themes and at others.

Thoughtfully, management theorists such as Boje (1995; Boje and Dennehy 1994), Calas and Smircich (1991, 1992) and Martin (1990) have surveyed the works of post-structuralists such as Derrida and Barthes and furnished us with readable road maps for the terrain of postmodern analysis, all despite the resistance of leading post-structuralists (e.g. Derrida 1991) to the appropriation of their techniques as methods. The approaches these theorists highlight can be grouped into two broadly defined categories. The first involves historical, genealogical and comparative approaches to discerning the symbolic webs of meaning in which texts are embedded and the *bricolage* of sign fragments on which they draw. The second involves reading for absences or 'gaps' – *différance* – in (or out of) texts to unsettle stable readings, challenge taken-for-granted hierarchies, and bring to the surface tacit contradictions.

As for postmodern, as opposed to modern or premodern, themes or conditions, Firat and Venkatesh (1995) and Boje (1995) can be read concomitantly in order to distinguish among the three. Their discussions can be summarised in the following sets of contrasts.

1 Postmodern discourses reflect a continuously symbolically constructed hyperreality, while modern ones reflect a stable unequivocal and knowable reality, and premodern discourses highlight the role of spiritual forces in shaping a reality beyond the comprehension in the mortal realm.
2 Postmodern discourses highlight the fragmentation and incoherence of human experiences, while modern discourses highlight coherent, rational narratives, and premodern ones rely on tradition, myth and religion to make sense of that which may seem arbitrary or disjointed.
3 Postmodern discourses highlight a culture of consumption, in which consumers are active producers of consumption symbols, while modern ones reflect a culture of production premised on the notion that production creates value while consumption destroys it, and premodern ones resist the separation and commodification of production and *laissez-faire* capitalism. It is worth noting

in general, but in particular with regard to this theme, Boje's contention that premodern discourse interpenetrates postmodern discourse: many elements of one appear, and are celebrated, in the other (1995: 1003).

4 Postmodern discourses feature decentred, historically constructed subjects, while modern ones portray human subjects as self-aware, cognitive, unified, independent agents, and premodern discourses do not differentiate a person from his or her social or religious role, and emphasise the embeddedness of individuals in contexts of family, community and nation.

5 Postmodern discourses juxtapose opposites through pastiche, while modern ones seek the logical unification and reconciliation of differences and paradoxes, and premodern ones rely upon tradition and custom to challenge dualities such as the separation of the political and the private.[1]

I want also to acknowledge here Firat and Venkatesh's (1995) argument that there exists, in postmodern conditions, some liberatory or emancipatory potential. Theirs is a call 'to practice unabashedly the conditions [of postmodernity] toward micro-emancipatory ends' (Firat and Venkatesh 1995: 245) since these conditions may free us from grand meta-narratives and unchallenged institutions that preserve a less than satisfactory status quo. They suggest, for instance, that the break between the categories of gender (feminine/masculine) and sex (female/male) allows greater latitude to men and women to represent themselves in transformative ways.

If we, provisionally, accept Firat and Venkatesh's arguments, we can easily extend them. *If* postmodernism has liberatory potential, then it might in some measure serve to break down some of the multiple boundaries between the mainstream and margin such that consumers who are in one or more categories that are systematically disenfranchised (whether based on race, ethnicity, class, income, sexuality, religion, age or some other factor) might benefit. But Firat and Venkatesh (1995: 245) note that the modernist institution of the market, which 'has become almost the sole locus of legitimation' even as other modern institutions have lost the confidence of their constituencies, must be challenged if the 'emancipatory potential of postmodernism is to be realised'.[2]

These observations lead us to look at mass customisation, which seems a promising development in some ways, to see the extent to which it is being constructed in a manner consistent with postmodernity. The search will require the techniques that have, above, been identified as postmodern approaches. The hunting grounds for purposes of this analysis will be, primarily, the articles which have appeared since 1993 in the *Harvard Business Review* that have been authored or co-authored by Joseph Pine and have been particularly focused on mass customisation. Passages from recent versions of a popular MBA-level textbook (the Canadian version of Philip Kotler's *Marketing Management*) will also be referred to. These texts have been chosen for two reasons. First, they are reflective of the discourses that have developed in association with the phenomenon since it began to emerge in the late 1980s. Second, they are aimed at (and have the potential to reach) a broad audience of practising or would-be managers, and as such are likely both to draw on and contribute to practitioners' social constructions of mass customisation as it fits within the institutionalised practices of marketing.

In the discussion below, I will first examine how the discourse of mass customisation is being constructed with a view to discerning how managers are being encouraged to understand it. I will then consider what is being left out of the discourse in order to understand how marginalised versus prized consumers might be affected by the emerging discourse.

WHAT IS MASS CUSTOMISATION MADE OF?

A favourite point of departure for reading texts is the top line – the title. In this case, as mentioned above, there is not one top line title, but a range. The fact that there is ongoing rhetorical play in the labelling of this phenomenon is itself interesting: the linguistic variability suggests, for the moment, a lack of stability and coherence in the social construction of the practices associated with the various terms, and perhaps an uncertainty as to how they fit within the extant institutionalised understandings of marketing. (This could be good news, if what we are hoping for are changes in those institutionalised understandings.)

The term 'mass customisation' appears to have been the first term introduced, and it remains the most common among those in use. The phrase was introduced by Stanley Davis (1987) in his hopefully titled tome *Future Perfect*, and was quickly adopted by Philip Kotler (1989), thus ensuring it a place in a significant portion of North American marketing texts. B. Joseph Pine II then took up the task of familiarising *Harvard Business Review* readers with his reading of mass customisation, first through a *Harvard Business Review*-published book (Pine 1993), and second through a series of articles in the journal (Pine, Victor and Boynton 1993; Pine, Peppers and Rogers 1995; Gilmour and Pine 1997).

While some writings on the subject seem to distinguish between mass customisation and one-to-one marketing (e.g. Pine, Peppers and Rogers 1995: 103), others discuss mass customisation as synonymous with targeting consumers individually (e.g. Kotler and Turner 1998: 250). The former view portrays mass customisation as that which builds (and improves) upon the manufacturing strategy of continuous improvement (see Pine, Victor and Boynton 1993), suggesting that customisation is what the engineering and production portions of the organisation do, while one-to-one marketing involves eliciting and using customer specific data, and is what the marketing department does. The latter view, in which mass customisation is synonymous with targeting segments of one and with one-to-one marketing suggests that the production and marketing departments are seamlessly integrated in serving individual customers, and that customisation presupposes targeting segments of one, just as targeting segments of one presupposes customisation. Given the unsettled nature of the meanings of the terms under consideration, it is all the more interesting to consider how the most commonly used among them is being constructed.

The term 'mass customisation' has been used creatively in various texts to form effective contrasts between it and other concepts against which it is rhetorically positioned as superior, most notably mass production (Pine 1993; Pine, Victor and Boynton 1993) and mass marketing (Kotler 1989; Pine, Peppers and Rogers 1995; Gilmour and Pine 1997). The following passage is illustrative of the ways that mass customisation is constructed as 'superior' to mass production and mass marketing.

> Most managers continue to view the world through the twin lenses of mass marketing and mass production. To handle their increasingly turbulent and fragmented markets, they try to churn out a much greater variety of goods and services and to target ever-finer market segments with more tailored advertising messages. But these managers only end up bombarding their customers with too many choices.
>
> A company that aspires to give customers exactly what they want must look at the world through new lenses. . . . Customization means manufacturing a product or delivering a service *in response* to a particular customer's needs, and mass customization means doing it in a cost-effective way. Mass customization calls for a customer centred orientation in production and delivery processes, requiring the company to collaborate with individual customers to design each one's desired product or service . . .
>
> In contrast, product centred mass production and mass marketing call for pushing options (and inventory) into distribution channels and hoping that each new option is embraced by enough customers to make it worthwhile. It requires customers to hunt for the single product or service they want from among an ever-growing array of alternatives.
>
> (Pine, Peppers and Rogers 1995: 103, 105; emphasis and parentheses in original)

Note first the assertion that 'most managers' see the world through the lenses of (and presumably practice) mass production and mass marketing. That such an assertion should be mounted in 1995 is interesting, given that the doctrine of market segmentation and targeting, which distinguishes itself from undifferentiated or mass marketing and the associated practices of mass production, mass distribution and mass advertising, has been publicly preached for many, many years (see, for examples in each of the last five decades, Smith 1956; Roberts 1961; Wind and Cardozo 1974; Hlavacek and Ames 1986; Robertson and Barich 1992). Consider, also, the description of mass marketing that is offered in the article advocating mass customisation versus that in a standard marketing textbook. According to the former, to mass market is 'to churn out a much greater variety of goods and services and to target ever finer market segments with more tailored advertising messages' (Pine, Peppers and Rogers 1995: 103); according to the latter, to mass market is to 'design a product and a marketing program that will appeal to the broadest number of buyers' and to employ 'mass distribution and mass advertising' to sell a 'narrow product line' (Kotler and Turner 1998: 268).

Table 13.1 Comparison of terminology used in association with mass production/marketing versus mass customisation

Mass production/mass marketing	*Mass customisation*
'churn out'	'efficiently provide'
'ever greater variety of goods and services'	'individually customised goods and services'
'bombarding customers with too many choices'	'elicits information from each customer about his or her specific needs and preferences'
'hoping that each new option is embraced by enough new customers'	'in response to a particular customer's need'
'pushing options (and inventory) into distribution channels'	'customer centred orientation in production and delivery'
'requires customers to hunt for the single product or service they want'	'collaborate with individual customers to design each one's desired product or service'
'generates a list of the most likely prospects and solicits them with offers . . . that the marketer has attempted to customize by guessing their tastes'	'conducts a dialogue with each customer – one at a time – and uses the . . . feedback to find the best products or services for that customer'

Source: adapted from Pine, Peppers and Rogers 1995: 103–5.

Whereas Pine and his colleagues depict targeting ever more finely segmented markets with an ever greater variety of goods as mass marketing, Kotler and his cohorts tend to characterise the *absence* of segmentation, targeting and product proliferation as mass marketing.

It is tempting to suggest that the texts advocating mass customisation misconstrue mass production and mass marketing, but to do so would necessitate the assumption that the signifiers have some fixed meaning, something a good postmodernist ought never to do. What is more fruitful – or at least more consistent with a postmodern approach – is to note how the vilified terms 'mass marketing' and 'mass production' are being derogatorily *attached* to practices which themselves have previously been portrayed as being in *opposition* to mass marketing. In order to create mass customisation as the 'good guy', alternative practices have to be re-created as 'bad guys' (or at least, less good guys), and borrowing currently stigmatised terminology such as mass production and mass marketing is a useful technique for this purpose.

We can also examine other significations of the terminology that is being used to denigrate existing practices and elevate advocated philosophies. The side-by-side comparison in Table 13.1 has been created for this purpose. To facilitate the comparison, one deconstructive tactic that could be dragooned into service is to look at gendered significations of the terminology employed. For instance, that which is labelled 'mass production and mass marketing' is described with a series of verbs that portrays the practices as both aggressive and hapless: mass producing and mass marketing involves 'bombarding', 'pushing' and 'soliciting' but these brutish efforts result, at best, in 'churning', 'hoping' and 'guessing.' If a persona were to be applied to this collection of behaviours, it might be that of a rather stupid (and probably male) thug attacking a target (probably female) (cf. Fischer and Bristor 1994) he only dimly understands. On the other hand, mass customisation is a much kinder and gentler creature: it is 'responsive', it 'collaborates', it 'conducts a dialogue' (if there is a feminine-sounding tone to these terms, it should not surprise us, as Fondas (1997) has noted how qualities that are culturally associated with females are appearing in the contemporary descriptions of managerial work). But it should be noted that mass customisation is also a smarter and more effective creature (consistent with traits culturally associated with males): it is 'efficient' and 'finds the best products or services'.

Does this mean mass customisation is suffering from confused sexuality? A more compelling reading would be that mass customisation is being socially constructed so as to end up being something of a poster-boy (or girl) for postmodernism. And there are a number of indications that the emerging discourse of mass customisation has a wide ripple of postmodernity running through it.

Most notable is the pastiche of terminology that is full of unreconciled oppositions. The description above of postmodern versus modern or premodern themes indicated that the juxtaposition of unreconciled opposites is one of the hallmarks of postmodernity. Perhaps the most obvious evidence of opposites cohabiting is the very name 'mass customisation': even popularisers of the term have been sensitive to the fact that it could well be considered an oxymoron (Kotler and Turner 1995; Hart 1996). Other such juxtaposed opposites can also be found. Consider the point raised by Gilmour and Pine (1997: 95): mass customisers 'have identified the dimensions along which their customers differ in their needs . . . points of *common uniqueness*' [emphasis added]. More subtle, but equally consistent with the symbolic pastiche of postmodernism is the language reflected in Table 13.1. The descriptions of mass customisation in terms that are at once masculine and feminine, rational and emotive, hard and soft, is the very stuff of postmodernism.

Other indications of the postmodern proclivities in the discourse of mass customisation can be found in the description of the consumer's role in the process of creating mass-customised goods. They 'codesign and even coproduce' tailor-made products and services (Pine, Victor and Boynton 1993: 118). This image of the consumer as the creator rather than merely the user of goods is very soothing to postmodern sensibilities.

So, too, are such ideas as 'multiple markets reside within individuals' (Gilmour and Pine 1997: 92). This phrase, reflecting the recognition that a given individual does not always want the same thing from the same product, links nicely with the postmodern emphasis on the fragmentation of experience. It suggests that, in this postmodern era, we are different people at different times and, as a consequence, we value different aspects of things at different times. Similarly, the organisation that is an effective mass customiser will, according to the writings reviewed, have employees whose working experiences are highly fragmented relative to those of employees working under other systems. Continuous improvement, an earlier process that is (according to Pine) superseded by mass customisation, required 'tightly linked teams' that 'typically interact with each other in a predictable sequential manner' and 'values that create a sense of community because the interests of the individual are subsumed within the interests of the team' (Pine, Victor and Boynton 1993: 109). Mass customisation, by way of contrast, requires 'a dynamic network of relatively autonomously performing units' that 'typically do not interact or come together in the same sequence every time' and are 'constantly changing' in a 'never ending campaign to expand the number of ways the company can satisfy customers' (Pine, Victor and Boynton 1993: 109).

Though other facets of the discourse of mass customisation that resonate with postmodern themes could also be mentioned, those above should be sufficient to back the suggestion that mass customisation *could* be regarded as having some element of the liberatory potential identified with postmodernism (cf. Firat and Venkatesh 1995).

And yet . . . not all is postmodern here. The unreconciled oppositions, the acknowledged creative role of consumers, and the emphasis on the fragmentation of experience all coexist with a very modern emphasis on rationality. Indeed, it is the market-based modernist criterion of economic rationality that is called upon to justify mass customisation. The practice is being socially constructed as a rational way to manage companies so as to control expenses, reduce complexity and outmaneouvre the competition. Two quotations have been selected to indicate the coherent rationale of modernist narratives lurking in the language of mass customisation. The first touches on the rational control of *companies* through mass customisation:

> Mass customization offers a solution to the basic dilemma that has plagued generations of executives. . . . [Previously] companies had to choose between being efficient mass producers and being innovative speciality businesses. Quality and low cost and customization and low cost were assumed to be trade-offs. . . . The development of . . . mass customization models [shows] that companies *can* overcome the traditional trade-offs. . . . Continuous improvement has enabled thousands of companies to realize lower costs than traditional mass producers and still achieve the distinctive quality of craft producers. But mass customization has enabled its adherents . . . to go a step further. The companies are achieving low costs, high quality, and the ability to make highly varied often individually customized products.
>
> (Pine, Victor and Boynton 1993: 111)

The next quotation positions mass customisation as a means toward the goal of the rational management of *customers*, not to mention besting of competitors:

> The twin logic of mass customization and one-to-one marketing binds producer and consumer together in what we call a *learning relationship* – an ongoing connection that becomes smarter as the two interact with each other, collaborating to meet the consumer's needs over time.

> In learning relationships, individual customers teach the company more and more about their preferences and needs, giving the company an immense competitive advantage. The more customers teach the company, the better it becomes at providing exactly what they want – exactly how they want it – and the more difficult it will be for a competitor to entice them away. Even if a competitor were to build the exact same capabilities, a customer already involved in a learning relationship with the company would have to spend an inordinate amount of time and energy teaching the competitor what the company already knows.
>
> Because of this singularly powerful competitive advantage, a company that can cultivate learning relationships with its customers should be able to retain their business virtually forever . . .
>
> (Pine, Peppers and Rogers 1995: 103–4)

Lest it seem I am unfairly characterising the development of a learning relationship as a means of controlling the customer, let me underscore the rationale that is offered for this rational argument: the purpose of the learning relationship is to keep the customer 'forever'. I note also the asymmetry in the learning relationship proposed: the company learns about the customer, but mention is never made of the customer learning about the company. Since relationship marketing has elsewhere been deconstructed (Fischer and Bristor 1994) and excoriated for failing to live up to its implied promises (Fournier, Dobscha and Mick 1998), little more will be said here about the linguistic liabilities of this metaphor. But it is important to point out that the persisting modernist rhetoric of control, including via 'learning relationships', suggests that mass customisation is not being constructed in a fashion that is as highly discontinuous with previous marketing practices as might be assumed.

To further the argument that the discourse of mass customisation may be less revolutionary than first it seemed, I would also draw attention to that in it which can be construed as premodern. The linking of mass customisation to premodern practices is, in at least one sense, quite explicit and common. Kotler and Turner, for instance, note that:

> the prevalence of mass marketing has obscured the fact that for centuries consumers were served as individuals [and that] it is the new technologies . . . that are permitting companies to consider a return to customized marketing, or what is called 'mass customization'.
>
> (Kotler and Turner 1998: 250)

As was noted above, Boje (1995) has drawn attention to the interpenetration of postmodern and premodern themes in discourses, and in particular to the way in which both share a tendency to portray consumption and production as inseparable. The linking of contemporary mass customisation to much earlier practices of having things tailor made – whether by a merchant or by oneself – helps in some measure to legitimatise mass customisation on the grounds that it represents a return to simpler (premodern) times when we produced what we consumed and consumed what we produced.

There is another, more subtle, way in which the discourse of mass customisation reflects premodern sensibilities as well. Premodern discourses, unlike modern or postmodern ones, evoke spiritual, mystical and/or religious factors beyond people's control or comprehension as forces which shape reality and make sense of that which seems arbitrary. And in the discourse being constructed to promote mass customisation, there is a tendency to reify, or deify, it by resorting to language that invokes forces mystical or religious. A sentence quoted in the introduction of this paper will serve as a nice initial indicator of the religious tonalities that resound in the words used to describe mass customisation. Like the kingdom of god, 'the paradigm of Mass Customization is at hand. . . . The time has come to shift to Mass Customization' (Pine 1993: 264).

Consider, further, the image of relationships between customers and suppliers that could or should last 'virtually forever' (Pine, Peppers and Roger 1995: 104) and in which the supplier seeks constantly to learn more about the customer in order to keep the customer forever. The picture being painted is not unlike familiar Christian images of the relationship between God and 'man'. Both relationships are, ideally, permanent. And both are relatively asymmetric. To put some meat on the bones of this image, consider an example that is suggested as the ideal of customisation that could be offered by a greeting card manufacturer. Rather than simply having electronic kiosks that enable people to create their own greeting cards (as Hallmark has done) it is suggested that:

> If a greeting card company were to harness the full power of mass customization and one to one marketing, it would be able to remember the important occasions in your life and remind you to buy a card. It would make suggestions based on your past purchases. Its kiosks would display past selections . . . to ensure that you don't commit the *faux pas* of sending the same card to the same person twice. . . . The more customers teach the company about their individual tastes . . . the more reluctant they will be to repeat that process with another supplier. As long as the company fulfils its end of the bargain, a competitor should never be able to entice away its customers.
>
> (Pine, Peppers and Rogers 1995: 104)

Here, more fully expressed, is the image of relationships between the customiser and the customer. On one reading, the customiser plays God; the customer plays God's subject. The customiser reminds the customer of what is important (teaches values), helps the customer avoid *faux pas* (sins) and prevents competitors (Satan) from enticing the customers away. Note that the analogy could be worked the other way, of course. On this alternative reading, it is the customer who, in the first instance (by buying cards repeatedly from the same vendor), is teaching values to the customiser; it is the customiser who must not sin against the all-powerful customer (who ultimately has the choice of taking her business elsewhere); it is the customer who saves the customiser from the perdition of losing to the competition by rewarding the customiser with repeat business so long as the customiser serves the customer faithfully.

One might rightly question who, in the relationship, is analogous to God and who to God's subject. But given the postmodern pastiche of unreconciled contradictions embedded in the discourse of mass customisation, the question is unanswerable. All that can be (or at least, all that is being) argued here is that religious or mystical elements are working to enshrine mass customisation itself as something not to be questioned.

The most recent writing on mass customisation argues that there are four 'faces' (or different types) of customisation. In this latest piece, it is interesting to note that what now counts as customisation is not only the type lionised in the example of the card company above. Rather, in Gilmour and Pine's 1997 *Harvard Business Review* contribution, mass customisation now has four faces (one more than the triune Godhead, I might note). The range encompasses collaborative customisation (in which the supplier engages the customer in a dialogue to help them articulate their needs, identifies the precise offering that fulfils the need, and makes the customised product to fulfil it); adaptive customisation (wherein the supplier offers one standard but customisable product that is designed so users can alter it themselves); cosmetic customisation (here the supplier presents a standard product to customers but changes packaging, pricing, promotion or some combination of the three to suit however the customer most likes the offering presented); and transparent customisation (meaning that the supplier provides individual customers with unique goods or services without letting them know explicitly that those products and services have been customised for them). While questions could be raised as to how greatly some of the faces of mass customisation differ from what companies have been doing for the past fifty years, I wish to remain focused on the rhetorical positioning of mass customisation. Gilmour and Pine (1997) are persuasively promoting mass customisation as a superior 'faith' in the following sentences summarising the four types and extolling the virtues of mass customisation in general:

> Customers do not value merchants who recite monolithic mantras on customer service; they value – and buy – the goods and services that meet their particular set of needs. There is a time to conduct a dialogue with customers and a time to observe silently, a time to display uniqueness and a time to embed it. Businesses must design and build a peerless set of customization capabilities that meet the singular needs of individual customers.
>
> (Gilmour and Pine 1997: 101)

The echo of the famous biblical passage that argues that 'for every thing, there is a season' associates mass customisation with the behaviour of those who know the will of God, and who follow the enlightened course of action as a result. The injunction that businesses *must* design and build mass customisation capabilities is couched in terms strong enough to hearken to the Old Testament passages where Noah is instructed by God to build the ark.

The cumulative discursive effect in the passages cited above is to construct mass customisation as a mantra: an alternative mantra to that of customers' servicer; a superior mantra. Moreover, the mantra is not a purely postmodern one that promises to challenge the status quo in ways that might benefit consumers. Rather, it is being constituted as a sort of expanding premodern creed that customisers cannot easily question unless they are willing to give up the rational, modernist quest for control.

The quasi-religious undertones which echo here give rise to the following question: if organised religion is (or was) the opiate of the (old) masses, then is mass customisation now being peddled as a new opiate for both the new masses *and* those who supply them with goods and services? Perhaps. And to the extent that mass customisation is being thus promoted, the question that we now turn to is: what does this mantra mean for customers who are marginalised versus those who are prized?

THE UNSPOKEN WORD

The preceding section was concerned with the bricolage of meanings that is contributing to the social construction of the meaning of mass customisation. This section turns its attention to the gaps or silences in the texts being considered. In particular, it is concerned with the silences surrounding the customer, especially the marginalised customer.

Ironically, given the mantra of customisation catering to each customer's uniqueness, the loudest silence in the texts concerns the potential *differences* among the customers who are to be served by mass customisation. The following passage suggests just how uniformly the potential consumers of mass-customised products and services are depicted: 'Customers, whether consumers or businesses, do not want more choices. They want exactly what they want – when, where, and how they want it' (Pine, Peppers and Rogers 1995: 103). Any consideration of the possibility that some customers – particularly ones who have been poorly served by marketing in the past – may indeed feel they suffer from a paucity of choices is absent.

This is not to say that the discourse of mass customisation suggests that all customers should be served equally by mass customisation. Again, however, the texts say little on the subject of which customers are most (or least) deserving of the heroic efforts associated with mass customisation. In the main, the notion of who should be served is conveyed not directly but rather through a discussion of the industries most amenable to customisation. Given the emphasis on a 'customer orientation' that is repeatedly touted in the texts here analysed, we might expect to find customers a major factor in determining when to customise. Instead, characteristics of *products* rather than those of *customers* are most often constructed as the factors determining who should be served by mass customisation. For instance, it may not be good for 'makers of products . . . whose revenue or profit margin per customer is too low' (Pine, Peppers and Rogers 1995: 106). Commodity product markets, and markets where regulation is a barrier, are also singled out as cases where mass customisation might not be applicable (Pine, Victor and Boyton 1993).

I could find only two passages that referred to some characteristic of customers as a criterion when deciding when to customise. The first said: 'many manufacturers, service providers, and retailers may find . . . it pays to establish learning relationships only with their best customers' (Pine, Peppers and Rogers 1995: 106). The second stated: 'For retailers, the message is clear: if they want to maintain or increase their competitive advantage, they must begin establishing learning relationships with their best customers today' (Pine, Peppers and Rogers 1995: 110). Note how the tentativeness of the first assertion gives way to the certainty of the second: the customers to be served are the *best* customers. A curious word, 'best'. Like any word, polysemous. And like many words, hardly neutral. It is charged with value: the best is the most desirable thing to be, the most desirable thing to have. And it implies some unidentified opposite. Who are the unmentioned others – those 'worst' customers? They remain faceless and unnamed – the undesirable, the unmentionable and the marginal.

One thing seems apparent. Because we hear so little about customers in the discourse of mass customisation, there is nothing in the rhetoric that will challenge definitions of 'best'. The status quo, in terms of who 'should' be best served, is likely to remain tacitly taken for granted. Thus, when we ask who is likely to be considered the target market for mass-customised goods and services, the answer is *not* likely to be those who are already marginalised by marketing. What I would like, briefly, to consider, is whether this is necessarily a bad thing.

THE VICTIMISED BENEFICIARIES OF MASS CUSTOMISATION?

Having argued that mass customisation is most likely *not* being socially constructed directly for the benefit of the masses, I turn to pondering some potentially paradoxical implications of this assertion. Simply stated, it may be that consumers reap certain benefits from escaping the interests of mass customisers. To launch this argument, I begin by quoting an extract from Fournier, Dobscha and Mick regarding the experiences of consumers who are, presumably, being targeted by forms of relationship marketing that involve attempts at mass customisation.

> The new, increasingly efficient ways that companies have of understanding and responding to customers' needs and preferences seemingly allow them to build more meaningful connections with consumers than ever before. . . . Companies may delight in learning more about their customers than ever before and in providing features and services to please every palate. But customers delight in neither. Customers cope. They tolerate sales clerks who hound them with questions every time they buy a battery. . . . They juggle the flood of invitations to participate in frequent-buyer reward programs. Customer satisfaction rates . . . are at an all time low.
>
> (Fournier, Dobscha and Mick 1998: 43)

What's wrong with this, you ask (or I presume to ask on your behalf)? Well, let's see what our discourse on mass customisation has to say. The technique I'll use here to see what might be lurking in the silences or submerged beneath the surface of the texts is a form of intertextualisation (cf. Calas and Smircich 1991), wherein the discourse on mass customisation is interwoven with another text to see what might be revealed. The text chosen is John Fowles' (1963) novel *The Collector*, which explores the connections between love for a thing and the desire to own and control it. In the book, Frederick (who prefers to be called Ferdinand), a butterfly collector obsessed with a young woman named Miranda whom he has been observing, lays careful plans to kidnap her and keep her with him until he can win her love and persuade her to marry him. He is successful in capturing her, but unsuccessful in winning her love; eventually, Miranda, who comes to call the collector Caliban, dies in his captivity. As the book ends, Frederick/Ferdinand/Caliban notices a young woman who looks much like Miranda and begins to consider capturing her in the same manner. Parallels with Shakespeare's play *The Tempest* involving a Ferdinand, a Caliban and a Miranda have been artfully constructed by Fowles. Parallels with a discourse on mass customisation were undoubtedly quite unforeseen, but can, after a postmodern fashion, be made.

Some selected passages of the mass customisation texts and the novel in question are juxtaposed below. The first concerns what kinds of things are worth having relationships with, or, simply stated, worth having. Buried in the texts on mass customisation is the acknowledgement that: 'Few companies will want to have such relationships with all customers' (Pine, Peppers and Rogers 1995: 111). Comparably, the collector in Fowles' novel is only interested in a particular kind of specimen, whether the collectable be a butterfly or human woman: 'A Pale Clouded Yellow, for instance. I always thought of her like that, I mean words like elusive and sporadic, and very refined – not like the other ones. . . . More for the real connoisseur' (Fowles 1963: 9). This first textual comparison serves mainly to reinforce the suggestion made above, that mass customisation is being socially constructed so as to serve only those who are, by some collector's or customiser's standards, the 'best' customers. Moreover, these best customers are unlikely to be those who have previously been considered secondary target markets or untargeted consumers. They are likely to be those already judged as desirable.

A second comparison can be drawn between the ways of describing how information on desirable customers/specimens is obtained. The following advice is offered to potential mass customisers: 'In industries where customers are anonymous . . . a company may have to use . . . approaches to persuade them to identify themselves (Pine, Peppers and Rogers 1995: 110). The collector's methods of obtaining information about Miranda are described by Fowles as follows:

> For several days I watched for her but didn't see her. It was a very anxious time, but I kept on. I didn't take a camera, I knew it was too risky, I was after bigger game than just a street shot. I went twice to the coffee bar [where she had previously been spotted]. One day I spent nearly two hours there pretending to read a book, but she didn't come. . . . Then one day . . . I saw

> her. . . . It was easy. I followed her. . . . That's how I found out where she came from. . . . It was a good day's work.
>
> (Fowles 1963: 25)

How does the portrayal of the collector gathering information about a specimen to be added to a collection differ from the image of the marketer gathering information about a consumer to be targeted by mass customisation? In the customisation text, the target is to be 'persuaded' to identify itself, whereas in the description of the collector the target involuntarily provides information about herself simply by going about her daily business. The interweaving of the two different texts raises the question about what might be implied by 'persuasion'. Is the potential customiser being encouraged to persuade the targeted consumer to leave a trail of data behind them as they go about their business so that they can be tracked, in much the same way as the collector tracks the movements of his target?

Once a consumer becomes a customer, the mass customiser is enjoined to pay special attention to any failures on its part in order to ensure that the customer is not lost, as the following passage indicates: 'Capturing customer feedback on capability failures is crucial to sustaining any advantage that mass customisation yields' (Pine, Victor and Boynton 1993: 118). The collector in Fowles' novel is also alert to every possible failure on his part to keep Miranda in his control once he captures her: 'I could go on all night about the precautions. I used to go and sit in her room and work out what she could do to escape. . . . There could always be something' (Fowles 1963: 25). The two passages juxtaposed here can be to used to create a reading of the phrase 'the advantage that mass customisation yields' which portrays that advantage as, essentially, keeping customers captive, preventing them from choosing to either buy from a different source, or simply cease buying.

Both the customiser and the collector are, by their own lights, intent on serving their respective captives well. The mass customiser is characterised as being 'in a never-ending campaign to expand the number of ways the company can satisfy the customer' (Pine, Victor and Boynton 1993: 109). The collector says of Miranda: 'I felt I would do anything to know her, to please her, to be her friend' (Fowles 1963: 18). This intertextualisation highlights the possibility that a captive customer who is satisfied in an ever greater number of ways is *still* a captive: the point of keeping the target satisfied is to continue to control them. And this control is intended to be permanent. Though other parallels could be drawn, the final one included here concerns the goals of the mass customiser and those of the collector. Pine and his colleagues assume that mass customisers should answer in the affirmative to the following question: 'Do you want to keep your customers forever? (Pine, Peppers and Rogers 1995: 108) The collector, too, is compelled to keep his Miranda forever. In the face of her pleas for release he says simply: 'I just want to be with you. All the time' (Fowles 1963: 71).

While I am quite willing to concede the point that mass customisers are not being explicitly encouraged to stalk and kidnap customers, I have gone through the textual gymnastics above to help shed light on why customers who are being so eagerly served by would-be mass customisers may not be responding with the expected enthusiasm. The point of view of the targeted specimen is likely to be at odds with that of the collector who would like to possess it/her/him. Similarly, those who are the least targeted by mass customisers may be less well served with goods and services made to please their every need, but may also be less bothered by intrusive efforts to capture and control them. It might, in many ways, be better to be an undesirable specimen.

(IN)CONCLUSION

As the title of this final section suggests, there are no definitive conclusions to be drawn from a diatribe such as this. The very point of postmodernism and postmodern analysis is that much remains unconcluded and inconclusive. The observations drawn would suggest that the machinations of modern marketing, including mass customisation, have some postmodern potential, but retain much that is modern.

The question raised is whether this a good or a bad thing for consumers. If they continue to be marginalised by the market, are they better off, or worse? I hope I have at least challenged the reader to think about this question, and to acknowledge that the answer is, very likely, both.

NOTES

1 This summary has been adapted from a version which appears in Fischer (2000)

2 A counter-argument regarding the liberatory possibilities of postmodernism might merit consideration here: If the market institutions which support the creation of selves through consumption serve to maintain the status quo of economic rationality, it seems postmodern consumer conditions may require and support modern market institutions. I will not, however, pursue this line of argument here.

REFERENCES

Boje, D. (1995) 'Stories of the storytelling organisation: a postmodern analysis of Disney as "Tamara-Land"', *Academy of Management Journal* 38, 4: 997–1015.

Boje, D. and Dennehy, R. E. (1994) *Managing in the Postmodern World: America's Revolution Against Exploitation*, Dubuque, IA: Kendall/Hunt.

Bristor, J. and Fischer, E. (1993) 'Feminist theory and consumer research', *Journal of Consumer Research* 19, 4: 518–36.

—— (1995) 'Exploring simultaneous oppressions: towards the development of consumer research in the interests of diverse women', *American Behavioral Scientist* 38, 4: 526–36.

Calas, M. and Smircich, L. (1991) 'Voicing seduction to silence leadership', *Organization Studies* 12, 4: 567–602.

—— (1992) 'Re-writing gender into organisational theorising: directions from feminist perspectives', in M. Reed and M. Hughes (eds) *Rethinking Organisations: New Directions in Organisation Theory and Analysis*, London: Sage.

Davis, S. M. (1987) *Future Perfect*, Reading, MA: Addison-Wesley.

Derrida, J. (1991) [1983] 'Letter to a Japanese friend', in P. Kamuf (ed.) *A Derrida Reader: Between the Blinds*, New York: Columbia University Press, 269–76.

Fischer, E. (2000) 'Consuming contemporaneous discourses: a postmodern feminist analysis of food advertisements targeted toward women', *Advances in Consumer Research* 27 (forthcoming).

Fischer, E. and Bristor, J. (1994) 'A feminist poststructuralist analysis of the rhetoric of marketing relationships', *International Journal of Research in Marketing* 11, 4: 317–31.

Firat, A. F. and Venkatesh, A. (1995) 'Liberatory postmodernism and the reenchantment of consumption', *Journal of Consumer Research* 22, December: 239–67.

Fondas, N. (1997) 'Feminization unveiled: management qualities in contemporary writings', *Academy of Management Review* 22, 1: 257–82.

Fournier, S., Dobscha, S. and Mick, D. G. (1998) 'Preventing the premature death of relationship marketing', *Harvard Business Review* 76: 42–51.

Fowles, J. (1963) *The Collector*, London: The Reprint Society.

Gilmour, J. H. and Pine, B. J., II (1997) 'The four faces of mass customization', *Harvard Business Review* 75, January–February: 91–101.

Hart, C. W. (1996) 'Made to order', *Marketing Management* 5, 2: 11–23.

Hlavacek, J. D. and Ames, B. C. (1986) 'Segmenting industrial and high-tech markets', *Journal of Business Strategy*, Fall: 39–50.

Kotha, S. (1995) 'Mass customization: implementing the emerging paradigm for competitive advantage', *Strategic Management Journal* 16: 21–42.

Kotler, P. (1989) 'From mass marketing to mass customization', *Planning Review* 17: 10–13.

Kotler, P. and Turner, R. E. (1995) *Marketing Management: Analysis, Planning, Implementation and Control*, Canadian 8th edn, Scarborough, Ontario: Prentice-Hall.

—— (1998) *Marketing Management: Analysis, Planning, Implementation and Control*, Canadian 9th edn, Scarborough, Ontario: Prentice-Hall.

Martin, J. (1990) 'Organizational taboos: the suppression of gender conflict in organizations', *Organization Science* 1: 334–59.

Mumby, D. and Putnam, L. K. (1992) 'The politics of emotion: a feminist reading of bounded rationality', *Academy of Management Review* 17: 465–86.

Pine, B. J., II (1993) *Mass Customization: The New Frontier in Business Competition*, Boston, MA: Harvard Business School Press.

Pine, B. J., II, Peppers, D. and Rogers, M. (1995) 'Do you want to keep your customers forever?', *Harvard Business Review* 73, March–April: 103–14.

Pine, B. J., II, Victor, B. and Boynton, A. C. (1993) 'Making mass customization work', *Harvard Business Review* 71, September–October: 108–19.

Roberts, A. A. (1961) 'Applying the strategy of market segmentation', *Business Horizons*, Fall: 65–72.

Robertson, T. S. and Barich, H. (1992) 'A successful approach to segmenting industrial markets', *Planning Forum*, November–December: 5–11.

Smith, W. R. (1956) 'Product differentiation and market segmentation as alternative marketing strategies', *Journal of Marketing*, July: 3–8.

Wind, Y. and Cardozo, R. (1974) 'Industrial market segmentation', *Industrial Marketing Management* 3: 153–66.

14 Marketing and the divided self: healing the nature/woman separation

Susan Dobscha and Julie L. Ozanne

INTRODUCTION

> Each of us reflects, in our attitudes toward our body and the bodies of other planetary creatures and plants, our inner attitude toward the planet. And, as we believe, so we act. A society that believes that the body is somehow diseased, painful, sinful, or wrong, a people that spends its time trying to deny the body's needs, aims, goals, and processes, whether these be called health or disease, is going to misunderstand the nature of its existence and of the planet's and is going to create social institutions out of those body-denying attitudes that wreak destruction not only on human, plant, and other creaturely bodies but on the body of the Earth herself.
>
> (Allen 1990: 52)

In this chapter, the split between mind and body that underlies a body-denying attitude is explored. First, a general introduction to ecofeminism is offered and ecofeminists' analysis of the mind–body duality is examined. Ecofeminist theory spans a wide range of disciplines and includes liberal, cultural and radical feminist positions. A common thread across these various approaches is the belief that the interests of women and nature should be aligned and those patriarchal systems that dominate and devalue them both must be questioned. Ecofeminism voices a powerful critique of existing institutions and structures and the dualistic thinking that underlies most social theorising.

Ecofeminists, however, have not fully explored the mind–body disconnection and how this disconnection is reinforced in the marketplace. Philosophical dualisms lie at the heart of the treatment of nature as a separate and foreign realm that can be controlled and harnessed toward human ends. When women internalise these tensions between themselves and their bodies, a painful disconnection arises for women that is often extended and bolstered in the marketplace. For example, within the marketplace, women's relationship to their bodies is often framed in terms of consumer decision-making problems to be solved, yet the marketplace solutions exact a price that harms both the women and the environment.

Ecofeminism seeks to explore non-dualistic and non-dominating ways of conceiving of the relationship between humans and nature, such as reconnecting women to their bodies. Quotes from in-depth interviews with a group of women who deeply value nature highlight the subversive power of women to transform themselves, and their relationship to nature and the marketplace.

ECOFEMINISM

Ecofeminists hold a wide range of positions, as varied as the scope of positions found within feminism (Warren 1987; Lahar 1991). Ecofeminism emerged as a distinct area of discourse in the 1970s when feminists began analysing the connections between feminism and environmentalism (e.g. Carson 1962; D'Eaubonne 1980; Ortner 1974; Ruether 1974; King 1981). Specifically, these early writers, as well as contemporary theorists, seek to understand the relationship between the subordination of women and the degradation of the environment. Beyond this shared interest ecofeminists ask questions that vary widely, from the impact of Western development on local natural economies (Shiva 1989), to issues of spirituality (Starhawk 1990), to toxic waste protests (Krauss 1993). Moreover, their positions vary broadly (Sturgeon 1997). One position is that patriarchal systems similarly devalue both nature and women. Women and nature share a common interest in dismantling these oppressive structures (Warren 1987; Plumwood 1993). Another position is that women's global roles in farming and caring for the home place them in proximity to environmental harms and, therefore, they are the first to notice and be affected by environmental pollution (Gibbs 1982; Wells and Wirth 1997). Still another view holds that women's reproductive system makes them inherently closer to nature and gives them a privileged insight into nature (Starhawk 1990). Thus, while ecofeminist theorists may all focus on the nature–women link, this link is seen by some writers as a basis of oppression while others see it as a source of insight (for a wider selection of ecofeminist approaches see Diamond and Orenstein 1990 and Warren 1997).

DUALISMS AS OPPRESSIVE

In this chapter, we emphasise ecofeminists' insights into the role of dualisms in the subordination of women and nature (Dobscha 1993; McDonagh and Prothero 1997; Dobscha and Ozanne 1999). Specifically, dualisms are oppositional terms: male/female, culture/nature, public/private, beautiful/ugly or good/bad. Dualisms are not just descriptions of differences. These dualisms form ideological systems in which men/culture/public are interlocking and reinforcing realms that are valued over the women/nature/private realm, and these divisions shape social practices. From this perspective, the masculine (i.e., active, rational, mental) is valued over the feminine (i.e., passive, emotional, physical) (Plumwood 1993). Masculine speech is the public speech of logic and consistency. Feminine speech is the private speech of feelings, chatter, gossip or oral histories through storytelling (Gluck and Patai 1991; Tseelon 1995).

Whilst Plumwood analyses these dualisms as far back as Platonic thought, the duality between nature and culture became prevalent during the Enlightenment (Merchant 1980; Tseelon 1995). Ortner (1974) argues that a cross-cultural division exists between nature and culture in which women are seen as closer to nature, while men are perceived as representing culture. Similarly, women are found in the private realm of the home, while men are found in the public arena of work. These systems naturalise divisions that are actually social constructions used to subordinate others: it is naturally women's place to be in the home, and nature is of course a tool to be used toward human ends.

If nature is devalued, then it can be asserted that the 'natural functioning' of the body – disease, ageing, bleeding, dirtiness and so forth – would also become discounted or distanced in favour of health, youth, cleanliness and neatness. The body already is philosophically marginalised in favour of the logic – and knowledge-producing mind, then becomes another devalued side of a hierarchical dualism. Therefore, all 'bodily' functions that are not clean or orderly are avoided, shunned, feared or ignored. As the opening quote by Paula Gunn Allen suggests, one's attitude toward one's own body may also reflect one's view of the natural world at large. This fear/avoidance of all that is natural in the body is manifest in a marketplace that offers products to facilitate the disconnection from the natural processes of our own bodies. The feminine hygiene industry, the household cleaning products industry and the beauty industry are three compelling examples.

In the next section, the separation of women from their bodies is explored in the areas of menstruation, the home and the body project. The participation of the marketplace in furthering this division is discussed. This chapter concludes with ideas for reconnecting women to their bodies within the context of a world dominated by a body-hate ideology. It also offers insights into how the marketplace could be re-framed to be celebratory of nature and women, rather than oppressive. But first, the methodology employed in this study is briefly reviewed.

METHODOLOGY

This study resulted from a two-year, in-depth look at a group of women from the south-eastern portion of the United States of America who viewed themselves as deeply connected to the natural world. A feminist methodology was employed, in order to 1) maintain the voice of the participant, 2) build trust between researcher and participant, and 3) empower the participant through her selection of topics covered during the interviews (Oakley 1981; Reinharz 1992; Hirschman 1993). To facilitate these goals, two forms of data collection were used: 1) engaged observation (Hirschman 1986; Hudson and Ozanne 1988; Belk 1991), and 2) multiple, in-depth interviews (McCracken 1988; Reinharz 1992).

Each participant was interviewed on three separate occasions and each interview ranged from one to three hours. These interviews took place in the homes of the participants and employed a relaxed conversational approach consistent with women-to-women talk (Oakley 1981; DeVault 1991). The women were encouraged to tell their stories, and questions of elaboration or clarification were asked. The first interview was guided by an initial set of broad questions pertaining to the women's relationship to nature and the marketplace. The second interview was guided by the content of the first interview, and the third interview consisted of a conversation concerning any unresolved issues related to the participants' commitment to the natural world (Dobscha 1995).

Data were then analysed using a three-stage hermeneutical process derived from the works of McCracken (1988) and Spradley (1979). This hermeneutical process first involved creating a text for each participant by reading and analysing the text as a whole, then creating a second text from the common elements among the participants, and finally creating a third text designed to combine the analysis with the women's original words.

It is very important to note here that these women were all one nationality; they all were born and raised in the United States of America. In addition, they were all Anglo-American and within the central socio-economic category of middle class. Therefore, our data will reflect the cultural idiosyncrasies of American culture and cannot (and should not) be generalised to women of other nationalities, classes or races.

DISCONNECTING SELF FROM BODY

Womanhood as control of cleanliness

Menarche, a girl's first menstruation, is dealt with differently across cultures with rituals of both inclusion and exclusion. In the twentieth century, an American girl's menstruation changed from a marker of her new reproductive ability (i.e., womanhood) to a hygienic problem to be managed in terms of staying clean, avoiding stains and buying the right product. Until the birth of mass production, women showed girls how to use rags or cotton as a means of absorbing menstrual blood. With the advent of the consumer goods revolution coupled with germ theory, feminine waste (which had been dealt with through a private, home-centred discourse) transformed into the more public *problem of hygiene*. Endorsed by doctors and facilitated by efficient distribution channels, middle-class women began ordering antiseptic napkins. The now very public issue of menstruation could be found in the hallowed pages of America's first mass-produced catalogue (Montgomery Ward as early as 1895 and Sears Roebuck in 1897) and later in advertisements in popular magazines (Kotex ads in the 1920s in *Ladies' Home Journal* and *Good Housekeeping*) (Brumberg 1997).

Menarche became one of many bodily functions in which the marketplace provided a 'quick fix' (Brumberg 1997). Most contemporary women remember shopping for bras and feminine hygiene products with their mothers: 'American girls and their mothers characteristically head for the mall, where coming-of-age is acted out in purchases – such as bras, lipsticks, and high heels, or "grown-up" privileges such as ear piercing' (Brumberg 1997: 33). Shared rituals of menarche now involve the ubiquitous viewing of commercially sponsored health films in gender-separated school classrooms. And advertisements for feminine hygiene products have consistently stressed the product as a form of social insurance to control against embarrassing bodily odours or stains (Brumberg 1997). Product innovations, whether improved absorbency, larger size or the latest 'technology' – wings – all serve to contain the problem of leakage and provide more assurance against the social dangers associated with menstruation. Ironically, this industry appropriates the language of feminism – concepts such as 'control', 'freedom' and 'liberation' – to bolster its market share (Treneman 1989).

Sharing a surprising similarity to the language of chemical spills, menstruation is constructed by marketing as a mess that needs to be contained. It represents a concrete instance of how the marketplace reinforces a disconnection of women from their bodies. Beyond the environmental implications of aisles of sanitary products that contribute to landfills, the disconnection from normal bodily processes reinforces an overall attitude toward all waste. Bodily waste becomes a metaphor for the planet's waste. It is 'contained' and then 'disposed'. Waste is neatly packaged, left at the kerbside, only to disappear magically. One informant, Rachel, bemoans people's lack of accountability for their own wastes:

> 'People want to have convenience; they don't want to have to deal with their messes. They just want it all to get [go away], a good example for me is that, I don't know if this is going to gross you out or not, but feminine hygiene products like disposable feminine napkins and tampons and all that – I don't use those. I use cloths and I wash them out. I have been doing that for a long time and it's not a big deal to me anymore. I just don't even think twice about it. So I go to the store and I look in the aisle full of all that shit, wrapped in plastic and it really kind of freaks me out that this is what everybody is using and it's all just going into the landfill! . . . [Menstrual blood] is actually like a really a potent, mysterious, fertile substance.'
>
> (Rachel)

The women in this study were connected to the waste that they created. For example, all the women viewed composting as a practical solution for many of their wastes.

> 'I don't throw out any food type products. Everything goes in there. We have compost. It's near that tree back there. And every once in a while I'll turn it over. And we do use it. We set up some beds for flowers. . . . Everything goes into the compost.'
>
> (Helen)

Robin compares her own comfortable attitude toward dealing with household wastes to her mother's more mainstream discomfort:

> 'My mom came and took care of the house while my husband and I went to New Zealand. . . . [So] she composted for the first week and wouldn't do it after because it stank. . . . We can't do anything that smells bad. . . . [In] New Zealand people have goats so their garbage gets translated into sweaters, which is kind of neat.'
>
> (Robin)

Thus, these women who had a deep connection to nature were more aware of and responsible for all of their wastes. This sense of accountability influenced their action in the marketplace where they sought to minimise the waste they created:

> 'All of the juices, things like ketchup, mustard, mayonnaise, anything like that, if it's in plastic, I won't buy it. It's like, sorry, I guess I really didn't need mustard today, I need to buy one that is in glass. That way I know that the material, when I'm done with what's inside of it, I can either re-use it again for a storage container or I can get it back to the recycling system so that it can be made into a new one.'
>
> (Terry)

> 'Another thing we do is we try not to use the car to go to town just for one thing. We'll try to have a [plan], that's why I had to go to the library, I have to go to the bank, I have to pick, to go to [store name], pick up the paper, and then go to [store name]. I try to have a whole series of things to do so I don't run back and forth every day. You can get into the habit of doing that if you're not careful. . . . Well, I am much more concerned about paper now. Just to give you an example. I mean all our scrap paper. I used to buy pads. I don't buy pads any more. I just use my scrap paper.'
>
> (Helen)

All of the women sought to do without many unnecessary products, use less when consumption could not be avoided, and re-use products rather than throw them away. These activities allowed the women to decrease the overall waste they created, a waste for which they felt connected and thus responsible.

Home as a temple of cleanliness

Despite changing roles, housework is still generally viewed as women's work (DeVault 1991). The goal of housework is to present a public masterpiece of efficiency and cleanliness (Oakley 1974; Cowan 1987; DeVault 1987). This work of 'keeping house' traditionally requires the use of harsh chemical solutions to maintain the level of cleanliness instilled in most women by their mothers and reinforced by advertising. Cleaning often involves covering up nature as manifested by dirt, odours, bugs, and the like (Gruen 1993).

The women in the study do not use harsh cleaners and most make their own benign alternatives (e.g. baking soda and vinegar). Robin figures that a strong product 'that cleans really well and kills germs . . . also kills cells and cuts the grease on your skin. So they're bad for you.' Helen also goes without buying any harsh cleansers. She states, 'For example, I used to buy stuff for the drains'. Now, she simply flushes the drains once a week with very hot water. She finds that this solution works just as well to prevent clogs.

But beyond rejecting cleaning products, many of the women rejected traditional norms of cleanliness. Robin questions ideas regarding cleanliness when she uses no pesticides: 'We put up with a lot of spiders and ants'. The women who were concerned about water issues chose to shower less regularly. Laura states, 'Some people think they have to wash their sheets every day. Heck, we're fairly clean when we get in them. . . . Or my towels, I dry myself when I've just taken a shower. Why would I have to wash my towel?' Similarly, Robin states, 'Like I'll use toilet bowl cleaner not regularly, but when things start to grow'.

The women referred to their attitude as 'letting go'. Cathy says:

> 'I'll let things go. I haven't cleaned my toilet all the time. I'll let it go. I have well water here and I have iron bacteria, so I get this orange fill. And it is completely harmless and it doesn't smell. I mean there is absolutely no, you know, it's not bad. So I'll let that go until I can't stand it, and then I squirt some of that stuff on it and clean it, but rather than every time, cause every time you clean it you have to flush it, which is wasting a couple of gallons of water. So, I just don't do it. And I think, well, if somebody is bothered by my orange toilet bowl, well, that's too bad'.
>
> (Cathy)

Robin and Cathy acknowledge that this norm collides with traditional norms, which is apparent from the social disapproval they receive from their mothers. Both Cathy and Robin's mothers are fanatical housekeepers with a myriad of chemicals in their arsenals. Here, Robin discusses her gradual shift away from her mother's style of cleaning:

> 'If I'm toilet training, this always happens when I'm toilet training a child you don't want to sit their bottom on a toilet seat that's just been cleaned with Lysol. Cleaning bathrooms and bathtubs concerned me right away that I was, I used the same chemicals basically that my mother did, and it concerned me that I was gonna be bathing my child in the bathtub that had just been cleaned with Clorox or Lysol or something like that. So I tended to not clean very much, like for a long time I just used Windex because it was easy and pretty inexpensive and it seemed to clean just about everything.'
>
> (Robin)

Helen remarked about the difference between herself and her mother:

> 'My mother had the cleanest refrigerator in the world. I mean she never saved anything. Everything went out to the garbage. Whereas like we, tonight

> we have leftover soup, and we have leftover linguini. So the linguini will go in the soup and that will be another meal.'
>
> (Helen)

Laura even kidded, 'If I ever get around to cleaning my house', and then immediately asked whether her anonymity would be preserved. Even though Laura cleaned infrequently to affirm her relationship to nature, she still feared the social evaluation that might arise if someone heard her confession that she rarely cleaned her home. While the women framed their actions as letting go of the standards of cleanliness instilled by their families and society, they were also struggling to escape from societal expectations that the home is the feminine domain and a measure of a woman's self worth (Dobscha and Ozanne 1999).

The home is constructed as a private feminine domain in which nature must be kept at bay; the home must be controlled, pure and clean. The marketplace encourages woman to labour using solutions that harm themselves and nature. The women in this study offer an alternative vision of 'letting things go'. While letting go may refer to relinquishing the social norms of cleanliness, the women's attitude also involves an acceptance and even a celebration of nature as manifest in dirt, dust and bugs.

Women's freedom to have the perfect body

The disconnection between self and body is perhaps even more pronounced in contemporary women's views of their bodies. To the extent that women internalise their subordination, they form a self-image from the perspective of the dominant group (Wolf 1990). They learn that 'their outer body's appearance represents and reflects their moral value; to be beautiful is to be good, and to be both, one must suffer – the female body must be scrutinised regularly, privately as well as publicly, restricted and laboured over continually' (Valentine 1994: 119).

Many women are dissatisfied with their bodies and their body size in particular. A contradiction exists between the perception of freedom by contemporary women and the need to police increasingly broader areas of their body.[1] The body is animal, appetite, hunger; the body must be denied and controlled. If the self is mirrored in the contours of a woman's body, then controlling the body and self are one and the same project. For example, Susan Bordo (1993) suggests that anorexics and compulsive body-builders share a similar preoccupation with gaining complete mastery over their bodies by controlling their urges in order to create a perfect body. Brumberg (1997) offers a similar insight in her analysis of the historical construction of the body for adolescent girls from Victorian to contemporary society. While the sexual coming of age with its distinctive bodily changes, such as breasts and menstruation, stays constant, it is the socio-cultural historical context that gives these physical changes their meaning. A young woman in the nineteenth century dealt with the 'anguish' of her changing adolescent body by improving herself through good works and spiritual development. Some concern existed about one's body; that is, small hands, feet and waist were preferred, and large robust bodies were devalued as indicative of a more brutish and working-class origin. In contrast, at the end of the twentieth century, the body has become an 'all-consuming project' for both women and girls. This project involves intense scrutiny of their bodies, weight, hair, complexion, face, thighs, hips, breasts, and so on (Brumberg 1997: xvii). Girls coming of age have always struggled with questions of identity. Yet, in today's culture, with its emphasis on physical beauty, women and girls judge their self-worth by their outer appearance. When this judgement falls short of an unattainable ideal, young girls enter the marketplace (Brumberg 1997).

The marketplace accentuates the fear felt by women of the natural ageing process. As one becomes more attached to the body as a project, one may fear wrinkles, flab, disease, all things that are part of nature and the natural course of life. Denzin (1984) calls this the divided self and suggests that guilt, shame and self-loathing dominate such a self (Valentine 1994). According to the extent to which we are engaged in the body project, we may become more disconnected from the nature of which we are a part. The freedom to express our postmodern self may involve violence to the self because we are still tyrannised by the ideal images of advertising that remind us of our failings. We now must have slim muscled bodies free of imperfections. We must be able to reveal beautiful midriffs so flat that they deny the existence of a womb and certainly make any evidence of childbirth invisible. One informant, Terry, emphasised advertising's role in this process:

> 'I think advertising and the marketplace is a very seductive and very powerful realm . . . I mean if somebody want's to come up with the money to make advertising and marketing techniques that would make people genuinely feel good about themselves [and] not worry and fret about the right fragrance, the right colour of eye shadow, the right body build, the right clothes. . . . They cause expectations in you of how your life and your relationships go and they don't! And so you are disappointed.'
>
> (Terry)

Dana explicitly points to the danger of an emphasis on the self and a preoccupation with mastery; this attitude of mastery when applied to nature may have bad results. Ann further suggests that when one moves away from this self-orientation, an earth-orientation is more possible.

> 'I hear a lot of this, you know, me, me, me, me. It really scares me. . . . I agree we are all important, we are all powerful, but it just seems like [they are] really focusing on the individual, instead of the community and groups and families. . . . Well, if we are so entirely important and reigning supreme, or whatever that means, then we should be able to control and manipulate anything around us to our benefit. So I think it could have a negative impact on the way we view the environment.'
>
> (Dana)

> 'Because they [environmentalists] really care inside. That's a rare quality in people usually. And they don't have a selfish viewpoint. I have the kind of viewpoint I hope more people get. And I think more people are realising that there is only one earth and if we don't protect it, it is going to be in bad shape.'
>
> (Ann)

The project of body/nature mastery contrasts vividly with the balanced lives sought by the women in our study. Most of the women wore no cosmetics and many bought their clothes at second-hand stores so they would not fuel a consumerist society. For example, Terry states that she does not wear make-up or fragrances and scoffs at marketing's attempts to portray consumer goods as a means of solving real problems. Similarly, Rachel states that she no longer wears make-up because it created a false persona.

> 'Not worry and fret about the right fragrance, the right colour of eye shadow, the right body build, the right clothes. I make coffee and now Mom and me are talking together. Whatever. Most of that stuff, I think, puts a real incredible stress intentionally on people's real lives because it doesn't work that way in real life. Making the coffee that smells real good is not going to resolve the argument.'
>
> (Terry)

> 'I can kind of see wearing make-up in a way. Because when I was younger I used to wear some make-up and stuff and I can kind of see the fun and the desire to change your looks or take something and, like put on this mask. I can kind of understand that. But it just seems like a lot of what is for sale is useless.'
>
> (Rachel)

Instead of creating alternative or false personas through such consumer goods as make-up, fragrances or fancy clothes, the women spoke of their quest to find a more balanced and harmonious existence with nature as an expression of their relationships with their selves and their bodies. Terry exemplifies this connection and how it plays out in what she buys as well as what she puts into her body:

> 'To live my life in such a way that I honour all the things that I know to be realities in the environment. I base all of what I do, how I live my life, what I buy, where I go, if I go on my understanding of what the world can support from each individual. As far as anything I use internally or externally on my body. I don't use any chemicals. If it's any type of cosmetics or anything, not that I use cosmetics anyhow but if it's any type of creams or lotions or any type of medicinal salves or anything else like that. I don't use anything with animal products in them. That again has just been a thing that I did not develop for a religious or a preaching reason. It just made sense to me. I didn't see any need to kill animals to make products when there were plenty

of alternatives that were lower down on the scale of the way the world works. And mostly I just ended up not liking them.'

(Terry)

The women in this study found that a deep connection to nature sustained them internally and externally. They shunned consumer goods not only for the negative impact they had on the earth but also for the negative impact they had on their own sense of self.

RECONNECTING SELF AND BODY

> A society based on body hate destroys itself and causes harm to all . . .
>
> (Allen 1990: 53)

> 'I think that our society works best – the consumerism society works best – when people are separated from themselves.'
>
> (Rachel)

As these two women suggest, to be disconnected from one's sense of self, especially in the form of the body, is to be disconnected from the powerful healing, calming and spiritual force of nature. When the self is divided and we obsess about the dirt, the wrinkles, the pain, and the changes, then we deny the body and its needs and natural passages. Perhaps a society based on body-love offers an alternative path. How can we as marketers play a role in fostering body-love instead of body-hate?

Erdman's (1994) look at the self-acceptance of body size by fat women offers some guidance as to what body-love might look like. The women moved beyond external measures of self-worth, such as the numbers on a scale and images in an advertisement. The women's process of acceptance involved being kind and gentle to themselves. They stopped living for a time when they would be thin and started creating the life they sought now. Their obsession with food changed to a focus on how eating and exercise can contribute to overall health. But they also radically challenged traditional meanings of obesity and constructed themselves as 'women of substance' who were more than the mere image of their bodies. They sought to be involved in political and spiritual activities that extended beyond themselves, 'the largeness of the body' reached beyond to 'the largeness of inner spirit' (Erdman 1994: 168).

Thus, a project of body-love might help heal the division between self and the natural body. An acceptance of the nature in us may also extend to an acceptance of the nature around us.

> 'Well, my relationship with nature is that I am part of it. I don't see any separation between what we call the natural environment and human beings except we human beings have built on it. . . . There is unity throughout the

> entire creation and nothing exists separately from the whole. . . . So I never ever thought any other way; I've never understood the idea that humans have dominion over nature. That's always been foreign to me. I never even realised that people even felt that way until – I can't tell you when that idea dawned on me, but that came as a surprise that some people felt they were completely separate from everything else in creation.'
>
> (Cathy)

> 'It's . . . all-consuming. . . . Everything I do is really based on my relationship with the natural world. And I feel real connected in a very deep way. . . . I just feel that I am just a part of it and that I don't really disconnect from it at all. I know a lot of people around here who feel so connected in such a deep way that it's a physical pain for them to see the suffering of the mother [earth].'
>
> (Rachel)

Body-love involves women reconnecting to the wondrous diversity of their bodies. Enjoying the flow, the fitting into an ongoing cycle of birth, growth, death and rebirth. This means that they must actively honour themselves and reject the images that say freedom is having a perfect body, a pure body and a clean home. Unfortunately, 'consumerist society', as Rachel calls it, is not set up to foster loving relationships with nature or with ourselves.

A marketplace based on connection

> A marketplace that is based on connections to nature and ties among people would look very different from a marketplace based only on economic efficiency. Some environmentalists have begun to live this credo in the form of LETS, Local Exchange Trading System. These cash-less communities establish trading circles for goods and services that are typically locally produced and distributed. Therefore, all members must contribute something of value, whether it is a trade, a service, or knowledge. These communities were designed in opposition to the mass-produced, mass-distributed exchange networks that these people feel promotes waste, over consumption, and a general disconnection from nature and selves.
>
> (Davies 1998)

While alternative systems of exchange do exist and new systems could be created, consumers can also work within their existing local markets to foster connections. For example, buying local produce from local farmers strengthens the community by supporting its own members. It may be perceived as a sacrifice to forgo the pleasure of eating out-of-season produce – a global marketplace means that those consumers of economic means may eat melons in winter. But pleasure can also be found in reconnecting to the seasons and what they offer: enjoying the lushness of ripe melons in summer, feasting on the bounty of the harvest, enduring the sparse offerings of winter, and savouring the greens of spring. The change of seasons provides comfort that binds one to people of the past, present and future. Joy exists in knowing the local farmers, their hardships of drought and their good fortunes of rain. And beauty exists in their weathered faces and dirty hands.

CONCLUSION AND FUTURE RESEARCH

Ecofeminist marketers must find the means to create these positive connections for both the people producing and consuming culture. However, before alternative ways of exchange can be enacted, current images in the marketplace that increase people's disconnection from themselves, others and nature must somehow be critiqued and resisted. In order for women to reconnect with their bodies, they must first understand where the disconnection stems from. If we deconstruct the images and products designed to disconnect from their otherwise very natural bodily functions ('feminine spray' is a classic example), what we find is a marketplace that is reinforcing negative images of self (McDonagh and Prothero 1997).

The women in this study offer guidance as to how affirmation of a central value, such as the importance of nature, weakens the power of other pulls, such as negative self-images. The women in this study were liberated and comforted by their connection to nature, which stands in contrast to women who engage in body mutilation, starvation and other forms of body-hate. Perhaps the first step is a refusal to hate one's body. Each person can rename the 'beautiful' glossy images instead as starved bodies in denial; each person can love the part of the body that they most despise; each person can affirm the different beauty that exists in all people. Thus, individuals can resist narrow ideals of beauty that disconnect people from themselves and others.

Future research in this area should first focus on the person–nature relationship. One assumption within much ecofeminist writing is that this relationship is stronger among women. Yet, in most traditional environmental studies, few gender differences exist with regard to environmental awareness or action. Therefore, researchers choosing to focus on the consciousness raising of consumers must first understand the equally complex relationship between gender and nature. How do men define their connection? Does it result in different manifestations and marketplace reactions?

Furthermore, environmental marketing research needs to turn its lens to more macro-level issues. For example, what is the role of culture, class, race and ethnicity on the person–nature connection? As stated earlier, this study was only of American women, most of whom lived fairly privileged economic existences; therefore, more insight is needed at the intersections of nationality and class and how this plays out in the marketplace.

Envisioning a field of marketing that fosters connections and builds community is no easy task. Traditional environmental research fails to acknowledge the deep connection to nature that many people feel and also fails to understand how this connection influences the movements of these people within the marketplace.

The women in this study enter the marketplace with a high level of distrust and fear; they are not the brand-fetish consumers of marketing texts. Neither are they the simplistic consumers as defined in most environmental marketing research where the level of 'greenness' is used to capture this connection uni-dimensionally. However, the complicated deep connection that they have to nature means that they enter the marketplace treading lightly and using only what can be returned to the earth. Given the urgency of the environmental problems facing all earth inhabitants, marketers need to turn their attention away from the goal of buying. The focus should be on how researchers can raise people's consciousness in order to foster a strong relationship with nature that can lead to a sustainable marketplace.

NOTE

1 While exercise and diet can result in healthier and stronger bodies, the concern here is that the goal of the body project is merely to create a work of art, which is viewed as an object that is separate and detached from the self (Bordo 1993). Whereas, experiencing the joy and wonder of one's own body growing stronger and more agile can reconnect the self and body.

REFERENCES

Allen, P. G. (1990) 'The woman I love is a planet; the planet I love is a tree', in I. Diamond and F. Orenstein (eds) *Reweaving the World: The Emergence of Ecofeminism*, San Francisco: Sierra Club Books, 52–7.

Belk, R. W. (1991) 'Epilogue: lessons learned', in R. W. Belk (ed.) *Highways and Buyways: Naturalistic Research from the Consumer Behavior Odyssey*, Provo, UT: Association for Consumer Research, 234–8.

Bordo, S. (1993) *Unbearable Weight: Feminism, Western Culture, and the Body*, Berkeley: University of California Press.

Brumberg, J. J. (1997) *The Body Project: An Intimate History of American Girls*, New York: Vintage Books.

Carson, R. (1962) *Silent Spring*, Boston: Houghton Mifflin.

Cowan, R. S. (1987) 'Women's work, housework, and history: the historical roots of inequality in work-force participation', in N. Gerstel and N. E. Gross (eds) *Families and Work*, Philadelphia, PA: Temple University Press, 164–77.

Davies, N. (1998) 'What is LETS?', Teifi Taf LETS-Introduction, Online. Available at http://www.teifitaf.freeserve.co.uk/intro.htm.

D'Eaubonne, F. (1980) 'Feminism or death', in E. Marks and I. de Courtivron (eds) *New French Feminism*, New York: Schocken Books.

Denzin, N. K. (1984) *On Understanding Emotion*, San Francisco, CA: Jossey-Bass.

DeVault, M. L. (1987) 'Doing housework: feeding and family life', in N. Gerstel and H. E. Gross (eds) *Families and Work*, Philadelphia, PA: Temple University Press, 178–91.

—— (1991) *Feeding the Family: The Social Organization of Caring as Gendered Work*, Chicago: University of Chicago Press.

Diamond, I. and Orenstein, G. F. (eds) (1990) *Reweaving the World: The Emergence of Ecofeminism*, San Francisco, CA: Sierra Club Books.

Dobscha, S. (1993) 'Women and the environment: applying ecofeminism to environmentally-related consumption', in L. McAlister and M. L. Rothschild (eds) *Advances in Consumer Research* 20, Provo, UT: Association for Consumer Research, 36–9.

—— (1995) 'Women and the natural world and their marketplace activities', unpublished doctoral thesis, Virginia Polytechnic Institute and State University.

Dobscha, S. and Ozanne, J. L. (1999) 'A critical ecofeminist look at the woman–nature link: exploring the emancipatory potential of an ecological life', unpublished working paper.

Erdman, C. K. (1994) 'Nothing to lose: a naturalistic study of size acceptance in fat women', in K. A. Callaghan (ed.) *Ideals of Feminine Beauty*, Westport, CT: Greenwood Press, 161–73.

Gibbs, L. (1982) *Love Canal: My Story*, Albany: State University of New York.

Gluck, S. B. and Patai, D. (1991) *Women's Words: The Feminist Practice of Oral History*, New York: Routledge.

Gruen, L. (1993) 'Dismantling oppression: an analysis of the connection between women and animals', in G. Gaard (ed.) *Ecofeminism: Women, Animals, Nature*, Philadelphia, PA: Temple University Press, 60–90.

Hirschman, E. C. (1986) 'Humanistic inquiry in marketing research: philosophy, method, and criteria', *Journal of Marketing Research* 23, August: 237–49.

—— (1993) 'Ideology in consumer research, 1980 and 1990: a Marxist and feminist critique', *Journal of Consumer Research* 19, March: 537–55.

Hudson, L. A. and Ozanne, J. L. (1988) 'Alternative ways of seeking knowledge in consumer research', *Journal of Consumer Research* 14, March: 508–21.

King, Y. (1981) 'Feminism and revolt', *Heresies* 4, 1: 12–16.

Krauss, C. (1993) 'Women and toxic waste protests: race, class and gender as resources of resistance', *Qualitative Sociology* 16, 3: 247–62.

Lahar, S. (1991) 'Ecofeminist theory and grassroots politics', *Hypatia* 6, 1: 28–45.

McCracken, G. (1988) *The Long Interview*, Newbury Park, CA: Sage.

McDonagh, P. and Prothero, A. (1997) 'Leapfrog marketing: the contribution of ecofeminist thought to the world of patriarchal marketing', *Marketing Intelligence and Planning* 15, 7: 361–88.

Merchant, C. (1980) *The Death of Nature*, San Francisco, CA: Harper & Row.

—— (1992) *Radical Ecology: The Search For a Livable World*, New York: Routledge.

Oakley, A. (1974) *The Sociology of Housework*, New York: Pantheon.

—— (1981) 'Interviewing women: a contradiction in terms', in H. Roberts (ed.) *Doing Feminist Research*, Boston, MA: Routledge & Kegan Paul, 30–61.

Ortner, S. (1974) 'Is female to male as nature is to culture?', in M. Rosaldo and L. Lamphere (eds) *Woman, Culture, and Society*, Stanford, CA: Standford University Press, 67–87.

Plumwood, V. (1993) *Feminism and the Mastery of Nature*, London: Routledge.

Reinharz, S. (1992) *Feminist Methods in Social Research*, New York: Oxford University Press.

Ruether, R. R. (1974) *New Woman New Earth*, Boston, MA: Beacon Press.

Shiva, V. (1989) *Staying Alive: Women, Ecology and Development*, London: Zed Books.

Spradley, J. P. (1979) *The Ethnographic Interview*, New York: Holt, Rinehart & Winston.

Starhawk (1990) 'Power, authority, and mystery: ecofeminism and earth-based spirituality', in I. Diamond and F. Orenstein (eds) *Reweaving the World: The Emergence of Ecofeminism*, San Francisco, CA: Sierra Club Books, 73–96.

Sturgeon, N. (1997) *Ecofeminist Natures*, New York and London: Routledge.

Treneman, A. (1989) 'Cashing in on the curse', in L. Gamman and M. Marshment (eds) *The Female Gaze*, Seattle: The Real Comet Press, 153–65.

Tseelon, E. (1995) *The Masque of Femininity*, London: Sage.

Valentine, C. G. (1994) 'Female bodily perfection and the divided self', in K. A. Callaghan (ed.) *Ideals of Feminine Beauty*, Westport, CT: Greenwood Press, 113–23.

Warren, K. J. (1987) 'Feminism and ecology: making connections', *Environmental Ethics* 9, 1: 3–20.

—— (ed.) (1997) *Ecofeminism: Women, Culture, Nature*, Bloomington and Indianapolis: Indiana University Press.

Wells, B. and Wirth, D. (1997) 'Remediating development through an ecofeminist lens', in K. J. Warren (ed.) *Ecofeminism*, Bloomington and Indianapolis: Indiana University Press, 300–13.

Wolf, N. (1990) *The Beauty Myth*, New York: William Morrow.

15 Gender and consumption in a cultural context

Janeen Arnold Costa

GENDER AND CONSUMPTION IN A CULTURAL CONTEXT

This chapter presents information and analyses that enhance our understanding of the interaction of culture, gender and consumption. In this cross-cultural study, I draw upon a database composed of the Human Relation Area Files, extant ethnographic research by other trained scholars, and my own ethnographic fieldwork. In searching for the influence of gender relations on consumption, and the ways in which gender influences what and how we consume on a cross-cultural basis, numerous considerations arise. While I cannot address every possible source or outcome of gendering, I consider the following: sexual division of labour; gender relations, identities and roles; the part played by the family and the household; and influences of globalisation, development and consumerism. The result is a framework designed to assess overall cross-cultural differences and similarities in gender as related to consumption in traditional and developing societies around the globe. Further research should elaborate upon and extend this framework.

PRODUCTION VERSUS CONSUMPTION

Much of the quantitative and some of the qualitative data concerning gender relations, identities and roles, sexual division of labour and other aspects of gender and society focus on issues of production rather than consumption. It is likely that this emphasis is at least partially related to the Western patriarchal discourse that informs the collection and interpretation of data. Western societies tend to emphasise production, primarily a male activity, and to ignore or underemphasise consumption activities, which in Western society are associated mainly with women. However, the focus on production within the data may also be seen as a reflection of economic reality, wherein the majority of people in the world are engaged in survival-focused production activities. Notwithstanding the fact that we all consume, it has been the need to produce adequately for basic necessities that has been the focus of much human activity.

This need to focus on subsistence and survival has been the case throughout much of human history. Since the beginning of the European Age of Expansion and the associated imposed transformation from subsistence to cash crop agriculture, the development of wage labour for industrial activities, and cash tax collections, this subsistence perspective has become a by-product of political, economic and military power. Prior to that time, and barring natural disasters such as drought or floods, most humans involved in hunting and gathering, horticultural or agricultural economic production were able to feed themselves and to meet sufficiently their needs for shelter and clothing. This was the case even within the agriculturally based civilisations, where some sectors of the population were relatively poor and surrendered a portion of their production as taxes. In those societies in which humans were largely involved in hunting, gathering, and/or horticultural endeavours, egalitarian access to resources guaranteed that virtually all would receive a portion of food, shelter and other resources (Sahlins 1972).[1]

Production and consumption are related activities, of course. Therefore, I intend to propose a framework partially based on an extrapolation from production issues to consumption practices, where necessary. However, substantial qualitative materials that provide valuable data and analyses directly concerning consumption are available in other disciplines, primarily in anthropology, sociology, political science and development economics. These materials are vast and untapped within the marketing field, and I am able to provide only a brief introduction to the sizeable collection of information. Nevertheless, patterns are quite evident within those materials that are discussed here.

METHODOLOGY

The findings reported herein are based on three data sources, which necessitated varied methods. I will continually draw upon the data from my ongoing field research in Greece. Beginning some twenty years ago and continuing to the present, I engaged in fieldwork and follow-up research using an array of qualitative methods, the most salient of which was the typical anthropological form of participant observation. For certain purposes, I collected quantitative data in Greece as well. The second data source of extant scholarly ethnographic or monographic work required extensive literature search, review and analysis. Finally, I utilised the Human Relations Area Files (HRAF). The files, now available as a website, provide coded and complete information on nearly 800 historic and presentday societies. Select ethnographic and other scholarly works provide extensive data on each society. The HRAF, in addition to aiding in the identification of important scholarly work for the purpose of intensive analysis, also allows for a search of coded information that provides brief glimpses into numerous societies on the basis of particular topics. These data not only furnished support for the framework or model but contributed to its development. As analysis proceeded, the HRAF supplied a basis for generalisability both of the overall findings and of the framework itself.

KEEPING IT IN CONTEXT

The social, historical and cultural contexts of a given research topic are often underemphasised in the marketing and consumer behaviour disciplines. For example, logistical analysis has been devoid of the notion of human influences, at least until the recent incursion of those who consider social context, resulting in the current discussion of 'relationship marketing'. In another instance, the symptomatic 'international marketing' textbook is often merely domestic US strategy writ large, with a few examples from Japan, China or Mexico thrown in. The latter often appear in small grey or blue boxes, along with colourful, ethnocentrically captioned photos representing those aspects of non-US practice that are 'interesting' to the American scholar and student. Consumer behaviour theorists have focused on the micro level of the human psyche since the 1960s; cognitive information processing continues to be the most predominant theory upon which research is based in the field in the 1990s. In summary, marketing and consumer behaviour scholars have often approached their topics using simplistic, microcosmic, context-avoiding models, the 'best' of which no longer concern themselves with an issue as bothersome as 'external validity'.

In general, my approach to the issues of gender and consumer behaviour is the opposite of the scholarship just described. Bringing in the anthropological approach in which I have been trained, I consider the most significant factors that affect the behaviour I study to be the social, cultural, historical, particularistic, systemic aspects of that behaviour. While I cannot deal with all of those aspects in this short chapter, I will pay attention to what appear to be the most significant factors. Briefly, these include gendered property ownership; practices of marriage, inheritance and postmarital residence; issues of power within the household; conceptualisations of male–female spatial domains; issues of social recognition and ways in which 'status' is construed; household and children-related expenditures; and past and present sexual and societal division of labour. The list is long, but the factors interrelate with one another, forming a cohesive framework for a preliminary assessment of the ways in which gender, culture and consumption interact.

The chapter concludes with a lengthy analysis of permutations in gender, production and consumption associated with 'development'. Societies throughout the world are changing remarkably as their economies are incorporated into the global economy. With tremendous societal force and impact, the 'integration' of local economies brings about alterations in the division and organisation of labour. Since, as will become apparent, much of gendered consumption is predicated upon gendered production, a reconfigured sexual division of labour dramatically affects gendered patterns of consumption. In the final pages of this chapter, then, I explore some of these altered patterns of gendered production and consumption in developing societies undergoing rapid social and economic change.

BRIEF LITERATURE SUMMARY[2]

In the anthropological discipline, the gendered nature of everything from products and property, to division of labour, social roles and created reality is well accepted. The pioneering work in anthropology in this area appeared in a book edited by Lamphere and Rosaldo in 1974, but numerous studies before that time reported on the way in which gender dichotomies pervade all societies. Since that book, the drive to understand gender and society has accelerated, and numerous books and articles in anthropology, sociology and other social science disciplines have been published. Many of these articles and books are seminal, and I have tended to emphasise the original works here.

In marketing and consumer behaviour, the understanding of gender is considerably less developed. The four conferences on gender in marketing and consumer behaviour (1991, 1993, 1996 and 1998) have been productive avenues for the presentation and precipitation of research. The proceedings of these conferences, as well as certain books and articles since that time, have contributed to the dissemination of extant and emerging knowledge in the area (Costa 1991, 1993, 1996; Fischer and Wardlow 1998). However, much remains to be done, and the contents of the book in which this chapter appears push back the frontiers of science and knowledge on this scholarly subject.

Among the most important books in other disciplines are those in the field of developmental economics, where much has been done on gender in developing economies. The literature is truly vast, and I will refer the reader only to a few works that have influenced substantially the analysis presented here. In *Women in Rural Development*, Satnam (1987) provides a useful early literature review of studies in both India and 'abroad' dealing with women's roles at home and in agricultural production, as well as the part played by women in family decision-making. These cited studies are a useful foundation for understanding the variety and nuances of gender and production in developing societies. Van den Hombergh's *Gender, Environment and Development: A Guide to the Literature* (1993) reviews other work and incorporates the issues of the environment and sustained development. In addition, *Women, Work and Gender Relations in Developing Countries*, edited by Ghorayshi and Belanger (1996), is just one of many books that provide powerful ethnographic case studies to enrich our understanding of both the similarities and differences of gender in a cross-cultural perspective within the context of global economic development processes; others include Massiah (1993) and Thomas-Slayter and Rocheleau (1995) on studies in Kenya.

The most important works that have contributed to my analysis, however, are those specific ethnographic studies undertaken by anthropologists and others throughout the world. The authors of these significant and substantial examinations of gender in traditional and developing societies explore the topic in its full complexity. The findings and implications of these studies are considered in greater detail in the following sections.

FINDINGS AND DISCUSSION

Moving beyond the basic knowledge of gender pervasiveness, I report here my preliminary findings on the issue of gender and consumption in cross-cultural and cultural contexts. All of the variables, factors or behaviours discussed here are interrelated, and any attempt to separate them one from another is fruitless and misleading. Therefore, while I look at each phenomenon, I cannot overemphasise their interconnectedness. Figure 15.1, which attempts to model this connectedness, should be seen as having fuzzy lines! The categories are not discrete, and the interactions and interrelatedness are underestimated through graphic representation. In short, I try to 'model' an interacting complex system. But, as with any such attempt, some misrepresentation occurs through attempting the abstraction itself!

GENDERED PRODUCTS AND ACTIVITIES

Perhaps the most important starting-point in presenting the data and analysis is the gendered nature of property, including objects, itself. Much of the property in virtually all societies, but particularly in traditional or developing economies, appears to be gendered. In American society, gendering of objects occurs in children as young as 5, and gendering is perceived through past and present association of particular names with particular products (Pavia and Costa 1993a, 1993b). The fact that property is gendered is accepted at face value in anthropology, sociology and other disciplines, based on innumerable research efforts and resultant publications (see, for example, Martinez and Ames 1997).

In Greece, space, as well as tangible and intangible products are all gendered. This genderedness is connected to other aspects of daily life, so that the items of the interior household are deemed to be 'female', as are any objects that are passed from mother to daughter through inheritance. Tools associated with agricultural production are considered 'male', and are not to be used or even touched by Greek women. In those parts of Greece where women own the farm animals, the tools used for them may be considered female, but this is relatively uncommon. Beyond this, ritual objects are typically female, as women are responsible for family spirituality and care of the dead and ill in Greek society. In some regions of Greece, men engage in holiday cooking, to avoid the 'contamination' of the food by women. The spit for roasting lamb is a good example of a male cooking tool, as are implements used to make certain holiday stews. However, since cooking is an 'interior' domestic task, most instruments used in the preparation of food would be considered female. In terms of space, the interior of the

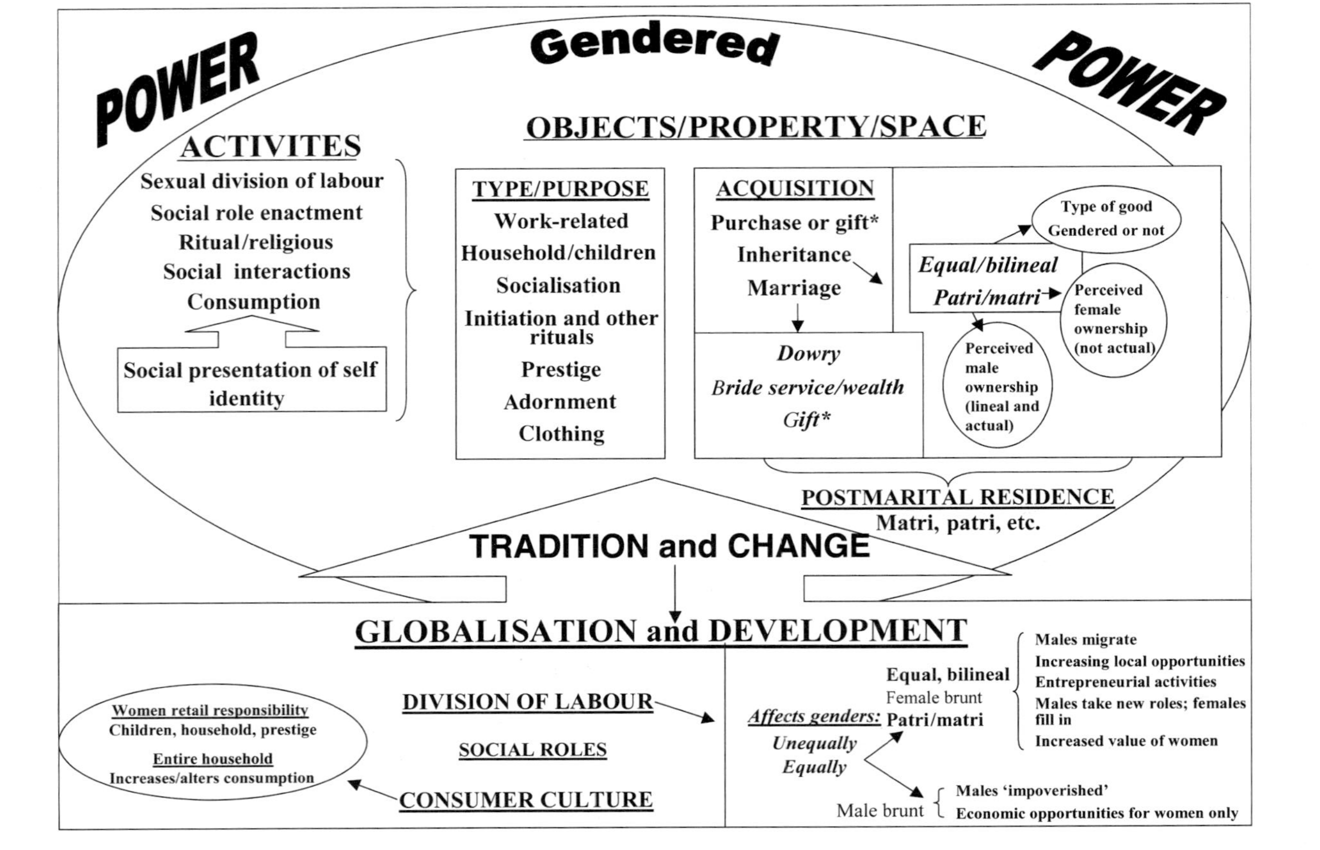

Figure 15.1 Consumption and gender
Note: *Not discussed in chapter

church, the home and its courtyard, and the cemetery are the domains of women. Alternatively, the exterior or courtyard and the steps of the church are male domains, as is the public square, the traditional coffee-shops and restaurants, and the agricultural fields (see Costa 1989 for further detail). Thus, the gendered nature of products in Greece is related to division of labour, social roles and cultural belief systems.

Other societies described in the HRAF or by other scholars indicate similar genderedness of products, to a greater or lesser extent than that found in Greece, but always present in some way. As in Greece, the gendered nature is related to other aspects of social and cultural life. Many traditional societies have objects that are associated with men or women by virtue of the activity for which they are used, based on sexual division of labour and of social roles. It is common for objects associated with productive activities outside of the home to be considered 'male', while those inside the home are 'female'. Among the Mataco of Bolivia and Argentina, for example, even the raw materials used in handicrafts are gendered (Alvarsson 1988).

Another domain in which gender roles are manifest is the conduct of ritual activities. Because rituals are performed by men in certain situations and societies and by women in other contexts, ritual objects are specifically male or female, depending on the genderedness of the ritual behaviour itself. As indicated above, cooking for ritual celebrations in Greek society is often gendered. However, women in Greek society are typically responsible for the majority of activities associated with sacred rituals. Women take care of the interior of the church, bathe and prepare the body of the deceased for burial, and decorate and maintain graves in the cemetery, for example. Objects and spaces associated with these activities are therefore considered female. Men would not want to touch them or use the objects or enter the ritual spaces. On Friday of Easter week, women decorate the *epitaphio*, or reproduction of Christ's tomb, with flowers. No males are allowed in or can touch the *epitaphio* at this time. Within the church itself, however, the sanctuary is entirely a male domain. Women are never allowed into this part of the church, both in traditional Greek villages and in cities in all societies where Orthodox churches are found. The objects therein, which are the most important and sacred objects in the church, are controlled by and are felt to 'belong to' the male priests and other males who serve in the sanctuary.

The ethnographic record reveals that religious and ritual objects and activities are gendered in societies throughout the world. When initiation into gendered roles such as male or female adulthood occurs in societies such as the Hopi or Navajo, the objects associated with those rites of passage are gendered, as are the ritual activities themselves (see Turner 1969 and van Gennep 1960 on rites of passage). The masks of African societies such as the Fang (Fernandez 1971); the paraphernalia, actions and communication forms in Igbo dances (Hanna 1979); and gendered secret societies such as those found among the Sherbro (MacCormack 1980) are all well-known examples in which objects and behaviours are gendered, and gender roles are manifest and maintained.

The devotion of specific space entirely to men or women is common in many societies. A 'men's house' is typical for male socialisation and manhood activities, as is a space for menstruating women in some societies (van Gennep 1960). In some cases, men and women sleep in separate structures. Industrial society equivalents of these spaces would include men's and women's clubs of various types, 'male-only' entertainment spaces, and separate bedrooms or even homes, in the case of the wealthy and upper class. Recent additions of 'female-only' entertainment should be included as a further example.

In considering the purported purpose of men's and women's houses, I should also comment upon regalia and ritual objects associated with menstruation, initiation into manhood and other gender-specific ceremonies. Although these are just one type of decorative or ritualistic object, they are clearly among the most gendered; these will often be 'off-limits' or 'taboo' to the members of the opposite sex. In any case, because they are associated with the clear physical changes or intentional body alterations (such as circumcision or clitorectomy, scarring or tattooing) that accompany the status change from generic child to sexual and gendered adult, the artefacts, tools and adornments that are used in these rites of passage are intensely gendered.

GENDER THROUGH ACQUISITION

Marriage exchanges

Turning now to ways in which men and women acquire objects that are considered to be gendered, I will discuss briefly the issues of marriage patterns on a cross-cultural basis. In general, the ways in which marriages are established create or enhance the gendering of objects. The most common forms of marriage exchange are the dowry and bride service or payment. In the dowry, common to African societies and some European societies, and pervasive in China, India and other Asian cultures, the woman's family provides objects for the establishment of the new household (see Goody 1969). These typically include virtually all household items such as dishes and implements; tablecloths, sheets, towels and other fabric items; and minor and sometimes major appliances. In the case of a wealthier family or when potential grooms are scarce (typically through a lack of local labour opportunities, forcing men to seek work in other cities or regions), all of the furniture for a new house, and even the house itself, may be offered by the bride's family.

The ownership of these various goods, all of which are typically considered to be 'female' in nature, varies from society to society. The objects or property may be considered to belong to both the male and female equally, to belong to the woman alone, or to belong to the man alone. In those cases where a woman's dowry objects are considered hers, she will have more power within the household and the marriage relationship. In times of trouble, she may threaten to leave and take her dowry items with her. Typically, her dowry objects are passed on to her daughter(s) at the time of her death. This is the case even when the dowry includes a house or portion of the house, as is common in Greece (Costa 1989). In modern times, cash is also an important component in many situations.

This customary form of dowry disposition, however, sometimes results in remarkable situations when the husband is allowed to keep the dowry upon the death of his wife. In India, this has led to the infamous 'wife burnings' in which marital discontent or the infertility of a wife has precipitated murder of the woman in this fashion. If the woman were to return to her family in the case of a divorce, she would be allowed legally to take her dowry objects with her. Since the husband prefers to keep the wealth of the dowry rather than to release it to his unhappy wife, the wife is abused and disposed of. The man is then free to marry again. Conviction of males for this crime is unusual. This particular case is seen to be an aberration that developed as a result of modernisation and materialism in Indian society, and is a consequence of mass urbanisation, where family members cannot protect their daughters as the women leave their traditional villages for distant cities.

Alternatively, a man may bring certain goods with him in establishing the marriage. In this practice, referred to as bride payment or bridewealth, however, the goods are given to the woman's family in exchange for her. Traditionally, these have been animals, tools or some other important object related to male productive activities or traditional wealth forms. The exchange of bridewealth items, like those in the dowry, pressures men and women to continue even unhappy or unproductive marriages, since it is most typical for a family to be required to return the objects should the marriage fail.

Inheritance and postmarital residence

The numerous forms of inheritance lead to very different gendering of inherited products and property, based on the gender of both the original and the new owners. For example, although dowry transfer occurs at the time of marriage rather than at the death of a parent(s), the dowry is often considered to be the woman's portion of familial inheritance. When one or both of the parents die in these societies, it is common for 'estate goods' to be divided among the male inheritors. In situations where property passes through the male line only, as it does for example in patrilineal societies, a certain male gendering bias may be attributed to the inherited objects. In the opposite case, in the more rare matrilineal societies, a similar gendering bias may occur. Of course, there are also instances of inheritance from both male and female lines in cases of bilineal families, for example. In these situations, particularly when the lines are still distinct, the inherited objects may be gendered as well.

Depending on the society, these inherited goods may continue to be seen as specifically belonging to the male or female throughout their lifetimes, or they may be considered as belonging to both the inheritor and his/her spouse. While this is clearly crossing the line into the issue of ownership, rather than genderedness of objects per se, it is important to remember that the inheritance pattern itself is often gendered. Thus, the objects may retain that genderedness, based on the particular objects themselves (household versus agricultural items, etc.), on the lines or manner of inheritance and on the gendered power that is inherent in owning those objects. Thus, as indicated above, retaining ownership of dowry products may give a woman relative power within a marital relationship.

Friedl's (1967) cross-cultural research indicates that 'gender equality' is based on the resources that men and women bring to the new household. Thus, in virtually all societies according to Friedl, women's prestige and power within the marriage rises when she contributes significantly to the family resource base, either through objects, housing or cash within the dowry, or currently through wages that accompany labour inside (in cottage industries) or outside the home. The latter practice is commonplace in developing countries, and it will be discussed in greater depth later in this chapter.

The gendering of products and spaces is also confounded by issues and patterns of postmarital residence. In cases of patrilocal residence, where a bride lives with the groom's family or in proximity to them, any objects she may bring with her may become less important as a source of power and ownership. Except for small, personal items, the objects she owns typically become part of the patrilineal family's resource base. However, in situations of matrilocal residence, a woman may retain clear ownership of property and objects, as well as substantial power derived both from those possessions and through the proximity of kin.

SEXUAL DIVISION OF LABOUR AND SOCIAL ROLES

It is clear that the sexual division of labour is an important influence in the gendering of products. In 'traditional' economic systems of non-agribusiness agriculture, pastoralism, swidden horticulture, and hunting and gathering societies the association of objects with the productive activities is very marked. The products associated with 'work inside the home', traditionally performed by women, are counterposed against those objects related to 'work outside the home', customarily undertaken by men. With a clear sexual division of labour comes an equally clear gendering of the objects associated with work.

This conspicuous differentiation of objects is based not only on labour roles or production, however. Social roles are also a powerful influence in this gendering process. In the vast majority of societies in the world, care of the household and raising of the children is the responsibility of women. Any objects associated with the social role of women in this context are often considered gendered, or 'women's things'. In contrast, men may be responsible for the social standing of the family in the community, for any negotiations with government and non-government organisations such as agricultural co-operatives, and for economic transactions of such basic types as banking and grocery shopping. Any products they may typically use in the enactment of these aspects of their role may be considered gendered, as 'men's things'. Chequebooks and banking literature, the grocery bag, paperwork associated with organisations, for presenting the members of the family as having adequate resources through the purchase and display of any prestige-based product, are all examples of objects that may be considered 'male' in a given society.

The enactment of social roles and the associated gendering of products can be a very nuanced process, resulting in complex associations of objects with either men or women. For example, in my research on the Greek *saloni* (parlour), I found that men and women displayed objects that reflect their pride and success in fulfilling various aspects of their assigned social roles. A woman serves homemade or traditional sweets and drinks in entertaining within the *saloni*. Many of her dowry items such as furniture, carpets, tablecloths and silver are exhibited within this room, and the family altar for which a woman is responsible is typically found here. Alternatively, objects purchased by men during their travels with the merchant marines are also displayed in the *saloni* and include 'Mexican velvet paintings, artificial flowers, Chinese silk tablecloths and tapestries, large ceramic animals, and other art objects purchased in foreign ports' (Costa 1989: 565). In rural Greece, men continue to bring in more wages than do women, and the objects purchased with this income can also be found in the *saloni*. These might include a stereo, television set, refrigerator and new dining set or sofa, for example. Thus, this room becomes a setting for the conspicuous public display of objects that represent successful enactment of Greek gender roles by both men and women.

BEYOND OBJECTS: CONSUMPTION AND GENDER

Perhaps, beyond the gendering of objects, the most significant aspects of gender in this context lie in the activities of consumption. I have tried to provide a broad exposure to various gendered products and properties, as well as the processes of marriage, inheritance and productive activity that contribute to this gendering. However, moving beyond the tangibility of products and property, we confront the vast array of gendered consumption activities, wherein specifically males or females are associated with, enact, influence and/or control specific acts of consumption.

The most powerfully gendered behaviours are those productive activities discussed above. In a comprehensive description and analysis of these behaviours, however, it is clear that consumption is an integral part of production, and vice versa. The separation of these two activities one from another is merely a heuristic, far removed from the actual behaviours in their calorie-producing, energy-consuming, income-generating, money-spending complexity. Thus, where a person produces, a person also consumes. In the following pages, while I am describing production specifically, the point is that both the activities and the objects used or consumed in the process of production are gendered.

Work is starkly dichotomised in most traditional and developing societies; certain types of productive activity are so gendered that the mere presence of a member of the opposite sex is discouraged or even proscribed. In Greece, it is said that menstruating women will spoil the wine during the grape harvest.

Menstruation is deemed to make Greek women even more 'dangerous' and 'polluting' than they are typically perceived to be, and the presence of a woman in such a condition can bring devastating results to any activity. However, in traditional Greek villages, even non-menstruating women should avoid the fields devoted to wheat, olive trees, currant vines or other agricultural products. Women, because they are perceived to be sexually dangerous and tempting, must remain in places where they can be 'protected'. Traditionally, it has only been in cases where a family is so poor that a woman must help in the fields, that her presence, and her working hands, have been tolerated.

Similarly, in Korea we find that the inside–outside gender dichotomy of activities is rigidly maintained. In this case, language itself reflects the binary gendered nature of the activities, so that Koreans use different words for labour, as well as for the head of household, depending on location of the activity and gender of the person undertaking the labour (Sorensen 1988).

In many of today's 'advanced industrialist' or 'developed' countries, a gender blurring of professions and occupations appears to be taking place. Salaries and wages, as well as percentages of male and female employees in a given line of work, are moving towards equity and equality. In those societies where labour activities indicate a blurring of gender lines, the gendered objects associated with those labour activities should also exhibit blurring, or 'de-gendering'. In developing countries, however, this process is barely beginning. In some cases, gendered distinctions in labour are actually increasing. I will return to this issue shortly.

While all societies have a sexual division of labour, some of the specific tasks associated with males and females are nearly universal. Thus, undertakings which require strength, short-term endurance, performance at a distance from the household, and group co-operation have traditionally been allotted to men, while the care of children, the household and activities close to home have been associated with women. Speculation as to why these patterns are so common revolves around questions of human evolution. Specifically, it is thought that men's hunting and women's childbearing formed the foundation upon which a more elaborate sexual division of labour and associated spatial domains were based (consult Sanday 1981; Friedl 1975). Regardless of its origin, however, the association of women with 'the home' or with 'private space' is pervasive.

Because the productive activities of raising children, feeding the family and caring for the household are considered 'women's tasks', and because these productive activities also involve a great deal of consumption, 'consuming' is typically considered to be the role of women. It has been common, for example, for economists and government officials to count only those activities that generate external income or wages as 'production' or 'labour'. Thus, when a woman performs the household tasks for which she receives no actual wages, she is not viewed as 'producing'. Instead, the focus rests on the expenditure of resources involved in her activities. As a result, women are often stereotyped as consumers rather than producers.

In Western societies, this generalisation is very apparent. In fact, the mythology of Western society is that 'men produce and women consume'. In this myth, men are deemed more 'valuable' as they are perceived to produce the wherewithal for the family's survival. At the cultural level, women's consumption activities are devalued, termed 'spending', and considered to be draining the wealth and resources of the family. With the increase of wealth and leisure time typical of Western industrial societies, women's roles as 'consuming experts' become filled with nuances of gift-giving, comparison shopping, web-surfing for various products, and the development of expert and niche-oriented knowledge. Nevertheless, the activities, regardless of the complexity and expertise required, are typically devalued. As a woman cares for her family and for their social relationships, invoking and carefully crafting her defined social role, she is nevertheless derided for the fact that her activities involve consuming or spending (for an interesting discussion and example, see Belk and Costa 1990).

In traditional and developing societies, it is also the case that women are often responsible for activities of the family and household that involve the use and distribution of household resources. Because these are consuming behaviours, the women in these societies are also seen as consumers. However, the division of production and consumption that is so apparent in Western societies is not as obvious in many non-Western societies. Although women are devalued for many things, it may not be specifically for their consuming roles in these societies. On the other hand, in societies such as China and Greece where the dowry has existed traditionally, it is thought that women 'take away wealth' from the family. In a way, then, the provision of a dowry may be seen as a situation in which daughters are viewed negatively as consumers. In China, for example, it is said that the birth of a daughter is 'a small happiness' because the daughter will eventually marry and thus drain the resources of the family through her dowry. Alternatively, the birth of a male child is greeted as 'a large happiness', because sons produce and bring in wealth to the patrilocal extended family household through their own brides' dowries (see Wolf 1975).

DEVELOPING, EXPANDING, MARKETISING

While it is appropriate to consider 'traditional' societal patterns on a cross-cultural basis, this information provides us primarily with an understanding of the variety, complexity and nuances of gendered products and consumption activities. As the world enters the new millennium (Christian dating), it is the changes in societies, the interrelationships, the globalising tendencies, the acculturation (in the anthropological sense, referring to changes that occur as dominant and subordinate societies interact) and the apparent spread of 'consumer culture' that begs for our attention. I now turn specifically to the topic of gender and consumption in 'developing' countries.

With development and the growing complexity of division of labour, as well as the movement of women from the interior of the home to public life, gendered associations of objects and activities are open to change. Still, culture is notably slow in changing, and the appearance of changing gender roles and genderedness of objects and space, is often misleading. My longitudinal study of Greece indicates a continued and pervasive gender dichotomy, where the specifics may alter for example, but the underlying division continues and is maintained. Nevertheless, developing societies are undergoing remarkable changes, particularly in the economic sphere and in terms of division of labour, and we can expect the specific details of gender and consumption to alter concomitantly.

The anthropological studies in this arena are multiplying, although it is seldom gender per se that is the focus of scholarly efforts. However, contained within the elaborate and incisive ethnographies are clear descriptions and analyses of gendered consumption behaviours. These behaviours tend to fall into specific patterns, the very existence of which is interesting in and of itself. That is, from the vast array of behaviours, types, and forms that I have briefly discussed in this chapter, we see only a few very specific patterns of gendered adaptations to the developing or modernising process. Keep in mind, however, that this apparent simplification of forms may be just that – apparent, rather than, real, manifest primarily in a still small but growing literature on the topic.

DIVISION OF LABOUR

In my opinion, the most significant alteration that occurs in peoples' lives in developing societies is the change in labour forms and relations. The demands and opportunities of developing economies manifest themselves in a variety of ways, but all represent an expansion of options for both men and women. This is not always, or perhaps not even often, to the benefit of members of those societies. The ways in which militarily or economically 'advanced' nations have evoked, even forced, changes in the labour pool of the countries which they conquer, control or influence are numerous and often debilitating to local populations. They can lead to poverty, starvation and cultural genocide. They can destroy the cohesion of families and larger kin groups. They can markedly affect religious, social, political and economic traditions. And they universally affect gender relations (see, for example, Amin 1977; Wolf 1982; Mies 1986; Chomsky 1994).

It is interesting that, despite the debilitation and destruction of certain aspects or ways of life, local people are often prone not only to accept the changes, but to embrace them enthusiastically. It is perhaps only from the elitist, paternalistic and romantic perspective, from the gaze of the etic-oriented social scientists or the intelligentsia of the society itself, that the negative aspects of the alterations are so clear. Whatever the case, the fact remains that the changes are dramatic and of continuing scholarly and social interest.

A typical pattern of gendered changes in the division of labour and in role enactment in general is for women to take on a greatly expanded list of duties and responsibilities. This shape of the developing division of labour in such economies may be related to a pattern of urbanisation that favours males, to expanding opportunities and forms of labour in the local community and/or to new forms of entrepreneurial activities, in which the entire household becomes involved in a given economic endeavour, or where a male may take responsibility for an enterprise and will leave the tasks he had traditionally undertaken to the female. In each of these instances, women are responsible for more and more labour in the developing economy.

Among the Iban of Southeast Asia, for example, men are often involved in a pattern of migration for labour opportunities referred to as *bejala*. In the absence of men, women are forced to undertake more of the responsibility for tasks in agricultural production and in maintenance of the home. Apparently, 'Men view bejalai as a way to escape the drudgery of farm work . . . [while] women in the downriver areas are not enthusiastic about bejalai . . . they resent having to bear the double burden of child-care and farm work without help' (Mashman 1991: 256). Stephen (1991) reports that Mexican Zapotec weaving opportunities fall equally to men and women, but 'women continued to perform all of the unpaid household labour in addition to weaving' (Tice 1995: 181). In rural Greek society, the pattern of urbanisation or male migrant involvement in the merchant marines has left many women in the villages to care for themselves and their families without the aid of males. In these situations, a woman may take on an increased number of tasks outside the home, including agricultural tasks in which her participation has typically been discouraged as 'shameful' (Costa 1988a). In both Iban and Greek societies, however, the objects associated with work outside the local area are sent back home and become a source of prestige for the family (Costa 1989; Mashman 1991). We will return to this point presently.

This particular pattern of labour is well established and has caught the attention of the UN and other social agencies, who find that women are bearing increased responsibility yet are also faring worse than men in terms of health and wealth. Ghorayshi and Belanger indicate that 'women, compared to men, in developing countries work longer, receive less money, have more responsibilities, have less schooling, and even absorb less calories' (1996: viii). Even in societies such as the Navajo, where women have relatively greater power through the existence of matrilineality and matrifocality, changes associated with 'development' have resulted in a relative decline in position and power for women.

It is also possible that women actually benefit from the increased availability of labour opportunities. As suggested by Friedl (1967, see also 1975), income-producing or other activities in which a woman augments the economic resources of the household generally raise her status within the household. Among the Kuna of Central America, Tice notes that women have benefited from the commercialisation of crafts they produce:

> . . . Kuna women have done quite well for themselves. They have (1) become active in marketing their [crafts], (2) retained their access to and control over land and over many other important economic resources, (3) entered regional and national politics and economic development planning processes,

> (4) learned business skills that have allowed them opportunities, and (5) controlled the income from the sale of [crafts].
>
> (Tice 1995: 182)

Tice's findings however, contrast markedly with women in similar cottage industry craft-producing situations. Among female lacemakers in Narsapur, India, for example, women are not allowed to participate in the marketing of their products, and male intermediaries become wealthy at women's expense (Mies 1982). Similarly, in Guatemala, the men control profits from fabrics and clothes that the women help produce (Ehlers 1990).

In an alternative pattern of gendered changes in labour roles, the responsibility for tasks may lead to relatively greater deprivation for men. In southern Italy, for example, those men who are unable to take advantage of the economic opportunities to the North, are left to meagre wages and under- or unemployment in the towns and villages of the South. Here, it is the women who have the greatest opportunity to provide for the family. Working as maids or in other female-dominated occupations that few Italian men would consider undertaking, these women literally take charge of the entire domestic economy. They both bring the resources and arrange for expenditure thereof. In an interesting twist of cultural practice, the public dominance of males continues. It is no longer the case that the males are dominant economically, however. Rather, the women exercise their considerable social power by allowing the male to appear prosperous, influential, and 'superior' in public view. All apparently understand that it is a social façade, however (Cornelisen 1977).

CONSUMER CULTURE!

As I indicated, to produce is to consume, and the objects and consuming activities associated with productive activities expand with the tasks and obligations of women in developing economies. However, a striking aspect of these economies is also the spread of consumer culture. The scintillating, inviting, prestige-bearing objects of Western society are sought, particularly by children, teens and young adults. Klein notes of the Tlingit, for example, that any 'extra money is often spent on children', and that, in wealthier families benefiting from changes associated with development, they buy 'luxury items . . . household goods and cars . . . boats' (Klein 1975: 216).

Returning to those aspects of culture that are more slow to change – the gendered social roles themselves – we find that it most often remains the woman's responsibility to control or influence consumption within her family. In Greece, my ethnographic studies reveal the continuing and even expanding role of women in this context. As her children, regardless of their age, seek the objects they view as exciting, status-enhancing and representative of desirable lifestyles, the woman responds. Not only does she try to find ways to allocate funds to meet their 'needs', she engages in active conspiracy with children to seek the father's approval and financing of purchases. When money is simply not available, the woman may respond by taking on some of the newly available economic activities in the local or regional economy (Costa 1988b).

Of course it is not only the children of a family who seek the products and experiences of 'modern life'. Cars and motorcycles, washing and drying machines, dishwashers, ovens and stoves, stereos, televisions and radios, computers and cellphones, branded T-shirts, jeans and athletic shoes, sunglasses and cosmetics, video and still cameras, VCRs, video films, and CDs, diamonds and gold, high-heeled shoes and leather boots, manicures and facials, rollerblades and Doc Martens, all are in demand in the developing societies of our global economy. In these cases, the consumption activity may be largely gender-neutral. Anyone and everyone joins in the near-frenzy of the shopping quest and the consumption display. Although older folks sit and wonder at the whirling consumption activity all around them, they often engage in the action themselves, receiving gifts from younger members of their families or enjoying the entertainment brought into their homes through television, stereos and VCRs. While the products themselves may be gendered, the process of consuming often is not.

Even in rural areas of developing countries, the availability of such products and services is increasing. Alvarsson found among the Mataco, for example, that, although they remain in their traditional territories straddling the Bolivian and Argentinian borders, 'they have given up the consumption of a great number of tubers, roots, and tree-fruits and prefer to acquire Western foods instead. They have stopped manufacturing traditional clothing and rely on Occidental ready-made clothes' (1988: 161). This is also noted by Sorensen (1988) in his study of rural South Korea.

Often, temporary visits or longer periods of employment in the urban areas are also occasions to purchase products that represent prestige and an urban style of life. Back in the rural areas, remaining family members display these objects proudly as emblems of the success of their migrating kin. The homes of rural Greeks are filled with items from the foreign countries visited by their male relatives in the merchant marines, for example (Costa 1989). In Asia, when Iban males migrate,

> . . . items brought back . . . symbolize knowledge of the world beyond, of trade and travel. . . . Major items . . . such as guns, outboard engines, chain saws, furniture, radios, sewing machines, and bedding . . . enhance the products resources . . . such items are not only useful but a source of status.
>
> (Mashman 1991: 257)

Finally, it may be the drive to consume these objects and to take advantage of new services that brings about social change in the rural areas and/or contributes to out-migration. When something cannot be found or achieved locally, migration is a response, as I found in Greece (Costa 1988b, 1989). The mass movement of people in China, for example, headed for such commercial centres as Hong Kong, Guangdong and Shanghai, is not only a response to diminished opportunities in rural areas. Often, young men and women seek the 'bright lights' of the city, willing to endure the long hours, the unfavourable working and living conditions. They come not only to make, and perhaps save, money; they also come to see a new and exciting lifestyle up close, to survey the consumption options and objects perhaps within, but typically just beyond, their reach.

CONCLUSION

Covering the entire range of gendered behaviours in the context of culture and consumption would require volumes. In this chapter, I have tried to expose the reader to some of the variety, complexity and nuance we find throughout the world today. Since there are clearly patterns to this variety, and relationships among the various behaviours and gender attributions, I have focused on those patterns. The descriptions and analyses I provide, as well as the 'model' represented in the figure, are thus intended to suggest both cultural diversity and adaptive similarities.

It has been a salient characteristic of studies within the marketing and consumer behaviour disciplines to take an ethnocentric approach. This is the case in virtually all sub-topics of the disciplines, so that frameworks and understandings developed in the United States and less so in Europe typically have been assumed to be 'universal', i.e., applicable to all societies. As more cross-cultural and international research has been undertaken, dramatic cultural diversity has surfaced, resulting in the need to adapt products, strategy, research procedures and other facets of marketing in the international business environment.

In the field of gender in marketing and consumer behaviour, the myopic and ethnocentric approach has been characteristic as well. Scholars continue to be satisfied with a finding that 'men and women behave differently', with little reference as to how or why. In order to begin to understand the nature of gendered variations in consumer behaviour, we must understand the cultural basis of both gender and behaviour in general. This chapter represents a preliminary attempt in this direction.

Some objects, other forms of property, and consumption activities are gendered in all societies. The process by which the gendering occurs varies, but certain patterns have emerged in this cross-cultural study. An important source of gendering is through the enactment of gender-specific roles. Productive efforts strongly affect the perceived gender of the objects, property and activities as enacted within the sexual division of labour. However, other aspects of gender roles (sometimes referred to as 'sex roles'), beyond economic pursuits, can similarly affect perceptions of the genderedness of goods and actions. Thus, items used in the care of children, in religious rituals or for social occasions are often gendered based upon the enactment of gender-dichotomised social roles. A further source of gendering occurs based upon the way in which property or goods are acquired. The gender of the person through whom an item is inherited can affect the perceived gendering of the object, so that, in a given family, property inherited patrilineally may be seen as male, while matrilineality would result in perceptions of femaleness. Similarly, objects acquired at marriage may be seen as gendered, depending upon the form of acquisition through dowry (female ownership) as opposed to bridewealth (male ownership).

Because development is occurring rapidly and extensively in many parts of the world today, and because it is a socio-economic process of great impact, we would expect development to markedly affect the relationship of gender and consumption. In assessing the dramatic influence of development in this domain, the most salient route by which alterations in patterns of gender and consumption are occurring is through the avenue of changes in the division of labour. Since, as we have seen, the sexual division of labour substantially contributes to perceptions of the genderedness of objects, any changes in production are likely to alter specific patterns of genderedness in consumption.

Furthermore, not only because of the intimate, concomitant interactions of production and consumption, but also because of the availability of wages which can then be spent on consumer products, development can lead to alterations in gendered consumption activities beyond those associated with production. As 'consumer culture' becomes an important facet of life among segments of developing societies, both women and men engage in different forms and increased levels of consumption. However, because women are typically responsible for the raising of children, it is women who are often compelled to find ways to meet the newly developed consumption needs of their children within the context of the changing society. Clearly, though, both men and women are significantly affected by the availability of and increasing demand for consumer products in many developing societies.

In conclusion, gender and consumption vary considerably on the basis of culture. Intimately connected to other economic and social processes, gendered consumption is most evident in the pervasive gendering of objects, other forms of property and consumption activities themselves. Woven into the fabric of society, this gendering cannot be separated from forms of the family and household, of inheritance, residence and marriage exchange, of the sexual division of labour, enactment of social roles and the presentation of self to society at large. In the context of widespread development, the social and economic changes contribute to significant alterations in these patterns of gender and consumption.

NOTES

1 I will not explore here the various methods of population control utilised to ensure that the population would not exceed the resource base. For example, these would include warfare, infanticide, and the abandonment of the very old or very ill in mobile hunting and gathering societies.

2 Some of the material presented in this chapter is 'common knowledge' within the anthropological discipline, with numerous articles and books devoted to the study of a given described phenomenon, making up a totality of knowledge concerning the topic. Thus, I occasionally present such information without full references.

REFERENCES

Alvarsson, J.-A. (1988) *The Mataco of the Gran Chaco*, Stockholm, Sweden: Uppsala University.

Amin, S. (1977) *Imperialism and Unequal Development*, London: Monthly Review Press.

Belk, R. and Costa, J. A. (1990) 'Nouveaux riches as quintessential Americans: case studies in an extended family', in R. W. Belk (ed.) *Advances in Non-Profit Marketing*, Greenwich, CT: JAI Press, 83–140.

Chomsky, N. (1994) *World Orders Old and New*, New York: Columbia University Press.

Cornelisen, A. (1977) *Women of the Shadows*, New York: Vintage Books.

Costa, J. A. (1988a) 'The history of migration and political economy in rural Greece: a case study', *Journal of Modern Greek Studies* 6, 2: 159–85.

—— (1988b) 'Systems integration and attitudes toward Greek rural life: a case study', *Anthropological Quarterly* 74: 3–90.

—— (1989) 'On display: social and cultural dimensions of consumer behavior in the Greek saloni', in T. Srull (ed.) *Advances in Consumer Research* 16, Provo, UT: Association for Consumer Research, 562–6.

—— (ed.) (1991) *Proceedings of the First Conference on Gender and Consumer Behavior*, Salt Lake City: University of Utah Printing Service.

—— (ed.) (1993) *Proceedings of the Second Conference on Gender and Consumer Behavior*, Salt Lake City: University of Utah Printing Service.

—— (ed.) (1994) *Gender Issues and Consumer Behavior*, Newbury Park, CA: Sage.

—— (ed.) (1996) *Proceedings of the Third Conference on Gender, Marketing and Consumer Behavior*, Salt Lake City: University of Utah Printing Press.

Ehlers, T. B. (1990) *Silent Looms: Women and Production in a Guatemalan Town*, Boulder, CO: Westview Press.

Fernandez, J. W. (1971) 'Principles of opposition and vitality in Fang aesthetics', in C. Jopling (ed.) *Art and Aesthetics in Primitive Societies*, New York: E. P. Dutton, 356–73.

Fischer, E. and Wardlow, D. L. (eds) (1998) *Proceedings of the Fourth Conference on Gender, Marketing and Consumer Behavior*, San Francisco, CA: San Francisco State University.

Friedl, E. (1967) 'The position of women: appearance and reality', *Anthropological Quarterly* 40: 97–108.

—— (1975) *Women and Men: An Anthropologist's View*, New York: Rinehart & Winston.

Ghorayshi, P. and Belanger, C. (eds) (1996) *Women, Work and Gender Relations in Developing Countries*, Westport, CT: Greenwood Press.

Goody, J. (1969) 'Inheritance, property, and marriage in Africa and Eurasia', *Sociology* 3: 55–76.

Hamamsy, L. (1957) 'The role of women in a changing Navaho society', *American Anthropologist* 59: 101–11.

Hanna, J. L. (1979) *To Dance is Human*, Austin: University of Texas Press.

Klein, L. F. (1975) 'Tlingit Women and Town Politics', unpublished doctoral dissertation, New York University, Department of Anthropology.

MacCormack, C. P. (1980) 'Proto-social to adult: a Sherbro transformation', in C. P. MacCormack and M. Strathern (eds) *Nature, Culture and Gender*, Cambridge: Cambridge University Press, 95–118.

MacCormack, C. P. and Strathern, M. (eds) (1980) *Nature, Culture and Gender*, Cambridge: Cambridge University Press.

Martinez, K. and Ames, K. L. (eds) (1997) *The Material Culture of Gender; The Gender of Material Culture*, Winterthur, DL: Henry Francis du Pont Winterthur Museum.

Mashman, V. (1991) 'Warriors and weavers: a study of gender relations among the Iban of Sarawak', unpublished MA thesis, University of Kent.

Massiah, J. (1993) *Women in Developing Economies: Making Visible the Invisible*, Providence, RI: Berg Publishers.

Mies, M. (1982) *The Lace Makers of Narsapur: Indian Housewives Produce for the World Market*, Westport, CT: L. Hill.

—— (1986) *Patriarchy and Accumulation on a World Scale*, London: Zed Books.

Pavia, T. M. and Costa, J. A. (1993a) 'The winning number: consumer perceptions of alpha-numeric brand names', *Journal of Marketing* 57, 3: 85–98.

—— (1993b) 'Alpha-numeric brand names and gender stereotypes', *Research in Consumer Behavior*, Greenwich, CT: JAI Press, 85–112.

Rosaldo, M. Z. and Lamphere, L. (1974) *Woman, Culture and Society*, Stanford, CA: Stanford University Press.

Sahlins, M. (1972) *Stone Age Economics*, New York: Addison-Wesley.

Sanday, P. R. (1981) *Female Power and Male Dominance: On the Origins of Sexual Inequality*, New York: Cambridge University Press.

Satnam, K. (1987) *Women in Rural Development*, Delhi: Mittal Publications.

Sorensen, C. W. (1988) *Over the Mountains are Mountains: Korean Peasant Households and their Adaptations to Rapid Industrialization*, Seattle: University of Washington Press.

Stephen, L. (1991) *Zapotec Women*, Austin: University of Texas Press.

Thomas-Slayter, B. and Rocheleau, D. (1995) *Gender, Environment, and Development in Kenya*, Boulder, CO: Lynne Rienner.

Tice, K. E. (1995) *Kuna Crafts, Gender, and the Global Economy*, Austin: University of Texas Press.

Turner, V. (1969) *The Ritual Process*, Chicago, IL: Aldine.

van den Hombergh, H. (1993) *Gender, Environment and Development: A Guide to the Literature*, Amsterdam: Institute for Development Research.

van Gennep, A. (1960) *The Rites of Passage*, Chicago: University of Chicago Press.

Wolf, E. (1982) *Europe and the People without History*, Berkeley: University of California Press.

Wolf, M. (1975) *Women in Chinese Society*, Stanford, CA: Stanford University Press.

Index